community LIVABILITY

What is a livable community? How do you design and develop one? What does government at all levels need to do to support and nurture the cause of livable communities?

Using a blend of theory and practice, experts in the field look at evidence from international, state and local perspectives to explore what is meant by the term "livable communities." Chapters examine the various influencing factors such as the effect and importance of transportation options/alternatives to the elderly, the significance of walkability as a factor in developing a livable and healthy community, the importance of good open space providing for human activity and health, restorative benefits, the importance of coordinated land use and transportation planning, and the relationship between livability and quality of life.

While much of the discussion of this topic is usually theoretical and abstract, Wagner and Caves use case studies from North America, Brazil and the United Kingdom to provide substantive examples of initiatives implemented across the world. This book fills an important gap in the literature on livable communities and at the same time assists policy officials, professionals and academics in their quest to develop livable communities.

Fritz Wagner is a Research Professor in the Department of Urban Design and Planning at the University of Washington (Seattle). He directs the Northwest Center for Livable Communities and teaches part-time. Before joining UW he was at the University of New Orleans where he founded the College of Urban and Public Affairs and served as its Dean.

Roger Caves is Professor of City Planning, School of Public Affairs, San Diego State University. He received his PhD in Urban Affairs and Public Policy from the University of Delaware in 1982. He is co-author of *Planning in the USA*, 2nd and 3rd editions (Routledge, 2003, 2008), editor of the *Encyclopedia of the City* (Routledge, 2005), editor of *Exploring Urban America*, and author of *Land Use Planning: The Ballot Box Revolution*. His research areas include urban planning, direct democracy, housing, information technologies and community development, and planning for sustainable development.

community LIVABILITY

ISSUES AND APPROACHES TO SUSTAINING
THE WELL-BEING OF PEOPLE AND
COMMUNITIES

Edited by
Fritz Wagner and Roger Caves

Routledge
Taylor & Francis Group
LONDON AND NEW YORK

First published 2012
by Routledge
2 Park Square, Milton Park, Abingdon, Oxon OX14 4RN

Simultaneously published in the USA and Canada
by Routledge
711 Third Avenue, New York, NY 10017

Routledge is an imprint of the Taylor & Francis Group, an informa business

© 2012 selection and editorial material, Fritz Wagner and Roger Caves;
individual chapters, the contributors

The right of the editors to be identified as the authors of the
editorial material, and of the authors for their individual chapters,
has been asserted in accordance with sections 77 and 78 of the
Copyright, Designs and Patents Act 1988.

All rights reserved. No part of this book may be reprinted or
reproduced or utilised in any form or by any electronic, mechanical,
or other means, now known or hereafter invented, including photocopying
and recording, or in any information storage or retrieval system,
without permission in writing from the publishers.

Every effort has been made to contact and acknowledge copyright owners.
If any material has been included without permission, the publishers offer
their apologies. The publishers would be pleased to have any errors or
omissions brought to their attention so that corrections may be
published at later printing.

Trademark notice: Product or corporate names may be trademarks or
registered trademarks, and are used only for identification and explanation
without intent to infringe.

British Library Cataloguing in Publication Data
A catalogue record for this book is available from the British Library

Library of Congress Cataloging in Publication Data
Community livability: issues and approaches to sustaining the well-being
of people and communities/edited by Fritz Wagner and Roger Caves.
   p. cm.
   Includes bibliographical references and index.
   1. Sustainable living—Case studies.   2. Community life—Case studies.
   I. Wagner, Fritz.   II. Caves, Roger W.
   GE196.C65 2012
   307—dc23   2011024743

ISBN: 978-0-415-77990-6 (hbk)
ISBN: 978-0-415-77991-3 (pbk)
ISBN: 978-0-203-14820-4 (ebk)

Typeset in Adobe Garamond
by Florence Production Ltd, Stoodleigh, Devon

Printed and bound in Great Britain by
TJ International Ltd, Padstow, Cornwall

CONTENTS

Acknowledgments	vii
FRITZ WAGNER AND ROGER CAVES	
List of Figures and Tables	ix
Notes on Contributors	xi
Preface	xv
DANIEL J. MONTI, JR.	

1	**Introduction to Community Livability**	1
	ROBERT K. WHELAN	

SECTION I: POLICY AND GOVERNANCE	7

2	**Public Policy Promotion of Livable Communities**	9
	JUDITH A. MARTIN	
3	**Variations in Regulatory Factors Affecting Neighborhood Livability: An International Perspective**	30
	ELISE BRIGHT	
4	**Creating Sustainable Communities – A Trans-Atlantic Perspective**	62
	DAVID SHAW, SIMON PEMBERTON, AND ALEXANDER NURSE	

SECTION II: EXPERIENCES IN COMMUNITIES	79

5	**Aging as the Foundation for Livable Communities**	81
	DEBORAH HOWE	
6	**Perceived Livability and Sense of Community: Lessons for Designers from a Favela in Rio de Janeiro, Brazil**	99
	VICENTE DEL RIO, DANIEL LEVI, AND CRISTIANE ROSE DUARTE	

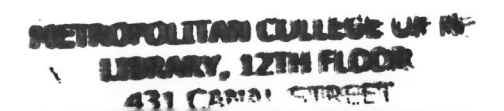

CONTENTS

7   Living Downtown in the Twenty-first Century: Past Trends and
    Future Policy Concerns   127
    EUGÉNIE L. BIRCH

8   The Cultural Component of Livability: Loss and Recovery in
    Post-Katrina New Orleans   158
    JANE S. BROOKS AND REBECCA HOUTMAN

SECTION III: SPECIFIC INTERVENTIONS   181

9   Public Participation in Neighborhood Planning, A Neglected
    Aspect of Community Livability: The Case of Seattle   183
    HILDA BLANCO

10 Envisioning a City's Green Infrastructure for Community Livability 198
    NANCY D. ROTTLE AND BRICE MARYMAN

11 Does Land Use and Transportation Coordination Really Make a
    Difference in Creating Livable Communities?   223
    RUTH L. STEINER

12 Livability, Health, and Community Design   249
    SARAH HEATON KENNEDY AND ANDREW L. DANNENBERG

13 Final Thoughts on Community Livability   274
    ROGER CAVES AND FRITZ WAGNER

    Index   276

ACKNOWLEDGMENTS

Fritz Wagner and Roger Caves

In producing this book we could not have done it without the unwavering support and encouragement of our wives Carol Caves and Margaret Wagner. We want to thank them for their understanding and patience. To Andreas Piller and Lori Tang, graduate students at the University of Washington; we cannot thank them enough for all the correspondence, editing, and advice given to make this book a reality. Our authors are the best and cannot be thanked enough. Their chapters are substantive and contributed much to our topic. Moreover, it was a great pleasure to work with them. We thank Bob Whelan and Dan Monti for the introductory contributions. Their work set the tone of our work and its focus. We also thank our respective departments at the University of Washington and San Diego State University. We enjoy their support and collegiality. Finally, we would like to acknowledge the late Judith Martin, University of Minnesota, a tireless advocate of livable communitites, and to others working to make our communities more livable for us and future generations.

LIST OF FIGURES AND TABLES

Figures

2.1	Demonstration Account Awards	14
2.2a and b	Excelsior and Grand, St. Louis Park	15
2.3	Heart of the City, Burnsville	21
4.1	Multiple Deprivation in Liverpool. Super Output Areas falling within the 1 percent most deprived and 10 percent most deprived nationally	67
6.1	Aerial View of Mata Machado	108
6.2	Site Map of Mata Machado	109
6.3	Main Entrance to Mata Machado	111
6.4	Mata Machado Site Plan and Study Areas	112
6.5	View of the Main *Praça*	113
6.6	Main Thoroughfare Leading to the *Praça*	114
6.7	Mata Matchado's Main *Praça*	115
6.8	Mata Machado's Main *Praça*	116
6.9	The River Cachoeira in Mata Machado	120
7.1a and b	Downtown Philadelphia and Downtown Phoenix	132
7.2	Comparative Population Growth Rates 1970–2000	133
7.3	Household Growth Rates Pass Population Growth Rates in the 1990s	136
7.4	Household Composition of Downtowns, Cities, and Suburbs, 2000	137
7.5a–d	Downtown Philadelphia	141–142
7.6a–e	Downtown Los Angeles	143–145
7.7a–c	Downtown Milwaukee	146–147
7.8a–c	Downtown Orlando	148–149
9.1	Seattle's System of Urban Village Centers	188
10.1	1908 Olmsted Plan for Seattle Parks and Boulevards	205
10.2	Seattle Watershed and Topographic Units for the Open Space Seattle 2100	208

LIST OF FIGURES AND TABLES

10.3	Photo of the Green Futures Charrette	211
10.4a and b	Visions for Seattle's Green Infrastructure, 2025 and 2100	212–213
11.1	Conventional Suburban Development versus TND	227
11.2	Context of Transit Oriented Development	229
11.3	Variables Affecting Individual Travel Behavior	237
12.1	Obesity in Adults in the US, 2009	251
12.2	Bike Traffic and Bikeway Miles in Portland, OR	253
12.3	Access to Healthy Eating	257

Tables

2.1	Communities Participating in LCA Programs, 2008, by County	13
4.1	Themes within Liverpool's Sustainable Community Strategy 2009–2024	69
5.1	Disability Status Ages 65 and Above: 2007	82
5.2	Elder-Friendly Community Characteristics	94
6.1	Livability Matrix	103
9.1	How features of neighborhood planning relate to criteria of participatory democracy	191
11.1	Actors in the Process of Coordinating Land Use and Transportation	239

NOTES ON CONTRIBUTORS

Eugénie L. Birch is Nussdorf Professor of Urban Research, University of Pennsylvania, co-director, Penn Institute for Urban Research (Penn IUR) and co-editor, City in the 21st Century series, University of Pennsylvania Press. Her most recent books are: *Global Urbanization* (Penn Press 2011), *Neighborhoods and Life Chances: How Place Matters in Modern America* (Penn Press 2011), *Women's Health and World Cities* (Penn Press 2011) (all edited with Susan Wachter and others), *Urban and Regional Planning Reader* (Routledge 2009) and *Local Planning, Principles and Practice* (ICMA 2009) (edited with Gary Hack, Paul Sedway, and Mitchell Silver).

Hilda Blanco is a Research Professor and the Interim Director of the Center for Sustainable Cities in the School of Policy, Planning, and Development at the University of Southern California. Professor Blanco has wide experience in planning, redevelopment, and community participation, including preparing the economic development strategy for Oakland, CA (1985 to 1987); leading graduate planning studios to redevelop low-income communities in Brooklyn, NY in the 1990s and to assist several communities in the Puget Sound in their planning efforts in the 2000s. She also served on Seattle's Planning Commission from 2005 to 2007.

Elise Bright is a Professor in the Department of Landscape Architecture and Urban Planning at Texas A&M University. She served as Director of the Master of Urban Planning program until 2010. She holds a BA in Government and Spanish from the University of Arizona, a Master of City Planning from Harvard, and a Doctor of Environmental Design from Texas A&M. Before joining A&M in 2006, Dr. Bright was on the faculty of the School of Urban and Public Affairs at the University of Texas at Arlington. She worked as a practicing planner for a decade before joining academia and continues to do plans for small communities whenever possible.

Jane S. Brooks holds the Jean Brainard Boebel Chair in Historic Preservation in the Department of Planning and Urban Studies at the University of New Orleans where she has been a faculty member since 1976. She established the Historic Preservation Planning concentration in the planning program and has been actively involved in community-based historic preservation activities in support of revitalizing diverse New Orleans neighborhoods. A native of New Orleans, she holds degrees in landscape architecture from LSU and the Harvard University Graduate School of Design.

NOTES ON CONTRIBUTORS

Andrew L. Dannenberg serves as a Consultant to and formerly was Team Leader of the Healthy Community Design Initiative in the National Center for Environmental Health at the Centers for Disease Control and Prevention (CDC) in Atlanta. He holds affiliate faculty appointments in the Department of Environmental and Occupational Health Sciences and in the Department of Urban Design and Planning at the University of Washington in Seattle.

Cristiane Rose Duarte is a Professor in the School of Architecture and Town Planning at the Federal University of Rio de Janeiro, Brazil. She is an architect and an urbanist with several articles and four co-edited books. Her work examines the social and anthropological dimensions of urbanism, and particularly favelas, and she managed the Favela Bairro project for Mata Machado in Rio de Janeiro.

Sarah Heaton Kennedy was formerly a Presidential Management Fellow and public health analyst for the Healthy Community Design Initiative in the National Center for Environmental Health at the Centers for Disease Control and Prevention (CDC). She currently works as a private consultant to communities, organizations, and local governments seeking to improve health outcomes through participatory community design interventions and innovative land-use strategies.

Rebecca Houtman is a 2010 graduate of the MS in Urban Studies program at the University of New Orleans. She currently serves as a fiscal analyst for the City of New Orleans Capital Projects Administration.

Deborah Howe is Professor and Chair of the Department of Community and Regional Planning at Temple University. She has spent the past two decades raising awareness of the importance of community planning for an aging society. Her current research addresses local land use policies that yield built environments that enable healthy, active lifestyles.

Daniel Levi is a Professor of Psychology at Cal Poly, San Luis Obispo. He is an environmental psychologist whose work examines public attitudes toward planning and resource management issues and the analysis of community responses to technology and environmental issues. He is author of *Group Dynamics for Teams* (Sage 2007, 2nd edn).

Judith A. Martin is Professor of Geography and Director of the Urban Studies Program, University of Minnesota, and editor of the University of Pennsylvania Press's *Metropolitan Portraits* book series. She has taught in Urban Studies, Geography, History, Art History and Architecture at the University of Minnesota, and has been a visiting professor at University College, London, the University of Munich, and the University of Amsterdam. She served on the Minneapolis City Planning Commission for 15 years and was president for eight. She has been awarded the University of Minnesota's Morse Alumni Teaching Award (1996), the University's Award for Community Service (1999), the College of Continuing Education Teaching Award (2005) and the President's Award for Outstanding Service (2009). Early publications focused on new towns, neighborhood development, historic preservation, and urban renewal. Recent interests have focused on metropolitan governance, regional planning, and urban design.

Brice Maryman is a Landscape Architect with SvR Design Co. He lives in Seattle where he designs and writes about high-performance urban landscapes. As a Lecturer at the University

NOTES ON CONTRIBUTORS

of Washington, he co-directed Open Space Seattle 2100 to "design Seattle's green network for the next century."

Daniel J. Monti, Jr. is Professor of Public Policy Studies at St. Louis University. He is the author of over forty scholarly articles and six books on subjects ranging from educational reform and inner-city redevelopment to youth gangs and American urban history. Professor Monti is an expert on community development and the public contributions of private enterprises. His research led to his creation of *InnerCity Entrepreneurs*, a Boston-based technical assistance program for growing small businesses, which has been utilized nationally to help tenant-managed public housing organizations and has spawned gang intervention strategies for school students. A former Woodrow Wilson Fellow, Professor Monti has consulted with private companies and agencies of the federal government.

Alexander Nurse is a postgraduate research student in the People, Space and Place research cluster, within the University of Liverpool's School of Environmental Science. His research focuses on Local Area Agreements as a method of delivering local public services, with an emphasis on the role of horizontal and vertical governance. This research is set within wider scholarly interests of public policy, governance and central-local relations from a planning perspective.

Simon Pemberton is Senior Lecturer in Urban Geography and Planning at the University of Birmingham, UK. He has wide-ranging research interests in community planning and livability, urban resilience and regeneration, the neighborhood impacts of "new" immigration and outcomes of state rescaling on urban and rural communities. Simon has published widely in all of these areas. He was also Director of the Merseyside Social Inclusion Observatory between 2004 and 2010, which sought to improve people's quality of life through a series of applied research projects focused on tackling social exclusion and multiple deprivation.

Vicente del Rio is a Professor at the City and Regional Planning Department, Cal Poly, San Luis Obispo. Previously to joining Cal Poly in 2001, he was at the Federal University of Rio de Janeiro for 23 years. He is an architect and urban designer who has worked and published extensively, including five books in his native Brazil. He is co-editor and co-author of *Contemporary Urbanism in Brazil: Beyond Brasilia* (University Press of Florida 2009).

Nancy D. Rottle is a Professor of Landscape Architecture at the University of Washington, where she teaches ecological design and directs the Green Futures Research and Design Lab. Her current research focuses on urban ecological infrastructure, community engagement and design for environmental literacy. She co-directed Open Space Seattle 2100.

David Shaw is a Senior Academic within the University of Liverpool's School of Environmental Sciences. He has a wide range of interests in the field of spatial planning and in particular is interested how the concept can provide an integrated framework for place making within both a rural and urban context. He is also interested in understanding how planning practice operates in different political contexts around the world.

Ruth L. Steiner is an Associate Professor and Director of the Center for Health and the Built Environment in the Department of Urban and Regional Planning at the University of Florida. Her research focuses on the interactions between transportation and land use, with a particular focus on planning for all modes of transportation including transit, bicycling, and walking. She received her B.A. in History from Lawrence University in Appleton, Wisconsin, an MBA from the University of Wisconsin in Milwaukee, and a Masters of City Planning and a PhD from the University of California at Berkeley.

Robert K. Whelan is Clinical Professor of Public Affairs at the University of Texas-Dallas. He is co-author of *Urban Policy and Politics in a Bureaucratic Age* and author of numerous articles and papers. His major current research interest is historical and theoretical approaches to US urban politics.

PREFACE

Daniel J. Monti, Jr.
Department of Policy Studies
St. Louis University

The authors assembled here have considerable knowledge – of both the bookish and practical kind – about the subjects discussed in their respective essays. Planners, policy experts, specialists in land use, housing, transportation, economic development, and the layout and revitalization of neighborhoods, they bring a common orientation to their work. They are fixers.

More precisely, they are the kind of men and women that people responsible for fixing things call upon when something about urban areas doesn't look quite right anymore, doesn't work the way it should, or needs a full-blown makeover. This means, among other things, that they have a profound appreciation for the importance of the places their plans and proposals would touch and for the impact their actions are expected to have on the people that live and work in these places.

The authors are inheritors and carriers of a tradition of reform that began early in the nineteenth century when men and women with considerable wealth, power, and prestige started identifying what was broken in their cities and spent a lot of time and money trying to make vital civic repairs. First as volunteers, and later as trained experts and institution builders, the writers here are handmaidens and carriers to that reforming tradition. Today, these full-time, professionally-trained, and relatively well-paid consultants and teachers are public intellectuals and often minor celebrities in their own right.

They all believe in the power and preeminence of *place* in everyone's life, especially the blocks, districts, and cities on which they happen to be working at the time. Their great regard for the pieces of territory they work on is best understood in words that any fan of the movie *Field of Dreams* would appreciate. However, instead of predicting that "if we build it, they will come," the Planner's Creed might more closely resemble: "If you rebuild it, people will come and somehow be made better and more whole."

In a "global" world where only a few of the largest and most powerful places seem to garner our attention or a "postmodern" world in which the only place that counts is the small piece where you hang your hat, contemporary planners and reformers are hopelessly and blessedly wedded to the notion that every city matters, that every place needs to be livable. What happens in one city is relevant to what happens in other cities, and what makes any city worth fighting for is precisely what makes them livable for everyone who happens to be there.

We have a shared preoccupation with the places we live and work, and making these places more congenial, more livable, is part of our cultural inheritance and legacy. To the authors assembled here, then, repairing these places is very much part of how we repair ourselves and our way of life. It is also the reason why people like the ones whose words are featured in this book keep writing and why what they have to say is worth listening to.

Chapter 1

INTRODUCTION TO COMMUNITY LIVABILITY
Robert K. Whelan
Clinical Professor of Public Affairs
University of Texas, Dallas

Community livability, like many concepts in city planning, is like Mr. Justice Stewart's definition of pornography in the early 1960s: he did not know exactly what it was, but he knew it when he saw it. Several years ago, David Godschalk (2004), a leading academic planner, noted that livability "does not come packaged in a single accepted definition." For Godschalk, the concept involves the everyday physical environment and placemaking. On the one hand, community livability includes traditional city planning ideals of economy, ecology, and equity. On the other hand, livability involves the use of public space, transportation systems, and building design. Community livability is a concept that is important at the level of the house, the block, and the neighborhood. It is also important in broader contexts, such as the metropolitan region.

As Hilda Blanco points out in Chapter 9 of this volume, many urbanists associate livability with social characteristics, as well as the physical aspects mentioned above. Blanco and others see such things as a sense of identity or belonging, population diversity, and economic opportunity as important for livability. The organization, Partners for Livable Communities, defines livability as "the sum of the factors that add up to a community's quality of life-including the built and natural environment, economic prosperity, social stability and equity, educational, entertainment, and recreation possibilities" (Partners for Livable Communities 2011). The essays herein address community livability in the broader sense of the PLP definition. Every topic in their definition is covered by at least one author, and, generally, by several authors.

Closely associated with community livability are the ideas of New Urbanism and smart growth. The Congress for the New Urbanism was founded in 1993 by Andrés Duany, Elizabeth Plater-Zyberk, Peter Calthorpe, and their associates. The CNU founders were primarily architects, but their principles are widely accepted by scholars and practitioners in contemporary urban planning. These principles include livable streets arranged in compact, walkable blocks; a range of housing choices for people of diverse ages and income levels; schools, shops and other community facilities accessible by walking, bicycling, or public transportation; and a human-scale public realm (Congress for a New Urbanism 2011). Many of these ideas are reflected by the authors of subsequent chapters in their discussion of livability issues.

The smart growth movement might be viewed as the political arm of New Urbanism. Smart growth advocates are especially concerned with addressing the negative consequences of suburban sprawl. The Smart Growth Network, a coalition of environmental and governmental groups, was founded in 1996 to address these concerns. Smart growth might generally be characterized as an effort to build housing, offices, and commercial facilities in close proximity to public transportation. One of the first principles of smart growth is neighborhood livability. These concerns are reflected in this volume's essays.

The above paragraphs give the impression that dealing with the problems of livability is a recent development. Here in the United States, livability has been a prominent concern of reformers since the urbanization and industrialization of the second half of the nineteenth century. Livability has been a central issue for American city planners since the emergence of the profession in the early part of the twentieth century. Underlying the City Beautiful movement, early city plans such as Daniel Burnham's Plan for Chicago, and the work of the McMillan commission in planning modern Washington, DC was a deep, enduring passion to make the city a more livable place by providing recreational space, by creating more attractive streets and public space, etcetera.

For those who came of age in the 1960s, Jane Jacobs is the person typically associated with viable urban neighborhoods. As we mark the fiftieth birthday of the publication of her classic, *Death and Life of Great American Cities*, Jacobs' prescriptions for neighborhood livability still ring true. Jacobs was not only a theorist. She lived in New York's Greenwich Village for thirty years, and she lived in Toronto's The Annex from 1968 until her death in 2006. These were neighborhoods with mixed land uses and cultural diversity. Social cohesion contributed to lower crime rates. The "eyes on the street" were assisted by the fact that the neighborhoods were busy around the clock. The attractive, viable older buildings were sometimes characterized as "blighted," probably because of proximity to choice urban real estate desired for development. Jacobs fought New York's urban renewal "czar," Robert Moses three times: to maintain Washington Square Park as a park, to keep the West Village out of urban renewal, and against the construction of the proposed Lower Manhattan Expressway. She won all three battles. Through her efforts, SoHo and other neighborhoods emerged, and Lower Manhattan retained its residential livability. After her move to Toronto, Jacobs fought the proposed Spadina Expressway. Partially as a result of Jacobs's efforts, the center of Toronto is one of the most livable places in urban North America (Jacobs 1961; on her work, see Flint 2009; Gratz 2010).

Much of our current concern with livability issues arose in the 1970s, particularly as a result of the energy crisis of that decade. A series of academic books appeared, arguing that rising gasoline prices would force people back to central city living. While this did not exactly happen in the manner suggested by these experts, Eugenie Birch (Chapter 7, this volume) traces the revival in downtown living to the 1970s decade. An entire literature on livability emerged. Foremost among these works is Donald Appleyard's *Livable Streets* (1981), a book said to influence urban policy makers in both the US and Europe (Ewing and Appleyard 2009). Writing before and after Appleyard, both Jacobs and William H. Whyte were concerned with the livability of streets, in particular, and cities in general. (A comprehensive bibliography on livability questions can be found on the International Making Cities Livable website.) The organization Partners for Livable Communities was started in 1977 to promote quality of life, economic development, and social equity. The group does this by providing technical assistance, leadership training, workshops and charrettes, and research and publications.

Chapter 1: **INTRODUCTION**

The major purpose of this book is to present practical, real world examples of issues confronting community livability. Much of the existing discussion of this subject is highly theoretical and abstract. Here, we try to give students and faculty substantive examples of how these issues play out in a variety of scales. The book is divided into three sections. The first part considers issues of policy and governance. How do urban livability concerns connect to economic competitiveness? What kinds of state and local policies would best promote livability? In the North American context, how do economic development and metropolitan governance issues contribute to (or detract from) livability? The second section considers specific experiences in communities. How is the livability experience impacted by zoning and other regulations? What kind of livability does our aging population have here in US cities? What is livability for a population living in poverty? Does it make a difference if we are talking about places outside the United States? What is the level of livability in American downtowns? How much does urban livability depend on a rich and vibrant local culture? The third part of the book looks at specific interventions. Did the institution of a neighborhood planning process in Seattle contribute to livability? How might the Open Space Seattle 2010 process add to livability? Does land use and transportation really make a difference in creating livable communities? How are community design and health linked to livability?

Plan of the Book

Section I: Policy and Governance

In the North American context, state and provincial governments play a critical role in relation to community livability. In Chapter 2, Judith Martin examines Minnesota's Livable Communities Act, passed in 1995. Minnesota is known as a state with a strong progressive tradition. Minnesota, in general, and the Twin Cities region in particular, are held up as national models in urban policy for their achievements in regional tax base sharing, affordable housing dispersal, and other regional governance efforts. Martin examines and assesses the efforts of five cities under the Livable Communities Act. Two of the communities are older, first-ring suburbs; a third community is an outer-ring suburb; another is an historic town facing urbanization because of its proximity to the airport, and the last case is in a section of downtown St. Paul. The author offers some thoughtful reflections on the possibilities and limits of state government intervention in making cities more livable.

In our teaching, we tend to emphasize the US experience. This is especially true in relation to zoning and other regulatory policies, which tend to be discussed in the context of American zoning only. Elise Bright's contribution (Chapter 3) is to place zoning and regulatory policies into a comparative context. In addition to the United States, she presents a discussion of zoning and regulatory policies in numerous nations in the British Commonwealth and Europe. Overall, the question is how zoning and other regulatory policies add to neighborhood livability. The author gives us a basis for comparison, offering both similarities and differences. Are there better ways to promote neighborhood livability than the traditional US model? If there are better methods, could we implement them here? The livability of residential neighborhoods depends on these policies.

Chapter 4 demonstrates that the British experience in building sustainable communities has similarities and differences with its North American counterparts. David Shaw, Simon Pemberton, and Alexander Nurse discuss the emphasis on placemaking and place-shaping in the UK. They do this in two ways: they first relate central government efforts at placemaking and place-shaping, followed by a case study of these efforts in Liverpool. The discussion of the national livability agenda is interesting; while much is new and innovative, many components of British livability policy are hardy perennials of urban governance, e.g. integration of service delivery. The three Liverpool narratives are instructive. The first vignette considers efforts at policy integration. The second narrative presents Liverpool's designation as a European Capital of Culture in 2008. The final case is the development of a partnership to deliver green infrastructure. Shaw *et al.* conclude that planning should be at the heart of place-making.

Section II: Experiences in Communities

The aging population of the US has been largely ignored in relation to urban livability issues; this is a main point of Chapter 5 by Deborah Howe. Howe shocks with statistics such as that half of the over-85 population suffers from dementia (see also Jacoby 2010) and provides a cogent discussion of the relationship of the built environment and aging. She then presents a series of planning principles for aging, followed by several aging-focused planning frameworks. Both of the latter sections are filled with numerous practical examples that should prove useful for practitioners.

How does poverty impact urban livability? Del Rio *et al.* (Chapter 6) present some interesting research from the Mata Machado favela in Rio de Janeiro. Before reading the chapter, students might look at Neuwirth's excellent and readable chapter in *Shadow Cities* as an introduction to the topic (2005: 25–65). Del Rio *et al.* base their research on interviews with residents and behavioral observations of the favela. The authors find "high levels of housing satisfaction and perceived safety, a strong sense of community, a vibrant social system, and a sustainable lifestyle" (196). The primary dislikes involved the lack of public sector services and private enterprises in the favela.

There may be as many myths about downtown residential living in the United States as there are about living in squatter settlements in Brazil. The downtown residential experience has often been romanticized by the US media; indeed, residents of US downtowns may share complaints with the residents of Brazilian favelas, including the lack of markets or grocery stores, for example. Fortunately, Eugenie Birch's Chapter 7 gives us a thorough description of downtown living in the US by tracking a number of variables using Census data for downtowns in forty-five US cities between 1970 and 2000. In brief, the chapter "describes the rise of downtown living, quantifies this shift, and outlines its nature" (232). Professor Birch concludes the chapter with some reflections for policy makers on development issues, demographic and market potential, and density.

The cultural component of livability is also often ignored by other works on the subject. In some places, however, culture may be a central aspect of urban livability. This is especially true for a city like New Orleans as it faces rebuilding after Hurricane Katrina, as Jane Brooks and Rebecca Houtman point out in their case study of New Orleans' Mid-City neighborhood in Chapter 8. Their examination of such cultural institutions as food, music, and Mardi Gras at the neighborhood level points to a need for cultural recovery – as well as physical recovery. Any relocated person will miss family, friends, neighbors, co-workers, church, etc. As someone who relocated from New Orleans, I can attest that I miss food, music, and special events – important components of New Orleans' identity – in addition to the above.

Section III: Specific Interventions

Section Three considers specific interventions in cities, and how they contribute to urban livability. Hilda Blanco in Chapter 9 examines Seattle's neighborhood planning program and its relation to livability. Using the concept of urban villages, the city hired community organizers (not urban planners) to implement the neighborhood planning process. Blanco concludes that the process contributed to livability because real plans were produced; residents, including usually under-represented groups, were involved in the process, and recommendations were actually implemented. Her chapter is a significant contribution to a rich literature (see Fung 2004 and Rohe 2009).

Nancy Rottle and Brice Maryman argue in Chapter 10 that urban green infrastructure is also important for livability. After presenting the concept of urban green infrastructure, which may be unfamiliar to some readers, the authors give us a case study of another Seattle planning process, the Open Space Seattle 2010 visioning process, which was done through a charrette planning process. Ultimately, some of the recommendations emerging from the process were adopted by the city, although the political process to implementation was somewhat tortuous.

Does land use and transportation coordination really make a difference in creating livable communities? This is the question posed by Ruth Steiner in Chapter 11. Steiner introduces some fundamental concepts in the relationship between land use and transportation coordination. These include "accessibility versus mobility, the scale of analysis, and the context of travel" (339). This is followed by a discussion of methods used to implement land use and transportation coordination: traditional neighborhood development, transit-oriented development, location efficiency, the jobs-housing balance, spatial mismatch, and transportation concurrency (340). After a thorough review of the literature, Steiner concludes that land use and transportation coordination does improve livability.

Sarah Heaton Kennedy and Andrew Dannenberg in Chapter 12 examine the relationship of livability, health, and community design. The authors review a number of factors which have been neglected in community design, including obesity, risk of injury risk, air quality, parks and green space, healthy food environments, noise, and mental health. They then turn to a number of alternative approaches to community design, including Smart Growth, Universal Design, Leadership in Energy and Environmental Design (LEED), and Health Impact Assessment. These should all provide food for thought for readers.

References

Appleyard, Donald with M. Sue Gerson and Mark Lintell, *Livable Streets*, Berkeley, CA: University of California Press, 1981.
Birch, Eugénie, Chapter 7, this volume.

Congress for the New Urbanism, http://www.cnu.org. 2011.

Flint, Anthony, *Wrestling With Moses: How Jane Jacobs Took On New York's Master Builder And Transformed The American City*, New York: Random House, 2009.

Fung, Archon, *Empowered Participation: Reinventing Urban Democracy*, Princeton, NJ and Oxford: Princeton University Press, 2004.

Godschalk, David, "Land Use Planning Challenges: Coping with Conflicts in Visions of Sustainable Development and Livable Communities", *Journal Of The American Planning Association* 70:1 (Winter 2004), 1–9.

Gratz, Roberta, *The Battle For Gotham: New York In The Shadow Of Robert Moses And Jane Jacobs*, New York: Nation Books, 2010.

Jacobs, Jane, *The Death And Life Of Great American Cities*, New York: Modern Library, 1993, originally published 1961.

Neuwirth, Robert, *Shadow Cities: A Billion Squatters A New Urban World*, New York and London: Routledge, 2006.

Partners for Livable Communities, *Culture Connects All: Rethinking Audiences In Time Of Demographic Change*, Washington: Partners For Livable Communities, 2011.

Rohe, William, "From Local to Global: 100 Years of Neighborhood Planning", *Journal Of The American Planning Association*, 75:2, (Spring 2009), 209–230.

SECTION I

POLICY AND GOVERNANCE

Chapter 2

PUBLIC POLICY PROMOTION OF LIVABLE COMMUNITIES

Judith A. Martin
Professor, Urban Studies Program
University of Minnesota

Introduction

The dreams and ambitions that feed Livable Community agendas nationwide have been on the minds of Twin Cities' policymakers for some time. Beginning in the early 1990s this region began to benefit from several quite distinct legislative and funding programs, all directed toward promoting a Livable Community agenda. In 1992, Minneapolis created the Neighborhood Revitalization Program (NRP), which redirected tax increment funding to broadly defined neighborhood improvement plans (Martin and Pentel 2002). In 1994, Hennepin County – Minnesota's most populated, with Minneapolis as the county seat – created a new funding stream around standard infrastructure investments. This program, Hennepin Community Works (HCW), was quite explicitly a "livable community" program, with a strong focus on transit corridors; its goal was to reshape declining inner city and inner suburban neighborhoods, create jobs, and foster environmental improvements (Martin and Jacobson 2008). To date these two programs have directed close to $500 million of new investment in Minneapolis and Hennepin County. Then the state stepped up to the redevelopment plate, as Minnesota passed Livable Communities legislation (LCA), a voluntary, incentive-based program (MN Statutes 1995). This program created a new funding source that has averaged $14.5 million annually, divided among three programs, for appropriate Livable Community projects throughout the entire 7-county Twin Cities area. Responsibility for administering the program was vested in the Metropolitan Council.

This chapter focuses on the latter program, which emerged after a decade of debate about the function and future of the Metropolitan Council (Martin 1998). LCA was intended to fund region-wide development and redevelopment projects by promoting increased mixed-use density that would connect to public transit systems and public spaces – all to lessen the negative impacts of urban sprawl. Over 100 communities in the Twin Cities have participated in this program since 1996.

The Metropolitan Council and the Livable Communities Act

While Livable Community projects typically exist at a neighborhood level, a regional approach to planning can better achieve these visions, if slowing down sprawl is a serious goal. As in

Toronto and Portland, the Twin Cities has long embraced a form of regionalism, primarily through the 1967 creation of the Metropolitan Council with its land-use planning and property tax sharing policies (Martin 1993). The Metropolitan Council is a planning agency that transcends the parochial interests of more than 200 local municipal and county governing boards. For over four decades, it has coordinated plans that cross these boundaries, particularly around sewer and wastewater treatment issues. It holds most of the responsibility to foster what most would recognize as Livable Community goals.

As in most other US metropolitan regions, the Twin Cities' region sprawled dramatically from the 1960s forward, even as a regional planning framework was emerging. The Metropolitan Council gained the power to review, and sometimes to modify, local land use plans to fit regional system goals in the early 1970s. What this meant in practice is that the Metropolitan Council signs off on the revised-every-decade comprehensive plans of each municipality. Despite this power, the region grew rapidly in the 1980s, especially at the far reaches of the interstate beltway. This then brought increasing policy concern about declining urban cores, increasing roadway congestion, and a loss of farmland and wetlands around the region. Little progress was made to address these concerns. Through the 1980s–1990s, a politically conservative legislative coalition resisted increasing centrally-led land-use planning.

But by the 1990s the legislature seemed to coalesce around emerging New Urbanist goals: to reduce sprawl through higher density infill development, to increase mass transit resources by linking high density residential areas with large job growth areas, and to bolster affordable housing in parts of the region with high rates of job growth. The Democratic legislature in the early 1990s passed several bills to alter and expand the Metropolitan Council – having it become an elected body, and requiring all municipalities to agree to affordable housing production goals. The Republican governor vetoed all of these. The Legislature even debated establishing an actual Urban Growth Boundary, to prevent any sewer or water service construction outside its border – unlike the existing MUSA (Metropolitan Urban Service Area) line, which manages these extensions, but does not prohibit them.

Tensions between these branches of state government over regional planning came to a head in mid 1990s. Following three cycles of vetoes, the Governor established an informal task force to develop a bill to address metropolitan growth issues. At the same time the 1994 Minnesota state legislative session began to set the stage for major changes to the Council itself. The Metropolitan Reorganization Act of 1994 was perhaps as significant as the 1960s legislation that originally created the Metropolitan Council. This legislation gave the Metropolitan Council greater operating control over the physical infrastructure of the Twin Cities region. Existing regional boards (Metropolitan Transit Council, Regional Transit Board, Metropolitan Waste Control Commission) were consolidated into the Council, which was also given the ability to issue bonds, to control wastewater treatment, and to control public transit siting, maintenance and operations (Orfield 1998). The Council's organizational structure changed as well: members had formerly served four-year terms with half appointed every two years; now they would serve at the pleasure of the Governor.

The Governor's task force then came forward with a plan to implement these changes. This plan became the 1995 Livable Communities Act (LCA), sponsored in the legislature by an inner-ring suburban legislator. It faced few hurdles as the both Governor and Curt Johnson, then-Metropolitan Council chair, embraced it from the outset. LCA would be a "carrot" approach

Chapter 2: **PUBLIC POLICY PROMOTION**

to development policy, not a big stick like an urban growth boundary. Thus it won support from unusual quarters: developers, Republicans, and suburban officials.

The LCA established new funds within the Metropolitan Council to promote specific types of new development. Municipalities could apply for funding from three separate accounts: the Tax Base Revitalization Account (TBRA), the Local Housing Incentives Account (LHIA) and/or the Livable Communities Development Account (LCDA). An advisory committee was also set up at the start. This group has usually been composed of experienced professionals (e.g. local planning directors). They evaluate proposals for these funds, and score them based on criteria established in legislation:

1. Projects must be located in cities where contribution net tax capacity exceeds distribution net tax capacity by more than $200/hh.
2. Projects must link employment opportunities and housing.
3. Municipalities must provide matching funds beyond a dollar-for-dollar requirement.

A community's readiness for a proposed project, as well as its need, were additional considerations, and projects were typically awarded extra points for sustainability and transit. LCA projects are expected to be a catalyst for ideas and projects that would simply occur in the market. In all cases the committee looks for partnership potential, and the usual pattern has been for the Metropolitan Council to accept the committee's recommendations (Barron 2008).

The TBRA mirrored traditional economic development incentive programs in many ways. It provides grants to municipalities interested in attracting companies either relocating to, or growing operations in, the Twin Cities. These funds are targeted for pollution cleanup, allowing land to be reused, and ultimately to increase living wage jobs and grow local commercial tax bases. Because the TBRA mimicked many existing state DTED (Minnesota Department of Trade and Economic Development) programs, most of these grants have been coordinated with grants from that agency.

The LHIA built on earlier failed legislation to extend the region's tax base sharing umbrella to housing; the ambition of this program is to diversify housing options across the region. The Metropolitan Council has long had a process to negotiate long-term affordable and lifecycle housing goals, sometimes called the "housing incentives program" which is separate from the LHIA process. This new funding source was directed toward affordable housing production in communities that have not yet met their negotiated housing goals, but were actively attempting to do so (Goetz 2000). LHIA provides an incentive to "make progress," but also expects municipalities to use some of their own tax base to meet these goals. Refusing to do so means paying into the LHIA account – for the first time financial consequences for uncooperative cities became a reality. LHIA and also helped to mute predictable negative responses to affordable housing by re-branding it as "life cycle housing" – for people in all stages of life, including local public servants and empty nesters – and recognizing that one size did not fit all. So, wealthy single-family home suburbs might propose affordable units, more compact units, or more rental property for fixed and low-income residents, while inner-ring suburbs with an aging housing stock might propose more single-family homes for younger families (Barron 2008).

The LCDA was the most unusual aspect of the 1995 legislation. It specifically identified the "type" of development that the Metropolitan Council would now subsidize. It offers competitive grants to municipalities for five specific kinds of development projects goals:

1   those that interrelate development or redevelopment and transit;
2   those that interrelate affordable housing and employment growth areas;
3   those that intensify land use that leads to more compact development or redevelopment;
4   those that involve development or redevelopment that mixes incomes of residents in housing, including introducing or reintroducing higher value housing in lower income areas to achieve a mix of housing opportunities; or
5   those that encourage public infrastructure investments which connect urban neighborhoods and suburban communities, attract private sector redevelopment investment in commercial and residential properties adjacent to the public improvement, and provide project area residents with expanded opportunities for private sector employment.

(Metropolitan Council 2005a)

The LCDA fund was designed to promote a New Urbanist agenda at the local level, but without a heavy hand. Participating in this program is a choice, not a requirement. No municipality has to diversify its housing stock or create high-density pedestrian-oriented development. But communities receiving LCDA funding do have to participate in the housing incentives (LHIA) program in order to receive grants. Since 1995, the LCDA program has leveraged more than 100 new development projects (Table 2.1).

The Livable Communities Act was a fairly dramatic move for the Minnesota legislature, though not as ambitious as the goals put forth by local Smart Growth and New Urbanist advocates. It lacked a strong regional vision for future growth. It lacked a clear regional transit plan or agenda. And requirements for suburban affordable housing were fairly modest. Despite these limitations, LCA did create new incentives in the direction of New Urbanist goals.

LCA Projects Examined

Having operated for over a decade, numerous LCA projects now dot the Twin Cities' urban and suburban landscapes (see Figure 2.1). The LCA "New Urbanist" projects examined here provide some sense of what has been accomplished to date. Most of these projects date from the program's earlier years, so have existed long enough to be considered on their merits.

It should be noted that most of the projects described here are rather sizeable. LCA funds have also been directed toward many smaller efforts, such as a modest brownfield clean-up, or support for a small affordable housing development. It should also be noted that for many communities the LCA application itself has been a learning process – many apply a second or third time before being approved. A community's need for a particular project is taken very seriously in this process. Given that many more communities apply than can be funded, a few rather wealthy metro communities (e.g. Plymouth and Woodbury) have been turned down, no matter how appropriate their proposal may be (Barron 2008).

Chapter 2: **PUBLIC POLICY PROMOTION**

Table 2.1 Communities Participating in LCA Programs, 2008, by County

Anoka	Dakota	Hennepin	Ramsey	Scott
Anoka	Apple Valley	Bloomington	Arden Hills	Belle Plaine
Blaine	Burnsville	Brooklyn Center	Falcon Heights	Elko New Market
Centerville	Eagan	Brooklyn Park	Lauderdale	Jordan
Circle Pines	Empire Twnshp	Champlin	Little Canada	Prior Lake
Columbia Hgts	Farmington	Crystal	Maplewood	Savage
Columbus	Hastings	Dayton	Mounds View	Shakopee
Coon Rapids	Inver Grove Hgts	Eden Prairie	New Brighton	
Fridley	Lakeville	Edina	North St. Paul	
Hilltop	Mendota Hgts.	Excelsior	Roseville	
Lexington	Rosemount	Golden Valley	St. Paul	
Lino Lakes	So. St. Paul	Hopkins	Shoreview	
Oak Grove	Sunfish Lake	Long Lake	Vadnais Hgts.	
Ramsey	W. St. Paul	Loretto	White Bear Twp.	
St. Francis		Maple Grove	White Bear Lake	
Spring Lake Pk		Maple Plain		
		Medina		
		Minneapolis		**Washington**
Carver		Minnetonka		
		Minnetonka Beach		Afton
Carver		Mound		Bayport
Chanhassen		New Hope		Cottage Grove
Chaska		Orono		Forest Lake
Cologne		Osseo		Hugo
Hamburg		Plymouth		Lake St. Croix Beach
Mayer		Richfield		Landfall
New Germany		Robbinsdale		Mahtomedi
Norwood/		Rogers		Newport
Young America		St. Anthony		Oakdale
Victoria		St. Bonifacius		Oak Park Heights
Waconia		St. Louis Park		St. Paul Park
Watertown		Wayzata		Stillwater
				Willernie
				Woodbury

Source: Metropolitan Council

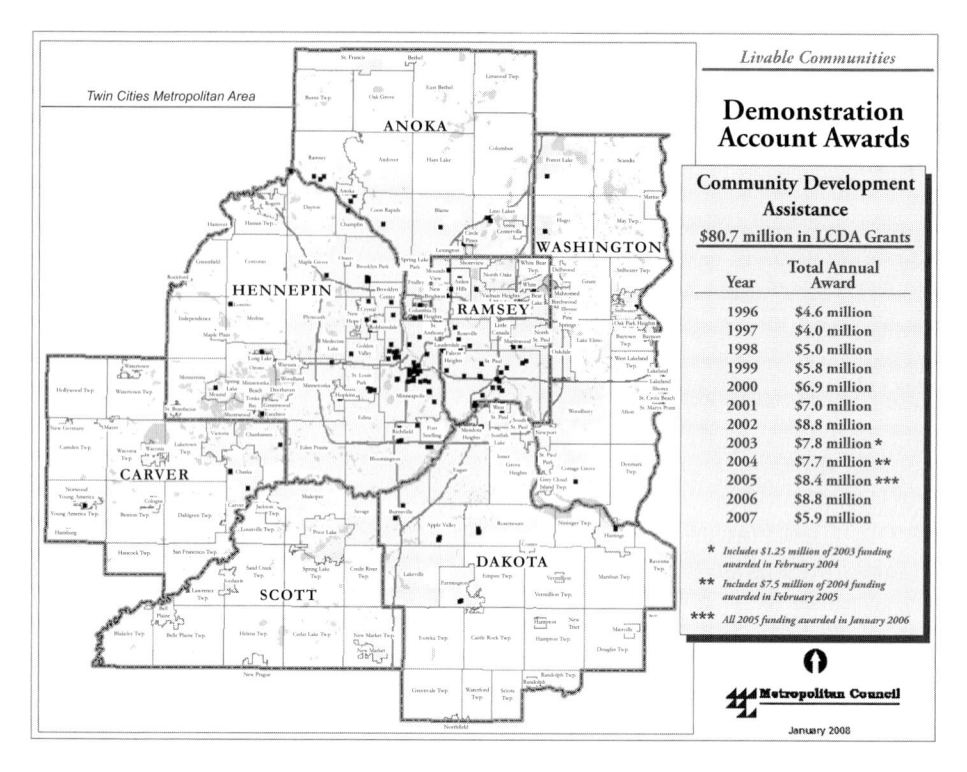

Figure 2.1 Demonstration Account Awards.
© Regents of the University of Minnesota. All rights reserved. Used with permission.

Excelsior and Grand, St. Louis Park

St. Louis Park, just west of Minneapolis, began life as an 1880s manufacturing suburb. Crisscrossed by trains and streetcars, it grew quite fast through the early twentieth century; growth then stalled until the postwar housing boom filled it in. Several important retail corridors were connected through St. Louis Park including Excelsior Boulevard, a four lane road extending west from Minneapolis' popular Lakes district and Highway 100, the Twin Cities' first limited-access beltway. One of the Twin Cities' earliest auto-oriented retail strips, Miracle Mile, sits near the intersection of Excelsior Boulevard and Highway 100. In the following decades, strip malls transformed Excelsior across St. Louis Park and beyond. As the postwar boom morphed into thousands of households "aging in place" by the late 1980s, St. Louis Park and other inner ring suburbs faced an uncertain future.

The community initiated a local community visioning process in the early 1990s, intended to help the city government better serve its constituents – by 1992, hundreds of St. Louis Park residents had participated in this effort. One theme that emerged very strongly from community meetings was a desire to create a central place, a town center designed for pedestrians, in St. Louis Park. Because the City was already discussing ideas for this project, and because its State Senator, Ted Mondale, was the chief LCA author, St. Louis Park was well positioned

Chapter 2: **PUBLIC POLICY PROMOTION**

for an LCDA application in 1996, the fund's first year. It was successful. The community proposed creating a prototypical New Urbanist development on Excelsior Avenue, just east of Highway 100 on the southern border of the 30-acre Wolfe Park.

The initial $139,000 grant paid for a community charrette process which plainly exceeded planners' expectations: they had to expand the room capacity to include 200 residents. A 25-year "Park Commons" plan to redevelop the 125-acre site around Wolfe Park emerged from this visioning process. The first stage, called Excelsior and Grand, opened in 2001 at the very

Figures 2.2a and b Excelsior and Grand, St. Louis Park. *Image from the Metropolitan Design Center Image Bank.*

15

center intersection. The City planned 92 apartments; 18 of these used public financing for low-income families. An additional 10 units were deemed live-work apartments, specifically set-aside for employees of the project's new retail spaces. The first phase also included 55,000 square feet of ground floor retail space, roughly half facing the busy Excelsior and the other half facing inward on Grand (Metropolitan Council 2005b). Project developers scored a major coup by attracting the region's first Trader Joe's market, guaranteeing that the retail spaces would draw well beyond the local market. A town green with benches, paths and public art, emerged in the center of Grand Boulevard.

In 1998, St. Louis Park received its second LCDA grant ($1.2 million) to complete the project's first phase. These funds were used for significant project elements: to subsidize structured parking in the center of each apartment structure (which is shared and publicly available); to locate bus stations at the center of the development; and to provide new sidewalks to connect all the project's elements internally, as well as connecting to surrounding uses. This made it possible for tenants to walk to a coffee shop, or to walk through Park Commons and Wolfe Park to the Park Nicollet health complex, which employs 4,500 people. Then in 2001, St. Louis Park received a third LCDA grant ($1.6 million), to complete all the public infrastructure improvements. The sidewalk and parking improvements allowed the second phase of the plan to begin, including 322 high-end lofts abutting Wolfe Park. These condominium units primarily house mainly young adults and empty-nesters. By 2008, the Excelsior and Grand project was substantially complete (McMonigal 2008).

Largely due to early and deep public involvement in planning, project supporters withstood the predictable opposition that a new and dense project such as Excelsior and Grand typically engenders. As elsewhere, local opponents feared increased congestion, the dangers of more rental property, and the density embodied in the four-story buildings – which do in fact tower over other local buildings. Several project opponents subsequently ran for City Council on an anti-development platform, but lost. After the project's first phase was completed, some of these former opponents even expressed approval, admitting that Excelsior and Grand did not fit their deepest fears embedded in the phrase "increased density."

Excelsior and Grand appears to be meeting many of the city's long-term housing goals. St. Louis Park adopted a 1997 resolution to increase its overall housing stock by 13 percent, or 2,617 units, by 2020. The city's original LCDA proposal estimated that 900 of these units could be accommodated in the Excelsior and Grand redevelopment area – this was later decreased to 660 units. Still, the development marks a major increase in density for St. Louis Park, given that the city cleared only 12 single-family homes for the whole redevelopment area.

Perhaps even more impressive, though, are Excelsior and Grand's retail successes. Apart from the most recent building, all of the commercial space is currently leased. The retail establishments are varied: boutiques, restaurants, salons, coffee shops, a specialized grocer, household furnishings, and an ice cream parlor. Patrons seem to come from the new homes, from the surrounding area, and from beyond St. Louis Park. Walking areas and outdoor seating are well used, as people are drawn to Excelsior Avenue, to the Grand Avenue shops, and to Wolfe Park.

St. Louis Park continues to promote connectivity to Excelsior and Grand. Bus stops along Excelsior Avenue have long linked St. Louis Park to South Minneapolis and downtown, as well as to the neighboring suburbs of Edina and Hopkins. But the new bus shelter at the project's center now elevates the visibility of public transit for the community. Yet another

Chapter 2: **PUBLIC POLICY PROMOTION**

LCDA grant was received to improve 36th Street (wider sidewalks, public art, a new bridge), connecting the high school and community center across Highway 7 to the Park Commons area. There are also new transit circulators linking the development to some nearby retail and medical areas (McMonigal 2008).

Though the larger Park Commons area currently lacks any high-speed transit option, an alignment has recently been set for the region's third LRT connection. The Southwest line will connect this area both to downtown Minneapolis and to suburbs farther out. Two station locations are nearby: Beltline, one-half mile away from Excelsior and Grand, and Wooddale, about three-quarters of a mile away. With a new dedicated transit-funding source, this line will likely be built by 2016. The prospect for continued dense development along Excelsior Boulevard appears poised to succeed.

Alternative transportation modes are also reasonably strong in this part of St. Louis Park. Regional bike paths connect Excelsior and Grand to South Minneapolis, and run through St. Louis Park out to Chanhassen and Chaska; another trail runs far out to Victoria, at the edge of the metro area. Walking paths through Wolfe Park connect residents to many employers – St. Louis Park claims that 10,000 jobs exist within a mile radius of the project. Reportedly some of the first residents were nearby hospital employees. Walking along Excelsior Boulevard remains challenging beyond the immediate project area. But some sections of Excelsior Boulevard are ripe for redevelopment, and improved pedestrian connections are appearing. With more structured public transit on the horizon, even more mixed-use development is increasingly viable in this section of St. Louis Park, given the success of the LCDA-supported projects to date, and the acceptance of the new levels of density.

Downtown Robbinsdale

Robbinsdale is another first-ring suburb, just to the west of Minneapolis' northern edge. With origins in late nineteenth-century truck-farming, it was a classic streetcar suburb well into the 1950s, with a typical Main Street feel along West Broadway Avenue. The small city was fully developed by 1970. Working-class families leaving North Minneapolis flocked to the area's modest single-family houses, creating a tight-knit community focused on baby-boomer children and their schools. A classic bedroom community, Robbinsdale had a modest job base, mainly anchored in a regional hospital. Among 44 cities in Hennepin County today, it has the fifth lowest commercial and industrial tax base per household (Metropolitan Council 2005b).

By the 1970s and 1980s, Robbinsdale faced demographic and commercial challenges, as did many other early suburbs. Though some of the Broadway Avenue retail center retained its original pedestrian flavor, a mix of more auto-oriented new additions slipped in over time, as gas stations eventually occupied several corner lots, and new parking lots interrupted pedestrians. State Highway 81, built one block east of Broadway in the 1960s, shifted retail front doors toward passing cars. By the early 1990s, local leaders were becoming concerned about the community's future, as younger families looked to nearby newer suburbs like New Hope and Maple Grove for larger homes and lots. With an aging population and housing stock, few jobs, and no destination commercial activity, Robbinsdale was facing decline. Property values stagnated throughout the 1980s – Robbinsdale had among the lowest property value increases and greatest poverty rate increases of any community in the Twin Cities (Orfield 1998).

A strong sense of community still persisted, and leaders worked to reverse the decline of their main street. For example, the city relocated a drive-through fast-food restaurant from West Broadway to a corner of Highway 81. But such efforts were sometimes stymied by legal actions, which have even preserved some "LULU" uses. In 1991, the Robbinsdale Economic Development Authority (REDA) commissioned a study of Broadway Avenue; this study ultimately recommended trying to create a sense of place in the old downtown by reconnecting pedestrians to the street and the buildings. REDA followed the study's recommendations, adding street amenities such as matching lampposts, trees, brick crosswalks, and attractive garbage cans and planters (Cornejo 1998). The goal, as elsewhere, was to unify the landscape with a common décor, and thus attract pedestrians, reinforcing a sense that you are in a small downtown, rather than on a suburban strip.

Then in 1993, REDA commissioned a market analysis for the downtown. The former Robbinsdale development director summarized this:

> The consultant's main recommendation was that Robbinsdale's best asset was our traditional, historic West Broadway . . . or rather what was left of it. They challenged us to rebuild, to infill, to increase the density of nearby residential, to add stores and services to the "hometown" mix we already had. They said we shouldn't try to "out suburb" the suburbs. "Hometown" is our market niche.
>
> (Cornejo 1998)

All of this worry and work strongly positioned Robbinsdale to receive a LCDA grant when the program appeared. Their 1996 application held a clear agenda for their downtown that aligned with the LCDA objectives. The plan proposed increasing pedestrian use of Broadway Avenue, boosting residential density, and developing multiple residential and commercial uses, linking all of the new uses to public transit. The City stated its public transit goal in its concept statement for Robbinsdale in the year 2020.

> People will come and go from Robbinsdale by many means including state of the art transit, the automobile, bicycle, and by foot. Multi-modal transportation brings to the businesses a new market from outside the community and support for a pedestrian scale Downtown.
>
> (City of Robbinsdale 2001)

In 1996 Robbinsdale received a $780,000 grant to jump-start several downtown redevelopment projects, and for single-family home acquisition. The grant was intended to increase density in and around the downtown corridor with new retail and residential development; to link downtown residents to public transit; and to allow Robbinsdale to increase the supply of larger single-family homes for younger families.

Two major projects were built using some LCA funding. First, Broadway Court, a 57-unit senior apartment building with ground level retail space, was the largest project, dwarfing the downtown's surrounding 4–10 unit apartment buildings. The design features a historic brick style, with balconies directly above the street and parking behind the building, "New Urbanist" to the core. Second, Hubbard Marketplace – one block away – is a renovation of

Chapter 2: **PUBLIC POLICY PROMOTION**

the 1940s three-story Art Deco police and fire station abutting the freight rail tracks. This became a transit depot with retail and office spaces, and an outdoor space for community events, including a farmers' market. LCDA funds were used to acquire and clear five lots for large single-family home construction, an example of life-cycle housing needs – local officials recognized that the community could not attract younger families without more homes with larger garages. Locally generated projects added streetscape improvements to link City Hall across Highway 81 to the redeveloped downtown, and a zoning revision for a second downtown block, which further encourages future compact, pedestrian friendly development along the Broadway Avenue corridor. Broadway's current auto-era landscape should eventually morph into something more akin to the same street in the early twentieth century. Buildings must now be close to the street, and must be 3–4 stories high, with ground-level retail (Robbinsdale City Code Sect. 521). Parking is to be hidden from view, and shop doors are to line the sidewalks.

Now, over a decade past the LCDA grant and several years after the projects' completion, downtown Robbinsdale still struggles a bit. It must be noted that legislative tinkering has played a role in this. In 2003, Minnesota's massive budget deficit led to a substantial cut in Local Government Aids (LGA). More recent legislative initiatives have reduced or eliminated redevelopment "tools" such as Tax Increment Financing and eminent domain, and relaxed rules about non-conforming uses, which have limited municipal abilities to be as proactive as in the past (Pearson 2008). Broadway Court's residents seem to provide a market for the transit center, but add little life to the retail shops. Most downtown Robbinsdale customers still arrive by automobile. Some storefronts on Broadway Court's block remain vacant, and the Hubbard Marketplace's major tenant is Metro Transit, the Twin Cities bus company.

Still there is potential here, given rising energy prices, as the plan proceeds slowly. There is space for, and interest in, a mixed income community close to downtown Robbinsdale, and transit services may prove the downtown's salvation. There is already a good bicycle connection between central Robbinsdale and Minneapolis. Owing to the success of the region's first line, there is ongoing analysis of LRT potential, coordinated with Hennepin County. Robbinsdale and other north metro communities, having beaten back a Bus Rapid Transit plan that would have missed the downtown and obliterated a remnant of WPA highway art, strongly support a Bottineau Boulevard light rail transit corridor. If this plan is approved and funded, likely given the County's strong interest in transit corridors, downtown Robbinsdale will be transformed in the next decade.

Burnsville's "Heart of the City"

Burnsville is an outer ring Twin Cities' suburb. Largely open space and farmland before 1960, it experienced intense growth from 1960 to 1980, as Interstate 35 split here to link St. Paul and Minneapolis to the south metro area, supplemented by the main east-west arterials, Highways 13 and 42. Nearly half of Burnsville's current housing was built in those two decades (US Census 2000). By 2000 Burnsville was the fourth-largest retail center in the state of Minnesota, largely due to good highway access. But many of its dozens of strip malls were beginning to struggle, with the Mall of America just to the north, and with newer development continuing south toward Lakeville.

Burnsville tried to be proactive about its challenges. Here, as in other communities, pleas for a more walkable town center were rising. This echoed strongly in an intensive 1995 "Partnership for Tomorrow" visioning process involving a thousand Burnsville residents, and area businesses. The Burnsville Economic Development Authority (BEDA) soon began planning a major 54-acre redevelopment centered on Nicollet Avenue and Burnsville Parkway, close to the intersection of TH13 and I-35W. The existing condition of Nicollet here was gas stations, convenience stores and surface parking lots, a clear representation of the recent past.

Burnsville leaders went looking for inspiration, taking in New Urbanist ideas and inspiration at a Chicago Smart Growth conference. Soon after, a streetscape committee that had evolved out of the "Partnership" process morphed into a planning committee for a large project to be called the "Heart of the City" (HOC). The vision was to create a distinct place where one did not currently exist – a "downtown" in Burnsville with new options for suburban living.

> The Heart of the City district will be designed to accommodate the pedestrian. One of the principles of the HOC district is to treat streets as public open spaces and linkages, not barriers . . . The Heart of the City district will resemble a traditional downtown and provide a variety of uses. Shopping, work, restaurants, entertainment, civic uses, cultural activities, parks, townhomes, condominiums and apartments are all permitted throughout the HOC district.
>
> (LCDA application, 14–15)

A "Heart of the City" Committee, with city staff and citizens would oversee the district's ongoing planning and development. The city hired a development firm, an architectural firm and a market research corporation to complete a design framework manual. This manual shares all of the now-traditional New Urbanist town planning goals, proposing to: create compact and mixed-use spaces; create green open spaces, accentuating the public over the private, and promoting a pedestrian atmosphere; it specifies brick, stone and glass building materials and frequent window locations to prevent "boring, blank walls"; it proposes building locations to closely line the streets and building alignments to form a "building wall"; and it proposes parking in the rear with much greenery, traditional overhanging signage and even street furniture. Ultimately, the manual led to a significant zoning change for this area (Burnsville HOC Manual 1999).

Although the first glimmerings of the Heart of the City project coincided with the 1995 passage of the LCA, four years of discussion and planning passed before the plan moved forward. Some residents, objecting to the potential for public subsidy and fearing the loss of the community's suburban character, opposed the project. The lone opponent on the five-member city council called the project "a financial rathole," (*Burnsville This Week* 1999). But supporters had done their homework. The city created a design committee to review every element of the HOC district, requiring developers to get the approval of this body. Early on, one developer proposed a traditional big box development in the district; the design committee strongly objected, and the City Council supported them by rejecting the proposal. This was a strong signal that Burnsville was committed to change. Following the 1999 passage of a new zoning district, Burnsville applied for and received a $1.6 million LCDA grant.

LCDA funds (from the first grant) went toward "street improvements." This involved constructing new streets on the east side of Nicollet, and in the area of the CDA town-homes

Chapter 2: **PUBLIC POLICY PROMOTION**

and other development, transforming a formerly inaccessible area into a "place." But the City's proposal also outlined the potential for significant private development, which began to emerge. In 2003, The Grand Market Place, a 133-unit apartment complex with 15,000 square feet of retail space opened. Fifty units here were rent subsidized, specifically reserved for residents below 30 percent of the region's median income. The City argued for this as part of the funding mechanism for the project, in line with Metropolitan Council goals (Pearson 2008). Increasing affordable housing units, with strong ties to public transit, appeared an obvious win-win.

In 2000, Burnsville again applied to LCDA for $2.5 million for Nicollet Commons Park. This grant created a centerpiece 1.5-acre park, just north of the Grand Market Place, which opened in 2004, with a watercourse and mini-amphitheater. Residents, bus commuters and visitors can use the 360 stall parking ramp built with a federal grant, and linked by circulator to the large Burnsville Transit Center across Highway 13.

Across Nicollet Avenue from the Grand Market Place, another large redevelopment emerged in the HOC area. The Dakota County Community Development Agency (CDA) completed 34 rental rowhouses for households below 80 percent of the area median income. HOC's largest development is Nicollet Plaza, a 17-acre site featuring 195 four-story condominiums (many facing the street), retail space turned inward to the development, 30 townhomes, and a new supermarket and commercial/retail strip with a bank and office building. Uptown Landing is another condo project with 111 units just east of Nicollet Plaza, and more townhouses and retail has been built. Altogether the HOC development includes 434 dwelling units, raising the density ratio in the immediate area to 20 per acre from virtually zero (City of Burnsville).

Figure 2.3 Heart of the City, Burnsville. *Image from the Metropolitan Design Center Image Bank.*

Source: © Regents of the University of Minnesota. All rights reserved. Used with permission.

The increased residential density is Heart of the City's great success. Since opening, Grande Market Place has been fully occupied, with a waiting list. The townhouses and condominiums, completed in 2007, have struggled along with the rest of the Twin Cities' and national market. The city has worked to improve the pedestrian experience, installing signed crosswalks, but Nicollet Avenue remains a four-lane, high automobile traffic street. The Nicollet Commons Park is a success; available for rental and with programmed events, it attracts an estimated 30,000 people to HOC annually. By January 2009, the city will have a new performing arts center, which will seat 1,000. Grand Market Square is close to full, with a culinary school/banquet center, shops, and a floor of offices; Grande Market Place has some vacancies, with expectations these will fill once the performing arts center opens (Pearson 2008).

HOC advocates wanted to create a new downtown in a sprawling suburb. To the extent that this is possible, it appears to be working. Burnsville residents are finding reasons to use the HOC district for recreation and entertainment. Many former single-family homeowners have chosen a new lifestyle here; and some who want a "downtown" lifestyle find HOC more affordable than either of the two downtowns. There are still few transit options, but an expected high-speed bus lane on I35W (under construction in 2008) will improve commute times for those working in Minneapolis. None of this will help the majority of suburban workers whose jobs are still not easily reached by transit. They can live in a downtown, but still have to drive.

Downtown St. Paul's North Quadrant

St. Paul's North Quadrant, the northeastern corner of the downtown, enclosed by the I–94 and I–35 interchange, was a sea of surface parking lots from the late 1970s to the late 1990s. Only a few blocks from St. Paul's commercial and government centers, parking rates here were cheap and spaces were available. The only other uses in the North Quadrant were some nonprofit agencies, a small grocery, a few bars and small businesses. Ideas for redeveloping the site dated to the 1980s, including an industrial facility, an office park, or the expansion of the St. Paul's Farmer's Market (Minneapolis St. Paul Business Journal 2000).

Several mid-1990s trends finally spurred North Quadrant redevelopment: first, the mayor was focused on downtown redevelopment and wanted increased housing options; second, city planning staff were strong proponents of New Urbanist designs and principles; third, St. Paul was cognizant of the "return to the city" downtown housing booms across the country, possibly even a bit envious of Minneapolis's central riverfront success; and fourth the Livable Communities Act provided funding for the early stages of planning and development.

Working with the Mississippi Design Center, the City hosted a community workshop to develop a plan for the North Quadrant. As in many other Twin Cities' communities, this plan can be read as a New Urbanist handbook. It recommended a locally-specific mix of the usual approaches: creating green space on the street by constructing a park; attracting pedestrians with landscaping, lighting and attractive walkways; slowing traffic and replacing surface parking with structured parking; constructing mixed use buildings at an appropriate scale and in context; and preserving sound historical buildings.

The plan moved smoothly from idea to action. While several business owners worried that new development would displace them, or make customer parking difficult, only a few were ultimately displaced; only one refused the City's purchase offer. The near-absent protest

Chapter 2: **PUBLIC POLICY PROMOTION**

about redeveloping a 15-block area in downtown owed largely to the North Quadrant's underuse. But the City Planning Department's cooperative tone, overall community participation in the vision process, and the eventual developer's full and enthusiastic participation with the neighborhood group likely helped calm concerned business owners.

Existing downtown residents welcomed a new residential neighborhood, and were impressed by the developer's plans. Most agreed that the development needed a major amenity to attract the first residents. As the only real amenity in the North Quadrant area was easy highway access, creating a one block square park in the middle of the project, eventually named Wacouta Commons, became a central goal. LCDA funding was needed for the park space, as Tax Increment Financing (TIF) could not be used for this purpose. A park could help draw people reluctant to live downtown, and the city viewed this project as catalytic, and necessary to attract private investment.

St. Paul received a $960,000 LCDA grant in 1999 for public infrastructure improvements. This grant allowed the City to realign a street to create a block large enough for a planned housing development. The grant also helped to straighten a curve along 7th Street, to slow traffic and improve safety for pedestrians. Over half this grant was applied toward the first stages of the park development, to acquire the land, and begin construction. The city formed a citizen committee of downtown residents to help design the park. They planned a playground for children, walking paths through the park, and a dog run along one side of the park. As housing would surround the park, the Committee agreed that it should primarily serve the new residents. Construction began in 2000 but despite an additional $500,000 LCDA grant in 2001, a tight budget prevented most of the park amenities from being completed until 2005.

With this commitment to a major amenity, residential construction in the North Quadrant took off as reasonably mixed-income neighborhood. The City's original LCDA application was for 210 rental units and 64 town-home and condo units built around the park. Two apartment rental buildings, Sibley Park and Sibley Court, were built, ultimately including 236 units, 10 units to replace demolished public housing, and another 32 Section 8 units. Two more upscale condominium and townhouse buildings, the Essex and the Dakota, with purchase prices between $200,000 and $400,000, expanded to 75 units. The 9th Street Lofts and Printer's Row, with more than 100 units, priced from $200,000–$600,000, also contain eight Habitat for Humanity units for low-income families. A 60-unit senior citizen rental building has also been built. St. Paul's 2001 LCDA application, which garnered another $500,000, estimated the North Quadrant would eventually include 600–800 housing units (North Quadrant website). St. Paul is nearing this goal. There is a certain pleasant uniformity to the North Quadrant, largely dictated by the existing converted warehouses. The fact that two local developers, Michael Lander and George Sherman, won all eight bids for North Quadrant buildings also contributes to this cohesion.

The project's retail spaces all face 7th Street, a major arterial abutting the project's southern boundary. There are very few vacancies. The early fear of business owners opposed to the project has been eased, as they are increasingly viewed as an asset to the neighborhood (Gilyard 2005). The community organization still hopes to draw a larger grocery store to the downtown, and patiently awaits the indoor expansion of the popular downtown farmer's market.

Because of its downtown location, the North Quadrant is an easy walk from most of St. Paul's bus routes, and from the largest employment center and retail spaces. Its design also promotes walking: the street grid was partially reconstructed to create short blocks; walkways across 7th Street link the neighborhood to Lowertown, the downtown artist-loft residential community; and the Sibley Court and Sibley Park complexes each have walking paths through their centers. All roads within the project's borders have on-street parking. Short blocks and four-way stops also help to slow traffic, and reduce through-traffic. To encourage street life, St. Paul prohibits any extension of its extensive skyway system to the North Quadrant. The developers chose to provide minimal parking of 1.5 stalls per ownership unit and 0.8 per rental unit, far below any other area in St. Paul, which also supports transit (Thompson 2008).

In what may seem a decision to limit density, North Quadrant building heights were limited to six stories, both to drastically improve ground cover and street life, and to recognize the historic character of the area. This was a deliberate choice to provide options in the downtown housing market. Several high-rise condo and rental buildings dating from the 1960s to 1980s had earlier saturated the downtown housing market, spurring little surrounding development. By drastically increasing density (80 dwelling units per acre), but limiting concentration on any one block, demand for new buildings continues. A six-story limit was also an economic decision, as any building above such a height would require a more expensive concrete frame. Still, there can be no doubt that the North Quadrant has been transformative for downtown St. Paul.

The Village at Mendota Heights

Mendota Heights is one of the Twin Cities' most historic communities, dating from initial settlement in the 1840s. Located just across the Minnesota River from the international airport, Mendota Heights is considerably smaller in scale than Burnsville or St. Louis Park. As with other Twin Cities' suburbs in the late 1990s, Mendota Heights was looking for redevelopment options, this one and others spurred perhaps more by the existence of LCDA funding than specific need.

Mendota Heights' LCDA project came later than some of the others described here; they did not apply until 2001 and 2002. The proposal was for a new "town square," appropriately enough on the site of the town's original nineteenth-century city hall and market-square. "The Village" comprises three "lifecycle neighborhoods," with street-level retail at the center. There are approximately 135 housing units: 39 two-story rowhouses; 36 two-story loft condominiums, and 60 high-density senior apartments (City of Mendota Heights). This project feels somewhat more private than Excelsior and Grand or Heart of the Cities, with secured fenced entries and private decks that mimic a gated community more than a new town center. Prices of the units started at $359,000 – far higher than the Twin Cities' median home price at the time. Sixty affordable units and some live/work units were included in the project as the Dakota County Community Development Agency (CDA), along with a private developer, is a partner in the development.

The Village's retail plan emulates that of Lake Forest, Illinois' Market Square, which pioneered the concept of a suburban main street shopping center. Nearly 47,000 square feet of retail space comprise "The Village," centered on a newly constructed town square. Plans called for a "mix of neighborhood convenience, specialty, and destination uses" – to create a central shopping district that Mendota Heights lacked. It now features various places to eat, shops, and commercial services. LCDA grants totaling over $1.1 million in 2002 and 2003 were used to build structured public-use parking to foster the commercial development (Kollman 2005).

Although access to "The Village" via Highway 13 exists and is well-marked, options for public transportation are not evident. Walking is focused on connecting to the town's park system, as sidewalks meander outward in that direction. This, in turn, connects to regional recreation trails that are a centerpiece of the Twin Cities. So, Mendota Heights is well-equipped for bicycle commuting, if not for mass transit.

Evaluating the LCDA Projects

Following the 1995 legislation establishing the LCA, dozens of projects are now completed and many more are underway. While the Metropolitan Council is generally positive about overall LCA efforts, there have been some challenges and some changes, some disagreements about the program's focus, and some politics. Local advocates of the program have often argued that it makes more sense to focus LCA funds on the region's core cities. In fact, the two big cities have always made more applications – in 2008 ten came from Minneapolis and St. Paul, eleven from all other cities (Barron 2008). The LCA point system itself is location neutral, searching only for worthy applications.

But in 2004, two separate sources of pressure led to a significant reassessment of the LCA program: outer-ring suburban legislators objected to the disproportionate funding of projects in Minneapolis and St. Paul; and questions began to be raised internally by some Metropolitan Council members about the program's actual purpose. The first concern ultimately led to increased project funding in outer-ring suburbs, as New Urbanist style projects have slowly spread all across the greater Twin Cities' region. The Metro Council did this by stipulating that Minneapolis and St. Paul could receive no more than 40 percent of any year's funding, reflecting the average that the two cities have been awarded over the life of the program. This change is consistent with evolving local politics (a Republican outer-ring suburban Governor since 2002, and a Republican controlled House until recently). A new Legislative Oversight Committee also came in to the picture.

The second concern led to changes in what the Metropolitan Council would fund going forward. Eligible uses of the funds would now be restricted to basic public infrastructure, such as streets and street extensions, sidewalks, trails connecting to transit, site assembly, and clearance; "add-ons" such as park spaces were no longer eligible, even though these might create more livability (Barron 2008). This then refocused the LCDA grants on projects that served a clear "public-purpose," without which a project could not move forward. The post-2004 Metropolitan Council has also been focused on programmatic results within a defined period of time (projects have two years to get underway, with an automatic one year extension). But they have been willing to allow changes in projects that are underway, for example accepting a shift from condos to rental units, given the current condo glut. Administrative changes also emerged, as the Advisory Committee's formerly open-ended terms were now limited to three years (Barron 2008).

These shifts make some wonder whether the Metropolitan Council is ignoring its own long-term plans outlined in the 2030 Regional Development Framework, adopted in 2001. While the Framework emphasizes growth along transit corridors, some of the newest exurban LCDA projects appear to contradict this principle.

In terms of functionality, some of the larger outer-ring suburban projects may face challenges. Indeed, one significant project, the Ramsey Town Center, a commuter rail station development, has languished since being approved, in part due to the developer's death. Lacking a tradition of former streetcar connections, or an existing town center – most second ring suburbs were farms for a century – many such communities are only now trying to define themselves for the first time, as their residents clamor for a "town center" or for places to walk. It is challenging for a New Urbanist development to succeed in exurban locations, surrounded only by low density, auto-oriented land uses. If Calthorpe is correct that "pedestrians are the catalyst which makes the essential qualities of communities meaningful," then the projects described above, and others coming forward, must work hard to ensure that they emerge as something other than one high density development after another in a sea of otherwise spread-out suburbs (1993: 17).

Perhaps a bit of density is enough though. As the Twin Cities is projected to add over 450,000 households by 2030, increased density in many locations could help moderate continued exurban sprawl (Metropolitan Council 2005b). As some fraction of the baby-boom generation leaves behind big houses on big lots, these LCDA projects everywhere could help keep people in familiar communities, but house them more efficiently. If Burnsville, for example, continues infill projects with higher densities, it could meet or exceed its projected share of Twin Cities' growth. At the same time, if it cannot replace some automobile trips with pedestrian and transit trips, traffic congestion and lessened air quality in the metro area will increase. The Burnsville transit center shows some promise that the "Heart of the City" can actually link pedestrians and public transit in an outer ring suburb. To do this though, Burnsville needs to get pedestrians in its new development across a busy highway safely and easily. Some of the existing transit investments make drawing more people to the street more possible.

Excelsior and Grand has a significant locational advantage over the Burnsville project, but its development plan was more pedestrian-oriented from the start – sidewalks were already in place. The design here links housing, retail spaces and jobs with sidewalks, benches, green spaces and parks – it successfully creates a more walkable community. It also has surrounding uses that offer potential for continued high density growth: aging commercial uses and existing low residential density on some blocks. Excelsior Boulevard is already an activity center, though in the form of a high traffic, four-lane highway which can be a bit daunting for slower pedestrians. St. Louis Park has created a central boulevard here to create a visual linkage through the city. Proximity to Minneapolis allows a quick commute to downtown, A bus link is in place, and light rail is coming. When it first appeared, Excelsior and Grand felt like a New Urbanist island in St. Louis Park. Recent developments have instead transformed this area into a regional node.

In Robbinsdale, the LRT discussion bodes well for the community's future; it will link to downtown Minneapolis and beyond. Today, this downtown struggles to fill its commercial spaces and add new housing. The elderly and low-income downtown populations provide a modest market for the retail spaces. So, despite a pedestrian-friendly, transit-friendly design, most people come to and from downtown Robbinsdale in cars. The centerpiece art-deco Hubbard Marketplace, a transit hub and farmer's market, struggles a bit with retail leasing. But Robbinsdale was careful not to push more development too quickly. Instead the city focused on improving its main street, awaiting a stronger market. This more gradual approach means that Robbinsdale might eventually have buildings built years apart, of different uses and with

Chapter 2: **PUBLIC POLICY PROMOTION**

different architectural styles, so its buildings will not all become unfashionable at the same time. Perhaps the "timeless" North Quadrant buildings, as developer Lander calls them, will also create a community with a long-term character. Here again, a more gradual approach yielded a park and maintained a church, creating a more natural looking urban community.

The North Quadrant also shows how even a big plan for a high density pedestrian community still needs a big push (like LCDA) before the market can successfully step in. Infrastructure projects funded by the LCDA, and other public programs, created a real non-highrise housing market in downtown St. Paul for the first time in more than a century. Other local developers, aware of Lander and Sherman's success, have successfully competed for several New Urbanist projects along St. Paul's redeveloping riverfront, creating a new pool of builders experienced with such projects. There is also significant potential to link all of these new downtown projects to public transit. Downtown St. Paul has many bus routes. By 2014 it will have a multi-modal terminus serving the region's second light rail line – the Central Corridor connecting to downtown Minneapolis – and the relocated Amtrak station. Bike commuting has increased in St. Paul as well, and the North Quadrant links easily to bike lanes and major regional trails.

Local advocates have argued that it would make more sense to focus LCA funds on the region's core cities. In fact, the two big cities have always made more applications – in 2008 ten came from Minneapolis and St. Paul, 11 from all other cities. The LCA point system itself is location neutral, searching only for worthy applications. Still the post-2002 Metro Council did stipulate that Minneapolis and St. Paul could receive no more than 40 percent of any year's funding, reflecting the average that the two cities have been awarded over the life of the program (Barron 2008). Thus LCA funds have recently been spread more broadly throughout the metro area, consistent with evolving local politics (a Republican outer-ring suburban Governor since 2002, and a Republican controlled House until 2006). This shift makes some wonder whether the Metropolitan Council is ignoring its own long-term plans outlined in the 2030 Regional Development Framework, adopted in 2001. While the Framework emphasizes growth along transit corridors, some of the newest LCDA projects appear to contradict this principle.

Ultimately, Livable Community projects here and elsewhere can only succeed if their development plans are integrated with regional transit planning. In the Twin Cities region, new transit planning waned a bit between 2003 and 2008, even as new capacity was added to the system. The Metropolitan Council even implemented service cuts in several of those years. With the passage of a dedicated transit tax in the 2008 legislative session (adopted by five of the seven metro counties), hopes are now high that transit planning – linked to land use planning – can begin to catch up to where transit advocates think it ought to be. The Twin Cities has not had a clear regional growth strategy to reduce auto trips and encourage transit, though recent gas prices increases seem to be adjusting behavior in this direction. Until significantly more transit options exist (rather than being in planning stages), many LCA projects will still struggle to become truly pedestrian and transit-oriented Livable Communities.

Given the political popularity of smart growth strategies nationally (Szold 2002) and the unexpected success of the Twin Cities' first light rail line, pressures for mixed-use development are already increasing dramatically. It is commonplace today to assume that increasing costs of driving and increasing bus/LRT ridership, combined with the widespread impacts of the foreclosure disaster, may well add to these pressures. But development will continue to occur throughout the entire Twin Cities and beyond. This remains a polycentric metro area, created by cheap auto travel and expansive roads. The legacy of such intense, transformative development will not disappear quickly. Still, the future Twin Cities will likely see intense growth in the urban and suburban centers, and along multiple transportation spokes. If more of this new development occurring along transit corridors can begin to link housing with job centers, as the new BRT lines, the commuter rail, and expected LRT lines will do, the LCA model, driven by frustrated public policy, will appear prescient indeed.

Acknowledgments

Critical research assistance from Lance Kollman, and especially Christopher Duffrin, was crucial to this project, as was the generous help of Joanne Barron (Metropolitan Council's manager of the LCDA program from its inception). I am also indebted to several local planners who read and commented on early drafts: Lucy Thompson (St. Paul); Meg McMonigal (St. Louis Park); Rick Pearson (Robbinsdale); Deb Garross and Skip Nienhaus (Burnsville).

References

Barron, Joanne. Manuscript review. 2008.
Burnsville HOC Manual, 2000 (includes LCDA application).
Burnsville This Week, August 21, 1999, p.7A .
Calthorpe, Peter. *The Next American Metropolis: Ecology, Community, and the American Dream.* New York: Princeton Architectural Press, 1993.
City of Burnsville. *Heart of the City.* Accessed August 4, 2010. www.ci.burnsville.mn.us/index.asp?NID=89.
City of Mendota Heights. www.mendota-heights.com/pages/whatsnew/village.html.
City of Robbinsdale. *Comprehensive Plan – Vision 20/20.* Adopted 11/20/01. http://www.ci.robbinsdale.mn.us/devtCompPlan.htm.
Cornejo, Dan, Renewing the old Urbanism: learning from Robbinsdale. *Planning Minnesota.* Newsletter of the Minnesota Chapter of the American Planning Association, June 1998.
Duany, Andrés, Elizabeth Plater-Zyberk and Jeff Speck. *Suburban Nation: The Rise of Sprawl and the Decline of the American Dream.* New York: North Point Press, 2001.
Duany, Andrés Elizabeth Plater-Zyberk and Robert Alminana. *The New Civic Art: Elements of Town Planning.* New York: Rizzoli, 2003.
Gilyard, Burt. Renaissance owner has big dreams, little money. *Finance and Commerce*, March 31, 2005.
Goetz, Edward G., Fair share or status quo? The twin cities livable Communities Act, *Journal of Planning Education and Research*, 20, 1, 37–51, 2000.
Kollman, Lance. Undergraduate researcher. 2005.
McMonigal, Meg. Manuscript review. 2008.
Martin, Judith A., In fits and starts, in *Metropolitan Governance: American/Canadian Intergovernmental Perspective*s, ed. A. Sancton and D. Rothblatt, Berkeley, CA, Institute of Governmental Studies Press, University of California, 1993.

Chapter 2: PUBLIC POLICY PROMOTION

Martin, Judith A., Renegotiating metropolitan consciousness, *Metropolitan Governance* (2nd edn), ed. A. Sancton and D. Rothblatt, Berkeley, CA, Institute of Governmental Studies Press, University of California, 1998.

Martin, Judith A., What the neighbors want, *Journal of the American Planning Association*, 68, 4, Autumn 2002 (with Paula Pentel).

Martin, Judith A., A county and its cities: the impact of Hennepin Community Works, *Journal of Urban Affairs*, 30, 3, 2008 (with Justin Jacobson).

Metropolitan Council. Metropolitan Livable Communities Act: accomplishments. Budgeted Funds 1996 through 2004. www.metrocouncil.org/services/livcomm/LCAAccomplishmentsThruDec2004.pdf, 2005a.

Metropolitan Council, Fiscal disparities taxes payable, http://www.metrocouncil.org/metroarea/FiscalDisparities2005/fiscaldisp.htm, 2005b.

Metropolitan Council, Excelsior and Grand, St. Louis Park, June 2006. www.metrocouncil.org/planning/tod/ExcelsiorandGrand.pdf.

Metropolitan Council Regional report (to the MN. State Legislature), June 2008.

Metropolitan Council, Livable communities program, July 2010. www.metrocouncil.org/about/facts/LivableCommunitiesFacts.pdf.

Minnesota Statutes, Sections 473.25 through 473.254.1995.

North Quadrant eyed for housing, *Minneapolis St. Paul Business Journal*: February 25, 2000.

Orfield, Myron, Conflict or consensus? Forty years of Minnesota metropolitan politics, *Brookings Review*, 16, Fall 1998.

Pearson, Rick. Manuscript review. 2008.

Robbinsdale City Code Sect. 521.

Szold, Terry S. Smart growth: form and consequences, *Land Lines*, 14, 3, July 2002.

Thompson, Lucy. Manuscript review. 2008.

US Census of Population, 2000.

Chapter 3

VARIATIONS IN REGULATORY FACTORS AFFECTING NEIGHBORHOOD LIVABILITY: AN INTERNATIONAL PERSPECTIVE

Elise Bright

Professor, Department of Landscape Architecture and Urban Planning
Texas A&M University

Introduction

As awareness of environmental issues rises, the true costs of sprawl become known, and the US population becomes increasingly characterized by the elderly and single parents, the goal of creating more livable communities based on the concepts of smart growth, sustainable development and New Urbanism has captured the American public. Communities such as Addison Circle and the Woodlands in Texas, Columbia and the Kentlands in Maryland, and redeveloped loft housing in downtowns throughout the country are experiencing very high demand and commanding premium prices; indeed, developers cannot keep up with demand for these "livable" areas despite a massive slump in real estate overall that has severely damaged the market for traditional single family homes in sprawling, car-centered developments.

This sea change in the amenities and basic structure desired by the public from their communities has led to a paradigm shift in plan implementation: planners and policymakers are now trying to develop regulations and financing mechanisms that ensure that new development will both create livable communities and encourage redevelopment of the existing built environment in America to make it more livable. Planners, elected officials and residents want more livable communities, and are creating high-quality plans to redirect urban life in America toward this vision. However, the tools to effectively turn these plans' visions into reality remain elusive: too often the new regulations are simply layered on to the existing ones, creating a development approval and enforcement maze that is not only confusing and somewhat contradictory, but often rests on shaky legal ground as well. For example, the regulations governing a single New Urbanist development can run fifty pages or more and still allow for so much discretion that defending them in court could be difficult.[1]

Other nations contain many livable urban neighborhoods which function in a political-social-economic context that reflects very different legal authority and cultural traditions regarding

Chapter 3: **INTERNATIONAL PERSPECTIVE**

plan implementation than those that underlie development in modern America. Some of these were built before local regulatory tools such as zoning were even dreamed of; by protecting the vibrancy and viability of these neighborhoods, however, the regulations that came to govern these areas do play an important role in their continued existence. Others were built after regulations were in place. What can we learn from this vast spectrum of experience in creating and protecting livable communities throughout the world?

This chapter will examine the regulatory tools used by planners and policymakers around the world to create, protect, and/or preserve livable communities. The chapter opens with a discussion of definitions of what makes a neighborhood livable. Next, the regulatory tools traditionally used in the US to achieve livability are briefly reviewed and critiqued. Our scope is limited to regulatory tools simply in the interest of space; it would take a book to cover the financial plan implementation tools (public private partnerships, tax abatement, fee rebates, etc.) alone. Our gaze then shifts to a world view, discussing basic differences in government regulation in various parts of the world and giving examples of plan implementation to create or sustain livable communities in some of these nations. The chapter concludes with suggestions for further research.

What Makes a Neighborhood Livable?

Planning is a systematic, creative way to influence and respond to a wide variety of changes occurring in a neighborhood, in a city, in an entire region, or around the world. Planners assist communities to formulate plans and policies to meet their social, economic, environmental, and cultural needs in the face of societal forces. Planners do so by identifying problems and opportunities, evaluating alternative solutions or plans, and communicating their findings in ways that allow citizens and public officials to make knowledgeable choices about the future. Planning can preserve and enhance the quality of life; protect the physical and natural environment; promote equitable economic growth; distribute services to disadvantaged communities; and, respond effectively to all development of all kinds.[2]

As this quote clearly shows, planning is deeply concerned with creating, enhancing and preserving livable communities. But what do we mean by that term?

A few years ago I went to a tiny Native American village above the Arctic Circle. It was only accessible by air. When I stepped out of the three-passenger Cessna that brought me there, hordes of humongous mosquitoes attacked. The land was gently rolling, barren, and extremely windswept. Even in July, it was cold. Clapboard and metal houses peppered the few unpaved streets, which existed mainly for the use of the town's lone pickup truck and the numerous ATVs that kids were riding; caribou hides festooned the porches of several homes, presumably to dry.

I made the five-minute trek to the other side of town and found the only tourist attraction, the Simon Paneak Museum. Inside, one of the founder's descendants sat alone at the counter, in front of a wall filled with fearsome-looking masks. She was friendly and articulate, educated, and had lived in the "lower 48" for some time, but chose to return to this barren outpost. "What's so good about life here? You seem to have so little!" I marveled. She thought for a long moment, then replied, "We share everything. When someone kills a caribou we all enjoy the meat. In the fall the whole community goes berry picking. When someone is sick, we all care for them. It's a real community."

If Census data were used to measure the quality of life here it would come out miserably: income was very low, as was the level of services – from street paving to medical care. But there was also much here that urban Americans lack: a high level of personal safety, a great social network, no traffic jams, plenty of leisure time, and what appeared to be a very low-stress lifestyle. Although poor, these people enjoyed a decent quality of life – superior in some ways to our own.

A review of many factors used to rank the quality of life in urban areas reveals that they fall into four broad categories: safety, shelter, services, and social capital.[3] Within each of these four categories, there are a multitude of more specific, measurable factors: for example, the safety category includes factors ranging from air pollution levels to arrest rates for drugs; it covers the full spectrum of factors that affect personal health and safety. The shelter category includes factors relating to the presence of a clean and attractive community appearance and the availability of decent, affordable homes; the services category includes measures of a wide range of businesses, entertainment and services nearby; and the social capital category includes less measurable factors such as community groups, friendly neighbors, and places to socialize.

In the US, most of the original neighborhoods were once good places to live; many could have served as models for the New Urbanism we seek to create today. But over time, their ability to provide a high quality of life for their residents declined. Crime rates have soared, buildings have been abandoned or fallen into disrepair, home ownership has declined, schools have failed, businesses have closed. Only social capital has survived, as those remaining band together to help each other and resist the adverse effects of declines in the quality of safety, services and structures. Now there is evidence that this "urban decay" is spreading to the older suburbs, and even residents of new suburbs sometimes fear for their safety. For many years the residents have reacted to this decline by fleeing to the suburbs, but this trend is now slowing and in some cases even reversing, as people find that the auto-dominated suburban communities not only lack easy access to a variety of services and housing types but are often wastelands for social capital – the very heart of the vibrancy found in many original neighborhoods.

Regulatory Tools in the United States

Zoning is the single most important, widely used regulatory plan implementation tool in the United States today. In the US it is essentially a police power given by the states to local governments that is designed to put restrictions and delineations of use rights on land. The term "zoning" as used here encompasses any regulation relating to the use of land that has different requirements for different parts of the city; thus parking, signage, landscaping and design regulations are included if they vary from zone to zone, but subdivision regulations are not included because they are required by law to be uniform throughout the community.

Zoning authority is derived from the Fifth and Fourteenth Amendments to the US Constitution, which established the basis for the "police power" as a reason for government to act. Under this power, government should act to protect public health, safety, morals, and

Chapter 3: INTERNATIONAL PERSPECTIVE

general welfare – hence the state's ability to establish police forces, provide fire protection, require testing of water supplies, zone property, etc. However, since the Constitution does not specifically list zoning as a national power, in the US the power to zone lies with each of the fifty states. This situation derives from the Tenth Amendment, which reserves for the states all powers not specifically listed in the Constitution as belonging to the national government. This is important because the restrictions on the national power to control land use that are contained in the Constitution itself have significantly shaped zoning, making it a fairly effective tool for preventing harm but a difficult instrument to use to create more livable communities.

Despite its roots in the Constitution (which was ratified in 1788), zoning was not invented for nearly another 150 years. By this time problems with incompatible land use were developing as the Industrial Revolution (followed by the car) reshaped urban land use, creating miserable conditions in some urban neighborhoods and increasing the effects of negative externalities in others as cities grew. Amid a growing public outcry that local government take action, in 1916 New York City passed an ordinance which divided the entire city into four zones: residential, commercial, "unrestricted," and "undetermined." Several other cities followed suit, but zoning's constitutionality was not clear until it was upheld in the *Village of Euclid v. Ambler Realty* case that was decided by the US Supreme Court in 1926, when the US Supreme Court declared a zoning law that restricted apartments to be valid.

During these early years it became clear that if local government was to have the authority to zone, laws were needed to delegate that power from the fifty states down to the local level. This transfer of authority occurs via state zoning enabling acts; today all US states have zoning enabling acts that are based on the Standard State Zoning Enabling Act (SZEA), a model that was written by staff of the national Commerce Department in the early 1920s.[4] This is important, because the language contained in that model has directed, and limited, the course of zoning to this day; and in many ways this model, along with the underlying Constitutional provisions, set American zoning apart from other implementation tools used around the world and seal its ineffectiveness as a tool for creating more livable places. Let us examine the specifics.

Issues and Problems with the Legal Framework of US Zoning

Who should decide on the appropriate level of limits to private property rights? In the US and most other countries that were once occupied by the British (from Canada to Saudi Arabia to India to New Zealand to Hong Kong), the job falls to government. This can be very tricky, and many court cases have hinged on the issue of whether government regulations such as zoning are an excessive use of the police power. The most common complaint is that the regulations are so restrictive that they deprive the private owner of the value of his or her property; this argument is known as the takings issue. In many nations, the government has so much power that individual property rights are trampled and the takings issue is nonexistent: for example, a friend from Iran watched helplessly as the local government sent a wrecking crew to bulldoze a path through the middle of his parents' sprawling home so a road could be extended. His parents received no payment, but they did retain ownership of the two ends of the home. In the US, this would be considered a taking of private property and the government would have to pay the owner for his loss.

Clearly, some government intervention in the land market is in the best interest of the people, to protect them from negative externalities – many costs of development are not included in the price of the land or building, and can significantly and adversely affect others. But overregulation can also be very destructive, even killing the private property market. The trick is to find the right balance.

One approach generally taken in the US is to support regulations designed to prevent harm (for example, restrictions on floodplain development) without extending them so far as to create benefits (for example, regulating the colors used in holiday lighting displays). But even establishing the level of regulation that is needed to prevent harm can be difficult because, for example, an activity that could be harmful in one place may be completely acceptable in another location. If you owned 3,000 acres in the country you could probably raise cattle, plant a field of corn, sell your produce from a roadside stand, build and operate a tourist hotel, build a house, even keep an elephant without harming your neighbors' health or safety. However, if you owned a vacant lot in the city then any of these activities could cause problems – or, as planners say, create negative externalities – for your neighbors, thus justifying their regulation under the police power. Local laws restricting deliveries, noise from parties, toxics in the local creek, storage of junk and stock and equipment, etc., will vary with the density of the community, the land use pattern, local tolerance, etc., but they are all based on this power. In the US, your right to use property as you please is not absolute, because of negative externalities; i.e. nuisances (noise), health threats (toxics), safety issues (traffic), and general welfare (unsightly storage, lowered property value) are all used to justify restrictions on private property rights.

Within this general framing of the issues, there are several which merit specific mention.

Variations in Local Power

In most states, the enabling act grants the power to zone to cities and counties; thus, all parts of the state are covered. Texas, however, did not grant zoning power to its counties, and since most of the explosive growth that has occurred in the state in recent decades has been outside the city limits, implementation of land use plans has been very difficult. Also, some cities – most notably Houston, one of the largest cities in the nation – have chosen not to zone. If zoning is not used, implementation must rely on a plethora of hodgepodge regulations and financial incentives to try to implement plans.

A few states have gone the other way, granting regulatory power to selected regional governmental organizations. This is very unusual; typically, regional comprehensive planning has to rely on financial incentives to obtain plan implementation (the US has some of the weakest regional and national land use control powers of any nation).

Uniform Powers in a Varied Landscape

The model state zoning enabling act gave local governments the power to:

- regulate height, bulk, yard size, population density, land use and location; and
- establish districts within the city, with different regulations applying in each – although within each district there cannot be variations in regulations.

Chapter 3: **INTERNATIONAL PERSPECTIVE**

The latter phrase has caused problems for planners for many years, as they struggle to find ways to tailor regulations to the unique aspects of each individual property and landowners' proposals without violating the requirement of uniformity within districts. Among the convoluted approaches employed to deal with this unfortunate restriction are the floating zone – a district included in the local zoning law like any other, but not mapped until the property owner asks for it; the overlay zone, which is included in the zoning law but is mapped on top of the existing zoning and adds restrictions to it; and the planned unit development (PUD or PD) zone, which is a (generally floating) zoning district that states general policies and restrictions in the ordinance but allows the specific regulations to be tailored to each parcel, at which time those specific regulations actually become part of the city's zoning law. Although this allows for maximum flexibility, it also produces many pages of amendments to the zoning law that must be monitored and enforced.

Regulatory Purposes v. Planning Goals

Zoning regulations can usually be used for the following purposes: reduce congestion; secure safety from fire, panic, and other dangers; provide adequate light and air; prevent overcrowding; provide adequate transport, water, sewers, schools, parks, and other public services; conserve land value; and promote appropriate land use. Note here that many purposes commonly found in comprehensive plans (for example, creating more aesthetically pleasing environments, protecting historic resources or wildlife habitat, ensuring a balance of jobs and housing, increasing urban density) are not purposes of zoning.

This narrowly defined scope has led to much uncertainty regarding how far regulations can go to create livable communities; often regulations have been passed that reflect the broader purposes of planning, in hopes that a legal challenge will not be mounted. Some states (for example New Jersey) have modified their enabling acts to broaden the purposes of zoning, and the American Planning Association has conducted extensive research and produced a new model enabling act that states can pass which is much more supportive of the New Urbanist/smart growth plan movement.

Interpretation by the Courts

If challenged in court, zoning regulations are presumed valid. This means that the burden of proof lies with the challenger, not the government. However, there are some restrictions on zoning's power that challengers have often used effectively, including:

- The idea that a few property owners should not be subjected to a big loss of property value or use for a small gain in protecting public health, safety, morals or welfare (that is, public gain and private loss resulting from the zoning should be in balance).
- The assertion that the regulations go beyond public protection from harm and actually create positive benefits. This usually stems from a zoning regulation that is based on the protection of general welfare rather than public health, safety or morals. The "general welfare" clause has been used to justify everything from preventing renovation of historic homes to requiring specific colors of paint, roofing materials, or even Christmas lights

- in some zones. Although the general welfare justification has surely been overused at times, the difficulty of using zoning to create positive improvements unrelated to basic protection of public health and safety severely limits its usefulness as a plan implementation tool for creating more livable communities.
- The idea that so much of the property's value is removed by the zoning regulation that in fact it is a taking of the property, so compensation must be paid. In the 1920s and for many years thereafter, virtually the entire value of the property had to be taken in order to claim damages under this provision; however, in the past three decades the courts have expanded the takings argument to encompass regulations that take only a part of a property's value (by, for example, downzoning property from retail to mixed office/housing), or take it temporarily (by, for example, restricting development of a property using a regulation that is later overturned in court). This expansion of the meaning of a taking has been frightening for planners, as they would not be able to move forward with innovative regulatory approaches designed to implement livability plans (for example, positive changes in appearance, density, etc.) if their local governments had to pay owners for small losses. This issue has spawned a movement – ironically called the Wise Use Movement – of landowners, mainly in the western states, that is pushing for changes in state enabling and/or other related laws that would ensure compensation for most regulatory changes, and some states have passed legislation along those lines. However, so far in most cases the new laws have proved to be unenforceable or so restricted that they rarely apply. Despite this apparent defeat, some who supported these bills have included provisions that require compensation not only for reductions in actual, current property value, but also for refusal to change the current regulations to allow more lucrative uses – an idea that would surely be the death knell of plan implementation if passed.
- The regulation is arbitrary and capricious because it is not consistent with a comprehensive plan. This one is interesting because although the enabling laws all contain provisions requiring that zoning be based on a comprehensive plan, in many state laws that term is never defined; thus a street map, or even the zoning map itself, can be called a comprehensive plan. Further, enforcement of this "consistency requirement" is also very lax in many states. For example, in Texas it is not uncommon for even major cities to complete their zoning before developing a plan. A significant minority of states take this requirement seriously, however; for example, the state of California requires that local plans meet a book-length set of standards and be approved by the state, and zoning can only rarely deviate from the plan. Planners in states that are lax about this have a more difficult time convincing their governmental officials to commit to the time and expense needed to complete a high quality plan to improve the livability of their communities.

US Zoning's Limitations as a Tool to Create Livable Communities

Zoning is an inflexible, rough tool to try to use to create livable communities. Many variations (for example special use permits, planned unit development districts, design regulations, overlay districts, vertical zoning, ballot box zoning, density (FAR) bonuses, development agreements, housing set-asides, special districts, and more recently unified development codes, traditional

Chapter 3: INTERNATIONAL PERSPECTIVE

neighborhood development zones, transit-oriented development zones, mixed use zones, smart codes, green development codes, LEED codes and form-based codes) have been tried in an effort to infuse zoning with more flexibility and broader scope. They are all tools that provide evidence of the paradigm shift in plan implementation that has occurred as we struggle to create – or recreate – the livability that once was common in our original neighborhoods, and is still the norm in many neighborhoods in a few US cities and in many other nations today.

Yet each of these efforts has flaws. New communities that incorporate clustering, form based design, amenities, green building, etc., can be sterile; development agreements can become big subsidies for small improvements in livability; and PDs often fail to achieve improvement in livability at all as enforcement becomes an administrative nightmare. Further, they often address only a part of the plan – for example, density bonuses are designed to provide a specific thing, such as affordable housing units, in exchange for an increase in the allowable development density.

When several of these tools are combined – as is often the case in both new master planned communities and declining existing residential areas – the result can be a maze of regulations and policies that require high-priced experts to incorporate them into development proposals. This leads to the biggest difficulty: being forced to utilize such a convoluted, piecemeal, indirect approach to land use control invites challenges from landowners on the many small portions of the regulations – for example, sign size or color – and these challenges so consume staff time and elected official patience that the real reason for the zoning – namely, to implement the comprehensive plan and create more livable communities – gets temporarily lost at best and entirely forgotten at worst. In short, in many communities there exists such a disconnect between the plan and the daily administration of the zoning that it is not uncommon for case after case to be heard and decided without consulting the plan. The relationship of the plan's general provisions to the specifics of zoning, and the importance of adhering to details of the regulations, may be unclear to the residents and elected officials who make zoning decisions. Decisions are often based at least in part on politics and personal connections rather than good planning.

Zoning is not supposed to be a straitjacket of regulatory minutiae; it is supposed to implement the community goals and vision for the future as expressed in the plan. Surely there is a better way.

A World View

Introduction

There are two main approaches to the control of land development: statutory (zoning and other government regulations, see above) and contractual. The contractual approach takes two forms, depending on whether the government or a private party owns the land.

When the government is the landowner, the public agency writes the plan requirements into the land lease contract with the private agents. The Netherlands, Israel and Hong Kong use this "contract" zoning. Zoning by contract in Hong Kong has been in practice since 1842 where lands with restrictive covenants or lease conditions put on by the local authority are allocated as leasehold lots by auction, sale, or grant to individuals. Urban land reforms in

China adopted Hong Kong's leasehold system with some changes: China makes a zoning plan or "detailed regulatory plan" before any land contracts between the government and individuals are possible. The lease is a civil contract between the government and the individuals; renegotiation for lease modification is possible.

When the planner-landowner is a private developer, development control often takes the form of contractual covenants and deed restrictions instead of zoning. Such contractual obligations putting restrictions on land development can be made by private individuals, filed with the deed when the property is sold, and then the contracts are enforceable either by the development's residents through their homeowners association, or by the government. Houston is a case in point (Siegan 1972). Houston land uses are controlled by private covenants, subdivision regulations and building codes instead of local government zoning regulations, yet the city enforces them. Land allocation with restrictive covenants and possible subsequent permission to change use is a scenario of initial assignment of property rights by contract (with government or among individuals, like Hong Kong and Houston respectively); subsequent change of rights is a much more difficult process than is a change of zoning, since covenants become part of the deeds themselves. Since contractual zoning is not subject to the requirements that apply to government laws, it can be far more restrictive; issues of property taking, protecting public health and safety, providing affordable housing, etc., are irrelevant.

A wide variety of possible combinations lies between the two extremes of government land ownership/complete control and private ownership/no significant government control. The combination used in any given nation may be vastly different than the US approach.

Whether land use control is statutory or contractual, the social and cultural conventions that are widely accepted regarding political behavior and operations are critically important in achieving successful plan implementation. In most of western Europe, North America, Australia, and scattered nations in Asia (Japan, for example) and the southern hemisphere, the rule of law is paramount; the residents hold their constitution in high regard and expect politicians to adhere to its provisions. A fairly substantial level of transparency in governmental decision-making is generally expected, as is public input into planning and regulatory processes – although these vary from nation to nation. Although bribes are occasionally given and corruption occurs, these are clearly viewed as illegal and morally wrong, and an average citizen who attempts to bribe a public official is in significant danger of being arrested. Political involvement, including voting, is encouraged but not mandated. If a substantial personal relationship exists between an applicant for development approval and anyone with approval authority, it is expected that the person with authority will remove himself from the decision-making process to avoid any appearance of conflict of interest. The result of this set of widely accepted social and cultural conventions is that plan implementation is strongly influenced by laws and regulations. In this setting, statutory approaches are often used; their effectiveness and scope is limited by the constitutions, laws, and mores of each nation. In cases (for example, Texas counties) where statutory authority is limited, contractual approaches may provide a solution. The Woodlands, Texas is a well-known example of excellent plan implementation in an area where zoning was not available, using contractual methods.

In many other parts of the world, these social and cultural conventions are weak or nonexistent. In these nations, government-authored plans are often not implemented; the best way to get a private development plan implemented is to cultivate a personal relationship with those who have approval authority. This relationship may involve bribery, kinship, business associations, etc. Many of these nations have laws and regulations regarding development that resemble those of the "rule of law" nations, but they have little effect on plan implementation. The national government is often not a democracy, or is one in which voting is mandatory and choices are limited. There is little or no transparency in governmental decision-making. A dichotomy exists between this separation of government from the people and the strong level of grassroots neighborhood decision-making and control that often exists in parallel – far stronger than that found in many of the "rule of law" nations. Problems of negative externalities are often handled directly by the affected parties, and some nations go so far as to leave development decisions up to the neighbors. Some of the most interesting, livable communities are found in these nations; some of the least livable conditions also occur there. The unpredictable nature of governmental decision-making may pose problems for foreign developers and landowners. Contractual approaches to plan implementation may work well in this environment.

With this framework in mind, let's take a closer look at implementation in some other nations.

England

England is the place with the greatest historical and political ties to the US. The legal system is based on the English one, the US concept of nuisance law derived from English precedent, and US cultural ties are extensive. Thus it seems logical to expect that plan implementation in England would resemble the US approach. In truth, though, they are very different. Since so much is shared culturally and legally, and England is replete with communities that embody the very essence of livability, it therefore seems likely that England will provide the US with fruitful ground for investigating more effective methods of creating livable communities.

Two of the biggest differences between the English and American systems are the level of national development control, and the resulting lack of zoning as we know it in the US. In 1947 the British government nationalized all development rights; since that time, zoning has gradually evolved to become a local development plan system where all development proposals are reviewed on their individual merits. In the English planning system, zones are created without prescribed prior uses (Ball 1994). This type of land use control could be considered a form of zoning only if one views each local planning area as one zone, within which all development goes through the development control process (Lai 1997) – a big stretch of the US definition of zoning. It seems to most resemble contractual zoning in a "rule of law" setting.

The English system is "unitary." This means that national land use planning policies and laws apply to the whole country, and they are mandatory. Central government departments ensure that local governments carry out the national land use planning policies and laws (for example, in 1990 a number of local councils were rebuked because they failed to get national Home Office approval of bylaws banning dogs in parks). The central government also has the power to control local authorities' borrowing, and to "cap" the amount that can be levied on local taxation (Cullingworth 1993).

English planning is conceived in terms of policies which will advance the public interest. This is in striking contrast with the United States, where the legal basis for government intervention lies in the police power: protecting private parties from harm.

Compared to the US, English courts have little role to play. They become involved only when it is alleged that an authority has acted contrary to the provisions of the planning legislation; issues of property takings, etc. are generally irrelevant. In place of the courts stands the central government (technically the secretary of state).

The English planning system provides for a great deal of governmental authority and discretion. The national and local governments are not constrained by the constitutional and enabling legislation restrictions that adversely affect US plan implementation.

Like the US, a major feature of the English system is that with certain exceptions, all development requires the prior approval of the local authority. This approval can be of three kinds:

1 Unconditional permission
2 Permission subject to such conditions as it thought fit
3 Refusal

Since zoning for various uses is not determined in advance, in effect the local government plan becomes the zoning. Landowners must comply with the provisions contained in the plan for their neighborhood, which can be as detailed as zoning regulations in the US.

This complete mixing of zoning with planning might be an improvement over the disconnected system now used in the US, and may not be as farfetched or legally indefensible as it first appears. The requirements for specific plans in California are akin to the English approach in both level of detail and involvement of the government in private land planning, and they have been upheld in court. On a broader level, one could view the national government powers in England as akin to the powers held by the states in the US; the difference being that those powers have been delegated to the localities in the US, but remain at the higher level in England. Perhaps it is worth considering returning some of those powers to the states.

Canada

As is the case in the US, services in Canada are provided by three levels of government: federal, provincial, and local. The federal government is a single, national government. The provincial level is made up of ten provincial and three territorial governments. The local level of government includes municipalities and school boards, as well as special agencies, boards, and commissions (Canadian Tax Foundation 2003).

In Canada the control of land and its uses is a provincial (a level of government similar to states in the US and Australia) responsibility. It is derived from the constitutional authority over "property and civil rights" granted to the provinces under the British North Canada (BNA) Act of 1867 and carried forward in the Constitution Act, 1982. The zoning power relates to "real property," or land and the improvements constructed thereon that become part of the land itself (in Quebec, "immeubles"). Each province has established municipalities and regions that are empowered to control the use of land within their boundaries. Provision has also been made for control of land use in unorganized areas of the province. In both areas, provincial tribunals are the ultimate authority for appeal and review. In Ontario a recent amendment permits the provincial government to exercise this power in that local plans must comply with provincial policy statements. More specifically,

Chapter 3: **INTERNATIONAL PERSPECTIVE**

An Official Plan for a municipality sets out the broad direction for land use in your municipality for 10–20 years. Official plans usually include policies about natural heritage features like wetlands, woodlands, wildlife habitat and rare species. The Provincial Policy Statement under the Planning Act guides the development of Official Plans and other planning documents. Zoning by-laws, site plan control, plans of subdivision, severances and other land use decisions by municipal councils are guided by Official Plan policies. Official plans are reviewed every five to ten years.

(Carolinian Canada 2004)

Each municipality may enact bylaws to control the use of land within its boundaries. Plans are made by the municipality, and the land area is divided into zones, each zone being set apart for certain defined uses. Plans are based on geographic features and existing development such as harbors, railways, highways, buildings and land use. Bylaws are then enacted to restrict the use of land in the defined areas to those uses established by the planning process. In rural municipalities, zoning is mostly used to protect agricultural land from urban or industrial development (Thomas 2008).

The planning system varies in its nature and extent among the ten provinces. Most provinces require approval of everything from municipal plans and zoning bylaws to flexible development agreements, and from standard subdivision controls to the transfer of air rights (Cullingworth 1993).

Another difference between Canada and the US lies in the powers available at the regional level. Canadian regions can truly function as levels of government; for example, until the late 1990s the cities in the Toronto area were governed by a single metropolitan government (Bright 2000). Planning districts consist of the area contained within the boundaries of several rural municipalities (Ashton 2006). They enable municipalities to work across boundaries to develop district development plans, which guide municipal zoning laws and local land-use decisions (Canadian Tax Foundation 2003).

Ontario has one of the most advanced plan implementation systems. Almost all municipalities have adopted official plans which set out objectives and policies concerning the use and development of the municipal area. Zoning laws passed by the municipality translate the broad policy into specific types of zones with specific uses contemplated for each zone category. The zoning law also sets out other standards and parameters such as setback, building height, maximum site coverage, and requirements for other matters such as parking. To obtain a building permit, whether for new construction or redevelopment, the proposed construction must comply with the standards set out in the zoning code (Kennedy 2004).[5]

Australia

Regulatory plan implementation in the US is similar to planning in Australia in some ways and different in others. The fundamental difference is that, like Canada, planning in Australia has retained more state government control over local planning, and this means that planning can occur in a strategic fashion rather than an *ad hoc* fashion.

To understand the planning system one must first understand the system of local government and its relationship to the state government. One of the fundamental differences between the American system and the system in Australia is that in the US, state and local governments are the heart of the democratic process. This means that in the US, the local governments have a great deal of power over local decision-making without any system of review by a higher level of government. In the US, generally there is no state or regional control or coordination over local planning, and therefore in many areas planning occurs in a regionally uncoordinated manner.

In Australia the basis for the system of government rests at the national and state levels; thus one sees more state-level control and more variation among states than is the case in the US. For example, most Australian states have zoning as well as development applications and the requirements for consent for particular activities. However, in most states in America there is no overall control of zoning and the elected city councils can change it with no reference to a broader strategic plan.

The state of New South Wales is the most extreme example of state-controlled land use regulatory power, as the state retains this power even in the municipalities. Many other Australian states resemble the US more closely than they do New South Wales, because most states and the Northern Territory have established local governments (also known as local councils). These handle community needs such as waste collection, public recreation facilities, and town planning.

Most states and the Northern Territory each have many local governments within their borders. The state or territory government defines the powers of the local governments, and decides what geographical areas those governments are responsible for. Each local government has the equivalent of a legislature and an executive only. The naming conventions for local governments vary across Australia. They can be called cities, shires, towns, or municipalities, but they are still controlled by the state or territory government above them. In the Australian Capital Territory (ACT), the responsibilities usually handled by local government are administered by a department of the territory government (www.australia.gov.au).

Most states also have county government, which has responsibility for the rural land, and within the county there are often a number of independent towns, which can range in size from less than 300 people to hundreds of thousands of people. Each of these towns has its own individual council. Each town council can also do its own zoning without any formal relationship or discussion with the surrounding county. It is not uncommon to have a rural county with some towns in it that have no zoning provisions at all, or indeed even whole counties may have no planning or zoning regulations. As Sinclair (2000) put it, "This is particularly true in Midwestern states where individual property rights are considered inviolate and any regulation or control is viewed with suspicion, even hostility. One of my colleagues from the Midwest has been told that zoning is the work of the aliens!"

This can create some problems, particularly where a town council may want to expand into a county area taking up good agricultural land. This can also work in reverse where a county can place development adjacent to a town with no provision for servicing by that town. County councils can also approve a shopping center on rural land adjacent to the town area, thereby causing the town's central business district to decline through lack of patronage by the residents (Sinclair 2000).

In America the planners usually have only very limited control over the aesthetics of a building or development. There is also a great reluctance to refuse permission for a development on aesthetic grounds (because, for example, it does not fit with the streetscape of an area).

Chapter 3: **INTERNATIONAL PERSPECTIVE**

The system of court review of applications is also different, because in Australia the person hearing the application is a person with legal training whereas in many parts of the US one can be a judge without legal training. Following are two examples that serve to illustrate the variety of planning approaches among states.

Western Australia

The central instrument of planning at the local level in the State of Western Australia is the Local Authority Town Planning (Zoning) Scheme. The *Town Planning and Development Act*, passed by the state parliament of Western Australia, empowers any local authority within the State to prepare a Town Planning (Zoning) Scheme with the general objective of securing suitable land use and development and for the various purposes, provisions, powers or works contained in the First Schedule of the Act. The *Town Planning Regulations (1967)* specify the form and content of Town Planning (Zoning) Schemes (Van der Kuil 1995).

Town Planning Schemes are given the force of law by the Town Planning and Development Act, which provides that a Town Planning Scheme, when approved by the Minister and published in the local newspaper, shall have full force and effect as if it were enacted by the Act. This is very different from the US, where plans have no force of law in most states but are viewed more as general, advisory documents.

The scheme consists of a Scheme Map(s) and Scheme Text supported by a Scheme Report. A Scheme Map zones land for particular purposes. The Scheme Text prescribes the uses which may or may not be permitted in the various zones through the means of a zoning table, and establish standards and conditions controlling the use and development of land in the different zones. The Scheme Report contains an analysis of the investigations and surveys made during the preparation of the scheme and an explanation of the proposals.

Recent changes to the Town Planning regulations include the introduction of planning policies relating to specific types of development and/or specific areas of the municipality; the introduction of various forms of policy plans and development plans to provide more positive guidance beyond the primary zoning for areas requiring comprehensive and coordinated planning; and the introduction of precinct plans based on the concept of defining the municipality into precincts with policies and proposals reflecting the needs and character of the particular precincts. Precincts are defined as "small pockets of the city with their own unique character, colour and charm" (www.melbourne.vic.gov.au).

Evaluation

Town Planning (Zoning) Schemes have been the subject of critical comment over a number of years. Schemes have been criticized as being negative and inflexible. The procedure for amendment can be cumbersome, time-consuming and expensive and the Minister (state level) . . . become unnecessarily involved in detailed local planning issues throughout the amendment process. Schemes are also regarded as legal instruments rather than planning documents and are of limited value in expressing a Council's strategies, policies and proposals for its municipality. However, the traditional form of Town Planning (Zoning) Schemes have a sound legal record and public acceptance.

In summary, I would have to say that the main benefit of having State Government review of planning decisions is that there is some ability to have planning occur in a strategic manner. A lot of my colleagues in United States comment about their frustration of not having the ability at the local level to work to a mandated strategy to ensure that development occurs in a planned and effective manner as well as great reluctance for Councils to work together on a common vision.

(Sinclair 2000)

The Australian system is an interesting mix of American and English features. Like the English system, the Australians do not differentiate between plans and zoning: the zoning is the plan. Like the US, Australian states have the most power over land use control; unlike most of the US, they have retained at least plan review power at the state level.

Ireland

Zoning of land occurs through the Development Plan process and is governed by the Planning and Development Act (2000). Under section 10(2)(a) a Development Plan must contain objectives in relation to the zoning of land. Under section 11(4)(d) the elected members of a planning authority may issue directions to the manager of a local authority regarding the preparation of any draft development plan.[6] Many of these directions relate to the zoning of land. The manager then prepares a draft plan, which is considered by the elected members. Prior to public display, this manager's draft plan may be amended and then becomes the elected members draft plan. Amendments also often relate to zoning (Tracey 2003).

In accordance with section 10(1), a Development Plan shall set out an overall strategy for the proper planning and sustainable development of an area. However there is no requirement inferred in the Act for elected members to give any planning reason when issuing directions in relation to what to include in the draft plan or when later they may amend the plan. Experience has shown that sometimes neither the planner's advice nor the manager's advice in relation to zoning issues is taken; the elected members do not have to give reasons as to why this advice is not taken.

The mechanism for zoning or rezoning lands remains the same as that in existence during the 1980s and 1990s. Elected local politicians in Ireland enjoy extensive powers in relation to the zoning of land for development purposes. All that is required to zone or rezone land is a simple majority of elected members. There is no third party appeal process, thus limiting the public's ability to question any zoning or rezoning decision by the Council."

This practice has led to serious public disquiet about the fairness of the whole planning system, and also disrespect for elected representatives as a whole, especially at the local-authority level, based on the perceived failings of a minority of councilors and parliamentarians.

The perception, if not the reality, of political corruption has risen sharply in Ireland in recent times. There is sometimes a perception amongst landowners that only "well connected" developers will be "bestowed" with the benefit of zoning by councilors although this is now changing. A number of improvements in relation to the zoning of land could ensure greater transparency and accountability, and reduce the public perception of unfairness in the system.

Chapter 3: INTERNATIONAL PERSPECTIVE

Thus there is a case for a review of policy structures, as an antidote to the perception of possible corruption. Greater attention needs to be paid to the "corruption proofing" of policies and institutional arrangements, in addition to the vigorous pursuit of wrongdoers (McCarthy 2003). The zoning of land under the present system invariably results in a windfall for the landowner with little common good accruing to the public and no benefit to those who are not zoned.

One tool which could ensure community benefit could be the introduction of an additional tax on profits (on capital appreciation) accrued to individuals as a result of lands being zoned for development (in particular agriculture to residential). These taxes would be paid to local government. It is hoped that this would allow planning authorities to engage in a more proactive manner; for example, the County Project Office, i.e. CPO (being better funded), could purchase lands that were not being released quickly enough and were inhibiting sustainable and comprehensive development of an area, and the local authority could then sell them on the open market to developers.

All draft development plans or draft variations of development plans (which provide for zoning of land) are subject to inspection and public inquiry by an independent, external planning inspector from the national Department of Environment and Local Government or An Bord Pleanala prior to its consideration for adoption by the Council (i.e. elected members).[7]

In summary, the making of development plans has focused primarily on "rezoning," and to the skeptic, the primary consideration appears to be "whose turn it is to become a millionaire," with decisions being made based on individual constituents interests over the common good. In this regard, some councilors seem to be unperturbed by the threat of public shame and less still the threat of legal consequences for their actions, Irish Planning Institute President Rachel Kerry explained.

> Recent examples of questionable or poor planning decisions taken by local Councilors against the advice of professional planners, such as in Loughrea, County Galway, where a majority of elected members on the Council decided to rezone one landowner's property for industrial development in the full knowledge that the land was earmarked for the building of the town's long-awaited bypass, with the Councilors eventually backing down following a standoff with the National Roads Authority, does not inspire confidence in the planning system.
>
> (Kerry 2003)

Zoning has tended to be restrictive in both urban and rural areas, and zoned land has acquired an artificial scarcity value. This problem is most acute in the Dublin area. Value, including the prospects of favorable zoning decisions, is affected by the availability of services such as water and waste disposal, whose provision is a monopoly of local government. Thus local councilors are important people to influence, as are certain key professional employees of local authorities. An entire industry of nationally-employed planners, private sector planning consultants, specialist lawyers, PR firms and political door-openers has grown up around the current Irish zoning arrangements (McCarthy 2003).

There has been pressure on local authority councilors from resident's associations, landowners and the development industry, regarding zoning decisions which is critical in the planning process. In existing urban areas, this pressure usually restricts housing supply (as the wishes of existing residents are the key political consideration), whilst in peripheral areas (where landowners are more influential) it often facilitates the zoning of land to enable green-field development. In Dublin there have also been delays in servicing lands, which were rezoned by politicians against the advice of local authority planners, due to the engineering and drainage work required (Williams 2002).

In summary, Ireland employs a system of local land use control that resembles that found in the US. However, the US Constitutional restrictions on taking private property only for public use do not apply in Ireland, thus opening the door to the government purchasing land then reselling it for development. Also, the national government plays a much larger role in Irish plan implementation than it does in the US As is the case in England and Australia, the plan is synonymous with the zoning law. Unlike those nations, however, it seems that corruption and deal-making are far more prevalent in Ireland than in the other two nations. Interestingly, if one examines the chart in Appendix D, one sees that the US ranks as having more corruption than does Ireland – a situation which is not well known in America and needs further investigation.

Singapore[8]

Singapore is a republic within the British Commonwealth, and has administrative and legal systems similar to England's. The head of state is the President, who has limited executive powers and is elected by popular vote for six-year terms. Pursuant to the Constitution, the President exercises executive competence over certain fiscal matters and the appointment of key civil servants. The head of government is the Prime Minister, who is the leader of the political party securing the majority of Parliamentary seats in general elections conducted every five years. The Prime Minister is assisted by a Cabinet, whose Ministers are appointed by the President and who are responsible to Parliament.

The Urban Redevelopment Authority is the national urban planning authority of Singapore, and a statutory board under the Ministry of National Development of the Singapore Government. Stringent planning and zoning laws attempt to ensure optimal usage of land and proper siting of polluting industries (URA Singapore 2003). The authority was established on April 1, 1974, and is of especially critical importance to the city-state, because Singapore is an extremely dense country where land use is required to be efficient, as there is a land shortage. The URA is also responsible for having their urban planning avoid segregation, as well as seeking ways to improve aesthetics and to reduce congestion. It is also responsible for the conservation of historic and cultural buildings and national heritage sites. The URA prepares long-term strategic plans (Concept Plans) and medium term plans (Master Plans) to ensure sufficient land for future development and to support continued economic growth. The URA oversees development of the Concept Plan, the current Master Plan, and supporting Special and Detailed Control Plans for different parts of Singapore (Lushhomeonline 2007).

The Master Plan is the statutory land use plan which guides Singapore's development in the medium term, over the next ten to fifteen years. It is reviewed once every five years, and translates the broad long-term strategies as set out in the Concept Plan into detailed implementable plans for Singapore. It shows the permissible land use and density for every

Chapter 3: **INTERNATIONAL PERSPECTIVE**

parcel of land in Singapore. The Master Plan incorporates amendments for the five planning regions (comprising fifty-five planning areas). It is accompanied by Special and Detailed Controls Plans which highlight areas subject to special guidelines (Republic of Singapore 2003). In sum, Singapore is like Britain in that there is no differentiation between plans and zoning. Since the nation is so small, it is not surprising that everything is handled at the national level.

Hong Kong

Zoning was introduced into Hong Kong by the Town Planning Ordinance of 1939. Then in 1959, a new section 16(1)(d) was introduced to the Building (Administration) Regulations of 1956 which allowed the refusal of building consent when a proposed development did not conform to the official zoning plans. Zoning regulations not only determine the type of use, they also regulate land and structure characteristics such as lot size, set back and building height (Pogodzinski and Sass 1991).

Since most residential development in Hong Kong is high-density development, and it is irreversible, it is desirable to have careful planning of land use.[9] One example is the Multiple Intensive Land use (MILU) system. MILU achieves intensification of land use through mixing residential, commercial and other uses at higher densities at selected urban locations, while being supported by an efficient public transport and pedestrian network. Successful case studies in Hong Kong have more than five uses, i.e. Residential, Commercial, Recreational, Community facilities and Transport facilities. The residential component in these projects is usually between 30 percent and 65 percent of the total gross floor area. The MILU concept is being implemented in subsidized public housing projects as well. Multiple land uses within the area, together with access to five or more modes of public transport and an accessible network of multilevel pedestrian links, are supposed to create the necessary variety, vitality and viability for a livable community.[10]

Although this sounds somewhat like the US system on paper, in reality it is quite different due to the close tie-in of zoning and plans: in Hong Kong, plans are done for many specific parts of the city and the plan itself is also the zoning map – hence the term "Zoning Plan." In effect it seems that each of these parts of the city would be operating under regulations similar to PUDs in the US, that is, several existing zones are mixed within the area according to a detailed land use/zoning plan. Unlike PUDs though, each of these detailed plans is actually listed in the ordinance specifically.

India

India suffers from inflexible zoning, rent and tenancy laws. Zoning laws, rent controls and protected tenancies "freeze" land in city centers that would otherwise be available for new retail outlets and flats. Protected tenants cannot be evicted, and will never voluntarily surrender their cheap tenancies, so their ancient buildings can never be renovated. These laws also restrict competition. For example, subsidized rents allow traditional inner-city counter stores to overlook their operational inefficiencies. But in Chennai, the capital of India's southern state of Tamil Nadu, where rent control and zoning laws are less stringent, modern supermarkets already account for almost 20 percent of total food retailing compared to less than 1 percent in cities with higher average incomes such as Mumbai and Delhi (Banerjee 2002).

Many urban governments lack a modern planning framework. The multiplicity of local bodies obstructs efficient planning and land use. Rigid master plans and restrictive zoning regulations limit the land available for building, constricting cities' abilities to grow in accordance with changing needs (World Bank 2008).

The Indian property market is extremely fragmented, thanks to zoning laws that specify land use based on pre- World War II English notions of what cities should look like. A legal "conversion" – using a vacant factory or farm for, say, retail or housing – is so difficult and time-consuming that many individuals and businesses cut corners, and bribery is rampant. It is only when the judiciary insists on a faithful enforcement of the zoning norms that one gets to understand just how oppressive the existing laws really are (Mukherjee & Gokcekw 2006).

Review and enforcing of all development control and zoning regulations occurs through the state governments (Kochhar 2006). However, the national government does play an important advisory role. For example, in an effort to create an appropriate and effective enforcement mechanism, the Indian Ministry of Home Affairs recently constituted an expert committee to develop model building laws, review the existing town and country planning acts, and develop zoning regulations/building laws. The committee report contains detailed recommendations for modifications in the existing town and country planning act, putting land use zoning regulations in place, and additions to development control rules and laws. The Ministry of Home Affairs has recommended the same to the state governments and union territory administrations for early adoption.

Recent tsunami waves on the east coast have further strengthened the need to have proper land use zoning regulations and safer construction in coastal regions. A series of workshops have been held in all states and Union Territories to disseminate the recommendations of the expert committee and further follow up action for amending the legal framework including development control regulations and laws for safety against natural hazards.[11] With all these actions and better enforcement there may be a road ahead for safer development and construction.

An Example of State Zoning Regulation

Haryana Urban Development Authority-HUDA

For the construction of buildings on parcels of land, HUDA has framed detailed building laws and zoning plans. Zoning regulation gives specific information regarding the extent of land development allowed on a particular piece of land depending on its land use (through FAR (floor area ratio), ground coverage, etc.) and also gives broad guidelines on the maximum height of building permitted, location and design of gates and boundary walls, exterior finishes and elevations, etc. This ensures that minimum standards of aesthetics and urban design are maintained. A copy of zoning plans for each sector or institution can be obtained from the office of the District Town Planner for a fee. (In India, Districts are bigger than towns and can encompass several towns, rural areas and villages.)

Chapter 3: **INTERNATIONAL PERSPECTIVE**

City and State Regulation

Hyderabad Urban Development Authority-HUDA

Though HUDA's statutory jurisdiction is confined to the HMA (Hyderabad Metropolitan Area), because of its expertise in handling problems of the largest and capital city of the state of Andhra Pradesh the state government has traditionally used HUDA to formulate urban development policies and to carry out studies for the entire state. HUDA has therefore produced major study reports in the area of building and zoning regulations. The Master Plan and Zonal Plans (done by HUDA) prescribe the land use and transportation network. Building and zoning regulations form part and parcel of the above plans in implementing the specific objectives and the development controls.

The Hyderabad Urban Development Authority is functionally a referral authority for development permissions. While all day-to-day cases (for example, individual residential building permits) are delegated to the respective local bodies, certain planning control powers are vested with HUDA: for example layout of developments, group housing schemes, all non-residential permits, etc. The HUDA reviews these directly, technically approves their development permissions, and forwards the technically approved plans to the local authority for approval, monitoring and enforcement.

A Sampling of Regulatory Approaches to Implementation in Nations Not Under British Rule

Belgium

Land use planning at the EU level clearly focuses on the municipality or functional urban region (mainly in Greece, France, Italy, and Sweden) with framework (master plan) instruments, and on specific areas within the municipality with regulatory instruments. In Belgium zoning also exists for sub-regions. The framework plans cover at least the whole of the area of the local authority's jurisdiction, and set out the broad land use and infrastructure patterns across the area through zoning or land allocation maps. The regulatory plan covers the whole or part of the local authority's area and indicates detailed site-specific zoning for buildings, land use and infrastructure. All the EU member states, except the United Kingdom and the Republic of Ireland, use detailed planning techniques (zoning instruments, building regulations, and other regulations for plan implementation) which play a determining role in guiding the location of development and physical infrastructure, and the form and size development takes (Albrechts 2004).

Each Belgian region has its own zoning and environmental rules. In addition, the municipalities and the provinces are also consulted for certain related matters. The following zoning-related legislation has been adopted by the regions: first, the Brussels Code for Land Planning; second, the Flemish Zoning Decree; and third, the Walloon Zoning Code (CWATUP).

Zoning is determined in every region at two levels: first, all plots of land have a general future use determined in a regional zoning plan, and second, this future use may be detailed in municipal zoning plans. In every region, buyers usually obtain zoning-related information from the local municipalities – possibly assisted by the notary, who has easier access (Global Legal Group 2007).

The Netherlands

The Dutch have a long and illustrious history of planning, and a long tradition of spatial (land use) planning. Their early involvement stemmed in part from their efforts to reclaim large areas of wetlands for agriculture, and from their major projects to protect parts of the country from being flooded by the North Sea. Even in the Middle Ages the development of polders (tracts of land enclosed by dikes) called for coordinated action of those who were to be protected by the dikes. This aspect of the Dutch heritage underlies the wide popular support for planning and land use controls, which are mandated by the national government and implemented locally (Faludi and van der Valk 1994).

The relatively high population density also provided a greater need for rules to regulate the negative effects of activities on neighboring households or firms. Strong population growth and urbanization at the end of the nineteenth century provided a major impetus for the "Housing Law" (Woningwet) of 1901, which is generally regarded as the starting point of modern Dutch spatial planning and housing policy. It enabled local governments to regulate land use in the interest of the construction of social (public) housing, using a zoning system. After World War II spatial planning intensified and became a national concern.

In the Netherlands, zoning plans are obligatory and have to be adapted regularly to changing circumstances. They are often restrictive, and a major task of spatial planning policy at the national level is to ensure that enough space becomes available to facilitate the demand for additional housing caused by the growth of the household population, and the demand for industrial location sites. The separation of these two types of land use decreases the negative external effects of the presence of industries close to residential areas. An important side condition in spatial planning is the wish to preserve the typically Dutch polder landscape in the western part of the country where pressure on space for residential and industrial purposes is also large. The destruction of this open landscape would imply the loss of an important positive external effect of agricultural land use. This may be of considerable importance in the area of spatial planning (Rouwendal and Van Der Straaten 2007).

Under Dutch law, every city is required to develop a comprehensive zoning plan, which must be approved by each district and regional government. Responsibilities of the central city government include the city's comprehensive land use plan, along with essential municipal services such as police, fire, water supply, and public transportation. The state or province coordinates regional plans for the central government. The province must also approve each city's plan for housing districts and determine if they are consistent with Dutch law. If the province rejects a plan, the national government reviews it.

In the Netherlands, zoning is based on spatial planning law. The process to change the zoning of a site is very difficult and requires the input of all community members and approval by the district council. Zoning imposes limits to those general uses in a particular geographic area.[12]

Residential development in the Netherlands involves many official approvals and processes. Beyond the soil protection law, Dutch housing law regulates the various aspects of home building. Once a site is approved for housing, a building permit must be obtained that requires soil tests. While building permits are obtained from the district council, soil cleanup plans are obtained from the province or one of the Netherlands' four major cities. Should a new owner decide to change the land use from industrial or commercial to housing, for example, the central city's government and district council's spatial zoning laws would apply. Thus, these zoning laws along with the Dutch housing laws and the soil protection act would make it very difficult to build housing (EPA 2008).

Dutch environmental policy traditionally focused on distinct environmental fields, such as noise, water, waste, air, and soil (Integrated Environmental Index for Application in Land-use Zoning) (Sol *et al.* 1995). As a result of manufacturing growth and intensive agriculture, parts of the Netherlands have become heavily polluted. In response to the problem, the national government enacted the Pollution of Surface Waters Act and the Air Pollution Act in the early 1970s, and later the Soil Protection Act. In each field standards, regulations, and legislation have been developed to deal with increased pollution problems. It was soon recognized that this sectoral (media-specific) approach was confusing, since several national and local governmental agencies had responsibility for administering the different regulations, and some policies overlapped. The time and expense of complying with the separate regulations was burdensome (Miller and De Roo 1996).

In recent years, Dutch environmental policy has shown a gradual shift towards a more integrated approach, focusing on five selected categories of sources (refineries, power plants, traffic, agriculture, chemical industry) and certain categories of effects (e.g. acidification). This dual source-and-effect oriented approach provided a base for the national environmental policy plan (NEPP), which was published in 1989 by the Dutch Ministry of Housing, Physical Planning and Environment. One of the policy instruments that has been emphasized in the NEPP is integrated environmental zoning aimed at improving the environmental quality around large industrial complexes. Further research is needed to identify the defining characteristics of this approach.

France

Those accustomed to detailed planning regulations found in the UK will rarely find the same experience in France. Clearly, there are exceptions, notably in relation to protected areas and buildings, but in general the French system is more akin to that of the US than Britain.

The main body of national rules governing new development and changes to existing buildings are called *Les dispositions imperatives du règlement nationale d'urbanisme (RNU)*. A small number of RNU have national authority and apply in all circumstances: for example, there are particular national rules called *Les Lois d'aménagement et d'urbanisme (LAU)* which apply in coastal areas and in mountain regions; these are the most powerful of the planning regulations and cannot be overruled in any circumstances, including local plans. Next in importance are incontestable regional directives called *Les directives territoriales d'aménagement (DTA)*. Although they may be regionally based, these directives are more often determined by the central government, and have a long term timescale.

The final set of national regulations is called *Les directives paysages* or *Directives de protection et de mise en valeur des paysages*. The regulations concern mainly planting requirements, the volume and height of buildings and external aspects of the development. They have influential authority in the determination of planning applications; however, if a local plan is in place, then the local rules take precedence. As a general rule, in the absence of a local plan, the RNU forbids new building outside built-up areas, except those relating to changes to existing buildings or agricultural uses (National Plans).

At a regional and county level the most significant planning regime is that of the *Schémas de cohérence territoriale (SCOT)*. The purpose of the SCOT is to delineate the major spatial development priorities for the area under examination over the medium to long-term. They may be best approximated to a county level "Structure Plan," familiar to those from the UK. The whole process is carried out on a collaborative basis involving the various levels of government in the region or the *département* (county). The plan is subject to a public review, and once approved, is valid for ten years. The level of preparation of SCOTs is very variable across the country as they were only introduced through a law in 2000. If a SCOT is not in place in any given area then the applicable regional/county plan will be the *Schéma directeur d'aménagement et d'urbanisme (SDAU)*, the predecessor of the SCOT.

Although not strictly speaking part of the land planning system, there is also a range of other plans focusing mainly on investment and regeneration. Perhaps the most interesting of these plans is the *Schéma régional de développement économique (SRDE)*. They also include *contrats d'agglomération*, which focus predominantly on city centers and larger towns, and *contrat de pays*, which are widespread across the country (French Planning System). Responsibility for the preparation of a local plan lies with the *commune* under the direction of the mayor. Until 2000 the local plans were called *Plan d'occupation des sols (POS)*, but since this time they have been replaced by the *Plan local d'urbanisme (PLU)*. The main aim of the change was to simplify the whole process and to reduce the complexity of the local plan. The purpose of the PLU is to determine a development plan for the *commune* (or the various *communes* that are party to the plan) and the general planning rules that will apply to the locality and to specific sites. The preparation of a PLU takes place in consultation with all the relevant statutory bodies and must be subject to a local public enquiry before it can be adopted. Once adopted it has legal, binding force. The PLU will establish planning zones for the area, the planning rules that will apply to new development, and information on major development constraints, all of which we can consider in a bit more detail below.

The PLU will divide the *commune* into four zones:

- Zone U – permits new construction on sites within or adjacent to areas with existing development, where the infrastructure exists or can be easily provided to enable development.
- Zone AU – for future development areas where infrastructure is already available, or where it is planned.
- Zone A – agricultural area; only agricultural related new construction is permitted.
- Zone N – protected areas where no new construction is permitted because of their sensitive historical, ecological or environmental nature.

The Planning Rules part of the plan will set out the general planning rules that will apply within each development area. In particular, it will set out rules on change of use,

Chapter 3: **INTERNATIONAL PERSPECTIVE**

permitted height of buildings, building arrangement, any architectural requirements, and public utility services and requirements. It will also set out the maximum permitted density of development on a site for new and existing buildings. These rules are called the *coefficient d'occupation des sols (COS)*. Using these rules it is possible to calculate the density of permitted development on a particular site, e.g. on an 800m² site a COS of 0.25 allows construction of 200m² of net surface area, called *surface hors oeuvre nette (SHON)*. If the property is located on a *lotissement* (housing development) then, in addition to the general planning rules, there are specific rules that apply to the *lotissement*, which are set out in a *cahier de charges*. These rules govern the management of the whole development.

The Development Constraints part of the plan will provide information on public spaces, public utilities, natural parks, major infrastructure projects, historic sites and monuments. The PLU should also identify major risk constraints. In the light of increasing flooding problems across the country, as well as problems with ground movement, the government is asking local councils to give greater attention to the identification of risk areas and to the preparation of risk prevention plans, called *Plan de prevention des risques (PRR)*. These plans should define those areas where construction is not permitted or where there are specific controls in order to reduce the risk of damage to property.

Where a PLU is in place, planning permission can be granted by the *mairie* (or inter-communal body); however, some smaller local councils are not able to offer planning services. In these cases, all planning applications are determined by the county planning and highways department, called the *Direction départementale d'equipement (DDE)*, in consultation with the *mairie*. Increasingly, the smaller local councils have worked together to produce a local plan (PLU) on an inter-communal basis. In the absence of a local plan there is a presumption that only new development within or adjacent to existing development areas, and with access to water and electricity services, will be granted planning permission for new buildings. It would however be possible to obtain planning permission for enlargement, modification or change of use of existing buildings.

Since the preparation of a PLU remains a significant task, and in smaller rural *communes* no such plan may exist, the government has agreed that smaller rural *communes* can prepare a *carte communale*. The main purpose of a *carte communale* is to identify those areas on which development is permitted and those where no development can take place. Unlike the PLU no specific planning rules can be established. It is a far less operational document than the PLU. Where development is not permitted then only extensions or changes to existing buildings will be permitted, although there is an exemption for agricultural buildings.

The preparation of a plan thereby avoids the need for consideration of individual applications on a case-by-case basis, as the plan will determine whether or not new development will be permitted. The plan may not necessarily cover the whole of the area, but merely that to which priority is being given, or which may be particularly sensitive. Where a plan is in place the *commune* has the right of pre-emption on the purchase of private properties that may be offered for sale within designated zones. This is a power that is used infrequently.

Contrary to PLU the *carte communale* carries no binding legal force. In the absence of detailed planning rules set out in a PLU then the *Règlement National d'Urbanisme (RNU)* apply.

The local council or central government may choose to declare a conservation area if they consider it to be an area of outstanding aesthetic or historical interest. There are three types of conservation area, as follows; there are also special rules relating to building along the coastline, in mountain areas and in proximity to a forest.

1. The area may be a *Secteur Sauvegardé*, which are zones designated within town or city centers. The designation is normally accompanied by a *Plan de sauvegarde et de mise en valeur (PSMV)*. Designation is at the discretion of the central government. The areas are often called *Malraux*, after the Minister who introduced the law and fiscal incentives available to those who invest in these areas. New designations are now rare, as they have been superseded by the ZPPAUP, below.
2. The *Zone de Protection du Patrimoine Architectural, Urbain et Paysager (ZPPAUP)* post-date the *Secteur Sauvegardé*, which they are tending to replace. They are determined by the local council. They are often smaller in size, based around an historic monument or sensitive areas in rural locations.
3. Although more of ecological than architectural interest there are also the *Zone naturelle d'intérêt écologique, faunistique et floristique (ZNIEFF)*.

In each case there are additional constraints on development and, in the case of (1) and (2) there may also be financial assistance towards the restoration of a property. There are formal procedures in place involving the public when the council is considering the creation of new conservation areas (French Planning System).

The French system is an interesting approach, quite different from that of both the US and England. The level of local control is more akin to the US system than the English, although the contents of a plan are set by national law. The apparent integration of planning with zoning is much closer to the English approach than to the American. The French zoning system seems to allow much more freedom to mix uses than does the typical US ordinance; its use of four suitability-based (i.e. based on the intrinsic suitability of each district as determined by environmental factors and infrastructure capacity) zones with density being the main governing factor in each zone might provide a simple, easily administered way to encourage mixed use, New Urbanist development, while focusing regulations on impacts and availability of public services.

Spain

In Spain, all properties fall into one of two categories of planning zone. For rustic (rural) plots (*suelo rústico*), the rural land law governs the building rules of rural sites. This varies among regions; for example in the regions of Catalonia, Pais Valenciano, and the Balearic Islands, *Ley 10/2004, de 9 de diciembre, de la Generalitat, del Suelo No Urbanizable* applies. However, in all regions some rural land is protected; all plots (parcels) fall under one of the two following criteria:

1. *Suelo no urbanizable protegido*. This is special, protected land which cannot be developed for residential homes.
2. *Suelo no urbanizable común*. This category has no special protection and can be developed for residential houses for private use.

For example, the development rights and restrictions of a rural plot in a *común* might be as follows:

- Plot size: minimum 10,000m^2
- Maximum building size: 2 percent of the plot size
- Floors: two. Height: seven meters

Thus with a 12,000m^2 plot you can build a home with 240m^2 on the ground floor and 240m^2 on the upper floor.

All rustic plots have aesthetic restrictions, with each planning zone having different regulations. Normally you have to build a typical regional-style building; for example you would not be given permission to build an *Ibicenco* (Ibiza-style) house in Valencia.

Urban plots (*suelo urbano*) are urbanized, serviced plots with access roads, water, and electricity. Each planning jurisdiction has its own rules although normally the plot size limitation is between 800m^2 and 1,500m^2, with the "habitable" space being about 20 percent of the plot. Each plot of land containing a chosen property has its own characteristics, in relation to its physical location within the total land area delineated, i.e. a town or city (municipality), which defines it from a municipal zoning point of view. This means that the ultimate use of the land is predetermined (e.g. multistorey building, single-family home with a maximum number of two stories, green area, road, ecosystem, reservation, maritime zone with no building allowed, etc.) and set forth in the municipal zoning laws.

Special consideration should be taken with regard to the land adjacent to the seashore; another official body, the Demarcación de Costas (Coastal Authorities, whose offices are located in the provincial capital), controls planning permission for coastal zones. Meanwhile, the planning information provided by the Town Hall will inform the purchaser whether or not the plot in question is located in such a zone. In case of dispute between the two authorities, the Coastal Authorities' decision rules (Countryside Properties).

The Spanish housing market is under threat from a growing number of accusations that local town councils are abusing their power to claim land for public developments – and dedicating land to resort communities and golf courses (Peralta 2007).

Germany

Zoning, an idea perfected by the Germans, was introduced into America and promptly stripped of any beneficial features. In the 1920s the US Department of Commerce drew up what was considered a model zoning enabling act. The model was principally the work of Edward Bassett and Alfred Bettman of the Ohio bar, who freely acknowledged their debt to the German experience. The then-Commerce Secretary Herbert Hoover heavily publicized the act and urged localities to adopt it. During the 1920s zoning became a kind of craze among municipalities. Thousands sought zoning information and eventually adopted the model zoning enabling act.

Yet there were significant differences between the German and American approaches to zoning. German zoning had its roots in the desire of residents of an increasingly crowded country to conserve unspoiled land and to protect residences against noxious industrial and commercial uses. But German practice for example, permitted duplex housing even in the most restricted residential zones. Duplexes both conserve space and, among other things, allow the elderly to be close to their adult children who might wish to have their parents close by but not in the same house. Many American ordinances initially contained flexible zoning provisions that allowed duplexes. Among such ordinances was the Euclid, Ohio statute that was upheld by the US Supreme Court in *Euclid v. Ambler Realty* that established the constitutionality of zoning. But the duplex feature has all but disappeared from most American ordinances.

The German practice subjected commercial uses in residential zones to performance standards allowing flexible land use. These permitted many forms of businesses and dwellings as long as they did not have certain adverse effects or consequences. For example, enterprises could be banned from an area if they released objectionable odors or noxious fumes. As economist and Nobel Prize winner F.A. Hayek wrote in his *Constitution of Liberty*: "Performance codes . . . impose fewer restrictions on spontaneous developments than 'specification codes' and are therefore to be preferred." The latter may at first seem to agree with our principles because they confer less discretion on authority. However, the discretion which performance codes confer is not of the objectionable kind. Whether or not a given technique satisfies the criterion of performance laid down in a rule can be ascertained by independent experts, and any dispute can be decided by a court. Nonetheless, in order to ease administration, and out of perhaps a justified mistrust of the integrity of zoning administrations, commercial uses were almost totally prohibited in American residential zones.

German zoning laws regulated residential areas through limiting the number of structures per acre; however, American zoning laws regulated residential areas through requiring minimum lot sizes and requiring residential structures to be a certain distance from thoroughfares.

Since their inception in the 1920s, American zoning laws have recognized constitutionally required variance. For example, when a government zones a parcel of property in such a way that all uses are barred, and as a result the property loses most or all of its value, the government is engaging in a taking of property. In such a case it would have to compensate the property owner for the loss. Further, in America zoning has mostly been under the purview of municipal governments, while in Germany the power generally remains with the equivalent of American state governments. Zoning in America gave rise to the evils of "spot zoning." In such cases, for example, a municipal council might rezone a particular parcel of land to satisfy a politically favored developer. This practice is less frequent in Germany.

A major goal of zoning in Germany was to limit despoliation of the countryside. Only recently has this become a concern in the less-crowded United States. Facilitating development in designated urban areas was an objective of the German system. But when zoning was introduced in America, the more generous provisions for citizen and neighborhood involvement allowed zoning to be used as a way to discourage development in built-up areas, and to defend the status quo. Ernst Freund, the first prominent American analyst of administrative law, as early as 1929 alluded:

> the [American] national temperament at present combines the lowest degree of local attachment with the highest degree of sensitiveness as to neighborhood associations. There is a subtle psychology about this sensitiveness; I think it is connected with our democratic institutions; where you haven't got natural class distinctions you make them artificially . . . People [in Europe] do not mind a little store around the corner a bit. When you go to Vienna you find that the palace of one of the great aristocratic families has a big glass work display room on the lower floor. We wouldn't have that in this country because it is not comfortable to our ideas.
>
> (Liebmann 1995)

Chapter 3: **INTERNATIONAL PERSPECTIVE**

Conclusions

This research has cracked open a door that leads to an intriguing view. Clearly there are many deep differences among the nations of the world with respect to implementing plans for more livable communities through regulatory means that are even evident in this small sampling – and there are some surprising similarities. Chief among these is the almost universal marriage of zoning and physical (or, as the Europeans say, spatial) planning; the plan is the zoning ordinance. This is certainly a very big step towards effectively implementing plans, one which is far from the system used in most US states today.

An interesting exception to the disconnect commonly found in the US between plans and zoning can be found in a few states such as California, in which the state law regarding planning and zoning has been interpreted (or even changed) to ensure better consistency between the two documents. In California zoning must be in accordance with the local plan, which can only be changed four times a year. Further, the plan must be approved by the state, and must comply with a book-length set of requirements specifying in great detail what sections should be included and what material should be covered in each section. California also has a state law establishing countywide LAFCOs (Local Area Formation Commissions), composed of representatives from the county and the cities within it. The LAFCO's main job is to establish boundaries around the cities beyond which urban growth is not allowed. Several other US states have similar provisions, but the majority is not even close to this model. In this regard, perhaps the laws and regulations found in California and similar states could provide a technique for tying zoning more closely to planning without violating US Constitutional restrictions on government intervention in the private land market.

Another tentative conclusion that leaps out from this preliminary research is the frequent use of techniques considered quite innovative in the US; specifically, the tailoring of regulations to individual parcels. This is done routinely in England, France and elsewhere; indeed, it seems that the French system approximates placing a form-based code (individually tailored design regulations done in accordance with the plan, with few or no use restrictions) everywhere, while the English system approximates use of PD zoning throughout the community (individually tailored design regulations, with uses specified according to the plan). In the US, PD zones are typically not a reflection of the plan but are often granted in exception to it, and form-based codes can be exceedingly complex; when either or both are used within a conventional zoning framework, the result is an administrative nightmare. Perhaps we can learn from our European cousins on how to better utilize these approaches.

Given the Constitutional restrictions placed on US property regulation, the best hope for improving American regulatory plan implementation may lie with the private sector. Private developers can place whatever restrictions they like on their property (as long as the restrictions do not violate any other laws, of course); justification on the grounds of preventing public harm or protecting public health, safety and welfare is not necessary. Not surprisingly, some of the best planned communities in the country have been done by private developers who wrote very strict regulations based directly on the plan for their development. The most noteworthy example is probably the Woodlands, Texas, a master planned community of nearly 18,000 acres with more than 80,000 residents located in the far north suburbs of Houston. Unlike most other planned communities of note, The Woodlands was built outside any city jurisdiction and in the only state where counties have no zoning power; thus all the land use regulation had to be done by the developer. The community's success, adherence to an environmentally sensitive master plan (40 percent of the land is preserved, including thousands of trees, floodplains, and most natural drainage areas), and very strict level of regulations give testimony to the thesis that livable communities can be successfully brought to reality even in the most hostile and ineffective public regulatory environments, if the private developer is required to provide the necessary restrictions that the governments in America cannot. Thus there seems to be some hope that much of the regulatory consistency we see with planning in England and other nations can be achieved in the US as well, if government planners will require more regulatory schemes be provided by local landowners when they first develop (subdivide) their property.

Finally, this research raises more questions than it answers. Some issues to clarify in future research include the following:

- When were the planning and zoning laws first passed, and were the British, French, Dutch, or Spanish in charge of the nation at that time?
- If so, what similarities and differences are there among the nations subject to that colonial power's rule?
- How does the current regulatory structure differ from that originally passed?
- Is planning separate from zoning (for example, is the plan map also the zoning map)?
- Is the government limited to taking private property for *public* use?
- Must government regulations be based on preventing harm, i.e. protecting public health safety morals and general welfare?
- Does the government own most of the land, and if so, does it make the land available for development?
- Does the government own the development rights for private land?
- What is the basic structure of government, i.e. are there local state and national levels or are there more? Are there three equally powerful branches (executive, legislative and judicial) or some other structure?
- Does the legal system have sufficient transparency in government to keep corruption and favoritism from running amok?
- Is there a tradition of resident input and control, or is the plan implemented from the top down?
- Is there sufficient respect for the law of the land by both residents and the government itself for implementation to take place?
- Is there respect for the plan?
- Is there a reasonably foolproof system for ensuring that the land use rules will be followed (i.e building/occupancy permits and recording of plats and deeds in the US)?
- How do the constitutions of the various nations differ with respect to powers of government to implement plans via regulations?

These and many other questions raised by this research remain to be addressed systematically in future research. Given the variety of approaches found in the small sampling completed so far, the future work should be most enlightening.

Chapter 3: **INTERNATIONAL PERSPECTIVE**

Notes

1. See, for example, the regulations governing the development of the New Urbanist community Addison Circle, Texas, or those governing the master planned community of the Woodlands, Texas.
2. Association of Collegiate Schools of Planning, *Choosing a Career in Urban and Regional Planning,* 2001.
3. Based on material in "Reviving America's Forgotten Neighborhoods: Addressing the Failure of Democracy to Produce a Civil Society in Our Inner Cities," by Elise M. Bright, PhD. Speech prepared for the Symposium on Democracy, Civil Society and Environmental Design sponsored by the College of Architecture and Planning, Ball State University, Muncie, Indiana, March 25–27, 2002.
4. Some of this material comes from Zhu Qian's doctoral dissertation, December 2008, Texas A&M University.
5. Canada also has Special Planning Areas (Round Table on Resource Land Use and Stewardship). Special Planning Areas are established by Government under the Planning Act to effectively promote and manage development and land use in accordance with Government's land use and development policies (www.gov.pe.ca).
6. The members of each local authority in Ireland are all called "Councilors" (for example, County Councilor, City Councilor, Town Councilor as appropriate). The number of members of each local authority is restricted by law; Schedule 7 of the Local Government Act, 2001 has set down the number of members of every county, city, borough or town council throughout the country. Councilors are directly elected in local elections by members of the local community. The number of Councilors elected to each local authority depends on the population of the local authority area (www.citizensinformation.ie).
7. *An Bord Pleanála* (the Planning Board) is a nominally independent statutory administrative tribunal that decides on appeals from planning decisions made by local authorities in the Republic of Ireland – Planning and Development Strategic Infrastructure Act, 2006.
8. (Tan 1998).
9. Impact of comprehensive development zoning on real estate development in Hong Kong by Raymond Y.C. Tse, Department of Building and Real Estate, Hong Kong Polytechnic University, Hong Kong.
10. Multiple and intensive land use: case studies in Hong Kong, S.S.Y. Lau, R. Giridharan and S. Ganesan, Department of Architecture, University of Hong Kong.
11. A Union Territory is a sub-national administrative division of India. Unlike the states, which have their own elected governments, union territories are ruled directly by the federal national government; the President of India appoints and Administrator or Lieutenant-Governor for each territory.
12. While the seller of a Dutch property must inform potential buyers of contamination on a site, the buyer must also perform their own "due diligence" investigation of the property.

References

Albrechts, L. (2004). Strategic (spatial) planning reexamined. *Environment and Planning*, 34: 743–758.

Alterman, R. and G. Cars, eds. (1991). *Neighborhood regeneration: An international evaluation.* New York, NY: Mansell Publishing.

Anglo Info. (n.d.). *Guide to building construction in Spain.* Retrieved May 7, 2008, from http://costablanca.angloinfo.com/countries/spain/build.asp

Ashton, S. (2006, Dec 18). *Planning districts regulation.* Retrieved Apr 2, 2008, from web2.gov.mb.ca: http://web2.gov.mb.ca/laws/regs/pdf/p080-249.06.pdf

Ball, M. (1994). The 1980s property boom. *Environment and Planning C: Government and Policy*, 26: 671.

Banerjee, B. (2002). Security of Tenure in Indian Cities. In Durand-Lasserve, A. and L. Royston, eds. 2002. *Holding Their Ground: Secure Land Tenure for the Urban Poor in Developing Countries.* London: Earthscan Publications Ltd.

Blatter, J.K. (2006). Geographic scale and functional scope in metropolitan governance reform: theory and evidence from Germany. *Journal of Urban Affairs,* 28: 121–150.

Bright, E. (2000). *Reviving America's forgotten neighborhoods.* New York: Garland Press.

Bright, E. (2001). TOADS: instruments of urban revitalization. In Wagner, F., T. Joder, and A. Mumphrey Jr., eds. 2000. *Managing capital resources for central city revitalization.* New York: Garland Press.

Canadian Tax Foundation. (2003). *The structure of Canadian government.* Retrieved Mar 27, 2008 from www.ctf.ca: http://www.ctf.ca/FN2003/chap01.pdf.

Carolinian Canada. (2004). Land use planning and conservation. Retrieved Apr 7, 2008, from www.carolinian.org: http://www.carolinian.org/ConservationPrograms_LandUsePlanning.htm

Countryside Properties. (n.d.). *Building regulations Spain.* Retrieved May 11, 2008, from Countryside-properties-spain: http://www.countryside-properties-spain.com/information/building-regulations-spain.htm

Cullingworth, B. (1993). *The political culture of planning.* APA Planners Press.

Cunningham, P. (1993). *The political culture of planning.* New York: McGraw Hill.

EPA. (2008, April 9). *International brownfields case study: Westergasfabriek, Amsterdam, Netherlands.* Retrieved Apr 22, 2008, http://epa.gov/brownfields/partners/westergas.html.

Faludi, A. and A.J. van der Valk. (1994). Rule and Order: Dutch Planning Doctrine in the 20th Century. *GeoJournal Library,* Vol 28. Boston: Kluwer Academic Publishers.

French planning system. (n.d.). Retrieved Apr 19, 2008, from French Property.com: http://www.french-property.com/guides/france/building/planning/.

Global legal group. (2007). *The International Comparative Legal Guide to: Real Estate 2007.* Retrieved Apr 28, 2008, from www.iclg.co.uk: http://www.iclg.co.uk/khadmin/Publications/pdf/1263.pdf.

Gould, J. (1986). *Quality of life in American neighborhoods: levels of affluence, toxic waste, and cancer mortality in residential zip code areas.* Boulder, CO: Westview Press.

Judd, D. and M. Parkinson. (1990). *Leadership and urban regeneration: cities in North America and Europe.* Newbury Park, CA: Sage Publications.

Kennedy, J. (Feb 2004). Land development considerations. *Real Estate Finance*, 11–12.

Kerry, R. (24 April 2003). IPI president calls for changes to restore public Trust. Irish Planning Institute: Dublin.

Kochhar, K., U. Kumar, R. Rajan, A. Subramanian and I. Tokatlidis. (2006). India's Pattern of Development: What Happened, What Follows? *Journal of Monetary Economics* 53: 981–1019.

Chapter 3: INTERNATIONAL PERSPECTIVE

Lai, L. (1997). The Property Rights Justifications for Planning and a Theory of Zoning. *Progress in Planning* 48 (3): 161–246.

Levitt, R., ed. (1987). *Cities reborn.* Washington, DC: Urban Land Institute, 26 (2): 63–66.

Liebmann, G.W. (1995). *Modernization of zoning.* Retrieved Apr 28, 2008, from www.cato.org/: http://www.cato.org/pubs/regulation/reg19n2f

Lushhhomeonline. (2007, June 29). "You ain't seen nothing yet." Retrieved Apr 24, 2008, from http://lushhhomemedia.com/2007/06/

McCarthy, C. (2003). Corruption in Public Offices in Ireland: Policy Design as a Countermeasure. *Quarterly Economic Commentary,* Autumn 2003.

Miller, D., and De Roo, G. (1996). Integrated environmental zoning: an innovative Dutch approach to measuring and managing environmental spillovers in urban regions. *Journal of the American Planning Association,* 62 (03): 373–380.

Mukherjee, R. and O. Gokcekus. (2006). Officials' Asset Declaration Laws: Do They Prevent Corruption? *Global Corruption Report.* pp. 326–327. Paris: OECD.

Nexia International. (2005). Real estate in Germany. Retrieved Apr 24, 2008, from http://www.nexia.com/publications_pdf/international_tax_matters/itm_real_estate_%20germany.pdf,

Peralta, C. (2007, Apr 20). *Uproar Over Land Grabs In Spain.* Retrieved May 5, 2008, from Planetizen.com: http://www.planetizen.com/node/23941.

Pogodzinski, J. and Sass, T. (1991). Measuring the Effects of Municipal Zoning Regulations: A Survey. *Urban Studies*, 28 (4): 597–621.

Republic of Singapore. (2003). Master Plan 2003. Retrieved Apr 28, 2008, from URA: http://www.ura.gov.sg/ppd/gazettedmp2003/index-frontmp2003.htm.

Round Table on Resource Land Use and Stewardship. (n.d.). Rural land zoning. Retrieved from http://www.gov.pe.ca/roundtable/index.php3?number=69477andlang=E

Rouwendal, J. and Van Der Straaten, J.W. (2007). Measuring Welfare Effects Of Spatial Planning. *Tijdschrift voor Economische en Sociale Geografie,* 98, 276–283.

Siegan, B. (1972). *Land Use Without Zoning.* Lexington, MA: Lexington Press.

Sinclair, I. (2000, June). Planning in the USA – The good, the bad and the ugly. Retrieved from http://www.ruralplanning.com.au/library/newsletter/June00.shtml.

Sol, V.M., Petronell, L.E., Aiking, H., and De Boer, J. (1995). Integrated environmental index for application in land-use zoning. *Environmental Management*, 19, 457–467.

Tan, A.K. (1998). *Preliminary Assessment Of Singapore's Environmental Law.* Retrieved Feb 10, 2008, from www.nUsedu.sg: http://sunsite.nUsedu.sg/apcel/dbase/singapore/reports.html#sec2.1.

The Village Building Co, Ltd. (2003, August). A case study in compatible land use. *Tralee News*, pp. 1–10.

Thomas, E.M. (2008). *Zoning in Canada.* Retrieved Mar 17, 2008 from http://www.thecanadianencyclopedia.com/index.cfm?PgNm=TCEandParams=A1ARTA0008779

Tracey, C.M. (28 July 2003). *The All-Party Oireachtas Committe on the Constitution.* IPI Council.

Urban Redevelopment Authority, Singapore. (2003). Retrieved Feb 12, 2008, from www.ura.gov.sg: http://www.ura.gov.sg/student/physicalplng.htm.

Van der Kuil, Peter. (1995, May). Town planning (zoning) schemes. *Planning Bulletin*, 2.

Williams, B.A. (2002). The expansion of Dublin and the policy Implications of dispersal. *Journal of Irish Urban Studies*, 1–21.

World Bank. (2008) Urbanization in India. Philadelphia: University of Pennsylvania Press.

Chapter 4

CREATING SUSTAINABLE COMMUNITIES – A TRANS-ATLANTIC PERSPECTIVE

David Shaw
University of Liverpool, UK

Simon Pemberton
University of Birmingham, UK

Alexander Nurse
University of Liverpool, UK

Introduction

For the last decade there has been a strong rhetoric in British policy-making about the importance of improving people's quality of life. Fundamental to this process has been the idea of "spatial planning," which is seen as an integrative device that moves beyond a narrow focus on land use planning and the regulation of development to integrate policies and programs from the public, private, and voluntary sectors, and considers the impacts on places and the way in which they function (Morphet 2010). This emphasis on placemaking and place shaping has been picked up by the main political parties and professional bodies. The Royal Town Planning Institute, the body that represents professional planners throughout the UK, for example, uses as its strap-line "The Mediation of Space: The Making of Place." National governments of different political persuasion have, in various ways, been advocating an approach which recognizes that all places have distinctive and diverse characteristics and that policy solutions should be focused on meeting the specific needs and challenges of particular localities. Nevertheless, the language and context of this agenda has recently changed. For example, the Labour government, which was in power from 1997 until May 2010, promoted the concept of "sustainable communities," which were:

> places where people want to live and work, now and in the future. They meet the diverse needs of existing and future residents, are sensitive to their environment, and contribute to a high quality of life. They are safe and inclusive, well planned, built and run, and offer equality of opportunity and good services for all.
>
> (ODPM 2005: 56)

Chapter 4: **TRANS-ATLANTIC PERSPECTIVE**

However, the current government, which since May 2010 is a Conservative and Liberal Democrat coalition, is now – at least in theory – advocating a new form of localism. In response to criticisms that both the system of spatial planning and an emphasis on sustainable communities under the Labour government failed to achieve meaningful consensus and agreement with respect to the key outcomes envisaged, this is informing – and indeed legitimizing – a "new" localist approach by the coalition. In essence, the system that is now emerging still relies heavily on consensus building through better public engagement but allies this to local area politics, although it remains unclear as to whether local people in reality will be given more power and responsibility to shape the communities within which they reside (Communities and Local Government 2010; Allmendinger and Haughton 2012).

Whilst there are very clear political differences in these two concepts, what they mean and how they should be delivered, there is a common theme which places a strong emphasis on the quality of a place and a placemaking agenda. These perspectives fit neatly with the concept of livability, and this chapter seeks to critically review the experiences in England over the last decade as policy makers have struggled to address social, economic, and environmental concerns of particular communities to make people feel more comfortable in, engaged with, and proud of the places they primarily associate themselves with. Enhancing this sense of civic pride and identity, which can be equated to livability, individual or collective well-being is evaluated at two broad scales. First, we review the way that central governments have been promoting this agenda, however it is described, drawing out common themes and contrasting perspectives. Second, we explore the way that some of these agendas have played out in Liverpool, a city in the North West of England.

Liverpool as a city evokes different feelings and emotions. From being a truly global city based around international trade in the eighteenth and nineteenth centuries (Wilks-Heeg 2003), the twentieth century saw the city experience a period of almost terminal decline so that by the mid-1980s it was being described as the "beaten city" of the Thatcherite decade and the "shock city" of the post-industrial age (Belchem 2006). Today the city (or at least the city centre) is seen as a renaissance city, but all the statistical indicators suggest that the city still contains some of the most deprived, disadvantaged, and socially excluded communities in the UK (Communities and Local Government 2007). One of the key indicators of well-being is life expectancy rates, and in Liverpool the average life expectancy for men is 73.6 and for women is 78.4 (Audit Commission 2010), compared with national averages of 77.7 and 81.9, respectively. Even within the city, men living in the most deprived neighborhoods are likely to live nine years less than those in the most affluent areas, and for women the differences are around eight years (Audit Commission 2010). We do not claim that Liverpool is an exemplar of best practice, but rather wish to use the city first, as a case study to explore how some of central government's policies have been operationalized at a local level, second, to review the extent to which past initiatives have achieved their outcomes, and third, to speculate about the future prospects of Liverpool as a city (and its communities) as the slow process of renaissance continues.

The Emergence of the Livability Agenda in the UK

"Livability," "quality of place," "sustainability," and "sustainable communities" have become the rhetorical terms or aspirations justifying almost all recent policy interventions. Whilst the

63

terms are often used interchangeably within a UK context, it is the notion of sustainable communities that until relatively recently had come to the fore. However, the concepts are vague and fuzzy. They are not readily amenable to precise definition, and they can be used at different spatial scales and within different policy frameworks.

In a UK context, Gallent and Wong (2009) have argued that the notion of livability emerged from the 2000 Urban White Paper (DETR 2000). Within this document a holistic and integrated approach, combining economic, social, and physical dimensions, was advocated to help the green shoots of recovery and to facilitate an urban renaissance, rather than an individual set of projects or programs which focused on particular issues or problems facing particular communities (spatially defined) or sectors of society (Robson *et al.* 2000). Furthermore, such an approach takes the argument away from one based on urban form which has tended, perhaps not unnaturally, to dominate the urban design literature (see for example Bramley *et al.* 2009; Biddulph 2010). Localities were expected to identify their key agendas for change and to work in partnership with other public, private, and voluntary sector bodies to create an action plan to try and address these critical place-based issues. A new institutional landscape was created with Local Strategic Partnerships (LSPs) being formed in localities, which were responsible for producing Sustainable Community Strategies (SCSs). The Local Strategic Partnership consisted of the key public, private, and voluntary sector organizations that had a central role in influencing a place and how it functioned. The SCSs were intended to evaluate the agendas facing an area and develop strategic priorities and action plans in an attempt to ensure that the well-being of individuals and communities could be enhanced in a structured and targeted manner. Ambitious "floor" targets were set at the national level as to what outputs localities were intended to achieve over a three-year programs, and the link between national targets, local diagnosis of place-specific issues, and an appropriate action plan were eventually facilitated by more formal contracts between central government and the LSP with the introduction of Local Area Agreements (LAAs). The LAAs were three-year funding programs whereby LSP partners agreed to work together to address issues that were of particular concern. But in practice there has been an academic debate as to whether this has really been a bottom-up approach based on local need, or whether local LSPs have framed their LAA priorities to coincide with centrally prescribed targets and aspirations (Coaffee and Headlam 2006; Nurse and Pemberton 2010).

Within this framework a number of key principles were readily apparent, some promoting positive intervention, others questioning the legitimacy of such action for local democracy. The fundamental aspiration could be seen as being derived from the UK's Sustainable Development Strategy, which was re-launched in 2005. In this document, the focus was "not only on creating sustainable communities but to give a new focus to tackling environmental inequalities as well" (DEFRA 2005: 4). In addition, one of the five guiding principles was to "ensure a strong healthy and just society which meets the diverse needs of all people in existing and future communities, promoting personal wellbeing, social cohesion and inclusion, and creating equal opportunity for all" (DEFRA 2005:18).

The key policy principles included:

- *Integration of service delivery.* There was a growing view that too many agencies across the public, private, and the voluntary sectors were delivering services to the public in a confused and inefficient manner. It was argued that by bringing service deliverers together they could work in partnership to ensure more focused delivery on the issues that really mattered to local communities. The new institutional landscape (briefly outlined above) was intended to serve this function of horizontal coordination.

- *Efficient and effective service delivery.* The integration of service delivery was intended to avoid duplication, repetition, and as a consequence lead to more efficient and cost effective service delivery. Hence there was an aspiration that these changes would encourage a modernization and transformation of public services.
- *Addressing place-based challenges.* The action plans within the SCS were intended to be focused on meeting the specific challenges and issues surrounding particular places.
- *Active co-production with user communities.* Key to the development of the SCS was listening and participation from stakeholders; this included both local communities themselves and also the various delivery agencies.

(Morphet 2010)

However, there were also criticisms of this approach:

- *Democratic deficits.* The LSPs were non-statutory bodies, and many local authorities initially feared that they might lose control. A democratic deficit was emerging whereby public spending in a locality was managed by individuals representing different interests, but not necessarily by those who had been elected. Having said this, the role of the local authority in "convening" the partnerships and their role in scrutinizing the delivery of police, health, and other public services attempted to guarantee that they remained central to the process.
- *Centrally-imposed localism.* Whilst there was a strong aspiration that decision making should be devolved to the most appropriate level, the importance of national targets and the requirement for detailed monitoring of LAA contracts against the agreed targets raised concerns as to whether this really was localism in action or central government retaining control through detailed performance management, though being less explicitly directive to the local governments.

The drive for efficiency savings in service delivery was enhanced with two further central government-derived projects, which were stimulated by the Treasury's desire for enhancing national economic growth. First, the introduction of Multi Area Agreements (MAAs) highlighted that some issues and elements of service delivery may require a more strategic cross-border approach, and that through partners working together across functional economic areas (FEAs), more effective and efficient service delivery could be achieved through economies of scale in service delivery (Pemberton and Lloyd 2011). Operating in a similar way to LAAs, groups of local authorities and other service deliverers therefore agreed to come together in order to try and address common problems through generating "freedoms and flexibilities" from central government. In this respect, MAAs could again be seen as a form of contract between central government and sub-regional consortia, whereby the consortia agreed to deliver various outcomes in return for additional flexibilities in how they could use government funding. Close scrutiny and monitoring of performance was an important aspect of these contracts.

Second, following various experiments – and just before the general election in May 2010 – the former Labour government launched its Total Place agenda. This advocated taking a "whole area" approach to the way that public services were to be delivered, either on an individual local authority basis, or collaboratively across a functional economic area. In theory, it would create the classic "win-win" situation, with 2 percent efficiency savings expected by 2013–14 and with an expectation that through dialogue and consultation, service delivery would better match the needs of citizens (HM Treasury and CLG 2010). However, whilst a number of pilot programs reported back on their initial activity – which highlighted difficulties in inter- and intra-scalar working (Pemberton and Lloyd 2011) – the program was quickly abandoned with the election of a new government that had differing ideological and political perspectives.

Nevertheless, in many respects the general direction of travel for public policy in the UK in terms of joined-up government, meeting citizen needs, and enhanced efficiency and effectiveness in service delivery (all of which were common themes under the Labour government) have been retained, although policy discourse and the context for action has changed. As already discussed, under the auspices of creating a "Big Society," the coalition government has sought to promote a new localism agenda advocating that local communities or neighborhoods take increased responsibility for determining and delivering services that are relevant and necessary to improve individuals' quality of life. Critical aspects of this approach include the decentralization of power, decision making, and service delivery, and with the potential for voluntary action to replace existing forms of (paid) public service delivery. But perhaps a key difference is through relating an emphasis on achieving consensus and public engagement to local area politics, although in practice the way that this plays out in terms of the extent to which the activities of certain groups (and institutions) is legitimized over others remains to be seen. Furthermore, the onset of the global recession has meant a changed context for public services and the balance between state-market-civil-society involvement in service delivery. Indeed, the sweeping public service cuts affecting central and local government is raising doubts as to whether the "Big Society" and individual and collective responsibility may ever be achieved. Perhaps nowhere is this more evident than in Liverpool, where the city council have pulled out of a national pilot testing elements of the "Big Society" approach as a consequence of national government cutting public expenditure in the city by £140 million from 2011/12. This in turn is now leading to many (promising) programmes targeting the most deprived areas of the city being withdrawn.

Livability and the City of Liverpool

The first two sections of this chapter highlight that over the past fifteen years, there have been on-going, yet varying, attempts by central government in the UK to focus on well-being and improving people's quality of life. The chapter now explores the extent to which such attempts have worked in practice by examining what has happened within the city of Liverpool.

Liverpool is currently ranked as the most deprived local authority area in England, and the second- and third-worst performing in terms of employment and income deprivation respectively (CLG 2007). Furthermore, at a neighborhood level (see Figure 4.1) it is evident that not only is deprivation concentrated within certain parts of the city, for example, in North

Chapter 4: **TRANS-ATLANTIC PERSPECTIVE**

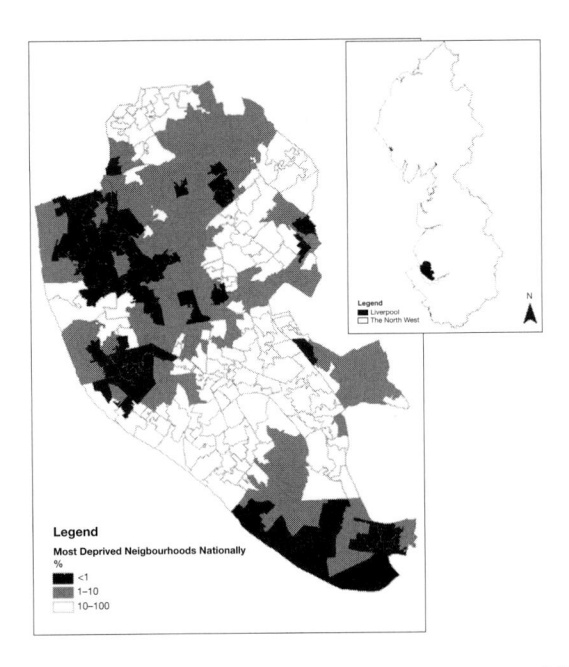

Figure 4.1 Multiple Deprivation in Liverpool. Super Output Areas falling within the 1 percent most deprived and 10 percent most deprived nationally.

Source: CLG 2007

Liverpool, it is also extremely widespread. Nearly one-fifth (19 percent) of Liverpool's Super Output Areas (an area of measurement containing approximately 1,500 people) reside in the 1 percent most-deprived neighborhoods in England, and in excess of half of the city is located in the 10 percent worst-performing neighborhoods. Beyond this, from an economic perspective it is clear that the city continues to underperform, with a current unemployment rate of 10.5 percent compared to a national average of 6.9 percent (Office for National Statistics 2010).

As already stated, we are not claiming that Liverpool is an exemplar of best practice; rather, it provides an interesting story (or perhaps more accurately a set of stories) to explore the extent to which the renaissance that the city has witnessed since the mid-1990s has sufficient "depth," and the extent to which various policy initiatives focused around enhancing livability are helping to deliver a better quality of life for the city's residents. In this respect, three vignettes are explored and all, in various ways, are interconnected.

We start from a partnership perspective by exploring how "Liverpool First" (the Local Strategic Partnership (LSP) for the city) came into existence and the roles and priorities of the Sustainable Community Strategy (SCS) that emerged. Liverpool First's focus was very much on improving the life chances of individuals living in the most deprived areas of the city, which according to any measure of social deprivation are the worst in the country. The second story then focuses around the idea of "city boosterism" that has been promoted, which has largely focused on the city centre. The designation in 2002 of Liverpool as one of two European Capitals of Culture in 2008 provided a timeline within which much physical regeneration in the city occurred. This place marketing of the city both as a tourism destination, but also as a place for substantial global investment continues today. However, what became clear, was that whilst 2008 Capital of Culture presented an opportunity to regenerate the city centre and improve the Liverpool "brand," this offered little to remedy the wider deprivation issues facing the city and within its poorest performing areas. Indeed, the final vignette reiterates the need to focus on the circumstances of individuals. We explore how effective partnership working has developed in the context of promoting green infrastructure, as well as its use as a mechanism for helping to improve people's quality of life in one of Liverpool's most deprived areas, namely North Liverpool.

Narrative 1 – Liverpool: A Divided City with the Need for Better Policy Integration

Liverpool's Local Strategic Partnership (LSP), known as "Liverpool First," drew together the three main elements of UK service provision (public, private, and voluntary) to create an Executive Board of partners which broadly reflected the main actors with responsibility for the delivery of public services in Liverpool. Ostensibly led by the city council, it also includes other public bodies responsible for public health and public safety (for example, the police and fire services). In addition, seeking to address concerns around the "democratic deficit," it engages democratically elected members of the council within its functions, is led by the Leader of the Council, and is assisted by a Chief Executive. The latter is a non-elected head of paid service, but who is a very powerful figure within most UK local authority structures. It also has representation from the city's business community through the Chamber of Commerce, as well as representatives from charitable and voluntary organizations.

The majority of English LSPs are administered directly by the local authorities themselves – in essence, they act as the accountable body. But Liverpool First operates "at arm's length" from the council. This means that it functions as a separate entity whose sole business is based around the running of the LSP and its associated functions. Indeed, Liverpool First has been described by representatives from the government's regional office (Government Office for the North West) as the "ringmaster" for the partnership itself.

The first key policy document that was produced by Liverpool First was a Community Strategy, which later metamorphosed into a Sustainable Community Strategy (SCS) in line with the Labour Government's Sustainable Communities agenda. The aim of the SCS document that was subsequently produced was to set out a long-term vision for the city over a period of fifteen years (Liverpool First 2008). The vision was based around five broad themes or policy imperatives of "Competitiveness," "Connectivity," "A Distinctive Sense of Place," "Thriving Neighbourhoods," and "Health and Wellbeing," each of which had numerous policy goals and targets and "lead" organizations for delivery (Table 4.1).

In line with criticisms nationally that SCSs were little more than "motherhood and apple pie visions" (Morphet 2010), a Local Area Agreement (LAA) was developed in Liverpool to take forward a programmed of activity within the context of the SCS over a (rolling) three-year period. Hence Liverpool First's LAA was signed off by the government in 2008 (a three-year contract), and included thirty-five "priority for improvement" indicators that had been taken from a nationally-defined set of nearly 200. The thirty-five that were selected for Liverpool were intended to best reflect the priorities set out in the SCS in order to deliver the long-term

Chapter 4: **TRANS-ATLANTIC PERSPECTIVE**

Table 4.1 Themes within Liverpool's Sustainable Community Strategy 2009–2024

Theme One: Competitiveness
- Increase job opportunities for the city's residents, matching the core city average employment rate by 2024

Theme Two: Connectivity
- Increase patronage on bus and rail, with a medium-term target of increasing bus use by 1 percent and rail by 7.9 percent by 2011

Theme Three: Distinctive Sense of Place
- Reduce overall vacancy levels in all types of housing across the city with a target of 5 percent by 2012
- Increase the proportion of owner occupiers across the city, with a medium-term target of 60 percent of all homes by 2012

Theme Four: Thriving Neighbourhoods
- Liverpool to be ranked by the Home Office as one of the Safest Cities in the UK by 2024
- The percentage of local people who feel they can affect decision making in their area will increase by 1 percent every two years

Theme Five: Health and Well-being
- Life expectancy at birth for both males and females will improve and be consistently above England's lowest ten rankings by 2024
- Liverpool with achieve top quartile performance in terms of supporting vulnerable people into employment and to live in their own home

Source: Liverpool First, 2008

vision for the city. But, as has already been highlighted, although local areas are in essence given a free hand to select any indicator they choose, as an area becomes more deprived, the extent to which this freedom presents itself in reality is greatly reduced (Nurse and Pemberton 2010). Liverpool is no exception to this trend. Questions can also be raised over the extent to which local areas can truly derive "bottom-up" approaches to tackling deprivation given the need to select indicators from the national set.

To deliver the goals of the LAA, partners were allocated to several working groups which broadly focused around the five SCS themes and related areas of activity detailed within the LAA. But an early concern that emerged of similar arrangements elsewhere was that instead of breaking down the silo mentality that has long been a criticism of UK governance (Sullivan *et al.* 2006), the approach simply acted to expand the silo, so that whilst partners would work together on their core business (in the context of the LAA) they would not look beyond the working group in which they were involved (Davies 2009). However, in Liverpool this was not generally the case and partners did appear to involve themselves within other working groups where at first glance they would not appear to have a core interest. One prominent example of this related to the Fire and Rescue Service, who beyond community safety did not have any obvious role in many of the other working groups. Yet in Liverpool they sought to involve themselves heavily in working groups focused on education and health, reasoning that both could have longer-term impacts in the reduction of instances of fires.

In order to gain some further sense of how the work of Liverpool First and the LAA contributed towards improving livability in the city, a number of examples are cited below. These take the form of an overview of current progress as well as illustrating how improvements to livability for particular individuals and communities have arisen as a result of partnership working.

One Place and Comprehensive Area Assessment

To monitor the success of LSPs, their LAAs, and the activities of constituent partners in their entirety (i.e. "One Place"), the Labour government introduced a system of Comprehensive Area Assessment (CAA). This operated on a "traffic light" style system, awarding green flags for what they deemed to be exceptional performance that others could learn from and red flags for areas that needed significant improvement. The results from such an approach were only published once, in 2010, before being scrapped by the coalition government, in part due to its cost and in part because of its unpopularity. However, the report, produced by the national Audit Commission (2010), offers a useful insight into how Liverpool was performing and achieving targets of relevance to the issue of livability.

Analysis of the report reveals that Liverpool was in receipt of one green flag for its efforts towards creating "thriving communities." The green flag was acknowledged for improvements in the "safer city" category, with best practice highlighted in reducing city centre crime and burglaries. The LSP and its constituent partners also won praise for taking concerted action to reduce the burglary rate by focusing on areas with a high burglary rate, many of which contained a high percentage of the city's student population. This resulted in a 60 percent drop in burglaries in those areas (Audit Commission 2010), and indicates the value of a strong partnership-based approach to addressing issues of livability.

Healthy Homes

Another prominent scheme that highlighted the drive to improve livability in the city was the Healthy Homes initiative, which was launched in 2009 and principally involved the city council, fire service, and numerous charities. The scheme focused on improving conditions in homes, particularly those which were rented by publicly registered landlords, noting that there was a strong inverse relationship between the quality of housing stock and the health of residents, including reduced life expectancy and lower economic activity for residents in substandard homes.

The scheme worked through an inspection process, investigating housing conditions that could lead to ill health, such as dampness or drafts, or posed a threat to the house itself, including fire risks. If a house was considered to be deficient in any of these regards, the council could instigate proceedings under UK environmental health law to compel the landlord or homeowner to rectify this and cover any associated costs.

Through this process, over 12,700 homes in the city were visited, with over 12,800 referrals made to other local partners, resulting in £2.5 million of investment to improve the housing stock (Liverpool City Council 2011). This high referral rate (indeed higher than the number of houses inspected) is attributed to the fact that during the inspections the visitors were able to talk to residents about a variety of pertinent topics, which resulted in referrals to dentists, doctors, the fire service, education services, employment agencies, and numerous relevant charities (Liverpool First 2010). All of these referrals, supplementary to the improvements within the home itself, have arguably helped to raise the living standards of those residents and improve conditions in the city.

Indeed, it has been claimed (Audit Commission 2010) that this scheme was a particular success in areas of the city that were in receipt of other government grants to promote "Housing Market Renewal," a program that aimed to regenerate some of the worst areas of housing in the city (and which has also been targeted in other areas of the North and Midlands of the UK). However, the CAA process also noted that outside these areas the scheme struggled to have the same level of impact, particularly within the private rental sector, where the housing stock was more likely to be of a poorer standard (ibid.). Despite this, in overall terms the scheme has shown some significant signs of success, particularly given that it has focused efforts to improve public health and livability in some of the poorest performing areas of Liverpool.

Sure Start Children's Centers

A third scheme that appears to have benefited from cross-partnership working is the "Sure Start" Children's Centers initiative. "Sure Start" (similar to the earlier US Head Start programs) has been targeted at the most disadvantaged areas and was designed, through early intervention, to provide children in such neighborhoods with learning and socializing support. There are currently twenty-five centers in Liverpool, principally run by the council, which are responsible for such provision. The Children's Centre's main function is to provide free education to children aged three to five, the point at which they would legally be required to enter full-time education, and each child is entitled to fifteen hours per week of education for thirty-eight weeks of the year.

Beyond this core educational role, the Sure Start centers draw upon other partners to provide services for parents as part of the previous government's wider employability agenda, which has been argued as diluting to the impact of such provision (House of Commons Children, Schools and Families Committee 2010). The centers can provide up to fifty hours of child care per week to a child, as well as providing advice to parents on benefits or tax allowances which may be available to help them to pay for the child-care service if required. This can allow parents to either find work or return to work, increasing economic activity rates within a local area, a key goal.

The continued presence of Sure Start Children's Centers is important beyond direct educational benefits. A recent national evaluation of Sure Start concluded that that the presence of a Sure Start Centre was more likely to lead to the improved physical health of a child who attended compared to one who did not. But crucially, it also noted that mothers whose children attended such centers reported greater life-satisfaction, a direct aim of the livability agenda (Department for Education 2010).

In overall terms, whilst the SCS approach was intended to be based around a long-term vision with a sustained program of activities, it can be difficult to get a real sense of how well these goals are being achieved. However, interim assessments and specific case-study examples associated with taking forward the SCS and LAA approach, as highlighted above, indicate the positive impacts that such forms of partnership working can have on improving livability, particularly in deprived areas. Hence a critical challenge for groups involved in these types of arrangements will be to maintain this level of working in the context of reduced public expenditure and a changing policy environment.

Narrative 2 – European Capital and Culture and the Emergence of the Renaissance City

The second narrative that runs in parallel is the way in which Liverpool emerged from what Murden (2006) has described as the "self-pity city" during the latter decades of the twentieth century to the aspiring "renaissance city" of today. It is a story of "city boosterism" and again there are several overlapping narratives that came together at a particular moment in time. Perhaps the most important story – although it is not the only one – is the story of 2008, when for a year Liverpool alongside Stavanger in Norway were the joint European Capitals of Culture (ECoC).

Other events and designations were important in respect of "boosterism," such as the city celebrating its 800th anniversary in 2007, and the waterfront being designated as a UNESCO World Heritage Site in 2004 as a Maritime Mercantile City. But the designation of Liverpool as the UK's nomination for the ECoC has been seen as the key catalyst for city renaissance (Shaw *et al.* 2009).

It was known that one city within the UK would be the ECoC in 2008, so the UK government launched a competition, inviting prospective cities to bid to win the title. Liverpool's bid was promoted around the theme of "The World in One City," which was centered on celebrating and reconnecting Liverpool with its historical global links based on trade and transport. The project was intended to deliver three key dimensions: first, improving the cultural infrastructure of the city, second, promoting an inclusive approach to culture and thereby facilitating community cohesion, and third, helping, through renewal, to create a premier European city. Internally this could be seen as a strong indication of the renewed sense of purpose and strengthened capacity in the city's governance structures. The decision in June 2003 that the bid was successful was greeted with a mixture of excitement, enthusiasm, and surprise in the city. Liverpool had not been the favorite but had beaten six other cities (shortlisted from an original list of twelve).

The success of winning the UK's nomination to become European Capital of Culture for 2008, following on from the City's 800th birthday celebrations in 2007, provided a tight and focused time frame galvanizing key actors into making important decisions to ensure projects were under construction on time. Various policies and programs became mutually reinforcing with culture being seen as an important driver of change, and there was a renewed self confidence in the city's ability to adapt. Whilst there has undoubtedly been a substantial amount of public, European, and national government funding supporting the regeneration, one of the notable features of the last decade has been the private sector's renewed confidence in the city, with a particular focus on the city centre.

From Anderson and Holden's (2008) perspective, this decision created a sense of hope and optimism around the city based on three distinct but inter-related dimensions. First, *advent*

Chapter 4: **TRANS-ATLANTIC PERSPECTIVE**

– the designation meant that something good was going to happen at some point in the future, in this case 2008; second *crystallization* – for most stakeholders and actors there was a focused deadline by which things had to be done and certain decisions had to made; and finally a *blank canvas* – whereby different individuals would have different hopes and aspirations for what the designation would bring.

In terms of livability and well-being the ECoC was expected to deliver across a range of activities:

- to positively reposition Liverpool to an international audience and encourage more visitors to the city and the North West;
- to encourage and increase participation in cultural activity by people from communities across Merseyside and the wider region;
- to create a legacy of long-term growth and sustainability in the city's cultural sector; and
- to develop greater recognition, nationally, and internationally for the role of arts and culture in making cities better places to live, work, and visit.

(Garcia *et al.* 2010)

One of the evident aspirations was the idea that cultural activities and local participation would enhance individuals' sense of civic and individual pride, which in turn might contribute to improved individual life opportunities. Kunzmann (2004) has identified seven key themes as a driver for city regeneration and renaissance:

- culture being used to promote and rebrand the city at all scales;
- culture being used to strengthen place identity and civic pride;
- cultural regeneration being used as a tool for facilitating the physical transformation of places. In Liverpool, a major redevelopment of the retail provision within the city centre combined with a transformation of the iconic Liverpool waterfront and building connectivity between the two was certainly facilitated through a desire – if not to get the city ready for 2008 – to entice visitors back through the transformations that were being undertaken (Shaw *et al.* 2009);
- culture providing entertainment for all;
- culture providing a catalyst for education;
- culture and creativity as a driver of economic growth; and
- culture as a tool to drive economic growth and recovery.

All can contribute to improving well-being within the city, and there was certainly a debate as to whether the lead-up to the event, and indeed the year itself, would provide wider benefits to all of Liverpool's residents. Indeed some of the key aspirations in the bidding document were that the event would leave a lasting legacy and that the approach would be one of widespread engagement. However, it would also be wrong to assume that any recent improvements in the economy of the city and the well-being of its residents could be ascribed solely to the ECoC event. Nevertheless, it has undoubtedly been a contributory factor in helping to galvanize action. In an attempt to try and understand the outcomes of ECoC, which was seen as a process rather than an event or series of events, a longitudinal evaluation was commissioned called *Impacts 08*. The two universities in the city were engaged by Liverpool City Council to consider monitoring impacts over time, rather than the usual post-event snapshot evaluation. Whilst there is no space to explore the detailed findings from this evaluation, a number of key headlines for livability stand out. Sixty-six percent of Liverpool's residents reported that they had engaged in more than one of over 7,000 events that had been organized during the year. Some 70,000 young people were actively engaged with cultural-educational activities in an attempt to raise their self-awareness and esteem. Local perceptions of a strong sense of place identity predominated, and a perception emerged that other people (particularly elsewhere in the UK) were now viewing Liverpool in a much more positive light, hence 99 percent of visitors like the "general atmosphere," 97 percent the "feeling of welcome," and 85 percent of Liverpool residents felt the city was a better place than before ECoC was awarded (a 20 percent rise on the 2007 survey). Visitor numbers were up by 35 percent to 27.7 million visits, generating spending of £617 million in the local economy. Finally, there was a greater sense of partnership working across many public, private, and voluntary sectors, which needed to continue if many of the longstanding issues of socio-economic deprivation in the city were to be addressed (Garcia *et al.* 2010).

Narrative 3 – Partnership Working in Delivering Green Infrastructure

Critical to the other two stories has been the notion of partnership working in terms of delivering common objectives, in what is often seen as a "win-win" situation. Whilst regeneration efforts have traditionally focused on physical regeneration or social well-being, more recently within the North West of England in general, and Merseyside in particular, the idea of green infrastructure (GI) contributing positively to sustainable communities has been gaining credence. Whilst many of the advocates of green infrastructure have highlighted the adaption and mitigation effects for adverse climate change scenarios, its increasing importance in delivering broader multifunctional benefits has also been pointed out.

Within the North West of England for much of the last five years, advocates of GI have been making the case for green infrastructure interventions and investments. Eleven economic benefits of a GI approach have been identified:

- gaining products from the land;
- promoting recreation and leisure activities;
- promoting tourism;
- improving labor productivity;
- promoting economic growth and investment;
- enhancing land and property values;
- promoting health and well-being;
- enhancing the quality of place;
- flood alleviation and water management;
- climate change adaption and mitigation; and
- protecting land and promoting biodiversity.

(NENW 2008)

Chapter 4: **TRANS-ATLANTIC PERSPECTIVE**

The advocacy has been so persuasive that GI is now being promoted by central government as a policy principle that needs to be integrated into spatial planning and the placemaking agenda. Published in 2009, "World Class Places: The Government's Strategy for Improving Quality of Place" (HM Government) saw that the quality and quantity of green infrastructure was one of the critical ingredients of placemaking. Subsequently, several national policy statements, which provide the policy framework within which local planning authorities have to operate, are now making reference to the need for planners to make explicit reference to GI in their plans. Hence Planning Policy Statement 12 (PPS12): Local Spatial Planning defines green infrastructure as "a network of multi-functional green space, both new and existing, both rural and urban, which supports the natural and ecological processes and is integral to the health and quality of life of sustainable communities" (Communities and Local Government 2008a: 5). A supplementary document to PPS1 (Delivering Sustainable Development: Planning and Climate Change) explicitly refers to the positive contribution that GI can contribute to "urban cooling, sustainable drainage systems, and conserving and enhancing biodiversity" (CLG 2008b: 15).

Liverpool City Council in collaboration with Liverpool Primary Care Trust, which is responsible for planning National Health Service (NHS) care for the people of Liverpool, commissioned the Mersey Forest team to develop a green infrastructure strategy for the city. The strategy is not really a plan in the statutory sense; it is more of a framework where a variety of different stakeholders who can make a difference can intervene, either individually or collectively as and when circumstances dictate (Mersey Forest 2010). The research has involved mapping the existing green infrastructure provision and evaluating both its current quality and functionality before identifying priorities for action.

The research indicates that from a health and well-being perspective the city faces many challenges. In terms of mental health, 30.3 percent of the city's residents are classified has having low mental well-being (the lowest in the region) and conversely, with only 5.7 percent of its population having the highest level of mental well-being, it is also by some margin the lowest in the region. Comparing thirty-two health indicators across the country, twenty-six of Liverpool's profiles were worse than the national average. In the areas of greatest deprivation, the well-being of the residents is even more precarious, and twenty-seven of Liverpool's thirty wards are included in the pentile of wards nationally that have the lowest life expectancy at birth. In terms of GI, the parts of the city that have both the lowest quantity, quality, and access to multi-functional green space are also those parts of the city exhibiting the worst indicators of health well-being (i.e. North Liverpool).

The plan then goes on to suggest that individual well-being could be enhanced through investment in green infrastructure. This is not advocated as a simple deterministic causal relationship, but recognition that there is a clear association between well-being and the quality of the built and natural environments, and that GI can make a positive contribution to enhancing life chances. The approach is not prescriptive, but rather advocates that all stakeholders explicitly acknowledge the importance of GI and "areas of opportunity" (i.e. those areas that are likely to be transformed) and "areas of need" (where there are identifiable deficits) which should be prioritized for action. North Liverpool satisfies both criteria.

A critical part of this work has been to engage with and secure "buy in" from other stakeholders who potentially can contribute to delivery. A series of workshops and seminars have been held, and the work has been endorsed widely. The advocacy that investment in GI can bring multifunctional benefits that will help to contribute to people's quality of life has been accepted. The key notion here is around "making a contribution," not to solving *per se* the many challenges facing individuals and communities in Liverpool.

Reflections and Future Challenges

The city of Liverpool has experienced an enormous transformation, and yet whilst the city centre is now a thriving space dominated by consumerist activities, including retailing, cafés and bars, and various cultural centers and venues, the city remains a divided one, corresponding to the notion of the "dual city" (Sassen 2000) with the relative life chances of many of its citizens remaining below average. This is not a new or recent phenomenon, and even at its zenith as a global city, poverty and deprivation were rife, and many philanthropic individuals in Liverpool strove to deal with these injustices (Belcham 2006).

More broadly, throughout this chapter a number of other important recurrent themes re-emerge. First, Liverpool and its citizens have created a distinct sense of place for which they are rightly proud. But underlying this sense of place and civic pride, deep social, economic, and environmental problems persist. The city has been subjected to (or benefited from, depending on your perspective) nearly every form of state intervention which has targeted regeneration, whether physical, social, or environmental on the areas of greatest need (currently measured through the Index of Multiple Deprivation). Whilst modest progress has been made, the fundamental underlying structural problems facing communities have not gone away. The three narratives outline different stories, programs, or projects that at their core have envisaged their success as contributing to improved social and economic well-being of Liverpudlians. These are only three of numerous activities that have attempted to deal with these issues. Common themes emerge such as joined up thinking and effective partnership working to deliver more targeted interventions with diminishing resource. But many are time-limited funding programs whose longevity is at the whim of central government or time-specific events. One of the critical questions is how these initiatives can become truly embedded in local context and hence sustain interventions over time. Such questions are particularly acute at a time of severe public spending restraint given that the city has the highest dependence on welfare for its citizens of any UK city – it is estimated that 28 percent of per capita income for citizens is based on welfare payments. Furthermore, the region is expected to witness a disproportionate number of job losses due to a high dependency on the public sector (Centre for Cities 2011).

In this time of turbulence, local authorities are increasingly being seen as a democratic and accountable power base within which difficult decisions have to be made. One of their key strategic documents, as we have noted in the context of SCSs, should be their local plan. This sets out what the vision for the city should be over the next ten to fifteen years and, just as importantly, identifies the mechanism through which this transformation will be realized. Spatial planning as currently defined goes beyond traditional land use planning, with its narrow regulatory focus, to think about bringing together other policies and programs about a place, how it functions, and what its priority needs are (CLG 2008a).

Planning is, or at least should be, at the heart of placemaking. But a key question to conclude upon is whether planners have the ability and confidence to create longer-term visionary policy frameworks that will guide other stakeholders in helping to create more fair and just communities. What we would suggest is that the evidence since the election of the coalition government in 2010 and the move to new scales (local, sub-regional) and structures of governance for planning does not entirely fill us with hope that those previously marginalized from decision-making processes will benefit significantly under the new arrangements (mirroring the thoughts of Allmendinger and Haughton 2011, forthcoming). Put simply, we would suggest that building on previous forms of partnership working, there is now a real need for a wider involvement and engagement of all those concerned with the livability agenda and a fundamental requirement for planning to address the "politics of consensus" in order to take forward some of the innovative approaches that we have began to highlight in this chapter.

References

Allmendinger, P. and Haughton, G. (2011) Postpolitical planning: a crisis of consensus, draft paper available from authors on request.

Allmendinger, P. and Haughton, G. (2012) *Post-political spatial planning in England: a crisis of consensus?*, Transactions of the Institute of British Geographers, article first published online: 12 Oct 2011. DOI 10.1111/j.1475–5661.2011.00468.

Anderson, B. and Holden, A. (2008) Affected urbanism and the event of hope, *Space and Culture*, 11(2): 142–159.

Audit Commission (2010) *Liverpool area assessment*, London: Audit Commission (http://oneplace.audit-commission.gov.uk/SiteCollectionDocuments/pdf/2009/AreaAssessment/AreaAssessment2009Liverpool_Full.pdf) accessed 3/3/2011.

Belchem, J., ed. (2006) *Liverpool 800: culture character and history*, Liverpool: Liverpool University Press.

Biddulph, M. (2010) Evaluating the English home zone initiatives, *Journal of the American Planning Association*, 76(2): 199–218.

Bramley, G., Dempsey, N., Power, S., Brown, C., and Watkins, D. (2009). Social sustainability and urban form: evidence from five British cities, *Environment and Planning A*, 41: 2125–2142.

Centre for Cities (2011) Cities outlook 2011, London: Centre for Cities.

Coaffee, J. and Headlam, N. (2008) Pragmatic localism uncovered: the search for locally contingent solutions to national reform agendas, *Geoforum* 30: 1585–1599.

Communities and Local Government Department (CLG) (2007) *The English indices of multiple deprivation*, London: CLG.

CLG (2008a) *Planning policy statement 12 (PPS12): Local spatial planning*, London: CLG.

CLG (2008b) *PPS 1: Delivering sustainable development: Planning and climate change, Supplement to Planning Policy 1*, London: CLG.

CLG (2010) *Decentralism and localism bill: An essential guide*, London: CLG.

Davies, J. (2009) The limits of joined up government: towards political analysis, *Public Administration* 87(1): 80–96.

Department for Education (2010) *The impact of Sure Start programmes on five year olds and their Families*, London: Department for Education.

Department of the Environment Transport and the Regions (DETR) (2000) *Our towns and cities: the future*, London: The Stationery Office.

Department of the Environment Food and Rural Affairs (DEFRA) (2005) Securing the future: delivering UK sustainable development strategy, London: HMSO.

Gallent, N. and Wong, C. (2009) An introduction to place making: spatial planning and liveability, *Town Planning Review*, 80(4): 352–358.

Garcia, B., Melville, R., and Cox, T. (2010) *Creating an impact: Liverpool's experience as European Capital of Culture*, Liverpool: Impacts 08.

HM Treasury and CLG (2010) *Total place: a whole approach to public services*, London: HMSO.

House of Commons, Children, Schools and Family Committee (2010) *Sure Start children's centres: fifth report of session 2009–10, Vol. 1*, Houses of Parliament, London: Houses of Parliament.

Kunzmann, K. (2004) Culture and creativity and spatial planning, *Town Planning Review*, 75(4): 383–404.

Liverpool First (2008) Liverpool 2024: a thriving international city, *Local Area Agreement 2008–11*, Liverpool First: Liverpool (http://www.liverpoolfirst.org.uk/sites/liverpoolfirst/files/laa_2008-10_2010refresh.pdf) accessed 2/3/2011.

Liverpool First (2010) City gains £1m for private tenants, Liverpool First: Liverpool (http://www.liverpoolfirst.org.uk/news/11_01_healthyhomes0) accessed 7/3/2010.

Liverpool City Council (2011) Healthy homes programme (http://www.liverpool.gov.uk/council/strategies-plans-and-policies/housing/healthy-homes-programme/) accessed 7/3/2011.

Mersey Forest (2010) Liverpool green infrastructure strategy: technical document (http://www.greeninfrastructurenw.co.uk/liverpool/Technical_Document.pdf) accessed 7/3/2011.

Morphet, J. (2010) *Effective practice in spatial planning*, London: Routledge.

Murden, J. (2006) City of change and challenge: Liverpool since 1945, in J. Belchem (ed.) *Liverpool 800: Culture, Character and History*, Liverpool: Liverpool University Press.

Natural Economy North West (NENW) (2008) *The economic value of green infrastructure*, (http://www.naturaleconomynorthwest) accessed 7/3/2011.

Nurse, A. and Pemberton, S. (2010) Local area agreements as a tool for addressing deprivation within UK cities, *Journal of Urban Regeneration and Renewal* 4(2): 158–167.

Office of the Deputy Prime Minister (ODPM) (2003) *Sustainable communities: building for the future*, (http://www.communities.gov.uk/documents/communities/pdf/146289.pdf) accessed 10/12/2010.

Robson, B., Parkinson, M., Boddy, M. and MacLennan, D. (2000) *The state of English cities*, London: DETR.

Shaw, D., Sykes, O., and Fischer, T.B. (2009) Culture, regeneration and urban renaissance: reflections of Liverpool's experiences as "European Capital of Culture," *RaumPlanung*, 143: 92–97.

Sullivan, H., Downe, J. *et al.* (2006) The three challenges of community leadership, *Local Government Studies* 32(4): 489–508.

Wilkes-Hegg, S. (2004) From world city to pariah city? Liverpool and the global economy, 1850–2000, in R. Munck (ed.) *Reinventing the City? Liverpool in comparative perspective*, Liverpool: Liverpool University Press.

SECTION II

EXPERIENCES IN COMMUNITIES

Chapter 5

AGING AS THE FOUNDATION FOR LIVABLE COMMUNITIES

Deborah Howe

Chair and Professor, Department of Community and Regional Planning
Temple University

If community livability is defined as a safe, engaging and healthy environment that allows us to carry out our daily activities, then senior citizens are shortchanged in most American communities. Our land use patterns and transportation systems have granted priority to the automobile. The real estate market has responded to the expectations of healthy adults with large houses, garages, and yards. The result is an environment that fails to offer viable transportation alternatives when an older person's health is such that driving is no longer feasible. A lack of sidewalks and comfortable places to sit and rest can limit physical activity to the detriment of overall health. And the housing stock is dominated by the single family house that is too large, costly and at times dangerous for an older person.

As we age, we find ways to cope, relying on family and social services to assist in overcoming the obstacles inherent in the built environment. This system, however, will be overwhelmed by major demographic changes. The large cohort of baby boomers entering retirement will swell the ranks of those aged 65+ from 35 million in 2000 to a projected 71.5 million in 2030 ultimately representing 20 percent of the US population (He *et al.* 2005). Against the realities of declining Social Security benefits, sky-rocketing medical costs, and higher fuel prices it is imperative to find ways in which older adults can maintain their health and independence allowing them to age with dignity.

The aging of America offers communities an extraordinary opportunity to critically examine the built environment from the perspective of older people in order to identify obstacles and opportunities for effecting changes. This involves understanding how the environment is experienced by individuals. It involves paying attention to such mundane considerations as cracks in sidewalks, a level of detail that is not normally considered in community planning. It involves a commitment to making our communities elder friendly through public policies and personal investment.

This chapter will explore ways in which we can transform the built environment in our communities to respond to the needs of an aging society. Concepts such as elder friendly community planning will be covered along with examples of how it is applied in support of public goals to create communities in which one can spend a lifetime. Specific alternatives will be presented such as accessory apartments and mixed use development. The unique needs of older people will be discussed in terms of effectively engaging them in local planning initiatives.

Particular attention will be given to implementing aging-sensitive development standards. The on-going incremental nature of development and rebuilding offers many opportunities for removing barriers in the existing environment.

Aging Is Not For the Faint of Heart!

Aging is a natural process that defines the arc of our lives. In childhood and youth we grow and develop with the expectation over time of gaining strength and independence. As adults we rely on a full range of mental, emotional, and physical capacities to pursue careers, raise children and fully engage in life's opportunities.

As we get older, time takes its toll affecting us in ways that vary significantly from person to person. In general, we lose muscle mass, flexibility and stamina. There can be hearing and vision loss. Cognitive functions can be affected with half of those aged 85 and older having some form of dementia. Reaction time lengthens. Many suffer from incontinence. These changes in combination with losses associated with the deaths of friends and loved ones can be manifested in depression and other mental health issues.

Medical advances and improved nutrition have dramatically lengthened life expectancy from 49 in 1900 to 77 in 2003. Those who reached age 65 in 1900 could expect to live an average of 12 more years. By 2003, a 65 year old could anticipate 18 more years (Arias 2006). Long life, however, raises the potential of living with disabilities. Estimates for 1990 reveal that 65 year old men faced the prospect of 7.6 years with a disability; women faced 9.0 years. Those who were 85 could have anticipated spending over 70 percent of their remaining time living with disabilities (Crimmins 1997). Over 14.7 million seniors reported some form of disability in 2007 with more than 6.3 million having a disability that limited their ability to go outside (see Table 5.1).

During the past century, the advent of Social Security and Medicare dramatically improved the financial circumstances of seniors which in combination with changing values about privacy enabled them to live in housing separate from their adult children.[1] In 2003, 10.5 million people aged 65 and older lived alone, 29 percent of all seniors. This percentage is higher for women and increases with age as spouses die. In 2003, 30.1 percent of men and 57 percent of women aged 85 and older lived alone (He *et al.* 2005). In 2005, nearly half of all elderly householders lived in suburbs; another quarter lived in rural communities. These percentages

Table 5.1 Disability Status Ages 65 and Above: 2007

Type of disability (in thousands)	*Total*	*65–74 years*	*75 years +*
Persons with a disability	14,735	5,674	9,061
With a sensory disability	5,893	1,847	4,046
With a physical disability	11,285	4,394	6,891
With a mental disability	4,467	1,426	3,041
With a self-care disability	3,772	1,134	2,638
With a go-outside home disability	6,354	1,731	4,623

Source: US Census Bureau 2009: Section 1 Table 35

Chapter 5: AGING AS THE FOUNDATION

are expected to increase over the next twenty years. Their housing is relatively large – three-fourths are single detached and manufactured homes averaging over 1,700 square feet on one third acre lots (US Census Bureau 2005).

Despite the perception of Americans as a nation of movers,[2] the elderly have deep roots in their homes. With an ownership rate in excess of 80 percent and a median duration of 25 years in their current home for owner occupants (US Census Bureau 2005), it is not surprising that eight out of ten respondents in an American Association of Retired Persons (AARP) survey of people aged 45 and older expressed a preference to age in place (Mathew Greenwald and Associates May 2003). Moves are expensive and stressful. They are a particular challenge for the elderly as they are forced to relinquish cherished possessions, comprehend a new locale at a time when their capacities may be in decline, and admit to a trajectory of decline. As difficult as it may be for an older person to remain in their home as they age, they may have no choice due to high costs and the absence of alternatives. Assisted living arrangements providing personal and custodial care can run $800–$4,000 per month. Skilled nursing facilities charge close to $200 per day.

Challenges associated with aging place considerable stress on caregivers. Baby boomers as a generation produced fewer offspring than their parents meaning more limited family resources for supporting the boomers when they age.[3] When seniors dominate the population profile, there are proportionately fewer workers supporting a dependent population. With the aging of society, it will become more difficult and expensive to secure professional caregivers. One recent study projects a national deficit of 340,000 registered nurses by 2020 (Auerbach *et al.* 2007). This underscores the imperative of finding ways to enable seniors to maintain their health and independence. While one's social network including family, friends and broader community support are critical to maintaining independence, a key factor is the built environment. We will turn to that next.

The Built Environment and Aging

The built environment frames our daily activities and thus has a huge bearing on the quality of our aging experiences. It reflects the sum total of individual development decisions against the background of public policies that set development standards. Local governments influence the development of the built environment through subdivision and zoning regulations which establish requirements for dividing and developing land including allowable uses; density; bulk standards such as building height and setbacks; and site development standards such as parking, landscaping, and requirements for sidewalks. Construction requirements are specified by building codes. These regulations have their origins in concerns with preventing public nuisances and preserving property values and at the same time protecting private property rights.

The single family home occupies the top of the American land use hierarchy and as such is so favorably treated by the regulatory framework that housing alternatives are excluded in many locales. Thus homeowners may find that they are not allowed to create accessory apartments out of their excess space to use for family members, caregivers or as a source of extra income. They may also be prohibited from entering into a house sharing arrangement because the zoning code limits the number of unrelated individuals who can live together. These homeowners might have considered making a housing adjustment by moving within their community thus preserving the relationships that they established over the years, but the zoning codes do not allow much other than the traditional single family home.

Ironically, the single family home is still promoted and purchased for senior housing. Builders are developing Active Adult Retirement Communities restricted to those aged 55 and above. These offer maintenance free living in single family, duplex and cluster housing with amenities such as exercise facilities, golf courses and pools. While this development type originated in the south and southwest, a 2005 study found more than 150 developments existing or under construction in Massachusetts containing over 10,000 units; an additional 14,000 units were proposed or permitted in 172 developments (Hendorfer 2005). Active adult developments are a predominately suburban phenomenon driven by local zoning regulations that favor senior development on the premise that it will not put a strain on the local school systems. In Anne Arundel County, Maryland, development is not allowed if the local school is at 15 percent above capacity, but age restricted developments are exempted. Given that 60 percent of the land in the county is in school districts that are over capacity, there is concern that the market will be overbuilt (Wan 29 May 2007). The Massachusetts study drew the same conclusion.

It is not simply the absence of housing alternatives that is problematic. The typical designs of single family homes present numerous obstacles to people with disabilities including steps to entrances, narrow doorways that cannot accommodate wheelchairs, bedrooms on the second floor and only partial bathrooms if any on the main floor. Hard to turn door knobs, sunken floors, outlets at floor level and high counters and sinks compromise the use of a home by someone with disabilities. Such homes are purchased by people who are considering the immediate needs of young, active families and not the future realities of aging in place. At the same time, builders are not giving consumers the option of a home with accessibility features. An analysis that looked at the lifespan of a newly built single family house and projected the probability of at least one occupant with a disability led to an estimate of a 60 percent probability of an occupant with a physical limitation and 25 percent with a self-care limitation. The study took this a step further and projected a 91 percent probability of a person with a physical limitation and a 53 percent probability for a person with a self-care limitation visiting the house (Smith *et al.* 2008).

The problems with the built environment extend outside the home. Zoning regulations that favor homogeneity by separating land uses result in communities where everything is far apart. Travel by automobile becomes essential which in turn overwhelms the roads making them more dangerous and less conducive to non-motorized travel such as walking and bicycling. Older adults are heavily reliant on automobiles with 90 percent of those over 65 licensed to drive in 2001. Given that eight out of ten will live in suburban environments by 2030 and have limited access to transportation alternatives, this reliance will increase (Urbitran Associates March 2005). The ability to drive safely is affected by the aging process. Problems with vision such as cataracts and difficulty with focusing, confusion and disorientation, slower reaction time, difficulty looking over one's shoulder, and reactions to medications such as drowsiness and dizziness are some of the factors that constrain the ability to drive and are the basis of calls for age-based driving skill tests and painful decisions by families and caregivers to remove driving privileges. While it is commonly assumed that seniors who no longer drive will resort to walking or using public transit, Rosenbloom *et al.* (2002) note that automobiles are actually easier for the elderly to use – people with health limitations often give up walking and the use of transit before ceasing to drive.

Elderly pedestrians and bicyclists face serious risks in negotiating the built environment. Because of problems with walking, maintaining balance, staying oriented and feeling safe in crowded places, the elderly may be fifteen times more likely to be injured or killed as pedestrians than as drivers (Rosenbloom *et al.* 2002). Elderly pedestrians represent one fifth of road users, but over half of all pedestrian deaths. A substantial proportion of elderly pedestrian injuries are from street-falls not involving cars. Poorly maintained sidewalks, illegally parked cars, crowds, street furniture, etc., can contribute to these falls (Rosenbloom *et al.* 2002). Suburbs are notoriously lacking in pedestrian amenities. Sidewalks are difficult to justify in low density environments where relatively few people walk and distances to destinations are too far. Some suburbs have evolved in areas with historically narrow roads that carry high traffic volumes, but have no room for retrofitting with sidewalks. Furthermore, the incremental and dispersed nature of development can result in a fragmented sidewalk system. Some suburbanites resist the notion of sidewalks as urban infrastructure which they specifically rejected in deciding to live in the suburbs.

One of the realities of poor walking environments in many American communities has been an observed decline in physical activity associated with more use of the automobile and less walking. Rates of obesity have correspondingly increased. There is a growing concern that the profound increase in obesity rates among adults will translate to a decline in longevity while increasing the length of time living with disabilities (Visscher *et al.* 2001; Preston 2005; Reynolds *et al.* 2005).

Clearly there is a need to take a hard look at American communities from the perspective of aging in order to set goals to proactively transform the built environment. The justification for this focus goes beyond meeting needs efficiently. An aging focus involves putting people into planning, framing a vision that speaks to the very essence of livability. In the extent to which we take actions that give people options for continued independence and provide appropriate levels of support as they age, we are communicating respect for elders and ensuring that they have a place and role in society. At the same time, meeting their needs involves creating the kind of environment that benefits other community members and achieves other public goals. Providing effective alternatives to automobile transportation, for example, can support people who do not drive and can contribute to improved air quality.

Principles of Planning for Aging

There is no single definition for communities that support aging. A variety of terms are used interchangeably including: elder friendly communities, aging friendly communities, communities for all ages, sustainable communities, aging-in-place initiatives, communities for a lifetime, lifecycle communities, aging sensitive communities and livable communities. There are several principles that should guide an aging-oriented planning process (Howe 1995: 17–18).

1. *Engagement.* An effective planning process fully involves both seniors and caregivers to ensure their perspectives are understood and their experiences appreciated. Aging is an intensely personal experience and the general tendency is to cope, doing what is necessary including scrambling to respond to crises. Those who are directly involved in these

situations need to be invited to share their experiences in order to identify opportunities to strengthen community support of the aging process. Outreach to minorities, those with low incomes, and the frail is essential. The notion of engagement also needs to address the appropriate involvement of different stakeholders to develop the constituency for elder friendly communities. Service agencies and businesses need to see how they can benefit from and contribute to dialogues about the needs of aging. In the extent to which advocates for children see opportunities for addressing their issues jointly with advocates for the elderly, then more momentum for change can be realized.

2. *Diversity.* An elder friendly community needs a diverse housing stock at a range of costs available throughout the community. These might include accessory apartments, duplexes, triplexes, condominiums, manufactured homes, housing in mixed use developments, senior housing and row homes in addition to single family residences. Assisted living and nursing facilities need to be appropriately sited and not relegated to the outskirts of communities or commercial zoning districts.

3. *Linkages.* An individual moves within an environment through a series of links from one place to another. Compromised links such as a dangerous intersection, an unpaved parking lot that is difficult to traverse in a wheelchair, a crime ridden neighborhood and an incomplete or poorly maintained sidewalk system can be insurmountable obstacles to someone with mobility limitations. The notion of linkages involves an attention to detail that is often overlooked in community planning: repairing cracks in sidewalks, providing benches and shade, ensuring signs are legible or developing a neighborhood watch program. Linkages are an important aspect of creating an environment that supports physical activity essential for maintaining health.

4. *Flexibility.* We need to guide development in ways that enable use by people with varying abilities and which facilitate cost effective adaptation in response to changing needs. Elementary schools could be designed for eventual conversion to a senior center and back again in response to a neighborhood's changing demographics. A single family house could be designed to enable the easy creation and later removal of an accessory dwelling unit enabling a homeowner to make changes that reflect changing income and household needs (Howe 1990). Universal Design is a new paradigm that takes into consideration a range of potential users and provides a space or product that is useable by people with varying abilities with minimal adaptations required.[4] For example, an outlet that is two feet off the floor is reachable by someone in a wheelchair. A grab bar can be easily installed in a bathroom that already has reinforced walls.

It is challenging to put these principles into action. Engagement involves hard work to get people to show up to meetings and to maintain their involvement over time. Programs and agendas need to be compelling and relevant. Involving seniors may require specific attention to the location of meetings relative to where they live, schedules that respect the tendency of many older adults who do not drive at nighttime, and the provision of transportation if needed. Meeting rooms need to be set up with comfortable chairs with arm rests and decent acoustics. Refreshments and meals can be an incentive for participation.

Engagement needs to be understood in terms of its potential for being time consuming and difficult – participants may not see eye to eye and could be obstructionists in terms of

Chapter 5: AGING AS THE FOUNDATION

trying to get things done. On the other hand, engagement can lead to the development of a powerful constituency for change. It also can be invaluable to individuals in affecting their understanding of aging issues and the choices they make as consumers.

Resistance to changes in development practices arises from fears of impacts on property values, prejudices against new residents, and concerns about additional costs of regulations. Thus it is not surprising that preliminary findings from a survey of planning and zoning practices in southeast Michigan jurisdictions revealed awareness among municipal officials of aging as a major demographic change, but an absence of zoning requirements that require the type of development that supports aging (Boyle *et al.* 2008).

Education is essential. As one example, zoning provisions allowing the creation of an accessory dwelling within the excess space of a single family dwelling are often resisted by neighborhood residents and local governments out of fear that accessory dwellings will undermine the single family orientation of a neighborhood and will subsequently lower property values. These perceptions can be addressed by systematically evaluating each issue by providing data from other communities that demonstrates that demand for accessory units is generally very low and thus they will not overwhelm any one neighborhood; the units usually have only one or two occupants, constrained in part by their small size; and they can be designed in ways that are compatible with single family homes. This latter point can be addressed by showcasing examples of well designed accessory units. Finally, specific concerns such as the impact of parking and the ability of emergency service providers to know where accessory units are located can be addressed through development standards such as requirements for minimum number of off street parking spaces and clearly marked entrances (Howe 1990).

In considering alternatives to support aging in place, it should be noted that it may be counterproductive to frame these options as specifically directed toward seniors. Again using accessory dwellings as an example – some municipalities are willing to allow these units, but want to limit their use to senior homeowners. A study of accessory dwelling owners in Seattle suggests that the more likely candidate for the creation of an accessory dwelling is a middle aged adult, an empty nester with excess space and the time, energy and resources to create such a unit (Chapman *et al.* 2001). Other municipalities limit accessory dwellings to those homeowners who can demonstrate a familial relationship to the ultimate occupants of the unit greatly reducing the flexibility of this option in enabling homeowners to meet changing needs.

There are intriguing indicators that change is happening in zoning and development practices. Retirees are driving a significant trend – cashing out their equity in suburban houses and moving to downtowns where they can enjoy rich cultural activities and other amenities that are emerging with urban revitalization. Along with single, young professionals and unmarried childless couples, seniors are creating demand for high density, loft and townhouse living thereby generating a housing alternative that did not exist twenty years ago. Cities small and large throughout the US are benefiting including Chicago, Pittsburgh, Rochester and Denver. The trend is also affecting suburban cities such as Evanston, Illinois and White Plains, New York (Huffstutter 3 March 2008; Brenner 19 February 2006). Downtown Bellevue Washington has 5,000 residents that did not live there ten years ago. Over 3,000 new condominium and apartment units are under construction and 2,500 more are in the permitting stage. Safeway grocery store owners expect half of all customers to their new downtown store to arrive by foot; there are 368 apartments above the new store and new mixed use complexes are planned nearby (Pryne 27 June 2008).

A study by this author of local land use policy innovation funded by the Robert Wood Johnson Foundation Active Living Program identified over 200 best practices communities that have mixed use zoning provisions and developments. The communities range in size from 711 (Calabash, NC) to nearly 3 million (Chicago, IL) in 39 states. Nearly 40 percent of respondents reported that accommodating aging was a stated goal in their master plan and/or their zoning code. Mixed use on a small scale is exemplified by the Androy Hotel of Hibbing MN. Built in 1919 with mining company money, it was a landmark hotel before falling into disrepair in the 1970s. In the mid-1990s, the hotel was renovated into commercial space and low-income housing for seniors. The first floor includes office space; a banquet facility; and a community room. There are 49 one- and two-bedroom apartments on the top three floors.

In Portland, Oregon, a new county library occupies the first floor of a building that houses 47 mixed-income apartments. It is within walking distance of stores, bus stops and a light rail station. Similar mixed use developments involving libraries and housing have been developed in St. Paul, Minnesota, San Francisco and Seattle. In Irvington, New York, a historic commercial building was transformed into a library and housing after a change in the zoning code allowed multi-family dwellings and mixed-uses in industrial districts subject to a special permit. All of these projects include housing that is targeted to households with low and moderate incomes. The housing in the San Francisco project is specifically for seniors.

One notion of incremental but profound change is "visitability," a term that originated in Europe. It involves requiring that all new housing be designed in a way that a person with disabilities could at a minimum enter a home, get through the doors and use the bathroom. To that end, there must be one zero-step entrance, doors with 32-inch clearance, and a bathroom on the main floor that is accessible by a wheelchair user. Proponents of these requirements contend that they add less than $100 to the cost of construction and not only reduce the isolation of people with disabilities, they enhance the feasibility of those who become disabled to remain in their homes.[5] By 2008, Arizona's Pima County "Inclusive Home Design" ordinance had produced over 15,000 visitable housing units and had survived a challenge by the building industry that reached the state Supreme Court (Concrete Change ND).

In Howard County, Maryland, provisions for Age-Restricted housing include Universal Design Guidelines that require that single family detached dwellings include a master bedroom and bath on the first level, a no-step access to the house, lever handles on all doors and reinforced walls for later installation of grab bars (Taylor 15 January 2007). Developers were not providing Universal Design nor were consumers demanding it, but clearly this type of regulation can incrementally transform the housing stock to the benefit of current and future occupants.

Meeting the needs of an aging society through community planning has parallels with the goals of various planning movements including Smart Growth, New Urbanism, Transit Oriented Development, Safe Routes to School programs, and Complete Streets initiatives.

Smart Growth involves a set of development and conservation principles such as mixed uses, housing and transportation alternatives, compact building design and investing in existing communities that underpins the creation of livable communities and at the same time protects natural resources.

Chapter 5: AGING AS THE FOUNDATION

New Urbanism is a community planning and design movement that is a reaction to low density sprawl and calls for infill and new development to recreate the pedestrian friendly, compact neighborhoods that evolved in American cities before the advent of the automobile.

Transit Oriented Development involves development designed to promote public transit use such as high density, mixed uses next to transit stops, pedestrian amenities and reduced parking for personal vehicles.

Safe Routes to School is a federally funded program devoted to encouraging children to walk or bicycle to school through road and sidewalk improvements, traffic enforcement, safety education, and promotions.

Complete Streets is a national movement to redesign road networks for a variety of users – pedestrians, bicyclists, motorists and transit riders – at the same time improving safety, environmental impact and aesthetics.

All of these initiatives call for new approaches to community design including features that could support elders such as transit access, housing diversity, mixed uses, and development of pedestrian amenities. Thus there are many opportunities to build bridges with other advocates to gain support and momentum for community transformation. At the same time, there are specific aspects of aging that are not fully reflected in these initiatives, including the following examples.

- New Urbanism has made great strides in encouraging compact, mixed use developments with sidewalks and a range of housing alternatives. Front porches are often required to connect the home occupants with activity on the street and garages are typically relegated to a subordinate position such as an alley in the back of a house. But New Urbanism does not speak to the internal design of houses such as having a bedroom and full bath on the first floor nor has this movement embraced the notion of visitability (Miller August 2007 and Smith 11 July 2005).
- Nuances of aging could and should influence efforts to improve pedestrian amenities. Traffic signals need to allow more time for elderly pedestrians to cross an intersection; limits on right turns on red may be warranted in some locations. Problems with balance suggest the need for railings along some paths and armrests on chairs and benches. Elders may be more comfortable visiting with friends when they are sitting at a right angle to one another rather than having to twist in order to talk with someone sitting to their side on a bench. Edges of steps need to be clearly demarcated. Sidewalks should be wide enough for someone with a walker to move comfortably without being jostled. Tree wells need to be designed and maintained so that elders do not trip on the edges.
- Elderly transit riders need legible signage on buses and on schedules. Drivers need to be aware that elderly riders may need more time and assistance in getting in and out of vehicles. Upcoming stops need to be clearly announced in transit. In addition, announcements should be made of which buses are arriving at a stop when the stop serves more than one route.
- The availability of clean, safe, and accessible public restrooms is very important for older adults, but this has not been in the forefront of concerns for these various planning design movements. Even healthy seniors may discover that they need to plan their daily travel routes relative to the location of public restrooms.

- Older drivers have longer reaction times and thus need advanced intersection signage and more turning lanes. Fog lines need to be maintained to assist in night time driving. Speeds may need to be lowered. The width of parking spaces may need to be increased.[6]
- Those involved with downtown revitalization are advised to specifically consider the needs of seniors in terms of walking, driving and signage. Barrier free design will be even more important: "Even though there are many applicable federal and state codes like ADA, downtowns need to go beyond the minimum to serve the public better. One broken, high, or dangerous curb can be an insurmountable barrier" (Alexander 15 April 2005: 2). Piles of snow on a sidewalk can be a minor annoyance for a young adult but a major problem for a senior who cannot afford the risk of slipping and falling.

Aging Focused Planning Frameworks

A growing number of initiatives speak to the notion of creating elder friendly communities. With essential leadership predominately from senior advocates and social service agencies, communities are being encouraged to systematically examine themselves from the perspective of the older adult and to develop alternatives for addressing the identified challenges. Here are some examples.

The AARP has embraced Livable Communities as a priority, a means of creating the kind of environment that supports people of all ages (Novelli 15 June 2005). In *Beyond 50.05, A Report to the Nation on Livable Communities: Creating Environments for Successful Aging*, AARP frames a concept of livability that seeks to guide community growth and change in terms of "a personal level, how the physical and social environments can promote independence among individuals and strengthen the civic and social ties among them" (Kochera *et al.* ND: 4). AARP offers a ten-question web-based livable community assessment that raises questions about places to socialize, walkability, transportation alternatives, safety and security and affordable housing alternatives (AARP ND). Each issue includes a discussion of its importance, alternatives, and relevant resources. *Livable Communities: An Evaluation Guide* provides a more extensive community planning resource (Kihl *et al.* 2005). It covers topics such as transportation and walkability, safety and security, shopping, housing, health services, recreation and culture, and care and support services.

As a component of its National Agenda for the Environment and the Aging, the US Environmental Protection Agency (EPA) sponsors a Building Healthy Communities for Active Aging National Recognition Program and provides resources to assist communities in developing programs and making improvements in the built environment that facilitate physical activity for older people (EPA ND). This focus is a natural outgrowth of the agency's Smart Growth Strategy providing support to communities in protecting the environment while encouraging economic development. The EPA has become a leader in promoting Smart Growth through advocacy and educational outreach, preparation and distribution of publications, provision of technical assistance and a national awards program.[7]

Partners for Livable Communities (Partners), a non-profit leadership organization focused on restoring and renewing communities, has partnered with the National Association of Area Agencies on Aging (n4a) to develop the Aging in Place Initiative. In addition to working

Chapter 5: **AGING AS THE FOUNDATION**

directly with communities to advance aging in place opportunities, Partners and n4a have collaborated with the International City and County Management Association (ICMA), the National League of Cities (NLC) and the National Association of Counties (NACo) with funding from MetLife Foundation to conduct a survey of municipal "aging readiness." The 2006 survey was sent to over 10,000 municipalities and counties. The conclusion "that only 46 percent of American communities have begun to address the needs of the rapidly aging population" is probably an overestimate given the low response rate of less than 18 percent (n4a *et al.* ND). There is no question, however, about the validity of the finding that few American communities have undertaken to comprehensively plan for the transformation of their communities into "elder friendly" or livable communities for all ages.

> Survey findings indicate that local governments generally offer basic health and nutrition programs, but as yet do not have the policies, programs or services in place to promote the quality of life and the ability of older adults to live independently and contribute to their communities for as long as possible. These services might include job retraining, flextime and other job accommodations; home chore services, home modification and senior-friendly housing options, tax relief, roadway redesign or public transportation assistance as well as volunteer opportunities targeted to older adults.
>
> (n4a ND: 1)

Partners and n4a again worked with ICMA, NLC and NACo in developing *A Blueprint for Action: Developing Livable Communities for All Ages* as a resource guide for communities interested in meeting the needs of their older adults (n4a *et al.* May 2007). The Aging Initiative features best practices on their website and has sponsored a series of regional conferences on aging in place themes throughout the US.[8]

Several states are developing programs to support community level planning for aging. Communities for a Lifetime is a technical assistance and recognition program established by Florida's Department of Elder Affairs in 1999.[9] Communities undertake a process to inventory services and opportunities that support independence and quality of life for older adults and initiate partnerships to promote senior friendly community amenities and develop partnerships to promote the development of senior friendly community amenities. The Bureau of Communities for a Lifetime has an explicit focus on elder housing, health promotion and disease prevention, volunteer and community services, senior employment, and transportation; communities can also seek technical assistance from other state agencies. To date, over 160 cities and counties have participated in this program.

In 2002, the Kansas Department on Aging initiated a Lifelong Communities Program which involves a state level review and certification of a community-based self study, action plan and its successful implementation.[10] Participating communities complete a standard community assessment tool that speaks to issues of government, community service, business, housing, transportation and health care. Twelve demonstration communities have participated to date with four receiving certification and road signs designating them as Lifelong Communities. The types of projects that these communities implemented included a community center, recruitment of medical personnel and development of a helicopter service for medical transfers, a caregiving training and support program, enhanced 911 services, exercise programs for seniors, housing rehabilitation and affordable housing projects, sidewalk improvements and curb renovations and transportation services for seniors.

In 2007, the Michigan Commission on Services to the Aging developed an Elderly Friendly Community Recognition Program entitled Michigan Community for a Lifetime (State Advisory Council on Aging *et al.* ND). Communities are allowed to use a national model for assessing aging-oriented assets or Michigan's Elder Friendly Community Assessment and Action Plan templates which addresses issues of walkability; supportive community systems; access to health care; safety and security; housing availability; affordability; modification and maintenance; transportation; commerce; enrichment; and inclusion. The five municipalities that received recognition were acknowledged for initiatives that included walkability plans and improvements, senior millage that enhances community resources, a leadership development program, a comprehensive community directory, code requirements supporting accessibility, community awareness and political support.

The Texas Department of Aging and Disability Services views communities as essential in creating the infrastructure that supports aging under the Aging Texas Well Initiative.[11] The department provides a detailed guide for undertaking this planning process with a particular emphasis on the six "Ps" of progress – policy must be translated into action, public funds are not the only answer, public awareness is an important strategy, partners are key to success, planning processes are a means to seek change, and progress is incremental.[12]

At the regional level, the Atlanta Regional Planning Commission is using the concept of Lifelong Communities to work with local communities in defining their unique aging-related concerns and crafting locally specific action plans. Particular attention is given to housing and transportation options, promoting healthy lifestyles, and expanding information and access to services. Accomplishments have included development of transportation programs, improvements to public transit, provision of preventive health screenings, and reviews of and changes to local zoning and housing policies.

The AdvantAge Initiative is a program developed by the Center for Home Care Policy and Research of the Visiting Nurse Service of New York.[13] It focuses on conducting a comprehensive survey of a community's older adults to provide information about how seniors are doing with particular emphasis on basic needs for housing and security, maintenance of physical and mental health, independence for the frail, disabled, and homebound and opportunities for social and civic engagement. The program has developed 33 quantitative measures for these four domains such as the percentage of people age 65+ who spend >30 percent versus <30 percent of their income on housing or the percentage of people age 65+ who had problems paying for medical care. In 26 cities and counties throughout the US and one state (Indiana), the AdvantAge Initiative is using survey data to assist communities to understand locally specific needs and to develop plans to develop elder-friendly, "AdvantAged" communities. The strength of this approach is that the survey instrument addresses need as well as the availability of services and the rigor with which the survey is administered enables communities to use the data directly in planning and implementation (Alley *et al.* 2007).

The Sustainable Communities for All Ages (CFAA) program is a planning and community development framework in which the opportunities for mutual inter-generational benefit are particularly well articulated. This process has been applied in numerous communities throughout the US. It involves engaging a broad cross section of community members in discussing issues

Chapter 5: **AGING AS THE FOUNDATION**

of generational concern such as child care, family wages, aging, etc. The issues and solutions are community specific ranging from a multi-generational community center in rural Concho, Arizona to an intergenerational leadership academy in Phoenix. CFAA planning efforts have led to pedestrian oriented improvements near senior housing and a child development center in Charlottesville, Virginia and the formation of a coalition to promote Universal Design in housing, transportation and land use (Jackson *et al.* ND).

The CFAA process seeks to engage people of all ages and backgrounds in exploring how generations can work together by devising shared solutions, promoting collaboration, and applying a long-term perspective. A toolkit providing guidelines and resources has been prepared to guide communities in facilitating this intergenerational planning process.[14] Key issues recommended for consideration include: lifelong education and civic engagement, community and economic development, individual and family wellness, affordable quality housing, land use, transportation, and natural resources. These issues include the tripartite of sustainability, i.e. equity, economy, and environment. The resulting goals and strategies blend both social and physical aspects of communities encompassing how people relate to one another as well as the community as a built environment. In terms of implementation, particular emphasis is given to "collaborative resource development" involving shared resources, blending funding sources, cultivating income-generating activities, and building leadership and volunteering capacities.

All of these planning frameworks emphasize the importance of focused, detailed and comprehensive community-level assessments of the aging experience. This is essential given the extraordinary diversity in American communities and its residents. Goals and implementation strategies need to be correspondingly different and must be rooted in a community's unique needs.

Another consistent theme is the emphasis on engaging older adults in defining the issues appropriate to creating elder friendly communities. This approach has been used in not only developing community assessment models such as, for example, AARP's Livable Communities: An Evaluation Guide and the AdvantAge Initiative's community indicators, but in their direct application at the community level. To supplement seniors' perceptions, Alley *et al.* (2007) consulted leading practitioners and researchers in the fields of gerontology, urban planning and community development to derive their collective understanding of the characteristics of elder friendly communities. Consensus was achieved on the characteristics listed in Table 5.2.

In a comparison with the concerns generated by seniors in the context of several national and local planning initiatives, the authors note the consistency between seniors' concerns and the researchers/practitioners with respect to the importance of safety, accessible services and respect for elders. The researchers/practitioners expressed additional concerns for caregiver support and age-appropriate exercise opportunities which may reflect current research and practice emphases. Perhaps most intriguing is that the researchers/practitioners called for attention to zoning reforms and pedestrian and traffic improvements, issues that were not emphasized by the seniors. Why does this differential exist? Do seniors fail to appreciate the fundamental relationship between the built environment and their aging experiences? Or is the built environment considered to be a given, not amenable to modifications?

While clearly various of these aging oriented planning initiatives have addressed aspects of the built environment that merit attention such as sidewalk improvements, the comprehensive

Table 5.2 Elder-Friendly Community Characteristics

- Accessible and affordable transportation
- Available in-home or long-term care services
- A wide variety of appropriate housing options
- Responsive health and long-term care
- Ability to obtain services with reasonable travel
- Personal safety and low crime rates
- Elders considered vital part of community
- Caregiver support services
- Accessible public and service buildings
- Elder-relevant issues present in local agenda
- Recognition of and response to unique needs of seniors
- A wide selection of services
- Adequate pedestrian and traffic controls
- Supportive zoning for senior housing
- Age-appropriate exercise facilities

Source: Alley *et al.* 2007: 7

nature of these assessment and planning efforts may result in less attention being given to the importance of fundamentally transforming the way we allow our communities to develop. This is not surprising given the extraordinary representation of aging service interests in leading these processes. It is imperative, however, that focused attention be given to the transformation of the built environment, even if that is difficult to achieve. The built environment is our legacy for future generations. Long after the last of the baby boomers, an aging-oriented community environment will be a livable community for all. Consider the following scenario:

> On first glance, it looks like a normal American community with single-family homes. But take a peek behind that house and you will see a tiny little cottage. Aunt Mary has lived there ever since she came home from the hospital. All the kids in the neighborhood head to her place after school because they can count on a handful of fresh-baked chocolate chip cookies. There is a little sign under the doorbell of the house across the street. It indicates that John Parker's door is at the right side of the house. He is a student at the community college. He is living in an accessory apartment that Betsy Roth created after her husband died. The extra income is helpful, and John's presence makes her feel more comfortable about living alone.
>
> The house over there is a duplex and down the side street is a triplex. They blend right in with the rest of the housing. There is even assisted care housing on the corner ... Martha Clarke, who lives in the neighborhood, has a mother in this facility. Martha likes the fact that her children can easily visit their grandmother without depending on a ride.
>
> The sidewalks are well-maintained which is important because the residents like to walk to the grocery store three blocks away. On any given day you will find old people,

Chapter 5: **AGING AS THE FOUNDATION**

teenagers, and mothers with strollers sitting on the comfortable benches in front of the store . . . The store offers delivery service for those who are housebound or need assistance with a particularly large purchase . . .

George Benson had to give up driving, but he still manages to get around on a tricycle. The bicycle paths are well-marked and automobile drivers, through years of public education and police oversight, are respectful of cyclists. When the weather is bad, George uses the bus. The service is frequent and on time, and the bus stops provide protection from bad weather. The drivers are patient and helpful. The transit authority makes a point of providing in-service training on the unique needs of older people.

Over there is Barton Brown's big old house. He's been there forever, and if he has a choice, he will live there until he dies. That may be unrealistic, but he is staying put for now. Whatever unfolds, Barton knows that he has options. When he has to give up his car, he will still be able to get around. If the house gets to be too much to handle, he can create an accessory apartment; he can rent one of those little houses two blocks away, or if his health dictates a need for a lot of help, then the assisted care housing might be a reasonable alternative.

Barton finds comfort in the knowledge that he will not need to move away from the place where he has set down his roots. He knows that he can count on his neighbors for support as he grows older. He is grateful to live in a community where people care about each other.

(Howe 1995: 25–26)

It is heartening to observe the variety of initiatives devoted to encouraging community planning with a focus on aging. A wide range of constituencies have become aware that the aging of society represents a major demographic shift that is at once both a challenge and a wonderful opportunity. It is also apparent that there is an extraordinary amount of work that needs to be done. For every community that is trying to address aging issues, there are hundreds if not thousands that have not even begun.

Notes

1   One could make the case that seniors are expected to live alone given the cultural emphasis on nuclear families.
2   Sixteen percent of the American population, 43 million people, aged 1 and older moved between March 1999 and March 2000. In contrast, only 4 percent of those between ages 65 and 84 moved during the same period (US Census 2000).
3   In 2002, 18 percent of women ages 40 to 44 were childless compared to 10 percent of the same age group in 1976. This same age group had on average 1.9 children in 2002 versus 3.1 in 1976 (Downs October 2003).
4   For more information see http://www.universaldesign.org/ (accessed December 22, 2009).
5   See http://www.concretechange.org/construction_costs.aspx for cost estimates (accessed December 22, 2009).
6   This might generate controversy as conflicting with climate protection and stormwater management goals to reduce impervious services.

7   See http://www.epa.gov/smartgrowth/ (accessed December 22, 2009).
8   See www.aginginplaceinitiative.org (accessed December 22, 2009).
9   See www.aginginplaceinitiative.org (accessed December 22, 2009).
10 See http://www.agingkansas.org/Choices/LifeLong/lifelongcommunity.htm (accessed December 22, 2009).
11 See http://www.dads.state.tx.us/services/agingtexaswell/index.html (accessed December 22, 2009).
12 Toolkit available at http://www.dads.state.tx.us/services/agingtexaswell/communityassessment/index.html (accessed December 22, 2009).
13 See http://www.vnsny.org/advantage/index.html (accessed December 22, 2009).
14 See http://www.viablefuturescenter.com/ (accessed December 22, 2009).

References

AARP (ND) Beyond 50: Livable communities quiz. http://www.aarp.org/families/housing_choices/other_options/a2005-06-20-livable_communities_quiz.html (accessed December 22, 2009).

Alexander, L.A. (April 15, 2008) Downtowns need to cater to the needs of a more mature population. *Downtown Idea Exchange*. http://www.downtowndevelopment.com/perspectives/dixperspectives041508.pdf (accessed December 22, 2009).

Alley, D., *et al.* (2007) Creating elder-friendly communities: Preparations for an aging society. Co-published simultaneously in *Journal of Gerontological Social Work* 49: 1/2, 1–18 and *Housing for the Elderly: Policy and Practice Issues* (ed: Philip McCallion) The Haworth Press, Inc., pp. 1–18.

Arias, E. (2006) United States life tables, 2003. *National Vital Statistics Reports*, 54: 14 Hyattsville, MD: National Center for Health Statistics http://www.cdc.gov/nchs/data/nvsr/nvsr54/nvsr54_14.pdf (accessed 22 December 2009).

Auerbach, D.I., Buerhaus, P.I., and Staiger, D.O. (2007) Better late than never: Workforce supply implications of later entry into nursing, *Health Affairs*, 26: 1, 178–185.

Brenner, E. (19 February 2006) Living in White Plains: A stalwart suburb gets a vibrant downtown *New York Times*.

Boyle, R. and Powell. M. (2008) The challenge of an aging society: Using planning, zoning and design to assist the elderly to age in place. Presentation at ACSP-AESOP Conference. Chicago, IL. July 8, 2008.

Chapman, N. and Howe, D. (2001) Accessory apartments: Are they a realistic alternative for aging in place? *Housing Studies,* 16: 5, 637–650.

Crimmins, E.M., *et al.* (1997) Trends in disability-free life expectancy in the United States, 1970–90, *Population and Development Review*, 23: 3, 555–572.

Concrete Change (ND) Is visitability legal? How courts have addressed visitability. http://www.concretechange.org/policy_legal.aspx (accessed 22 December, 2009).

Downs, B. (October 2003) Fertility of American women: June 2002. *Current Population Reports, P20–548*. Washington, DC: US Census Bureau. http://www.census.gov/prod/2003pubs/p20-548.pdf (accessed December 22, 2009).

Chapter 5: **AGING AS THE FOUNDATION**

Environmental Protection Agency (EPA) (ND) Building Healthy Communities for Active Aging: National Recognition Program. http://www.epa.gov/aging/bhc/about.htm (accessed December 22, 2009).

He, W., Sengupta, M., Velkoff, V.A., and DeBarros, K.A. (2005) US Census Bureau 65+ in the United States: 2005. *Current Population Reports, P23-209*. Washington, DC: US Government Printing Office, 151. http://www.census.gov/prod/2006pubs/p23-209.pdf (accessed December 22, 2009).

Hendorfer, B. (June 2005) *Age Restricted Active Adult Housing in Massachusetts: A Review of the Factors Fueling Its Explosive Growth and the Public Policy Issues It Raises*. Boston, MA: Citizens Housing and Planning Association. http://www.capecodcommission.org/housing/AgeRestrict HousingMA2005.pdf (accessed December 22, 2009).

Howe, D.A. (1990) The flexible house: Designing for changing needs, *Journal of the American Planning Association,* 56: 1, 69–79.

Howe, D. (1995) Community planning in an aging society, in *Expanding Housing Choices for Older People*. Conference Proceedings: AARP White House Conference on Aging Mini-Conference, held January 26–27, 1995, Washington, DC.

Huffstutter, P.J. (March 3, 2008) High-rise project divides residents in Chicago suburb: Big-city woes will follow, critics say, *Los Angeles Times*.

Jackson, J., Beiber, K., and Dressel, P. (ND) Creating viable futures: a case example from the Jefferson area board for aging (JABA) Charlottesville, VA. http://www.jabacares.org/uploads/documents/Cvile_Case_Study_FINAL_5.3.07.pdf (accessed December 22, 2009).

Kihl, M., Brennan D., Gabhawala, N., List, J., and Mittal, P. (2005) Livable communities: An evaluation guide, http://assets.aarp.org/rgcenter/il/d18311_communities.pdf (accessed December 22, 2009).

Kochera, A., Straight, A., and Guterbock, T. (ND) Beyond 50.05, *A Report to the Nation on Livable Communities: Creating Environments for Successful Aging*. Washington DC: AARP Public Policy Institute http://assets.aarp.org/rgcenter/il/beyond_50_communities.pdf (accessed December 22, 2009).

Matthew Greenwald and Associates. (May 2003) *These Four Walls: Americans 45+ Talk about Home and Community*. Washington, DC: AARP. http://assets.aarp.org/rgcenter/il/four_walls.pdf (accessed December 22, 2009).

Miller. J. (August 2007) Accessibility: How much is too much? *The Town Paper* http://www.tndtownpaper.com/Volume9/accessibility_how_much_is_too_much.html (accessed December 22, 2009).

National Association of Area Agencies on Aging (n4a), MetLife Foundation, International City/County Management Association (ICMA), National Association of Counties (NACo), National League of Cities (NLC), Partners for Livable Communities (PLC). (ND) The maturing of America: Getting communities on track for an aging population. http://www.aginginplaceinitiative.org/storage/aipi/documents/maturing_of_america_reformatted_for_printing.pdf (accessed December 22, 2009).

National Association of Area Agencies on Aging, Partners for Livable Communities (Partners), and MetLife Foundation (May 2007) A blueprint for action: developing a livable community for all Ages. http://www.aginginplaceinitiative.org/storage/aipi/documents/Blueprint_for_Action_web.pdf (accessed December 22, 2009).

Novelli, B. (15 June 2005) Livable communities as an AARP priority in *Universal Village Livable Communities in the 21st Century Conference Proceedings*, 10–15. http://www.aarpinternational.org/usr_doc/livablecommunities.pdf (accessed December 22, 2009).

Preston, S.H. (2005) Deadweight? The influence of obesity on longevity. *The New England Journal of Medicine*, 352, 1135–1137.

Pryne, E. (27 June 2008) New Bellevue Safeway caters to urban dwellers. *Seattle Times*. http://seattletimes.nwsource.com/html/businesstechnology/2008021192_safeway28.html (accessed December 22, 2009).

Reynolds, S.L., Saito, Y., and Crimmins, E.M. (2005) The impact of obesity on active life expectancy in older American men and women. *The Gerontological Society of* America, 45, 438–444.

Rosenbloom, S. and Stahl, A. (2002) Automobility among the elderly: The convergence of environmental, safety, mobility and community design issues. *European Journal of Transport and Infrastructure Research*, 2: 3/4, 197–214

Smith, E. (11 July 2005) Activists call "new urbanism" to account over lack of visitability http://www.raggededgemagazine.com/focus/esmithnewurbanism0705.html (accessed December 22, 2009).

Smith, S.K., Rayer, S., and Smith, E. (2008) Aging and disability: Implications for the housing industry and housing policy in the United States. *Journal of the American Planning Association*, 74: 3, 289–306.

State Advisory Council on Aging, Michigan Office of Services to the Aging, Michigan Department of Community Health, Michigan Vital Aging Think Tank, and Michigan State University Extension (ND) Michigan Community for a Lifetime: Elder Friendly Community Recognition Program History and Project Development Report, http://www.michigan.gov/documents/miseniors/7-_Michigan_CFL_History__Project_Dev_199548_7.pdf (accessed 15 August 2008).

Taylor, C. (15 January 2007) Aging populations inspire "universal design" housing. *NACO County News*. http://www.naco.org/CountyNewsTemplate.cfm?template=/ContentManagement/ContentDisplay.cfm&ContentID=22282 (accessed December 22, 2009).

Urbitran Associates, Cambridge Associates, and Howard/Stein-Hudson Associates. (March 2005) *Strategies for Increasing Safe Mobility for Older Residents*. North Jersey Transportation Planning Authority. http://www.njtpa.org/plan/Element/Safety/Safety_study/documents/olderdrivers.pdf (accessed December 22, 2009).

Visscher, T.L.S. and Seidell, J.C. (2001) The public health impact of obesity. *Annual Review of Public Health*, 22, 355–75.

Wan, W. (29 May 2007) Rules about crowded schools fuel the graying of Arundel, *Washington Post*. http://www.washingtonpost.com/wp-dyn/content/article/2007/05/28/AR2007052801456.html (accessed December 22, 2009).

US Census Bureau (2000) Chapter 3: People on the move, Geographic mobility, 1999–2000, *Population Profile of the United States: 2000* (Internet Release) http://www.census.gov/population/www/pop-profile/files/2000/chap03.pdf (accessed December 22, 2009).

US Census Bureau (2005) American housing survey for the United States: 2005. *Current Housing Reports Series H150/05*. Washington DC: US Government Printing Office. http://www.census.gov/prod/2006pubs/h150-05.pdf (accessed December 22, 2009).

US Census Bureau (2009) Statistical abstract of the United States: 2010 (129th edition) Washington, DC http://www.census.gov/compendia/statab/ (accessed 21 December 2009).

Chapter 6

PERCEIVED LIVABILITY AND SENSE OF COMMUNITY: LESSONS FOR DESIGNERS FROM A FAVELA IN RIO DE JANEIRO, BRAZIL

Vicente del Rio
Professor, City and Regional Planning Department Professor, Psychology and Child Development Department
California Polytechnic State University San Luis Obispo

Daniel Levi
Professor, Psychology and Child Development Department
California Polytechnic State University San Luis Obispo

Cristiane Rose Duarte
Professor, Faculdade de Arquitetura e Urbanismo
Universidade Federal do Rio de Janeiro

Livability and sense of community became popular notions widely utilized in planning and design – particularly in publications on new urbanism and smart growth – to justify contemporary theories and projects, and they are increasingly dominant in governmental policies. Although these are subjective notions and their effectiveness depend fundamentally on the relationship between users and the built environment, current literature pushes us towards design tenets and criteria that are action-oriented and rely almost exclusively on physical and measurable aspects.

Current research and literature concentrate on a very limited strata of socio-economic groups – high and middle high income – and mostly ignore what livability and sense of community might be for lower-income and culturally diverse populations. Specific cultural, social, political, and economic contexts of other countries, and particularly of the developing nations, also play very minor parts in determining any variation on the current notions of livability and sense of community that have been leading planning and design theory.

This may lead us to unpredictable results since different individuals and social groups have different perceptions of what makes a livable community, and they experience sense of community differently. As happened many times before in planning history, we run the risk of adopting a deterministic approach and simplistic models as remedies to cure all urban maladies.

In this chapter we explore the notion of livability and its strong connection with sense of community. We discuss how the nature, number, and quality of environmental transactions made within a community are important components of the community's *perceived* livability and sense of community, and thus to their satisfaction with the place they live in. Environmental transactions are the social interactions and networks born from environmental conditions but which will ultimately operate independently from them. The more environmental transactions they experience, the more livable a community would feel to its residents.

We were also curious to test if livability and sense of community are different for the poor, and specifically for the poor of a diverse socio-cultural context. Would residents of a poor community feel a stronger sense of community than those of a better-off community due to more intense environmental transactions? How would understanding this change our views about planning and design? To contribute toward an answer, we conducted a study of Mata Machado favela, a squatter settlement located in Rio de Janeiro. Our results clearly indicate that some variables do coincide with current literature in new urbanism and smart growth, but others point dangerously to other directions that are worth further attention and research.

Design, Livability, and Sense of Community

A New Design Paradigm

"Livability" and "sense of community" have become catchy labels in planning and design. New urbanism, smart growth, and more recently sustainable urbanism have embraced them; they feature in most missions for plans and projects; and the political discourse has adopted them at the national, regional, and local levels. The loss of sense of community was recognized as the major problem in modern cities by neo-traditional and new urbanist models, and it became a fundamental social goal behind contemporary planning and design (Katz 1993; Duany *et al.* 2001). Livability became the fourth variable in Godschalk's famous sustainability model – ecology, equity, and economy – which was transformed from a triangle to a prism with livability at the apex (Berke *et al.* 2006).

On one hand, this represents a major breakthrough to our disciplines since it matches planning and design decisions to sustainable development, and particularly to the social and psychological realms. But on the other hand, it can be a real problem and lead us to another mismatch between good intentions and the end results. Although we all have a pretty good idea of what we want for ourselves and for the place we live in, the notions of livability and sense of community are blurry at best. Their meanings are subjective, vary in time, and rest solely on the users of the final built environment. Different people have different perceptions of what makes a community livable and thus they experience quality and sense of community differently. Since it is so difficult to define livability and sense of community with the precision that is necessary to orient decisions and action, planning and design often relies too much on physical aspects and measurable qualities.

Chapter 6: **LESSONS FROM A FAVELA**

From ancient urbanism to modernism to new urbanism and smart growth, there has been a firm belief that improvement in social behavior derives from improvements in physical design. This is more disturbing today due to the expansion of numerous formulaic criteria for "good" planning and urban design, mostly derived from new urbanist theories. This is particularly important in how we think of residential environments and plan at the scale of a neighborhood or a home's immediate vicinity. An overview of current planning and design literature, or a simple analysis of the Charter of New Urbanism and the material marketed by the Congress of the New Urbanism, will clearly indicate this tendency. New urbanism has been presented as a rediscovery of the traditions that have shaped the most livable and memorable communities (Bressi 1994; Dutton 2000) and that it will promote the return "to a cherished American icon: that of a compact, close-knit community" (Katz 1994: ix).

The problem is that the social doctrine of new urbanism was translated into a popular design manifesto and that "the social prescription of new urbanism is based on spatial determinism" (Talen 1999: 1,364). Brown and Cropper (2001) stress the dangers of assuming a direct correlation between design and social and psychological goals which new urbanists imply in their designs. Patterson and Chapman's *New Urbanism Index of Neighborhood Characteristics*, derived from a content analysis of new urbanism concepts found in the literature, includes twenty-nine items, all reflecting physical design features (Patterson and Chapman 2004). The emphasis on design and measurable aspects are also found in the American Institute of Architects' principles for livable communities, the Smart Growth Network's *101 Policies for Implementation*, the ideas from the Local Government Comission's Center for Livable Communities, and the American Planners Association criteria for evaluating great neighborhoods.[1]

By and large, most popular design tenets and guidelines for a livable environment and sense of community are based on a deterministic approach that assumes the built environment is the primary determinant of human behavior and satisfaction. In a recent study of fifteen planned communities in the US, Brower (2005) concluded that although a unified design can help create community, the appropriate social setting requires much more than following certain design criteria. The presumption of the "power of design" in creating community and determining behavior is in no way different from the wrongful modernist theories of Le Corbusier and the Charter of Athens. What is particularly disturbing is, as happened before in planning and design history, we are running the risk of imposing a new paradigm and a new set of values and models as remedies that will cure urban maladies and lead us to idealized built environments. We must therefore begin by asking what the people we are planning and designing for perceive as good and bad in the environment. What do they understand as livability and community?

Characteristics of Livability

What are the characteristics that make a livable environment for people? In the classic social sciences literature, livability is described as "the sum total of the qualities of the urban environment that tend to induce in a citizen a state of well-being and satisfaction" (Sanders 1966: 13). Livability is best defined at the local scale as it refers to the quality of life for a group of people who live in a particular place (AIA 2005; Gutberlet and Hunter 2008). Livable environments are places that people like, satisfy their needs, promote human health, and contribute to a sustainable environmental system. Researchers and governments have used a variety of indicators to evaluate the sustainability and livability of communities. For the purposes of this chapter, the livability of residential environments relates to features that promote residential satisfaction, a sense of community, and environmental sustainability.

Research on communities in the US suggests that residential satisfaction primarily relates to four factors: the physical condition of the buildings; the size of residences and how they are structured to manage crowding and privacy; safety and the perception of safety; and relations with neighbors (Bell *et al.* 2001; Brower 1996 and 2005). The physical condition of buildings concerns the quality of materials, construction, and design of the residence and their maintenance. Crowding relates to both residential density and how the residence structures space to give people control over their social interactions (Evans *et al.* 1996). Perceptions of safety are related to the actual amount of crime in the area, social fear of crime, and the physical and social characteristics of the neighborhood that create defensible space (Taylor *et al.* 1984). Good relations with neighbors provide emotional and social support to residents and are encouraged by a variety of neighborhood design features, such as walkability, density, and local social spaces such as shops, parks, and recreation areas (Brown and Cropper 2001).

Residential satisfaction research shows that people differ on their residential preferences (Brower 1996). It is not a measure of the environment, but a measure of the fit or congruence between the individual and the environment. For example, good relations with neighbors are more important for residents of low-income housing than more wealthy residents (Amerigo and Aragones 1997). One of the reasons for this preference is that low-income residents are more dependent on social supports and community surveillance by neighbors to provide a sense of safety (Leeds 1969; Perlman 1976; Wilson-Doenges 2000). Access to public transportation is also more important to low-income residents since they cannot afford cars.

A sense of community includes both neighboring interactions and a cognitive and emotional connection to the people and place. The benefits of neighboring and a sense of community include greater residential satisfaction, community participation, perceived safety, social bonding and support, and perceived control over one's environment (Unger and Wanderman 1985). At a cognitive and emotional level, a sense of community relates to a sense of membership and belonging, influence on what happens in the community, fulfillment of needs, and shared emotional connections among the residents (McMillan and Chavis 1986). Research supports a connection between residential design and neighboring, but the connection between design and sense of community is weak (Talen 1999). A sense of community also relates to non-design variables such of homogeneity of residents and length of time living in a place.

The importance of neighboring and a sense of community and how this relates to the environment differ among types of people. Although all communities are based on people sharing common interests and values, there are also communities of place (McMillan and Chavis 1986).[2] These are communities formed by social relations between neighbors and other residents that live in a recognizable geographical area, supported by various environmental characteristics (Nasar and Julian 1995). Low-income residents are more likely to focus on community of place and view neighbor relations as more important (Amerigo and Aragones 1997).

Chapter 6: **LESSONS FROM A FAVELA**

Table 6.1 Livability Matrix

	Residential Environment	*Neighborhood and Community*	*Environmental Sustainability*
Livability			
Physical condition of buildings	**	*	*
Crowding, privacy and density	**	*	*
Safety and perception of safety	**	**	
Neighboring and sense of community	**	**	
Compactness and density	*	**	**
Mixed land use	*	**	**
Access to sustainable transportation	**	**	**
Natural environments and parks	**	**	**

** very important topic; * somewhat important topic

Environmental sustainability concerns the environmental impacts of residential environments and the relationship between environmental features and human health and satisfaction. Sustainable development relates to urban designs that lower energy and resource use and pollution (Jabareen 2006). Sustainable design concepts include compactness and density, mixed land use, sustainable transportation, and integrating nature into the urban environment. Compactness and density minimize sprawl and transportation use, protect the surrounding rural environment, and reduce energy consumption and pollution. Mixed land use reduces the use of cars for commuting, shopping, and recreation. Sustainable transportation uses walking, cycling, and public transportation to reduce energy consumption and pollution. Especially for low-income communities, the key to sustainable transportation is to provide convenient, safe, and affordable access to people for meeting their needs. Natural areas within and surrounding a community reduce pollution and help to preserve ecological diversity.

The characteristics of sustainable development have important physiological, psychological, and social effects on the residents. Although density may increase crowding, it helps to promote neighboring and a sense of community (Brown and Cropper 2001). Mixed land use has also been linked to increases in neighborhood social interactions and a sense of community (Nasar and Julian 1995). Sustainable transportation promotes neighborhood interactions and human health (Frank *et al.* 2003). Natural environments in urban areas increase neighborhood interactions and safety (Kuo *et al.* 1998), reduce stress and promote health (Ulrich 1984).

The livability of a residential environment relates to a variety of factors that impact residential satisfaction, a sense of community, and environmental sustainability. The relationship of these factors to the impacts is presented in Table 6.1.

Livability as Person-Environment Fit

The relationship of the environment to residential satisfaction and a sense of community depend on a variety of psychological, sociological, and cultural characteristics of the residents (Unger and Wandersman 1985; McMillan and Chavis 1986; Brower 1996, 2005; Talen 1999; Brown and Cropper 2001). Livability comes from the transaction of people and their environment. The transactional perspective emphasizes that environmental, psychological, and behavioral factors are in a reciprocal relationship with each other (Altman and Rogoff 1987). The environment affects how people live and function, and people change their environment to make it more suitable to their needs and lifestyles.

Livability relates to the fit or congruence between people and their environment. People do not passively accept the environments they live in. If they can afford it, they tend to move to an environment that better fits their expectations and needs; if they are poor and lack the resources to do so, they modify the environment to fit their needs. Environments vary in how well they support user needs or promote certain types of behavior, and people vary in their desires, needs, and goals. Therefore, there is not one best type of livable environment; there are a variety of types that relate to the differences among people. There is also a lack of agreement among academics and planners about the best urban form to promote sustainability (Jabareen 2006).

Brower's (1996) analysis of successful residential neighborhoods in urban areas suggests a typology of alternative types of livable urban neighborhoods. Preference for the different types of neighborhoods depends on the characteristics of the residents and the surrounding urban context. These types suggest there are a variety of approaches for creating livable environments.

In Brower's typology, the type of neighborhood most similar to the favela is the "small town neighborhood," which is also similar to neo-traditional and New Urbanist designs (Katz 1996; Dutton 2000). It is mixed-use with the commercial uses typically in the center or along major thoroughfares that connect to the outside. The neighborhood is self-contained and only partially open to the outside city. Consequently, the commercial area depends on the local residents rather than on external shoppers. It has a strong sense of community – residents know each other, there are common socializing places, and it is usually distinct and bounded with a strong local identity. A small town neighborhood is an internally walkable environment, although residents may have cars that they use for transportation to work and shopping.

A small town neighborhood is more characteristic of working-class than middle-class people. These neighborhoods often attract immigrants and minority groups who depend on the social support that the neighborhood provides. Although this design is popular with contemporary urban designers (especially New Urbanists), the small town neighborhood has several potential problems. Many urbanites shop via car in larger stores to save money, so the local stores often lose viability. The strong local social networks that make this environment work require a stable resident population. When populations change frequently, there is less opportunity for a sense of community to develop and less support for local stores. Because of improvements in transportation and communication, residents may have interests and social relationships that are not local, which reduces their desire for neighborhood interactions and sense of community.

The Mata Machado Favela in Rio de Janeiro

A Retrospect of Favelas

The most enduring images of Rio de Janeiro are of its mountains, beautiful beaches and tropical landscapes, but also of its numerous favelas, the word commonly used in Brazil for squatter

Chapter 6: LESSONS FROM A FAVELA

settlements. Originally, the word favela indicated a group of poorly constructed shacks or buildings erected on land to which the residents had no legal titles, and devoid of public infrastructure and services such as water supply, piped sewage, and garbage collection (del Rio 2005).[3] For many years, the typical *favelado* (resident of a favela) was a migrant to the big city from poor rural areas in search of better living conditions and work opportunities.

The social representation of favelas as a spontaneous and anti-hygienic settlement formed by disorganized migrants detached from city life, and of *favelados* as marginals to society prevailed until the mid-1970s (Perlman 1976; Valladares 2005). New social research by pioneers such as Mangin (1967), Turner (1969), Leeds (1969), Perlman (1976), and Leeds and Leeds (1978) changed this understanding by showing that a squatter settlement was not a problem but a functional solution for its residents. A favela provides easy access to nearby work and services, free access to land, and a cohesive social network the residents can rely on for their common needs. Research showed that these localities have a complex net of internal relations and social cohesiveness because of their shared origins, needs and dreams, the self-help and community initiatives to improve home and place, and their political alliances to fight the government against eviction.

By the early 1980s, urban social movements became catalysts against governmental programs that eradicated the favelas, fighting to regularize their land tenure and to grant *favelados* with right to the city just like any other citizen (Valladares 2005; del Rio 2009). Since then, the prevailing theoretical framework shifted from the theory of marginality to that of social and environmental exclusion, where individuals are "restrained or not enabled to access public services, goods, activities, or resources" (Gutberlet and Hunter 2008: 4). The National Constitution of 1988 recognized citizens' rights to the city and its services, and protected the squatters' right to their land after five years of un-refuted occupation (Fernandes 2007; del Rio 2009). In 2000 a constitutional amendment listed housing as one of the basic social rights of all citizens, together with education, health, work, security, social security, and protection to maternity and infancy. The favela was finally being recognized by society, together with the collective and individual investments of *favelados*. Respect for these communities was due to the move towards social equity and recognition of their value as a way to help respond to housing demand.

In the past two decades with the ghost of eviction gone and the political climate in their favor, *favelados* invested in the quality of their houses and communities. State and local governments have also been investing in programs to expand public social and infrastructural services into the favelas. These changes have deconstructed our understanding of what a favela is. Presently, the only aspect that is common among favelas is that, although protected by law and a *de facto* situation, their residents still lack appropriate titles to the land they settled on. There are extremely miserable favelas of wood shacks along canals in the far suburbs of Rio, as there are well-off favelas where all buildings are brick and mortar and the community has access to all public services. Many favelas are extremely dynamic and function almost as small towns, where one can find several services, stores, hotels, bars, public services, and even banks and post offices. Santa Marta, a favela of 10,000 residents in Botafogo, south zone of Rio, offers free wireless internet to the whole community. Rocinha, a favela of almost 100,000 residents spreading from Gavea to São Conrado, also in Rio's south zone, has hundreds of businesses including banks, pharmacies, a McDonald's franchise, internal bus routes, and a community operated radio station, web portal, and cable TV channel.[4] In early 2010, the state inaugurated a 150,000 sq. foot sports complex there – including a soccer field and swimming pools – which will offer 22 different types of sports to the favela residents who see that as not only a recreational asset but as opportunities for personal success.

Available data clearly indicates that in the past decades there has been an increase in the quality of life of *favelados* in Rio de Janeiro, particularly in terms of access to public services and income generation. Undoubtedly the major reasons were the new constitution, the expansion of citizenship, the halting of the inflation spiral, and the increase of the purchasing power of the poorer groups. A study by Cavallieri and Oliveira (2006) for the city of Rio shows the evolution of quality of life indicators in favelas. While in 1960 only 16 percent of domiciles were hooked to city's drinkable water pipes, 79 percent had electricity, and one percent of *favelados* had more than 8 years of education, in 2000 those numbers jumped to 92 percent, 99 percent, 14 percent respectively. By 2000, 81 percent of domiciles in favelas were owned by the families living there, 76 percent had access to a sewage collection system, and 98 percent had access to garbage collection. Another recent survey by sociologist Alba Zaluar in several favelas of Rio revealed that 94 percent of domiciles had a TV set, 59 percent had a DVD player, 55 percent had a cellular phone, and 12 percent had a computer.[5] This study also showed that only 15 percent of respondents would like to move from their favela, revealing a great attachment to place and community.

Besides the expansion of the notion of the rights to the city and the better of living conditions in general, two major phenomena continue to affect Rio's favelas. First, the demand for appropriate and affordable housing continued to increase. The economic crisis of the 1980s and the implosion of the State apparatus after Brazil's re-democratization put a halt on the old top-down housing solutions.[6] At the same time, the market was affected by inflated real-estate and land prices. While population growth in Rio's favelas has been decreasing in the last forty years, it remains significantly higher than that of the "formal city": 2.4 percent versus 0.4 percent between 1999 and 2000 (Cavallieri and Oliveira 2006). In 2010 the city of Rio de Janeiro had over 6.3 million residents, 20 percent of which were living in its almost 1,000 favelas according to census data and city estimates.[7]

The other major phenomenon that affects Brazilian society and particularly the favelas is the alarming increase in criminality and drug related violence of the last twenty years. In fact, Perlman (2010: 21) affirms that "the most devastating change that has occurred over four decades" in favelas was the rise of drug trafficking and the take-over of community control by drug lords and militia. Perlman continues pointing out that the "loss of trust, community unity, and freedom of movement" besides the erosion of social capital are among most perverse consequences (Perlman 2010: 21). The narco-traffic became the most disturbing problem in Rio de Janeiro both inside and outside the favelas. Public perception has also become more negative towards favelas that are increasingly more identified with crime (Valladares 2005). Due to their morphological conditions and difficult accessibility, and to the historical absence of the State and public services within their territories, the favelas of Rio became strategic centers for drug trafficking and distribution (Leite 2005). Gangs control most of the favelas by terror, battle over their territories, and victimize the *favelados*. But the police is also feared by the *favelados* for their indiscriminate brutality and ill-conducted operations against the gangs inside their settlements. In her original 1969 survey, Perlman found that only 16 percent of

Chapter 6: **LESSONS FROM A FAVELA**

the *favelados* stated that "crime and violence" were their main complaints about Rio, versus 60 percent of the respondents in her second study in 2003 (Perlman 1976 and 2003). This is particularly true in favelas that are easily accessed from major drug consumer markets, the higher-end city districts such as Leblon, Ipanema, and Copacabana.

However, an interesting development has been happening in the last two years that is changing the public perception of *favelas* and the life of *favelados*. Pressed by the need to prepare the city for the 2014 Soccer World Cup and the 2016 Olympic Games, the three levels of government (city, state, and federal) forged an alliance to come down hard on narco-traffic and free *favelas* from their control. After a coordinated action between the military and the state police that invade the favela (arresting or killing drug traffickers, and apprehending truck loads of weapons and drugs), a *Unidade de Policia Pacificadora* – UPP, or unit of pacifying police, is left permanently there.[8] This specially trained police group is meant not only to make sure organized crime does not come back, but also to provide community support and strengthen public social programs. In 2008 the first UPP was installed in Favela Santa Marta and operates with 123 police, and by the beginning of 2011 there were seventeen favelas served by UPPs.

Although critics point out that the UPPs are politically motivated and predict they will be pulled off after the 2016 Olympics, that real estate prices in favelas with UPPs have increased up to 400 percent (what evidently affects the poorer and renters), and that residents are now disturbed by the rapid increase in tourism in their communities, this has been a very successful and well-accepted program by both the favelados and the general population.[9] The results of an independent survey shows that the majority of the residents of favelas with UPPs approve the program, feel that their communities are safer, and that they feel more respected as individuals; they are happy they can move freely and their kids can play safely outside now.[10] These are indicators that no doubt affect livability and sense of community.

History of Mata Machado

Considered a favela, the Mata Machado community is located in Rio de Janeiro's Alto da Boa Vista district. Its main entrance is at Estrada de Furnas, the only thoroughfare linking Tijuca, one of the city's most traditional middle-class residential neighborhoods, to Barra da Tijuca, a modernist district planned by Lucio Costa in the late 1960s and Rio's major expansion area to the west. The community is limited by Estrada de Furnas, two rivers (Cachoeira and Gavea Pequena), forested areas that are a preservation zone, a small residential area mostly comprised of single family homes, and a walled property (Figures 6.1 and 6.2).

Nested in a small valley up in the mountains, Mata Machado is surrounded by Floresta da Tijuca, the world's largest urban forest off approximately 12.8 square miles. This large *floresta* resulted from the reforestation of vast coffee plantations in the mid-nineteenth century by a small contingent of soldiers and slaves in an effort to protect the city's fresh water resources. Listed as a national park since 1961, the *floresta* is one of Rio's major tourist and recreation attractions, and its main entrances for visitors are not far from Mata Machado.

The first families of Mata Machado settled in the area in the 1940s (Duarte *et al.* 1995). They migrated from São Fidélis, an essentially agricultural municipality in the north of Rio de Janeiro State. They came in search of work opportunities and better living conditions. The common origin of these families worked as a magnet to attract other families from São Fidélis.

Figure 6.1 Aerial View of Mata Machado. *An aerial view showing Mata Machado favela as limited by the forest (right and top of photo), river Gavea Pequena (forested corridor in the center) and the road Estrada de Furnas (in the lower portion).*

Source: Photo by Osvaldo L. de Sousa Silva

The natural assets of the site – surrounded by forested mountains with plenty of springs with drinkable water – favored the pioneers who utilized local woods to build their shacks (Duarte and Brasileiro 2001).

According to Soares (1999), the forest surrounding Mata Machado has been one of the major reasons for the community's affective ties to the place. Since the favela was originally located in an uninhabited area relatively far from the city, the first families survived by raising small animals and planting vegetables until their absorption into the city's job market.

By the 1950s, the residents of Mata Machado were leaving their agricultural practices to participate in the growing local industrial sector. At this time, fiscal incentives by the city encouraged the opening of a few isolated medium-sized factories in the Alto da Boa Vista district. One example was the *Fábrica de Artefatos de Papel* (paper artifacts factory) located on a parcel of land between Estrada de Furnas and Mata Machado which later became a vinyl record factory (Polygram of the Philips group). These factories greatly benefited the local community. In the 1960s, a real-estate market boom caused property values to rise in the whole city and encouraged the construction of new middle- and high-income housing in the

Chapter 6: **LESSONS FROM A FAVELA**

nearby areas. While on one hand this increased job opportunities – particularly in construction and domestic labor – for Mata Machado residents, on the other hand it exposed the favela as an "eyesore" that devalued the surrounding properties in the emerging real-estate market.

In the late 1960s and early 1970s, the tough planning policies and programs supported by the military regime of the time put pressure on Rio's favelas (Perlman 1976; Azevedo 1999; del Rio 2009). The Mata Machado residents' association (Associação de Moradores de Mata Machado; AMMM) expanded its role from supporting social relations to a more active role in controlling growth and new constructions within the favela. This was a much needed strategy to fight the negative perception of the *favelados* in Rio, which socially stigmatized the residents of Mata Machado and exposed them to government programs to evict "unhealthy housing" (Perlman 1976; Valladares 2005). The AMMM managed to convince politicians and government officials to include their favela in a cutting-edge community upgrading program by CODESCO, the city's community development company. The program had been relatively successful in a handful of other favelas in Rio, such as Morro do Pasmado and Bras de Pina, and although a project was done for Mata Machado, the agency was shut down in the late 1960s before having the chance of implementing it. Those were times when the tightening of the military regime dictated the end of alternative and democratic experiments such as CODESCO's, and housing policies shifted to a more technocratic and quantitative approach (Perlman 1976; Azevedo 1999; del Rio 2009).

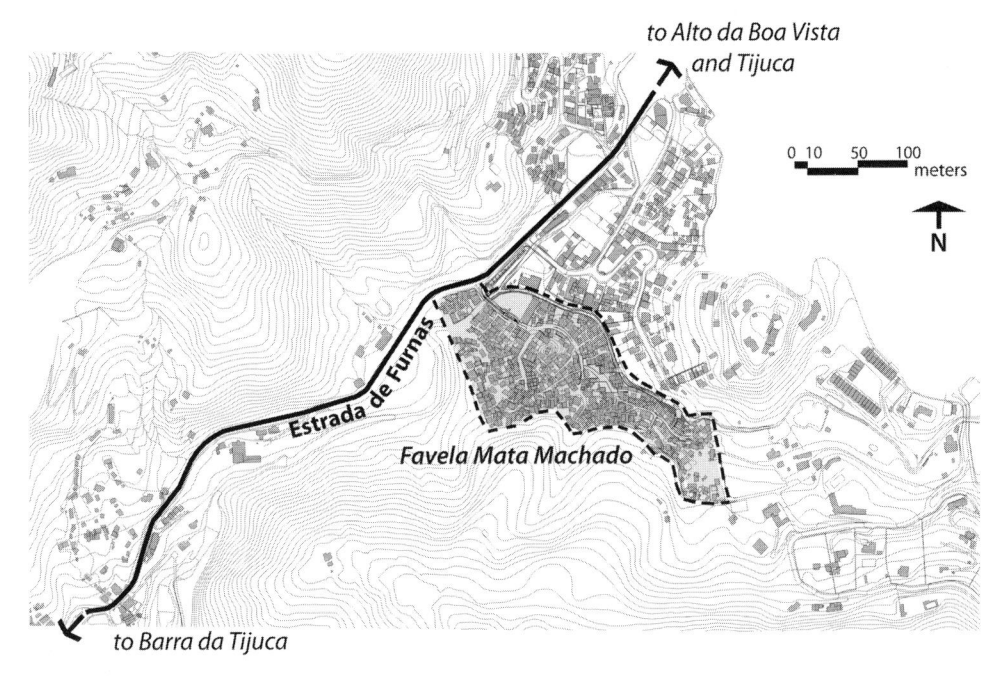

Figure 6.2 Site Map of Mata Machado.

Source: Map by Rodrigo Sgarbi, adapted by V. del Rio

However, with CODESCO's project in their hands, the Mata Machado residents' association started to work on upgrading their favela through a series of self-help initiatives, which included the sharing of costs of building materials. Hundreds of yards of sewage and water pipes and electricity cables were installed by the residents themselves. These were not necessarily environmentally friendly solutions. For instance, the piped raw sewage still ended in the local rivers due to the lack of an appropriate sewage treatment system in the surrounding area. Community works, the constant fight against eviction, and the awareness of the need for community union and organization strengthened the attachment to place and social cohesion in Mata Machado. According to Soares (1999), the strengthening of the residents' association also helped to limit the emergence of groups linked to drug traffic within the favela, a fact we verified during our fieldwork.

With the weakening of the military regime and the return to a full democracy in the 1980s, Mata Machado was left alone and continued to flourish as a strong community. In the mid-1990s, when the second generation of descendants of the first settlers was born, the community was included in Favela-Bairro, an important city program to upgrade small favelas, integrate them to the "formal city," and transform them into *bairros* –neighborhoods (Duarte and Magalhães 2008). Favela-Bairro was meant to provide communities with infrastructure and public facilities, better accessibility, and land titles, but in the case of Mata Machado only part of the designers' proposals was built (Duarte *et al.* 1995; Duarte and Magalhães 2008). For instance, although all housing units were connected to a piped sewage system installed by the city, the untreated sewage is still pumped into the river since it was never connected to the main lines in Estrada de Furnas. Most importantly, the residents never received land deeds, one of the most important goals of the original program. Nevertheless, the community considers that all the improvements that they have received resulted from their active residents' association, their legitimate representative during all the difficult times they faced (Duarte and Brasileiro 2001).

The Community of Mata Machado

Coincidentally, Mata Machado was the first favela visited in Rio by journalist Robert Neuwith, as he describes in his *Letter from Brazil* (Neuwith 2000). He was impressed by the quality of the community's social organization and its built environment, and felt that it was "almost suburban: a bucolic community of modern houses on shady streets that fan out from a central plaza." Indeed, the history of this favela, its relatively high-quality environment, and the existing facilities makes it a very special residential place among Rio's favelas.

When one drives up Estrada de Furnas and stops at Mata Machado's major entrance, most of the settlement comes immediately into view, sloping gracefully uphill with its spaces mingling with the sparsely urbanized and heavily forested surroundings (Figure 6.3). A river that springs higher in the mountains not far from Mata Machado runs between the settlement and the Estrada. In one of its margins, the city is replacing the old abandoned factory with an elementary school. It is anticipated to upgrade the soccer field and equip the open space once construction is over. Due to the site's mountain climate (much cooler that in the lower valleys of Rio) and the ever-present surrounding forest and trees in the favela (scattered in public spaces and in private yards), one feels a strong presence of nature at Mata Machado.

Chapter 6: **LESSONS FROM A FAVELA**

Figure 6.3 Main Entrance to Mata Machado. *The main entrance to Mata Machado from Estrada de Furnas. The settlement reflects the topography and is surrounded by the ever-present forest.*

Source: Photo by C. Duarte

The major thoroughfare into Mata Machado runs from Estrada de Furnas to its central open space, which the community calls "*a praça*" (the square) (Figure 6.4). Along it one finds one to three-story high residences, several small bars and shops selling food, produce, general goods, and clothes, service shops such as electronics and TV repairs, and small shrines. Commercial uses do not seem to be particularly attracted by the open spaces that are informally generated by the winding alleys. They thin out as one goes deeper in the settlement. The edges of the *praça* are mostly taken by residences but one also finds the community center (a three-story building with the residents' association and several offices serving a state community development agency), a couple of small shops, a small building used as a police station, and the day-care center and the elementary school – both run by the city government.

Confirming our initial perceptions, a recent study on the socio-economic characteristics of favelas in the city places Mata Machado in the upper stratum compared to other such communities and to the average socio-economic status in Rio's metropolitan region (Cunha 2000). The community has fewer dependents (family members under 15 years of age), more aged residents, and fewer people who cannot read or write than other favelas. More than 45 percent of the work force had job contracts, 16 percent worked as independent contractors, and only 28 percent of

111

Figure 6.4 Mata Machado Site Plan and Study Areas. *Mata Machado and the two areas of behavioral observations.*

Source: Map by Rodrigo Sgarbi, adapted by V. del Rio

the heads of families were jobless. Mata Machado's poverty level is among the lowest among Rio's favelas.

Besides being a community of place, the residents of Mata Machado also belong to many other communities of interest, with origins both inside and outside the favela itself. There are religious communities, soccer groups, and school buddy networks that connect the *favelados* with the broader community. Interestingly, since 2006 there is an internet Orkut community for Mata Machado, which is described in cyber-space as "this community is for you who live, know, have visited, cannot stay away from, or knows someone who lives in Mata Machado; the greatest community in Alto da Boa Vista."[11]

The last available census data indicates that in 2000 Mata Machado had 16.2 acres and a population of 2,491 people in 603 dwellings – an average of 3.72 persons per domicile and a gross density of 153 persons per acre. A city's research unit that uses aerial photography to monitor the growth of favelas registered that Mata Machado's area expanded only by 1.1 percent (7,680 sq. feet) between 1999 and 2004 (Lopes and Cavallieri 2006). From our talks with city council staff and community leaders, this is a stable community and its social dynamics have not changed substantially over the years.

Chapter 6: **LESSONS FROM A FAVELA**

The Study

Methods

Our analysis of the Mata Machado favela used multiple methods. Background information on the history and characteristics of the favela, maps, aerial photographs, several visits, and on-site observations and interviews were used to examine the social, physical and environmental conditions of the favela (Figure 6.5). Structured behavioral observations during one Sunday examined the social use of the community streets and public spaces. In-depth interviews with residents examined housing characteristics and satisfaction, perceived safety, neighboring behaviors and sense of community, and transportation.

Results and Discussion

Behavioral Observations

On a sunny Sunday at 2:00 pm it took us a little over three minutes of slow walking to cover approximately 600 feet (partially on an upward slope) between Mata Machado's entrance at Estrada de Furnas to its "core" – the larger open space serving as the main *praça*. Shared by vehicles and pedestrians, this thoroughfare is the principal access into the favela; its physical

Figure 6.5 View of the Main Praça. *Residents people-watching and socializing in front of their homes and at outside tables of a busy bar along the main thoroughfare on a Sunday afternoon.*

Source: Photo by V. del Rio

DEL RIO *et al.*

conditions (narrow width, irregular geometry, vehicles parked on both sides, and human activity such as tables and seats in front of bars) limit vehicular circulation significantly generating a "natural" traffic calming solution. During our walk we observed 101 persons in different activities along the thoroughfare: engaged in social activities and playing (40 adults, 15 teenagers, and eight children); walking (15 adults, ten teenagers and nine children), and standing next to buildings and observing the passers-by (four adults). This result, obtained in a very short time period of a day when most people do not work and are participating in leisure activities, indicates that the favela's main thoroughfare doubles as a highly utilized public space vital for the life of the community.

In subsequent visits to Mata Machado we noticed similar patterns of behavior while walking around the settlement. Recurrent activities for adults in public spaces included socializing in front of their houses or just standing there watching passers-by, playing an informal soccer game in the street, and sitting outside bars drinking and eating (Figure 6.6). As far as children are concerned, social activities included playing, flying kites, and just hanging out. Towards the mid afternoon, the crowds next to the bars got bigger and louder as more chairs and tables were added to serve the increasing number of clients. The vast majority of the clients were males and soccer seemed to be their main discussion topic that day.

Behavioral maps were done for the main access area and for the *praça* on a Sunday afternoon, during a five-minute observation period. The access area is approximately 300 feet long and 36

Figure 6.6 Main Thoroughfare Leading to the *Praça*. *The busy main thoroughfare leading to the praça at the core of the community, on a Sunday afternoon.*

Source: Photo by V. del Rio

Chapter 6: **LESSONS FROM A FAVELA**

feet wide, with a short landscaped median separating the two lanes of the thoroughfare into different levels. In the median two benches lay shaded by a big tree, there are regular sidewalks along this stretch of the thoroughfare and a small bridge over Cachoeira River. The main thoroughfare starts sloping up soon after this access area as it bends to the left towards the core of the favela and the *praça*. Within this small area we counted 27 persons (25 adults and two children) of which nine were walking (eight adults and one child), 13 adults and one child were socializing (six standing up; eight sitting), three adults were observing the activity in the street together (two standing up; one sitting), and one adult was working as a seller outside his store.

The second behavioral map was done at the *praça*, an irregular triangular-shaped open space with approximately 20,000 square feet. The Favela Bairro project had upgraded it by providing curbs and sidewalks, storm water drainage, and a few benches and tables around the edges which defined "sub-spaces" mostly in the shade. The square's edges are defined by residential and mixed-use buildings, a couple of small stores and bars, and small public facilities: a day-care center and a primary school run by the city, a police station, and the residents' association which shares a three-story building with private educational facilities on top, the highest building in the square (Figures 6.7 and 6.8). On the same Sunday afternoon, during our five-minute observation, we noted 45 persons using the *praça*: teenagers walking (16) and sitting down (2); children at play (8) and walking (4); and adults socializing standing up (6) and sitting (4), or simply observing passers by (four sitting down; one standing up).

Figure 6.7 Mata Matchado's Main *Praça*. *A partial view of the main praça, showing a three-story mixed-use building on the right, the primary school run by the city, and children escorted from the day-care center, on Thursday afternoon.*

115

Figure 6.8 Mata Machado's Main *Praça*. *At the main* praça, *older residents talking by the building holding the residents' association and the local offices of a social works foundation run by the state government, on Thursday afternoon.*

Source: Photo by V. del Rio

During other visits to Mata Machado during week days, we observed a similar pattern but with fewer people socializing and smaller groups overall. We observed more people doing errands, such as walking to and fro from shopping and work, and to and fro from school with their children. All small stores and service shops are open on weekdays, and one can find people using the public spaces for their professional activities, such as the two mechanics who mend cars parked in the main square, having appropriated part of it as their shop's territory. In one of the square's corners, the residents' association office seems to always attract people, since we observed people standing by its door, waiting or socializing, a number of times.

During our visits and behavioral observations we were never interrupted or suffered any hostile looks. In the few times that we had to identify ourselves and ask permission to take photos or observe groups in more detail, people were helpful and inviting.

These observations show that Mata Machado's public spaces are heavily utilized during the day for pedestrian circulation, socialization, and hanging out. The reasons for this high level of activity include:

1   strong social cohesion and sense of community;
2   users perceiving the public space as a safe haven;

Chapter 6: **LESSONS FROM A FAVELA**

3   lack of outdoor space inside their residences;

4   the settlement's morphology: a limited number of streets, irregular geometry, and numerous sub-spaces along the streets that can be appropriated for social uses;

5   limited local availability of formal recreational spaces (partially because the major space that is used as a soccer field was temporarily closed to serve the construction of a new school next to it).

Interviews

Twenty residents of Mata Machado participated in an in-depth interview about living there. They were selected randomly during site visits or from recommendations by other residents; 60 percent of the interviewees were men and 40 percent were women. All of the participants had lived in the favela for over 20 years, and 25 percent of them were born there. Most had moved there from other parts of Rio rather than migrating from rural areas or other cities.

Housing Characteristics and Satisfaction

About half of the participants in the interviews lived in houses within Mata Machado, while the others were living in apartments or renting parts of houses. The definition of a house in the favela is confusing because of the organic relationships among residences. In most cases, the resident or a family member owned the place where they were living. Three-fourths of the households had children. Half of the residents lived in households of three to five people, a third of the residents lived in households from 6 to 10 people, and the remaining households contained up to 17 members. Similarly, other favelas and as existing demographic data shows, the residential density was substantial.

A set of four questions developed by Francescato *et al.* (1979) was used to measure housing satisfaction. Ninety percent of the residents said they were either satisfied or very satisfied living in Mata Machado. Ninety percent also said that they had no plans to leave the favela or planned to live there forever; a one resident noted "I will move only if I win the lottery." They were then asked whether if they moved, would they go to another community like this one? Forty percent of the residents said they would move to a similar type of community, while the remaining respondents were divided with some saying they would move to a rural area rather than continuing to live in Rio. Furthermore, 75 percent of the residents said they would recommend living here to family or friends.

The residents were asked a series of questions about their perception of safety in the favela. All of the residents said they felt safe living in the community, and most of them felt very safe living there; as one of the residents said, "one can leave a kid tp play in the street around here." They felt safe when they are alone in the community both during the day and at night. In addition, all of the residents believed the favela was safe compared to other communities in the city. Our team shared the perception of safety during our field work, and existing data confirm that Mata Machado has very low crime and drug related problems.

Overall, the responses to these questions show high levels of residential satisfaction. The residents live with high housing density, but they are very satisfied with their living conditions and feel safe living in their homes and community.

Community

Two types of information were collected about community issues from the interviews. The first set of questions examined residents' behavior in the community. This included questions about where people went and the types of activities they performed. The second set of questions examined residents' psychological sense of community. These questions were based on the McMillan and Chavis (1986) model of sense of community and included measures of people's emotional connection to the community and their ability to influence and work with their neighbors. In addition, behavioral observations were used to document the use of public spaces in the favela.

The first set of behavioral questions about the community examined where people interacted. When asked "which places in the community do you usually go to," about half of the participants mentioned public open spaces such as the *praça*, the open spaces, and thoroughfares. The remaining responses were divided into private places (people's homes), public indoor places (such as temples and community centers), and commercial places (primarily bars, which were both indoor and spilled out into the streets). When asked where do people from the community usually meet, the responses were fairly similar, with half of the residents mentioning public open spaces and the remaining responses split between public indoor places and commercial places. When people were asked where they normally meet friends, the two primary answers were in public open spaces and private homes.

The second set of community behavior questions examined the types and locations of various activities. Most (70 percent) of people's leisure activities occur indoors either at home or at church. These activities included watching TV, arts and crafts, and socializing with others. Outdoor leisure activities included socializing with others in public spaces or spending time at the beach, forest, or soccer field. About half of the residents attend church regularly and about one-third of them participate in other church activities. Their churches are either inside of the favela or next to the community within walking distance. About one-third of the residents either participate in the residents' association or have participated in the past. The fact that the residents' association charges a modest annual fee may explain the low participation rate. In addition, the favela residents trust that the residents' association is taking care of the community's problems, a fact proved by Mata Machado's history, so they feel less need to participate actively. Seventy-five percent of the residents have children. Most of the children attend school near the favela or in outside districts. Almost all of the children play in the favela, either in public spaces (such as the street or soccer field) or at the homes of friends.

The results from the interviews were confirmed by the behavioral observations. There was a substantial amount of social activity in the streets and public spaces. The amount of public social activity was significantly more in the favela than in many residential areas throughout the city, and certainly in most residential gated communities. Many of the community gathering places were outdoor public spaces or bars and restaurants that were open to the street. Overall, these behavior measures show a community where most residents socialize within the community and are regularly involved in community activities.

The interview contained a series of questions examining the residents' psychological sense of community. Most of the residents (75 percent) felt that the people in the community are like a big family; in the words of one resident, "nobody moves from here . . . we all know each other." All of the residents believed they had friends they could count on in the community, and most felt they had many friends they could count on. About two-thirds of the residents believed they could have an influence on what happens in the community. Less than half of them agreed that they often get together with neighbors to solve community problems. The reasons for not working regularly with neighbors on community problems included dislike of getting involved in politics, lack of important community problems, and belief that others were in charge of solving the problems. Almost 90 percent of the residents felt emotionally connected to the community. Overall, these results demonstrate a strong psychological sense of community among the residents of the favela.

Environmental Sustainability
One important part of environmental sustainability is related to transportation issues. Results of the interviews showed that only 25 percent of participants owned cars. When asked what type of transportation they used most frequently all participants said buses. For shopping, only 20 percent usually shop within or near their community. Most of them regularly travel to large supermarkets in other parts of the city because they are cheaper. Many said that they wished there was a large supermarket near Mata Machado. Most of them take the bus for this shopping trip, although some residents share with friends. About two-thirds of the residents get to work via the bus, while the remaining walk to work. When recreating outside the favela, about two-thirds of them use buses, with the remainder either walking or driving.

Observations and analysis of the physical aspects of the favela were used to examine issues of environmental sustainability. Evidently, due to poverty, their use of energy and other resources is relatively low. Development in the community is compact with high residential densities, and a mix of land use including residences, small retail, service shops, backyard family run industries, small shrines, and a handful of public buildings. Due to its compact development and morphological conditions, the most popular means of transportation within Mata Machado is walking; some residents use bicycles and small motorbikes, which became a popular taxi service in many Rio's favelas. Bus routes to downtown and to Barra da Tijuca, (where many residents shop and work) serve Estrada de Furnas and stop at the entrance to Mata Machado, easily reached on foot from all parts of the favela.

Although there is not large park within the favela, residents use the natural forested areas surrounding Mata Machado and the Floresta da Tijuca national park for recreation. The favela has numerous small public spaces, most simply a "spontaneous" widening of the thoroughfares, some trees and, of course, the popular central *praça*. There are a number of infrastructure problems, the the most serious being the lack of sewage treatment since the pipes installed by the city continues to pump into the local river (Figure 6.9). Residents recognize pollution of the river as a problem but are also cognizant that they are in the hands of the ever-changing city and state politics for a definite solution. Garbage is not much of a problem, since the city collects it on a regular basis, although they depend on the residents to bring their garbage to containers close to a thoroughfare that can be served by trucks. Unfortunately, the river still serves as a dump site for some.

Overall, Mata Machado receives a mixed evaluation on environmental sustainability. Residents live in a compact development and rely on buses or walking to reach places. For a long time now, the favela has not expanded into the surrounding natural environment, something that is controlled to some extent by the community itself.

Figure 6.9 The River Cachoeira in Mata Machado. *The river Cachoeira runs through Mata Machado, next to Estrada de Furnas. Despite the sewage and storm water collection systems installed in the favela, they never were connected to the city's regional system and still flow into the river.*

Source: Photo by V. del Rio

Residents' Worldview

Geertz (1978) defines worldview as the set of moral, ethical, and esthetic values of a given social group. Because it is an essential part of human culture, understanding the worldview of a particular social group can help to explain the behaviors, cognitions, and attitudes that shape the group's social lives. When a social group is composed of individuals with different worldviews, conflict is inevitable. On the other hand, when a social group shares the same worldview, their aspirations, expectations, and responses to daily difficulties function as social cement; the place they live is perceived as supportive of an effective community.

In Mata Machado, there was a strong level of agreement with the three interview questions dealing with the expectations that respondents had for themselves and for their children: (1) What would constitute a better life for you? (2) How would you like your children to be living ten years from now? and (3) What can you do to reach this goal?

Most respondents (45 percent) gave a strong value to dignifying work as a means of enrichment, not only from an economic but a moral point of view. To the residents, a man's dignity is demonstrated through his work, and future success is related to a secure job position and ethical political leaders – 25 percent of respondents stressed the importance of making the right political choices. For their children, the residents of Mata Machado talk about continuity. They wish their children will follow their ideas and continue their life projects, completing to build the life that the older residents initiated when they moved to the area. They expect their children to reach their parents' goals by means of a quality education that will guarantee access to work (50 percent of responses). In the same way, residents also expressed the importance of communicating with their children and being their role models as a means to complement the education they obtain from school (40 percent of respondents).

The fact that their favela had never been razed by the authorities appeared in almost all respondents' answers (80 percent) to these three questions as an important factor in generating a strong community, in providing continuity to their children's education and as a foundation for the search for a dignified job. They recognize their community as a place that provides the security and support necessary to support a tranquil conviviality and prepare the lives of the future generations.

Overall Evaluation of the Favela
The residents were asked to list three things that they most liked and disliked about their community. Among the things they liked, the most frequent responses were the sense of community among residents, the natural environment surrounding the favela, and the tranquility of the place. Other positive responses include the community organization, safety, transportation, and their dwelling. The primary dislikes that residents had about the favela related to the lack of services which the public sector should be providing for (such as sewage and water, health centers, and schools) and the lack of private facilities within the favela (such as markets, pharmacy, theater, and bank). Other negative responses include inadequate bus connections, social issues, and maintenance problems.

Conclusions

A favela is a good example of viewing livability from a transactional perspective that focuses on the relationship or fit between people and their environment; it is a highly livable environment. The results of our study in Mata Machado show high levels of housing satisfaction and perceived safety, a strong sense of community, a vibrant social system, and a sustainable lifestyle. From a sustainability perspective, the favela is a compact and dense environment with mixed land uses; it has natural areas within and surrounding the community; and the residents rely on sustainable transportation approaches.

As in other favelas, in Mata Machado the first settlers faced many difficult challenges, and since they lacked alternatives they joined together to take control of the situation. Over the years, the residents created physical and social systems that provide a livable environment that is responsive to the residents' needs, because it evolved as a reflection of those needs. It is also a sustainable environment because the residents have limited choices – they are poor and their development has been constrained. By working with the limitations of social, economic, and environmental forces, the residents have created a livable environment that coexists well with the surrounding environment. In a similar way, the residents developed a highly cohesive community because of their needs for social support, safety, and protection from external forces.

A favela is not a designed environment, but an evolving one. In Mata Machado, the residents constructed their homes over several decades using vernacular architecture, available materials, and the desires and abilities of the residents. They have created an environment that uniquely matches their needs, even though they are poor and have often faced external resistance rather than support. In the process of creating their environment, the *favelados* created cohesive social and organizational systems to support the construction process, provide safety and social support to residents, and deal with the external environment. The physical and social environments were created together in the same process, mutually reinforcing each other during the development of the settlement.

The result of this development process is a favela that provides satisfying housing to low-income people, safety and social support for the residents, and a strong community system. What the place lacks and the primary problems for residents are things outside their control. It lacks adequate infrastructure like sewage treatment, because the government was unwilling to provide it. It lacks sufficient commercial development, because the population in Mata Machado is too small to support large stores by itself.

In some ways, the development of Mata Machado seems to be the opposite of New Urbanism or of several of the livability guidelines developed by planners and designers. These rules are based on "the belief on the power of design" (Brower 2005); an assumption that if developers follow the "right" procedures, then residents will have a livable environment with high levels of housing satisfaction, safety, community, and sustainability. Our study suggests that while a favela has physical qualities that would probably not be recognized by new urbanists, it is able to create a highly livable environment without the qualities they say every city should have. Rather than have experts tell them how to live, residents of the favela create a livable environment that is congruent with their unique personal, social, cultural, and environmental situation. It is the creation process that helped to develop the environment and social system that makes the favela such a strong community and a livable environment.

Acknowledgments

The authors would like to thank architect Rodrigo Sgarbi for drawing the base maps and for his help in the field studies. We are also indebted to Professor Sidney Brower for his comments on an earlier draft.

Notes

1. The AIA's *Livability 101: What Makes a Community Livable* (2005) is available from http://www.aia.org/liv2_template.cfm?pagename=liv_liv101 (retrieved on 08/15/08); the Smart Growth Network's *Getting to Smart Growth – 100 Policies for Implementation* (volume I, 2002; volume II, 2003) are available upon request from the International City/County Management Association (www.icma.org); the Local Government Commission is at www.lgc.org; the APA's criteria for great neighborhoods is cited in Mark Hinshaw's article "Great Neighborhoods" in *Planning* magazine, January 2008.
2. In a personal communication, Sidney Brower (by email, 9/2/09) rightly suggests that the common interests of a community may "derive specifically from living together (for example companionship or good neighborliness). People who live in the same place may or may not have strong place-based interests (may not be good neighbors), or they may also have additional interests in common (such as a church membership or lifestyle)."

Chapter 6: LESSONS FROM A FAVELA

3   For the origins, dynamics, and main aspects of favelas in Rio see, for instance: Perlman 1976, Pino 1997, Neuwith 2005, and Fabricius 2008. On the formation and evolution of the favela as a sociological representation see Valladares 2005.
4   Rocinha is one of the cases studies in R. Neuwith's book "Shadow Cities" (2005).
5   Research results quoted in an article published by the newspaper *O Globo*, 08/21/2007, page 16.
6   For an account of the evolution of state policies and programs for low-income housing see Azevedo (1999).
7   See Instituto Brasileiro de Geografia e Estetistica http://www.ibge.gov.br and http://www.armazemdedados.rio.rj.gov.br (access on 5/18/11).
8   See, for instance, the state police official website at http://upprj.com. Christopher Gaffney, a visiting professor at the Federal University of Niteroi – Brazil, has an interesting article on the UPPs at www.geostadia.com/2010/08/unidades-de-policia-pacificadora-police.html (access on 5/18/11).
9   The data on real-estate prices is from the newspaper *O Globo*. See http://oglobo.globo.com/rio/mat/2010/05/29/imoveis-em-favelas-com-upp-sobem-ate-400-916732643.asp (access on 5/19/2011).
10 Research contracted by O Globo newspaper from the Instituto Brasileiro de Pesquisa Social and published in January 2010. Downloadable from http://www.ibpsnet.com.br/v1/index.php?option=com_content&view=category&layout=blog&id=34&Itemid=57 (access on 5/18/2011).
11 In August 26, 2009 the Orkut community for Mata Machado had 166 registered members.

References

Altman, I. and Rogoff, B. (1987) "World views in psychology: trait, interactional, organismic, and transactional perspectives," in I. Altman and D. Stokols (eds.) *Handbook of Environmental Psychology*, volume 1: 7–40, New York: Wiley-Interscience.

AIA – American Institute of Architects (2005). *Livability 101: What Makes a Community Livable*, http://www.aia.org/liv2_template.cfm?pagename=liv_liv101 (retrieved on 08/15/08).

Amerigo, M. and Aragones, J. (1997) "A theoretical and methodological approach to the study of residential satisfaction," *Journal of Environmental Psychology* 17: 47–57.

Azevedo, S. (1990) "Housing policy in Brazil: 1964–1986," paper presented in the Housing Debates/Urban Challenges Conference, Paris.

Bell, P., Greene, T., Fisher, J., and Baum, A. (2001) *Environmental Psychology*, 5th edition, Mahwah, NJ: Lawrence Erlbaum Associates.

Berke, P., Godschalk, D., and Kaiser, E. (2006) *Urban Land Use Planning*, 5th edition, Chicago, IL: University of Illinois Press.

Bressi, T.W. (1994) "Planning the American Dream," in P. Katz (ed.) *The New Urbanism: Toward an Architecture of Community*, New York: McGraw Hill.

Brower, S. (1996) *Good Neighborhoods: A Study of In-town and Suburban Residential Environments*, Westport, CN: Praeger.

Brower, S. (2005) "Community-generating neighborhoods," in B. Martens and A. Alexander (eds.) *Designing for Social Innovation: Planning, Building, Evaluating*, Cambridge, MA: Hogrefe and Huber.

Brown, B. and Cropper, V. (2001) "New urban and standard suburban subdivisions: evaluating psychological and social goals," *Journal of the American Planning Association* 67(4), 402–19.

Cavallieri, F. and Oliveira, S. (2006) *A Melhoria das Condições de Vida dos Habitantes de Assentamentos Precarios do Rio de Janeiro – Uma Avaliação Preliminar da Nota 11 dos Objetivos do Milenio.* Rio Estudos # 234. Rio de Janeiro: Instituto Pereira Passos/Secretaria de Urbanismo, Prefeitura da Cidade do Rio de Janeiro.

Cavallieri, F. and Lopes, G.P. (2008) *Indice de Desenvolvimento Social – Comparando as Realidades Microurbanas da Cidade do Rio de Janeiro.* Rio de Janeiro: Instituto Pereira Passos, Prefeitura da Cidade do Rio de Janeiro.

Cunha, M.B.A.M. da (2002) "Perfil sócio econômico das favelas da cidade do Rio de Janeiro," paper presented at the 15th ENESTE – Meeting of Students of Statistics, Natal RN, Brazil, July 2000. Online. Available HTTP: http://www.iets.org.br/biblioteca (accessed 10 August 2008).

Del Rio, V. (2005) "Favelas," in R. Caves (ed.) *Encyclopedia of the City*, Abingdon: Routledge.

Del Rio, V. (2009) "Introduction: historical background," in V. del Rio and W. Siembieda (eds.) *Contemporary Urbanism in Brazil: Beyond Brasilia,* Gainesville, FL: University Press of Florida.

Duarte, C.R. et al. (1995) *Diagnóstico de Mata Machado – Programa Favela-Bairro.* Project report. Rio de Janeiro: IPLANRIO, Prefeitura da Cidade do Rio de Janeiro.

Duarte, C.R. and Brasileiro, A. (2001) "A volta da política da bica d'água: uma experiência de urbanização de favela no Rio de Janeiro," in A. Martins and M. de Carvalho (eds.) *Novas Visões: Fundamentando o Espaço Arquitetônico e Urbano,* Rio de Janeiro: Book Link.

Duarte, C.R. and Magalhães, F. (2009) "Upgrading squatter settlements into city neighborhoods: the Favela-Bairro program in Rio de Janeiro," in V. del Rio and W. Siembieda (eds.) *Contemporary Urbanism in Brazil: Beyond Brasilia,* Gainesville, FL: University Press of Florida.

Dutton, J. (2000) *New American Urbanism: Re-forming the Suburban Metropolis*, Milan: Skira.

Evans, G., Lepore, S., and Schroeder, A. (1996) "The role of interior design elements in human responses to crowding," *Journal of Personality and Social Psychology* 70: 41–6.

Fabricius, D. (2008) "Resisting representation: the informal geographies of Rio de Janeiro," *Harvard Design Magazine* 28: 4–17.

Fernandes, E. (2007) "Constructing the 'right to the city' in Brazil," *Social Legal Studies* 16(2): 201–19.

Francescato, G., Weidemann, S., Anderson, J., and Chenoweth, R. (1979) *Residents' Satisfaction in HUD-Assisted Housing: Design and Management Factors,* Washington, DC: US Department of Housing and Urban Development.

Frank, L., Engelke, P., and Schmid, T. (2003) *Health and Community Design,* Washington, DC: Island Press.

Geertz, C. (1977) *The Interpretation of Cultures*, New York: Basic Books.

Gutberlet, J. and Hunter, A. (2008) "Social and environmental exclusion at the edge of São Paulo, Brazil," *Urban Design International* 13: 3–20.

Jabareen, Y. (2006) "Sustainable urban forms: their typologies, models, and concepts," *Journal of Planning Education and Research* 26: 38–52.

Katz. P. (1994) "Preface," in P. Katz (ed.) *The New Urbanism: Toward an Architecture of Community*, New York: McGraw Hill.

Chapter 6: **LESSONS FROM A FAVELA**

Kuo, F., Bacaicoa, M., and Sullivan, W. (1998) "Transforming inner-city landscapes: trees, sense of safety, and preference," *Environment and Behavior* 30: 28–59.

Leeds, A. (1969) "The significant variables determining the character of squatter settlements," *America Latina* 12(3): 44–86.

Leeds, A. and Leeds, E. (1978) *A Sociologia do Brasil Urbano*, Rio de Janeiro: Zahar.

Lopes, G.P. and Cavallieri, F. (2006) *Favelas Cariocas: Comparação de Areas Ocupadas 1999–2004*. Rio. Estudos # 233. Rio de Janeiro: Instituto Pereira Passos/Secretaria de Urbanismo, Prefeitura da Cidade do Rio de Janeiro.

McMillan, D. and Chavis, D. (1986) "Sense of community: a definition and theory," *American Journal of Community Psychology* 14(1): 6–23.

Mangin, W. (1967) "Latin American squatter settlements: a problem and a solution," *Latin American Research Review* 2: 65–98.

Nasar, J. and Julian, D. (1995) "The psychological sense of community in the neighborhood," *Journal of the American Planning Association* 61(2): 178–84.

Neuwith, R. (2000) "Letter from Brazil," *The Nation* 271(2): 29–31.

Neuwith, R. (2005) *Shadow Cities: A Billion Squatters, a New Urban World,* New York: Routledge.

Patterson, P. and Chapman, N. (2004) "Urban form and older residents' service use, walking, driving, quality of life, and neighborhood satisfaction," *American Journal of Health Promotion* 19(1): 45–52.

Perlman, J. (1976) *The Myth of Marginality: Urban Poverty and Politics in Rio de Janeiro*, Berkeley, CA: University of California Press.

Perlman, J. (2003) "The chronic poor in Rio de Janeiro: what has changed in 30 years?" paper presented at the Conference on Chronic Poverty in Manchester, England, April 7–9, 2003. Online. Available HTTP: http//www.megacitiesproject.org/Chronic_Poor_in_Rio_30years.pdf (accessed 24 August 2009).

Perlman, J. (2010) *Favela – Four Decades of Living on the Edge in Rio de Janeiro*, Oxford: Oxford University Press.

Pino, J.C. (1997). *Family and Favela: The Reproduction of Poverty in Rio de Janeiro*, Westport, Conn.: Greenwood.

Sanders, I.T. (1966). *The Community: An Introduction to a Social System,* New York: Ronald Press.

Soares, F.F. (1999) A favela e a floresta: um estudo das relações entre homem e meio-ambiente – O caso Mata Machado, unpublished MSc thesis, Rio de Janeiro: Programa de Pos-Graduação em Urbanismo, Faculdade de Arquitetura e Urbanismo, Universidade Federal do Rio de Janeiro.

Talen, E. (1999) "Sense of community and neighborhood form: an assessment of the social doctrine of New Urbanism," *Urban Studies* 36(8): 1361–79.

Taylor, R., Gottfredson, S. and Brower, S. (1984) "Understanding block crime and fear," *Journal of Research in Crime and Delinquency* 21: 303–31.

Turner. J. (1969) "Uncontrolled urban settlement: problems and policies," in G. Breeze (ed.) *The City in Newly Developed Countries: Readings on Urbanism and Urbanization,* Englewood Cliffs, NJ: Lawrence Ehrlbaum

Ulrich, R. (1984) "View through a window may influence recovery from surgery," *Science* 224: 420–1.

Unger, D. and Wandersman, A. (1985) "The importance of neighbors: the social, cognitive, and affective components of neighboring," *American Journal of Community Psychology* 13(2): 139–69.

Valladares, L. do P. (2005) *A Invenção da Favela: Do Mito de Origem a Favela.com*, Rio de Janeiro: Editora FGV.

Wilson-Doenges, G. (2000) "An exploration of sense of community and fear of crime in gated communities," *Environment and Behavior* 32(5): 597–611.

Chapter 7

LIVING DOWNTOWN IN THE TWENTY-FIRST CENTURY: PAST TRENDS AND FUTURE POLICY CONCERNS

Eugénie L. Birch

Professor and Chair of Urban Research, Department of City and Regional Planning
University of Pennsylvania

Over time, public and private officials have tried to re-invent downtowns, employing a wide variety of revitalization tactics.[1] Presently, many are enamored with finding new residential uses for old buildings or precincts.[2] They have focused on housing in order to address a longstanding problem: the loss of economic activity in their central business districts as offices and retailers relocated to the suburbs. In this effort, they have adopted the mantra of fostering a "24-hour downtown" to animate their barren blocks.

Many downtowns, especially those in the Northeast and Midwest, have assets that support residential use. Among them are: a stock of older, architecturally interesting buildings (offices, warehouses), one or more natural features (riverfronts, canals), a rich cultural heritage (museums, art galleries, bookstores), a strong entertainment sector (restaurants, night clubs, sports stadiums and arenas), and specialized services (health, higher education). They also have social capital or leaders such as a relatively new cadre of downtown advocates, exemplified by business improvement district directors. Finally, they have nearby jobs. Less-endowed downtowns encounter difficulties in pursuing a residential strategy and may, in fact, be misguided in trying such an approach. Promoting downtown housing even in the most amenable places requires having strong, proximate employment and providing amenities and attracting such supportive services as grocery and dry cleaning establishments not ordinarily found in downtowns.[3]

Downtown Living as a Niche Market

Downtown living represents an emerging alternative to suburban choices.[4] While the population is small and, in fact, not comparable to that of the suburbs, an analysis of metropolitan data reveals that downtown living represents an important niche in the residential real estate market. It is located in a physically limited or bounded area. It is focused on a small place in a city, the traditional central business district and its environs. Being a specialized commodity, it does not, at this time, even constitute "citywide" living.[5] But in strong markets, it does have the potential for spillover effects. In Philadelphia, for example, the vibrant downtown housing market has stimulated residential growth in adjacent neighborhoods.

In contrast, the suburban scene encompasses a broad-gauged, unsegmented housing market in a loosely bounded physical area. Underlining these differences in scale and circumstances are dramatic variations in the number of units and growth rates between the two. Between 1970 and 2000, downtowns had a net gain of about 50,000 dwelling units (12 percent growth rate) while suburbs gained 15 million (61 percent increase). Even when downtown living increases as it has in the years since the 2000 Census, it has a long way to go to catch up with the suburbs.

Despite these figures, downtown living provides visible and tangible evidence of urban vitality that has important psychological and economic impacts. The occupation of vacant, centrally located buildings, the increased presence of people on formerly empty streets, and investment in supportive commercial activities and amenities all present worn-out downtowns in a new light. The presence of a new, highly-educated population has the potential to attract new "creative class" jobs. Downtowns are now "players" in the residential real estate market. And the real interest of downtown residential data is the trajectory of the trends in different cities and regions.

Studies on the Rise of Downtown Living

Since 1990, many have tracked the rise of downtown living, its strengths and, more recently, its pitfalls.[6] Journalists from individual cities first noted this trend in local newspapers. Later, analysts from the Brookings Institution and the Fannie Mae Foundation recorded the phenomenon more systematically. Academic researchers followed, assessing the topic in greater depth.[7] All left no doubt that the number of people living downtown had increased between 1990 and 2000. Census results for 2010 are not available at this writing, but other sources reveal a continuation of the trend. In fact, the 2008 financial crisis had a lesser effect on downtown than on suburban housing in some places.[8] These accounts documented growth in terms of population data and, to some extent, attempted to classify and explain the phenomenon. They profiled individual residents, highlighting their ages, household sizes, levels of education, and income but did not systematically evaluate these qualities. They did not detail downtowners as a group or fully illuminate the housing market they represented, nor did they explore the depth and extent of its growth. In general, they never looked farther back than 1990, nor did they pay attention to the range of cities beyond the largest places.

This chapter fills this vacuum for the 1970 to 2000 period. When the American Community Survey releases its census-tract level data, the author will update these findings. In the meantime, this discussion outlines general patterns. It explores US downtown development briefly, explaining the origins of today's residential approach, and delineates the methodological difficulties of defining downtowns. It focuses on the growth of the downtown residential market compared to cities, suburbs, regions, and the nation, offering an assessment of which cities and regions have attracted downtown residents. And it describes downtowners, their households, race, age, and education. Its most unique feature is to map the variegated character of downtowners' median income and overlays this analysis with race.

Chapter 7: **LIVING DOWNTOWN**

Understanding downtown residential patterns is useful to many involved in the contemporary policy arena. Local officials focused on the care and nurturing of downtowns have a direct interest because they are generally alert to new revitalization tactics, of which downtown housing is one. Environmentalists, smart growth advocates, and those warning of climate change view the growth of downtown residential areas as a viable alternative to suburban sprawl and an effective means of reducing greenhouse gas emissions. Checking greenfield development with office/warehouse conversions and urban infill are among the objectives that downtown housing meets. These topics have become especially important in light of rising fuel prices and the strong call for walkable cities from planners, developers, and others.[9] Economists involved in retooling the American economy by strengthening knowledge-based industries see downtown living as one element in a "creative cluster" strategy that matches high-value jobs to the young and well-educated, people for whom quality of life issues, often an urban lifestyle, are important.[10] Other interested groups include real estate entrepreneurs, chamber of commerce leaders, and such design professionals as historic preservationists and new urbanists, especially those involved in downtown HOPE VI projects.

Evolution of Today's Downtown Residential Trends

The movement of households into downtowns in the late twentieth century signifies a dramatic change in the land use patterns of these areas. Downtowns, labeled Central Business Districts (CBDs) in the mid-twentieth century, traditionally contained offices, large warehouses, and the occasional factory.[11] Downtown living was usually restricted to hotels, clubs with sleeping facilities, flophouses, and jails. The salient features of downtowns were: first, their economic dominance in their metropolitan areas, second, accessibility, third, high density development, and fourth, high land values and property assessments.

Downtowns peaked in the 1920s and then began to change.[12] Many CBD functions migrated to "uptowns" or "midtowns" within cities and, still later, these activities moved to "edge city" and "edgeless" city locations.[13] This movement accelerated in the postwar period, accompanied by the rise of suburbs facilitated by favorable tax and mortgage insurance practices and massive federal investment in the nation's interstate highway system.

By the late twentieth century, downtowns typically contained a cluster of signature or Class A office buildings, aligned in an identifiable skyline branding important corporations; masses of partially or under-occupied Class B and C buildings; and heavy doses of parking and discontinuous ground-floor retail located along key streets or in the lobbies of major office buildings. Adjacent to this core were warehouses and factories, often abandoned. In addition, larger downtowns had convention centers, associated hotels, and sports stadia. A few still hosted businessmen's clubs. Along with these features, many downtowns experienced retail remnants, especially the major department store, whose main facilities had moved to the outskirts. Detroit in the late 1980s is an extreme example: Hudson's Department Store, the Hilton Hotel, and multiple office buildings stood entirely empty; nearby the mirrored windows of the Renaissance Center, a 2.2 million square foot complex, opened in 1976, that drained any remaining office, retail, and hotel activities from the surrounding downtown, reflected this devastation as a three-mile elevated People Mover circled the area, linking a few active places like the old baseball stadium and the Renaissance Center.

From 1949 to the present, public officials and private investors have employed federal programs to buttress downtowns. At first, they used urban renewal along with subsidized interest programs – 221(d)(3) and 221(d)(4), the Internal Revenue Service, sanctioned private-activity bonds for specified redevelopment projects, and later turned to community development block grants and tax credits for historic preservation and low-income housing.[14] They sought to strengthen their downtowns with festival malls, stadiums, convention centers, hotels, housing, and other attractions.[15]

With regard to housing, cities employed public housing, urban renewal (with associated low-interest financing programs), and low-income housing tax credits to build more units located in or adjacent to downtown. In the late 1950s and early 1960s, several cities consciously deployed urban renewal funds to foster middle-income residential development as an alternative to the suburbs. Lower Manhattan (Manhattan Plaza), Midtown New York (Lincoln West), Boston (West End), Detroit (Lafayette Village), Philadelphia (Society Hill), San Francisco (Golden Gateway Center), and Los Angeles (Bunker Hill Towers) are examples of such practices. Often, these places provided the seeds of today's downtown housing resurgence. However, political opposition brought these projects to a screeching halt by the late 1960s.[16]

On the whole, the attempts to stem the outward movement of traditional downtown activities, especially offices, department stores, and hotels, largely failed. Today, for example, only 33 percent of the nation's office space is located in downtowns. Some downtowns have captured a larger percent – San Francisco, 72 percent; New York, 63 percent; Seattle, 57 percent; Chicago, 55 percent – and others much less – Miami has 12 percent; Houston, 21 percent; Philadelphia, 28 percent; Detroit, 32 percent; and Boston, 37 percent.[17]

Today, housing has become a critical piece of the evolving strategies for downtown revitalization. With abundant supplies of sound but underutilized properties, favorable transportation networks, and "character" – an ambience of density, mixed use, grittiness, and/or the possibility of unique dwelling units – many downtowns successfully compete with suburbs for certain consumers. In these circumstances, some view the residential approach as "a land use of last resort," while others label it the "SoHo Syndrome," an essential element of grass-roots, preservation-based activity that rejuvenates downtown districts.[18]

Tracking Downtown Residents

To assess the extent of current residential trends, the author employed data from the US Census Bureau to explore population and household growth rates and several demographic characteristics – race and ethnicity, age, education, labor force participation, and income – in three geographic areas: downtown, city, and suburbs. These characteristics were tracked from 1970 to 2000 in forty-five cities for forty-six downtowns chosen for their size and location from among the nation's 243 cities having a population of 100,000 or more.[19] The sample covers 37 percent of the most populous US cities (representing 59 percent of the nation's urban population), including 100 percent of the top ten, 62 percent of the top fifty, and 19 percent of the remainder (see Appendix A – Sample Cities). With regard to the four US Census regions, 11 percent of the downtowns are in the Northeast, 21 percent in the Midwest, 26 percent in the West, and 41 percent in the South. In terms of a region's urban population, the selected cities encompass 77 percent of the Northeast's total, 63 percent of the Midwest's, 54 percent of the South's, and 50 percent of the West's.

Deriving a spatial definition of "downtown" is the most challenging aspect of this research because no commonly accepted physical standard exists. Some equate downtowns with the Central Business District (CBD). (For several decades the US Bureau of the Census issued CBD data, simply designating one or two census tracts in selected cities; however, it discontinued this series in 1984.) Others have attempted to define downtowns as the area within a specified radius (one mile, one-half mile, etc.) from a city's so-called "100 percent corner," viewed as the highest-valued intersection in terms of real estate.[20] This concept poses difficulties when attempting a uniform application to different-sized cities. Even among the top 100 most populous cities, one-half mile from the "100 percent corner" in a physically small city can reach into its suburbs. In the end, the author relied on local knowledge and experience, asking public officials in the sample cities to define their own downtowns by census tracts as of 1999 to 2000. These boundaries are used as the basis of the time series dating back to 1970.[21] The author checked these definitions through field visits. [22]

The resulting sample yields downtowns that vary in population and geographic size. As a group, they provide a general view of downtown living and, individually (or grouped according to size or location), they demonstrate important variations. The sampled downtowns, whose populations range from 97,000 (Lower Manhattan) to 443 (Shreveport, Louisiana), fall into five population categories: Extra Large, 50,000 or more (11 percent of the sample); Large, 25,000–49,999 (13 percent of the sample); Medium, 10,000 to 24,999 (26 percent of the sample); Small, 5,000–9,999 (20 percent of the sample) and Extra Small, less than 5,000 (33 percent of the sample). Taken together they represent under 1 million people (470,000 households) in cities containing 39 million inhabitants surrounded by suburbs holding about 70 million residents.[23]

Downtowns in the sample range in size from almost seven square miles (Detroit) to under one-quarter square mile (Shreveport). Divided into four spatial categories, the sample contains 4 percent of downtowns five square miles or larger; 38 percent, 3 to 4.99 square miles; 38 percent, 1 to 2.99 square miles; and 18 percent under one square mile. All together, the sample downtowns cover 123 square miles and are located in cities covering approximately 8,000 square miles surrounded by 155,000 square miles of suburban territory.

Finally, the sample downtowns have variable densities, measured as the number of people per acre, ranging from slightly more than 2 (Jackson, Mississippi) to 76 (Lower Manhattan). Four percent of the downtowns have 50 or more people per acre. The building type accommodating such downtown densities is usually a multi-family structure, which could be a former office building or loft, an attached townhouse, or a new apartment building. Thirteen percent of downtowns have 20 to 49 people/acre; 18 percent, 10 to 19 people/acre; and 31 percent, 5 to 9 people/acre. Dwellings at these densities are most likely low-scale converted buildings – lofts, warehouses, office buildings – whose floor plates allow capacious dwellings prized by the young, highly-educated professionals who form the dominant group of downtown residents. Thirty-five percent of the downtowns sampled have population densities of fewer than five people per acre. This could encompass the single-family housing stock found in a historic district or in new construction on cleared or formerly-vacant sites. In addition, this density could also reflect a transition stage in which a former office or loft district could be in the process of being converted and therefore has few residents.

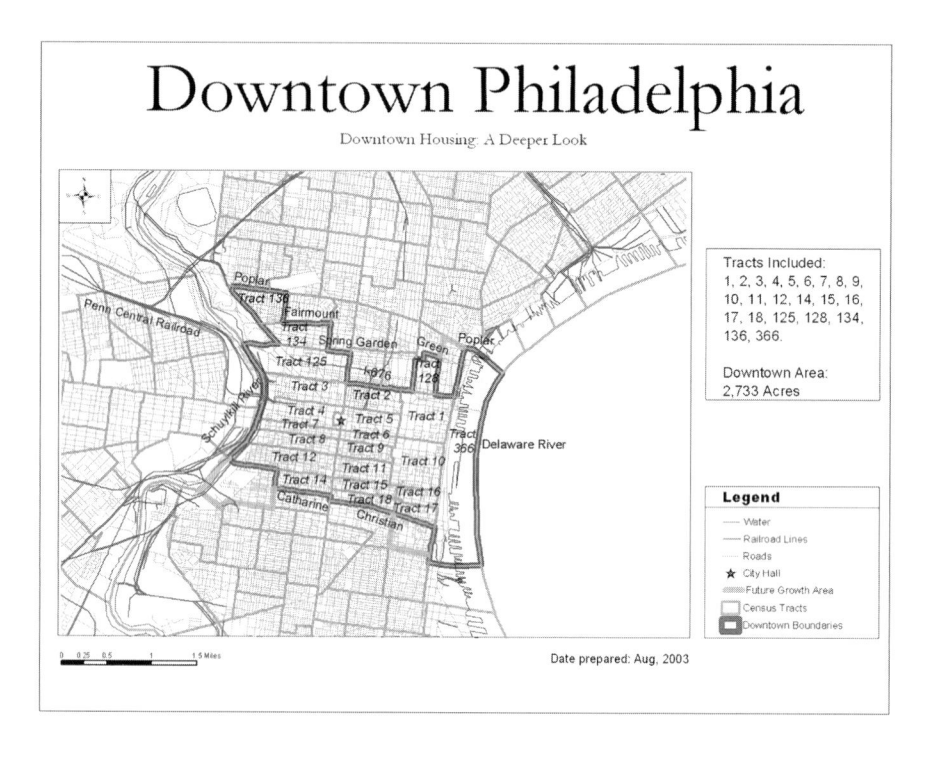

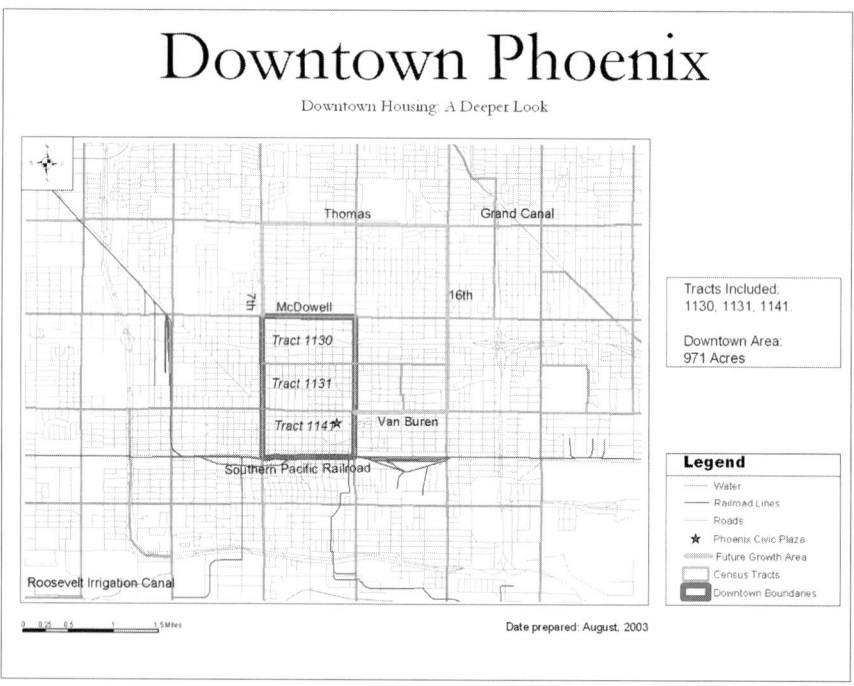

Figure 7.1 Downtown Philadelphia and Downtown Phoenix. *Downtowns vary in size, as Philadelphia and Phoenix demonstrate*

Chapter 7: **LIVING DOWNTOWN**

Downtown Population Growth

Between 1970 and 2000, downtown population declined slightly (–0.2 percent) from 934,060 to 931,814. Overall, 35 percent of the sample downtowns experienced some degree of growth, ranging from 2 percent to more than 200 percent. The remaining downtowns had losses from –0.4 percent to –67 percent. At the high end, Lower Manhattan added 37,000 residents, followed by Chicago (21,000), Los Angeles (14,000), and Seattle (10,000). At the low end, Detroit lost 31,000, followed by St. Louis (–15,000), Indianapolis (–9,500), and Orlando (–9,000). As downtown populations shifted, the population in the sample's cities grew 9 percent, their suburbs by 62 percent, and the nation by 37 percent.

While this chapter uses Census data from 1970 to 2000, recent evidence indicates that the impetus for downtown living has continued in the past eight years and is broadening. However, in the current housing crisis, developers in some cities have experienced and will continue to experience severe credit crunches, making multi-family investments more difficult. Nonetheless, in the first decade of the twenty-first century, downtown living is increasing in the sample cities and elsewhere. Data shows that Philadelphia is up 13 percent; Washington DC, 31 percent; San Diego, 68 percent; and Lower Manhattan, 145 percent.[24]

Population Growth by Decade

While the population data above provides a general assessment of change in downtown living, it misses an important part of the story, its volatility, that the following decade-by-decade analysis reveals. Downtown population declined by 11 percent in the 1970s, slowed its downslide in the 1980s, increasing by 0.4 percent, and turned around dramatically in the 1990s, exhibiting an 11 percent increase. And as the population of sample downtowns fluctuated wildly, their cities and suburbs exhibited different trends. The cities recorded a much slower rate of decline (–4 percent) than downtowns in the 1970s, had a much more substantial

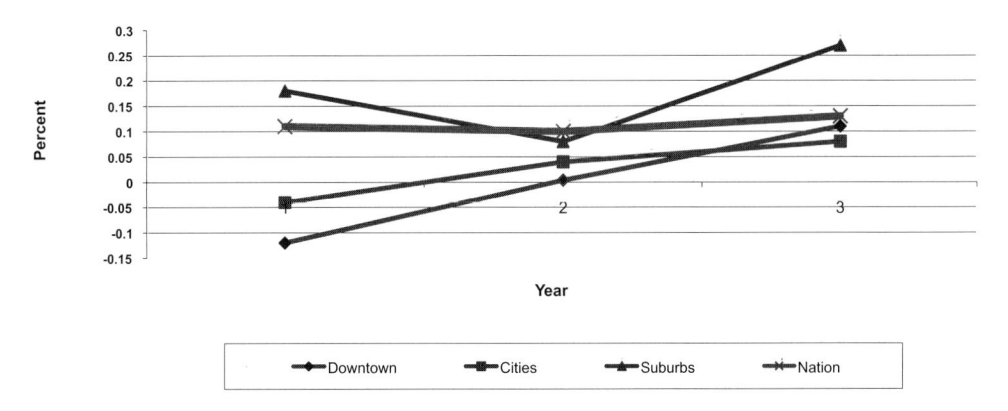

Figure 7.2 Comparative Population Growth Rates 1970–2000. *Comparative Downtown Growth Rates for Downtowns, Their Cities and Suburbs, and the Nation, 1970 to 2000*

turnaround (+4 percent) in the 1980s, and doubled that rate to 8 percent in the 1990s. In contrast, the suburbs had consistently positive growth (18 percent, 8 percent, and 27 percent) for these three decades. The national growth pattern was also positive in this period (11 percent, +10 percent, and +13 percent). Notably, *for the key decade, the 1990s, the downtown growth rate surpassed that of their cities.*

The 1970s were calamitous for most downtowns, as forty, or 87 percent of the sample, experienced decreasing populations.[25] By the 1980s, as the downward trend slowed, fewer downtowns – twenty-one, or 46 percent of the sample – decreased in population.[26] In the 1990s, the balance shifted. Only thirteen downtowns (28 percent of the sample) experienced decreases, and none more than 25 percent. At the same time, thiry-three places increased their downtown populations.[27]

This change-by-decade analysis illuminates three phenomena. First, 15 percent of the sample had losses in all three decades, while 11 percent had gains in each time period.[28] Second, the gains of the 17 percent of the downtowns showing great improvement (25 percent or more) in the 1990s are deceptive because in the previous decade, all but one had lost population in amounts ranging from –18 percent to –7 percent.[29] Third, in 40 percent of the sample, some gains included an increase of the incarcerated.[30]

Timing, Size and Other Characteristics of the Growth of Downtown Living

The decade-by-decade analysis also highlights the variable downtown development histories among cities. Some places, such as Des Moines, Indianapolis, and Minneapolis, have gains in one decade and losses in another. Others, such as Norfolk and Albuquerque, display enormous percentage gains on small numerical bases. *However, the most important finding is evidence of a much earlier beginning to today's downtown living trend than previously believed.* Forty percent of the sample experienced continuous positive growth since the 1980s. Of these, 11 percent began their increases in the 1970s. The remaining breakdown is as follows: 31 percent experienced growth between 1990 and 2000, 16 percent suffered losses in all three decades, and 13 percent had losses in the 1990s but earlier growth.

Changes in the Average-Size Downtown

The growth patterns reported above yield important changes among the array of sample downtowns. The average size of larger places rose but their number fell. The smaller places also increased average size and became more numerous. This phenomenon is best observed within the size-categories outlined earlier in the study (Extra Large, 50,000+; Large, 25,000–49,999; Medium, 10,000–24,999; Small, 5,000–9,999; and Extra Small, less than 5,000). Among the Extra Large downtowns, the average population rose 22 percent to 80,488, up from 66,231, but the number of downtowns in this category decreased by 20 percent. The average population among Extra Small downtowns increased 25 percent, rising from 2,800 to 3,500, and the number of Extra Small downtowns increased 56 percent after Austin, Colorado Springs, Des Moines, Lexington, and Phoenix experienced city-wide population losses.

Chapter 7: **LIVING DOWNTOWN**

Implications of Population and its Changes for Downtown Living

This assessment of population growth suggests existing and potential concerns for downtowns and their leaders. For example, high-growth-rate-low-population downtowns confront different issues than high-population-low-growth-rate downtowns. Contrast downtown Albuquerque, whose 46 percent increase in the 1990s made it the fifth-fastest growing place in the sample, but whose low number of residents (1,800) placed it second from the bottom in population, with downtown Philadelphia, a downtown with a slow growth rate (5 percent) but the presence of nearly 80,000 residents. Albuquerque has difficulties in attracting such support services as a grocery store or dry cleaner, while Philadelphia spends its time mediating between the often-at-odds-needs of residents and such other users as office workers and tourists.

The population trends not only describe current conditions but also hint at the future. Today, most downtowners live in three regions: the Northeast Corridor, the Midwest Circle, and the California Coast. Almost two-thirds (62 percent) are in the sample's ten most populous downtowns, and nearly half are in only six places: Lower Manhattan, Boston, Philadelphia, Midtown Manhattan, Chicago, and San Francisco. However, if up-and-coming cities, those that added 3,000 or more inhabitants in the 1990s (e.g. Seattle, Portland, Atlanta, and Dallas), maintain current growth rates, they will either join or surpass others currently having high concentrations. For example, if Seattle extends its 1990s growth rate for another ten years, it could move from 22,000 to 38,000, and if Detroit stays on its current track, it will lose about another 1,000 residents, falling to 36,000.

Looking at the performance of individual downtowns by decade underscores the variability among places and provides a timeline and geography of downtown living. Most important, it provides a platform for understanding another critical point in the downtown living story: *that the population growth rate was lower than the household growth rate between 1970 and 2000,* as will be seen in the next section.

Growth of Downtown Households

More important than the minimal population change (–0.2 percent) between 1970 and 2000 was the accompanying 8 percent increase in the number of downtown households (and of occupied housing units), from 435,159 to 469,366, in the sample cities. *Households*, not population, drive the housing market and define demand that, if sufficiently strong, stimulates an increase in the supply of dwellings.[31] The growth in households (and occupied housing units) demonstrates that more consumers are attracted to downtowns today than in the past. In many cases, the increased demand for housing matched decreased calls for Class B or C office buildings, warehouses, and factories, making them logical candidates for residential adaptive reuse.

Between 1970 and 2000, slightly more downtowns (39 percent) experienced household increases than did those (35 percent) that experienced rises in population. Their growth rates ranged from 1 percent to 94 percent. The remaining downtowns had losses from –3 percent to –47 percent. Those with the greatest gains were Lower Manhattan (+20,000), Chicago (+19,000), Boston (+9,000), and Philadelphia (+8,000), while Detroit (–15,000), St. Louis (–4,000), and San Antonio (–3,000) had the greatest losses.

By decade, household growth also had a slightly different pattern from that of population. In the 1970s, downtown households declined 3 percent (population fell 11 percent); in the 1980s, they dropped 2 percent (though population increased 0.4 percent); then, in the 1990s, their 14 percent growth rate surpassed the 11 percent population increase.

These trends played out in the timing of household increases in individual downtowns as well. A slightly higher percentage of downtowns sustained household increases (13 percent) than population increases (11 percent) for all three decades. However, while they fell behind population in the 1980s (17 percent of downtowns increased households compared to 29 percent of downtowns increasing population), in the key 1990s decade, the percent of downtowns with household increases (43 percent) jumped ahead of downtowns with population rises (31 percent). As with population, household growth rates for cities (39 percent) and suburbs (98 percent) far surpassed those of downtowns.

Nationally, downtown household patterns parallel those of population, but the level of concentration is slightly higher, as more households (66 percent) than population (62 percent) are in the Northeast Corridor, Midwest Circle, and California Coast. The line-up is also different. For example, Philadelphia, Chicago, and Midtown Manhattan lead in households, while Lower Manhattan, Boston, and Philadelphia have the highest populations.

This phenomenon underlines the importance of scrutinizing households, not only population, in studying the rise of downtown living. This is exemplified by several downtowns in the top ten that have higher household than population growth rates including Philadelphia (households +20 percent, population –2 percent), Baltimore (+15 percent, –13 percent), Boston (+25 percent, +2 percent), Lower Manhattan (+94 percent, +61 percent), and Chicago (+77 percent, +39 percent).[32]

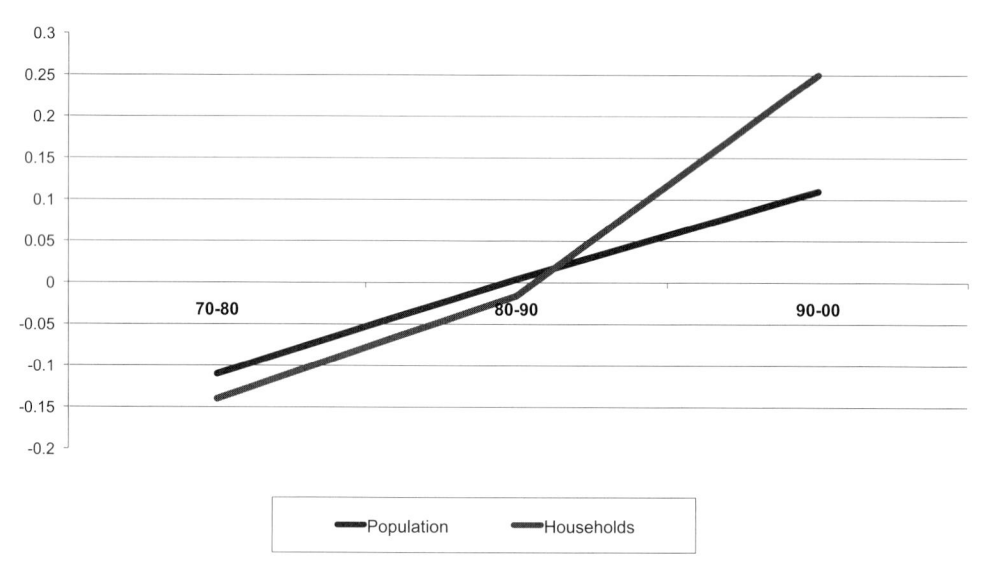

Figure 7.3 Household Growth Rates Pass Population Growth Rates in the 1990s.
Household Growth Rates Pass Population Growth Rates in the 1990s

Chapter 7: **LIVING DOWNTOWN**

Household Composition and Homeownership Rates

Besides the growth rates and amount, the type of household (family or non-family), its size (one-person, couples, presence of children), ownership patterns, race, age, level of education, and income are key market determinants of the demand for downtown dwelling units in terms of location, floor space, and amenities.

In 2000, 71 percent of downtown households were in non-families, compared to 41 percent in the cities and 29 percent in suburbs. (Half of the total downtown households are single-person.) Historically, downtowns have sheltered non-family households. Thirty years ago they were 61 percent of the total but had very different socio-economic characteristics. (The comparable figures in cities were 28 percent and 16 percent in suburbs.) Within non-families, the single-person component has declined considerably. In 1980, the first decade that the Bureau of the Census broke out elements of the non-family grouping, the single-person household was 84 percent of the non-family category; it is now 71 percent. The other component in this group, unrelated individuals living together, gained a greater share because it had a 44 percent growth rate in the past twenty years.

Within family households (29 percent of the total), the largest element is families without children (19 percent) in 2000. Of the 10 percent that are families with children, married couples are 5.4 percent and female-headed families are 4 percent.[33] Since 1970, fewer families are living downtown, female-headed families have held steady, and married couples without children have increased. Slightly countering this trend today are reports from several cities including Philadelphia that indicate an increase in children downtown.[34]

In looking at household composition in comparison to the rest of the city and the suburbs, the differences in the non-family and family components stand out. As Figure 7.4 demonstrates, downtowns are twice as likely to have non-families as the suburbs and 1.7 times

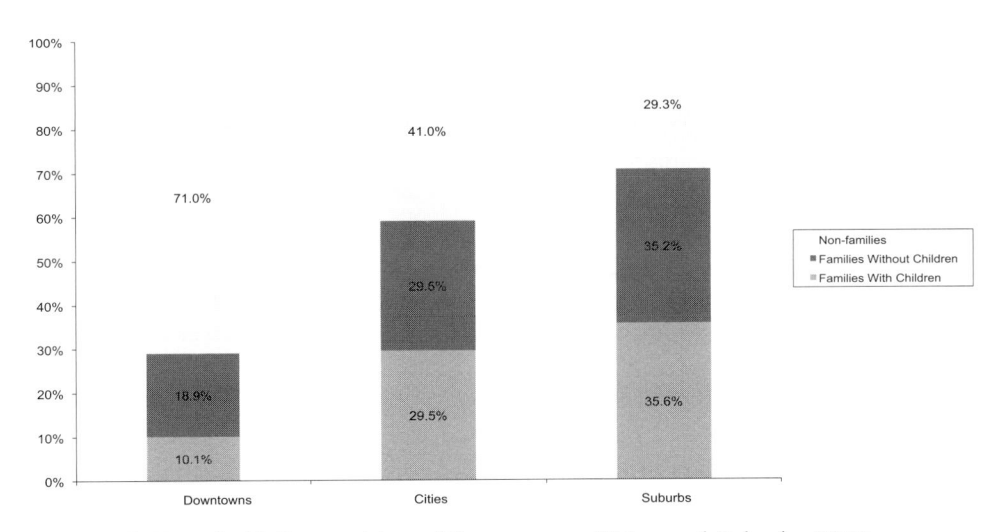

Figure 7.4 Household Composition of Downtowns, Cities, and Suburbs, 2000.
Household Composition: Downtown, City, and Suburb

as likely as cities. Downtowns have far fewer families with children; the suburban figure of 36 percent and the city figure of 29 percent highlight the low downtown figure of 10 percent.

As households and housing units had a 12 percent increase between 1970 and 2000, homeownership rates in the sample downtowns grew 145 percent, yielding twice as many homeowners in 2000 as in 1970. Although homeownership rates doubled by 2000, increasing from 10 percent to 22 percent, they still lagged their city (41 percent) and suburban (61 percent) counterpart rates. The majority of downtown households rent. And the downtown housing market has met this specialized demand by creating units suitable for small, childless households, often at suburban, garden apartment densities.

Racial and Ethnic Composition of Downtown Households

Downtown populations are in flux with regard to race and ethnicity. The racial composition in the downtowns presents a complicated picture, shaped, in part, by local conditions and, in part, by broader factors, including immigration and the location of jobs and housing units.

Between 1970 and 2000, as population grew moderately (4 percent), there were substantial changes among its components. Overall, the number of Whites fell 11 percent and African-Americans were down 16 percent. Making up the difference were Asians and "Others," who grew 279 percent in the same period.

Looking at the groups by decade reveals an important dynamic. In the first twenty years, the combined decline of Whites and African-Americans amounted to 15 percent in the 1970s and 3 percent in the 1980s. Meanwhile in the 1970s, the Asian and "Other" categories rocketed up 126 percent, but their growth rate slowed in the 1980s. By the 1990s, Whites reversed their decline with an 8 percent increase, while African-Americans continued to slide an additional 1 percent. Asians and "Others" increased another 40 percent, with the Asians growing 36 percent and the "Others" 42 percent.

In 2000, the downtown population was majority White (58 percent), with African-Americans (22 percent), Asians (12 percent), and "Others" (8 percent) accounting for the remainder. The Hispanic population, which has remained relatively stable since 1980, was 12 percent of the total. This downtown population is more diverse than its suburban and national counterparts, which have smaller proportions of African-Americans (suburbs, 10 percent; nation, 12 percent) and Asians (suburbs, 6 percent; nation, 8 percent). The proportion of Hispanics is approximately the same between the three scales.

Age and Educational Levels of Downtowners

A distinguishing feature of downtown populations is the growing dominance of adults aged 18 to 64 (83 percent of the total), especially younger adults as, 18- to 34-year-olds compose the largest segment (45 percent). Among them, the 25 to 34 age group represents almost a quarter (24 percent), followed by the 18- to 24-year-olds (21 percent). Completing the adult component are the 45- to 64-year-olds (21 percent), and the 35- to 44-year-olds (17 percent). The young (under 18) and old (over 65), almost evenly divided, provide the remaining 23 percent.

Thirty years ago, downtown populations were not so heavily weighted to younger adults. In 1970, children and the elderly accounted for more than one-third (36 percent) of

Chapter 7: **LIVING DOWNTOWN**

downtowners and the 45- to 64-year-olds about one-quarter (24 percent). In the ensuing decades, the shift occurred as the 25- to 34-year-olds grew an astonishing 92 percent while those under 18 declined by 72 percent.

This downtown age profile is quite distinct from that of the sample's cities and suburbs. The most dramatic differences are in the 25- to 34-year-olds, who account for only 15 percent in the suburbs and 18 percent in the city. In addition, the dependent population (those under 18 or over 65) constitutes a much larger proportion in the suburbs (38 percent) and cities (36 percent) than in downtowns (23 percent).

One of the most startling changes in the past thirty years has occurred in the educational profile of the downtown population. In 1970, 55 percent of the downtown population had no high school education, and only 13 percent had bachelor's degrees or higher. This rate was comparable for the rest of the city at that time (51 percent, no high school; 11 percent, bachelor's or higher) but was higher than that of the suburbs (38 percent, no high school; 14 percent, bachelor's or higher). While national educational attainment has improved over the years, the achievement levels for downtown populations have grown disproportionately, especially with regard to college and advanced degrees. In 2000, 44 percent of downtowners had bachelor's degrees or higher. This is well above the rates for the nation (24 percent), cities (27 percent), and suburbs (30 percent). Improvement occurred at the other end of the scale as well. Downtowners with no high school education shrank to 22 percent, and cities and suburbs showed similar improvements of 25 percent and 16 percent, respectively. The national rate is 20 percent.

Median Income in Downtowns

One critical factor about downtown residents is their median income. As the data are collations of census tracts yielding an income array for each downtown, deriving a single figure for downtown median income is not feasible. Further, such a figure would be deceptive because it would disguise the mosaic of contemporary downtown living, hiding the significant variations that exist at all geographic levels, especially within blocks.

One measure of downtowners' economic status compares the highest and lowest median incomes in each place with the city and MSA medians. By way of reference, in 2000, the median income for all US households was $41,994; for metropolitan areas, $44,755; and for MSA-central-city households, $36,964. In the sample, the MSA median incomes range from $63,297 in San Francisco to $23,483 in Miami, and the city median incomes range from $55,221 in San Francisco to $25,928 in Cleveland.

In general, downtowns contain both some of the most- and least-affluent residents of their surroundings. For example, twenty-five downtowns (54 percent of the sample) have at least one tract whose residents' median income surpasses the city median. The range is 106 percent to 532 percent. And twenty (43 percent of the sample) fall into this category compared to the MSA.

At the other end of the scale, thirty-six downtowns (78 percent of the sample) have lowest-median-income tracts whose level is 50 percent or lower than that of their cities. And a few downtowns house only lower income residents. For example, in downtown Boise, Des Moines, and Lexington, the highest median income tract is 50 percent or less that of their surroundings.

For the sample downtowns, the median income ranges vary widely within the two categories, highest income and lowest income tracts. Among the highest median income tracts, Dallas at $200,001 was the highest and Des Moines at $16,875 was the lowest. Among the lowest median income tracts, Chicago at $4,602 was the lowest and Norfolk at $46,081 was the highest.

Notably, for nineteen downtowns (41 percent of the sample), the general perception of downtown affluence is not a reality because in all cases, their highest- and lowest-income tracts are under the median for their cities and MSAs. These downtowns, primarily in the South and West, include Denver, Seattle, San Antonio, and Chattanooga.

Micro-Level Distribution of Median Income and Selected Other Characteristics

Another way to present a portrait of downtowners is to map median income by tracts, showing the range and its pattern. Mapping other demographic characteristics, like race or ethnicity, adds depth to the analysis. While coverage of the full sample and all its characteristics is beyond the scope of this chapter, looking at a small selection of downtowns (Philadelphia, Los Angeles, Milwaukee, and Orlando) vividly underlines how micro-level spatial analysis provides a context in understanding actual downtown living conditions and settlement patterns. The intent of this exercise is not to compare one downtown against another, but to highlight the spatial arrangements in each downtown. The data reveal both the range and location of median income and of race and ethnicity, factors that create distinct markets for residential projects. In the first decade of the twenty-first century, downtown leaders have labeled these areas, giving them marketable identities and dispelling any notion of downtowns being unitary places. For example, Cleveland has five districts – Flats, Warehouse, Historic Gateway, Playhouse, and Quadrangle – and Seattle has nine – Pioneer Square, Seattle Waterfront, Retail Core, West Edge, Belltown, Chinatown/International, Pike/Pine, First Hill, and Denny Triangle.[35]

Philadelphia

Philadelphia has the highest number of downtown households in the sample, contributing 10 percent of the total. Most Philadelphia downtowners are more affluent than the city, as 81 percent of the households live in tracts that have median incomes above the city's ($30,746), and about 15 percent live in areas with median incomes almost two times higher than the surrounding metropolitan area (MSA median, $47,536).

Among the array of twenty-two tracts that compose the downtown, the median income is $39,051 and the mode is $38,026 – higher than the national median income for cities and lower than the national MSA figure. However, the spread between the highest and lowest median incomes is $79,000, with the highest being 2.8 times the city median and 1.8 times the MSA median, and the lowest being 27 percent of the city and 18 percent of the MSA. The lowest are found in two pockets of poverty, representing 2 percent of the downtown's households that exist side by side with those in the more affluent areas. These areas shelter non-White populations with Asians dominating one and a mixed group (White, 55 percent; African-American, 28 percent; and Asian, 13 percent) in the other.

Chapter 7: **LIVING DOWNTOWN**

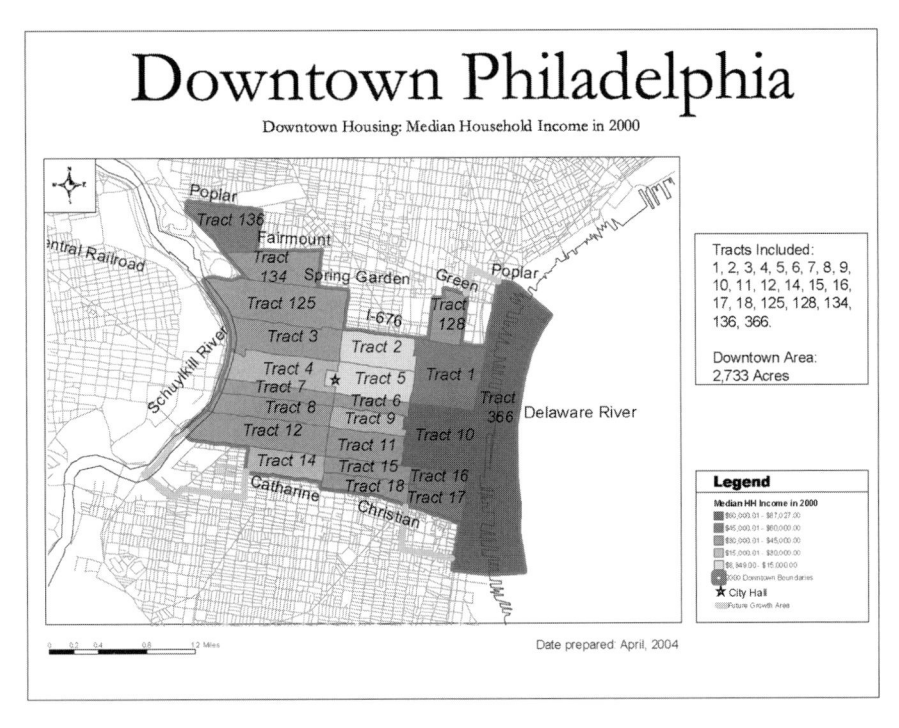

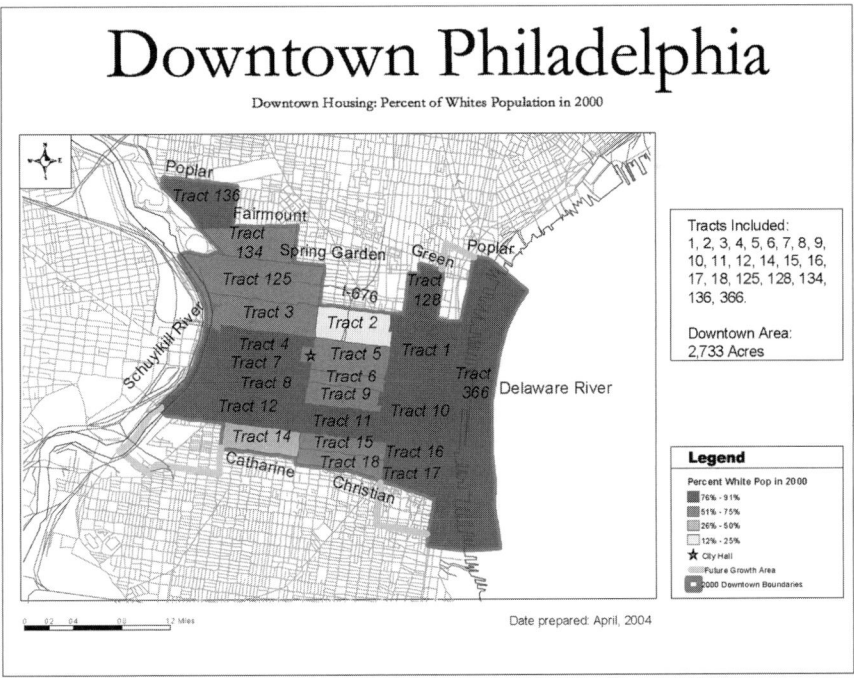

Figures 7.5a and b Downtown Philadelphia. *Downtown Philadelphia Median Income and Race, 2000*

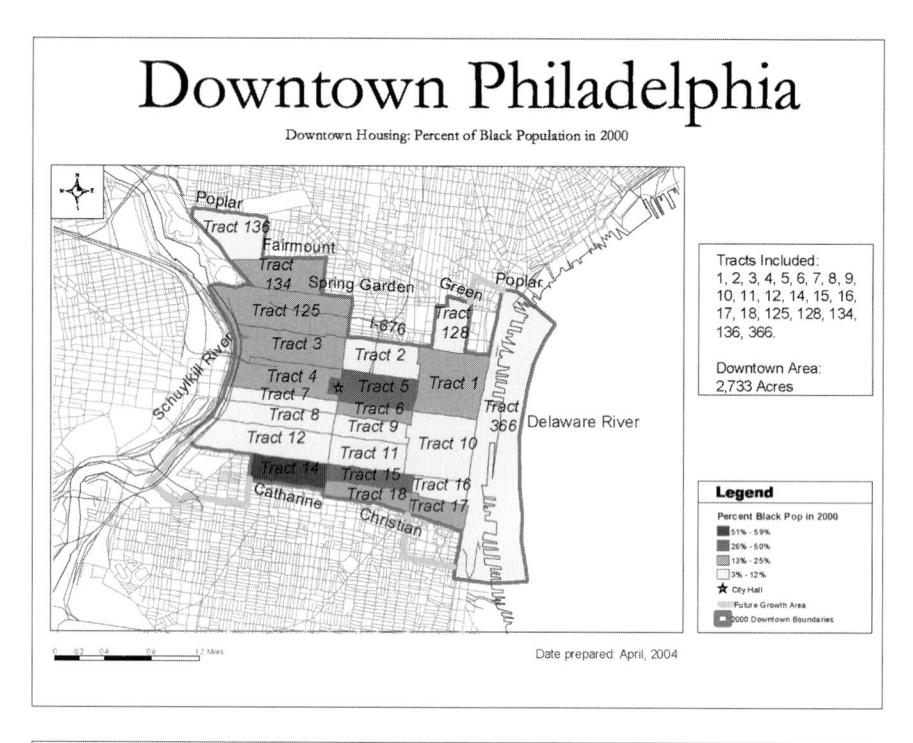

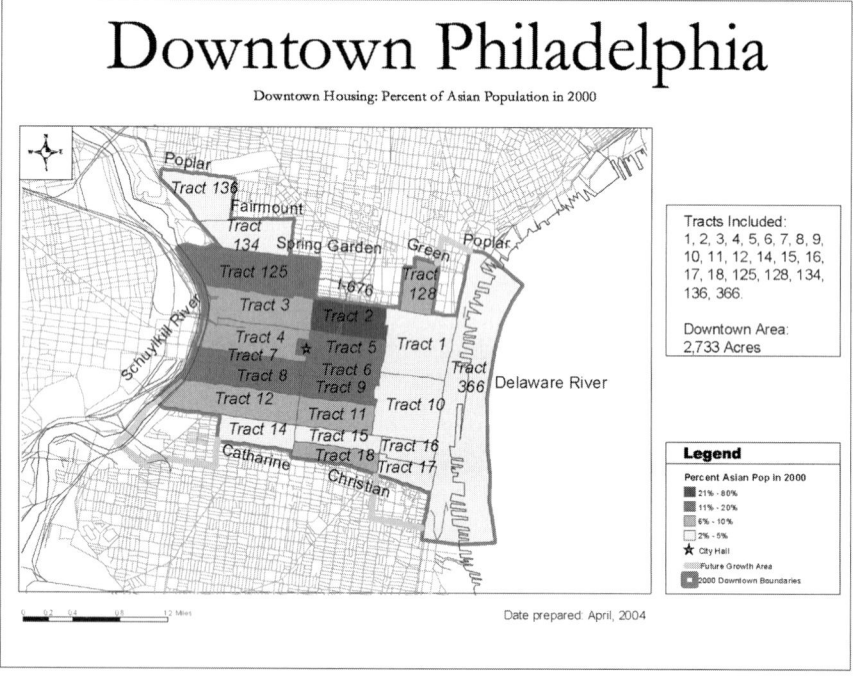

Figures 7.5c and d Downtown Philadelphia. *Downtown Philadelphia Median Income and Race, 2000*

Chapter 7: **LIVING DOWNTOWN**

With regard to race, Philadelphia exceeds the sample in the proportion of Whites (76 percent) and has smaller proportions of African-Americans (13 percent) and Asians (8 percent). And it is far different from the surrounding city (45 percent White, 43 percent African-American, and 5 percent Asian).

Los Angeles

Los Angeles is tenth in the household ranking, contributing 3 percent of the total. This downtown provides a substantial contrast to Philadelphia. None of the twelve downtown tracts have a median income higher than the city ($36,687) or the MSA ($42,189). In fact, the highest downtown median income is 70 percent of the city's median and 60 percent of the MSA's. In the array, the median is $17,115, and the range between the highest and lowest median income is approximately $20,000.

Los Angeles downtowners are much more diverse than the sample norm, 51 percent are either Hispanic or Asian. These populations are spatially concentrated within sub-districts, with the Hispanics dominant in 41 percent of the tracts and the Asians congregated in 50 percent of the tracts, all different. Ten of the twelve downtown tracts have White populations ranging from one-quarter to one-third of the total.

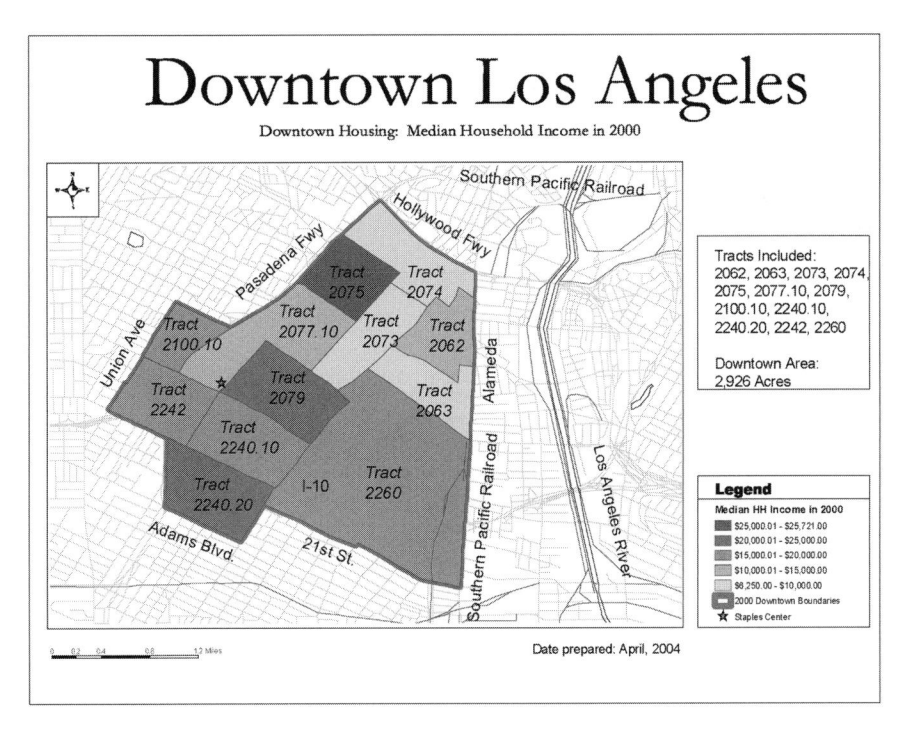

Figure 7.6a Downtown Los Angeles. *Downtown Los Angeles Median Income and Race, 2000*

143

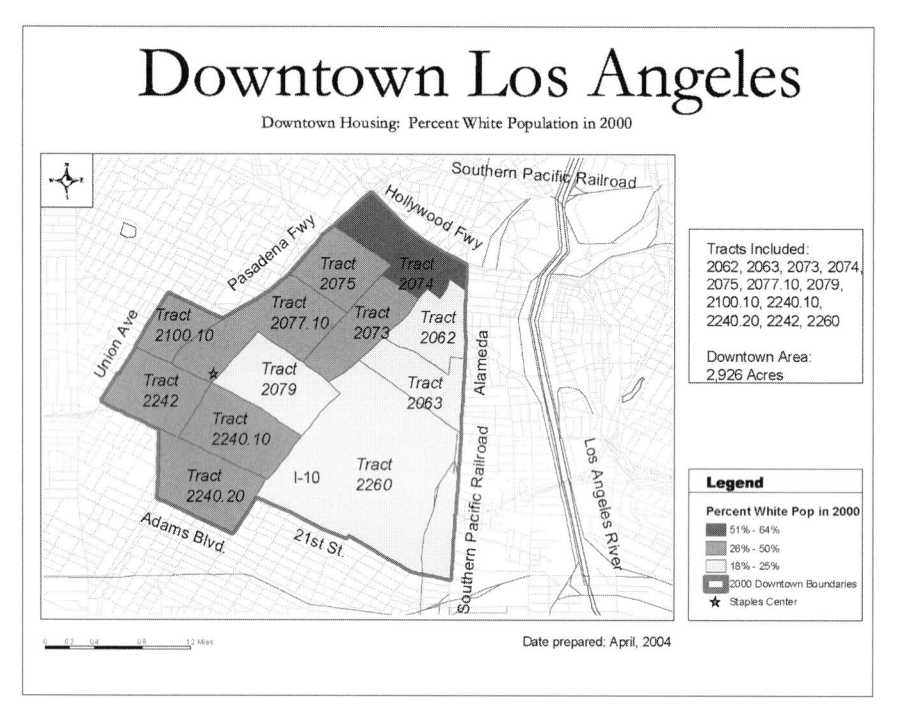

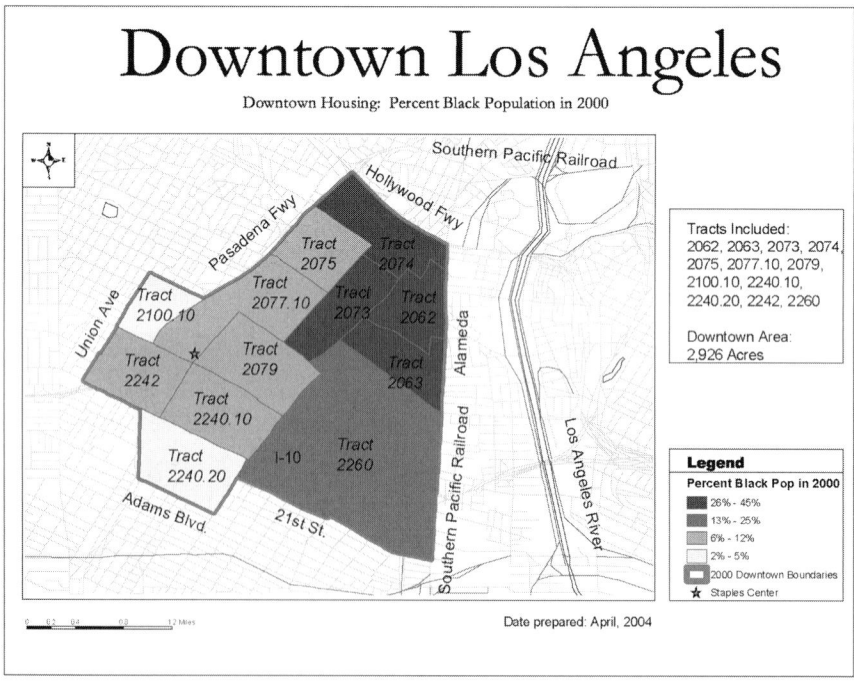

Figures 7.6b and c Downtown Los Angeles. *Downtown Los Angeles Median Income and Race, 2000*

Chapter 7: **LIVING DOWNTOWN**

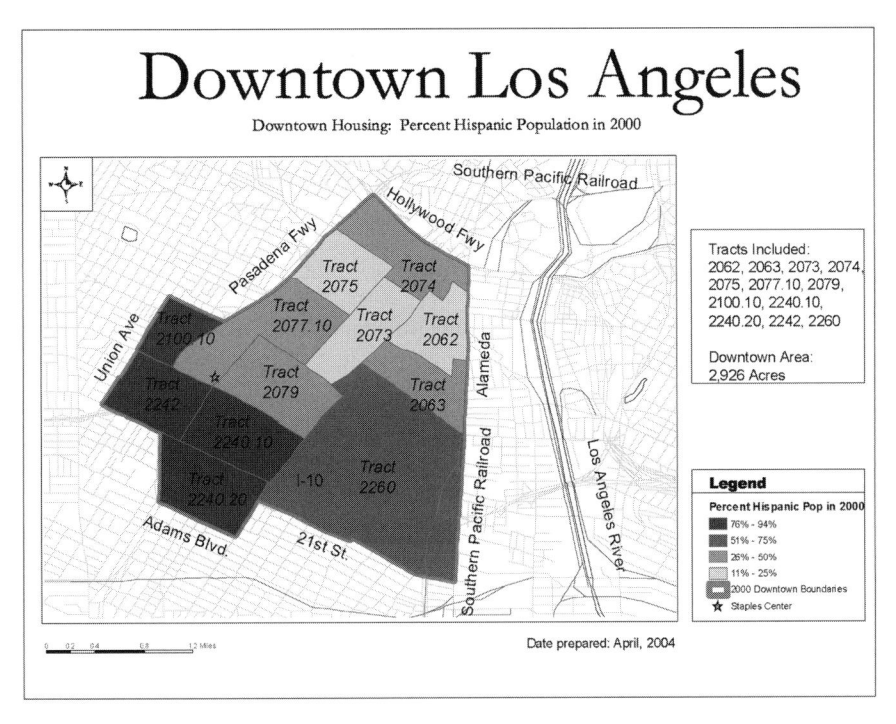

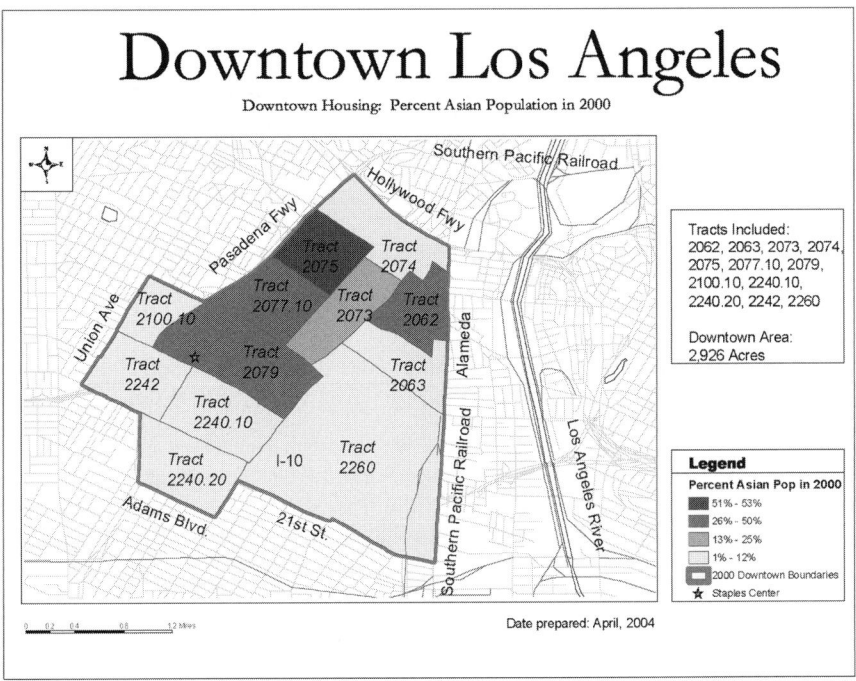

Figures 7.6d and e Downtown Los Angeles. *Downtown Los Angeles Median Income and Race, 2000*

145

Milwaukee

Milwaukee is seventeenth in the household rankings, contributing 2 percent to the total. Only 7 percent of the downtown households live in tracts whose median income exceeds that of the MSA ($45,901) but 36 percent surpass the city's ($32,216). The highest median income is 1.2 times the MSA and 1.6 times the city median. The lowest median income is 35 percent of the city and 24 percent of the MSA median. In the ten-tract array of downtown median incomes, the median is $31,938. The range between the highest and lowest tracts is about $42,000.

Whites comprise 71 percent of all downtowners and are the dominant population group (79 percent to 86 percent) in 80 percent of the tracts. African-Americans are the largest component in the remaining 20 percent of tracts, contributing 69 percent of the households in one and 80 percent in the other.

Orlando

Orlando, ranked twentieth in downtown households, contributes 2 percent of the housing stock. Of its downtown tracts, one (holding 11 percent of the households) has a median income above that of the MSA ($41,871). Two tracts (holding 42 percent of the households) are above the city median ($35,732). The lowest is 27 percent of the city median. Among the six-tract

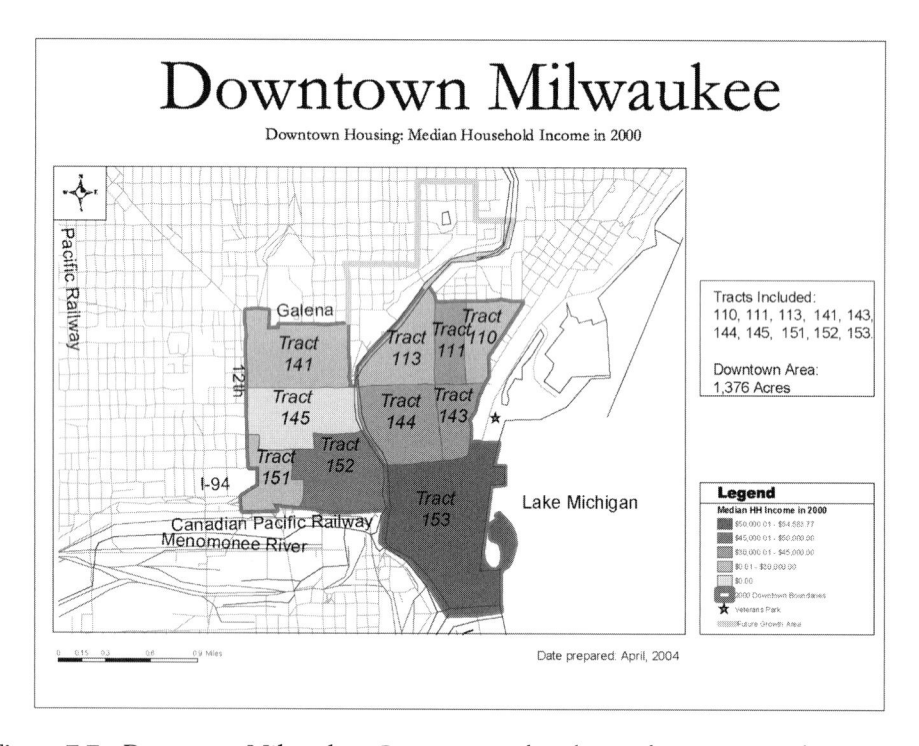

Figure 7.7a Downtown Milwaukee. *Downtown Milwaukee Median Income and Race, 2000*

Chapter 7: **LIVING DOWNTOWN**

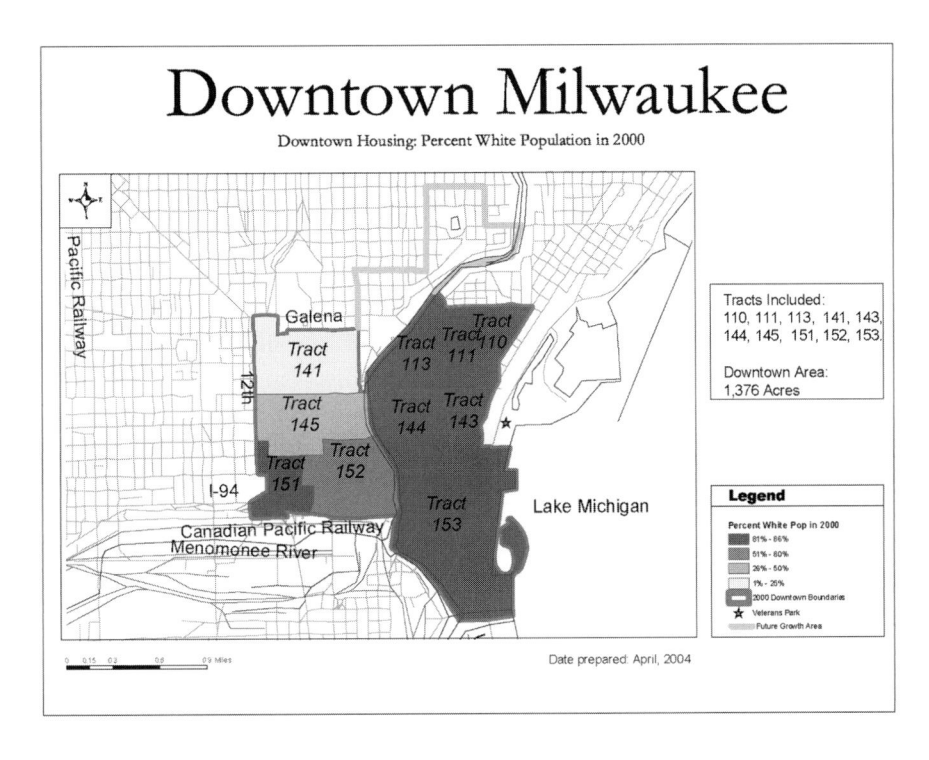

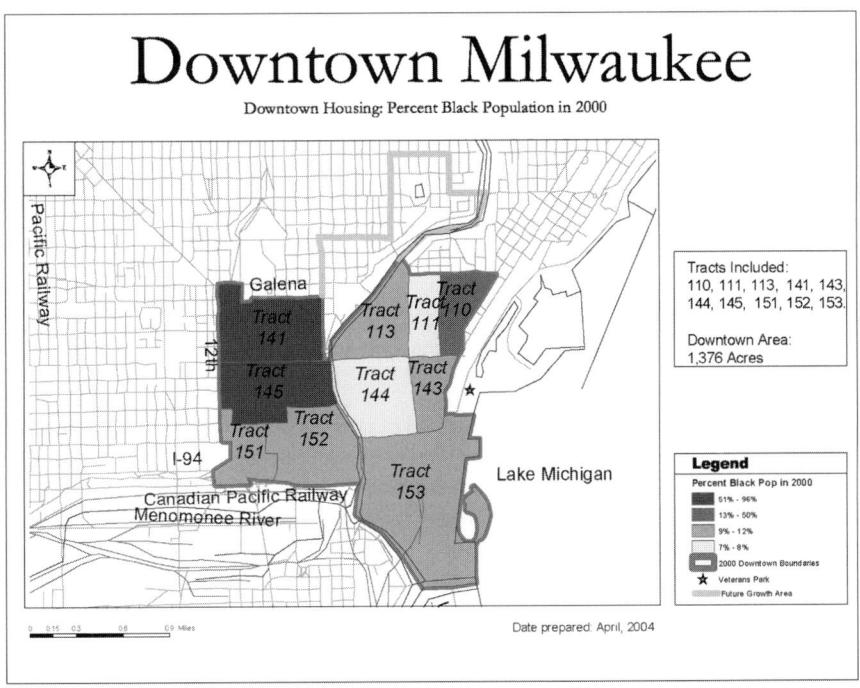

Figures 7.7b and c Downtown Milwaukee. *Downtown Milwaukee Median Income and Race, 2000*

147

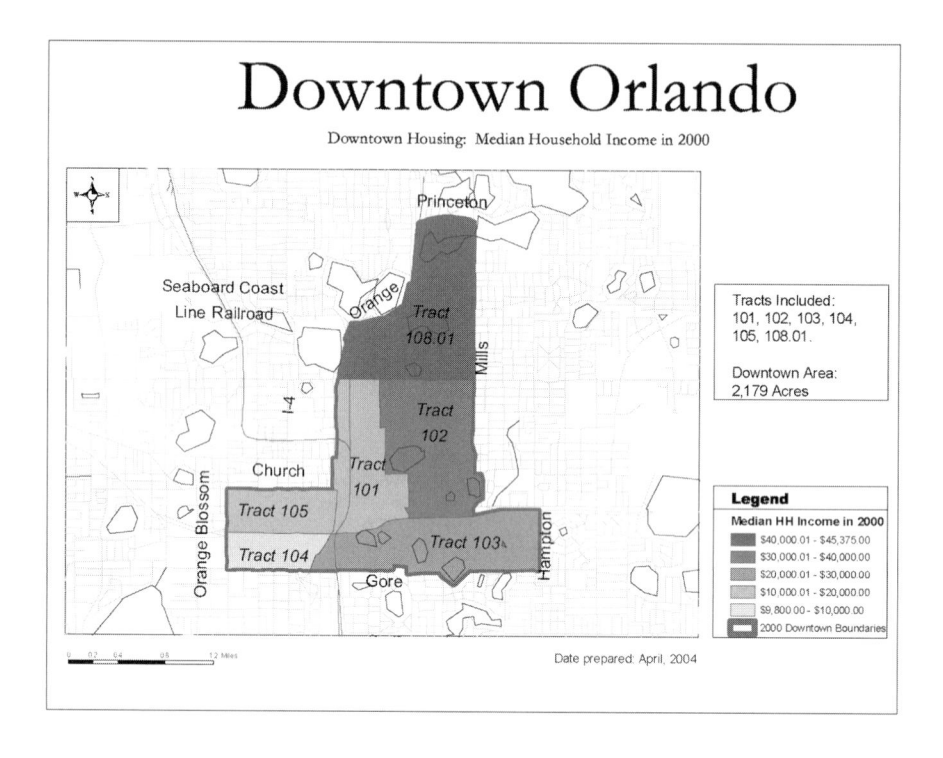

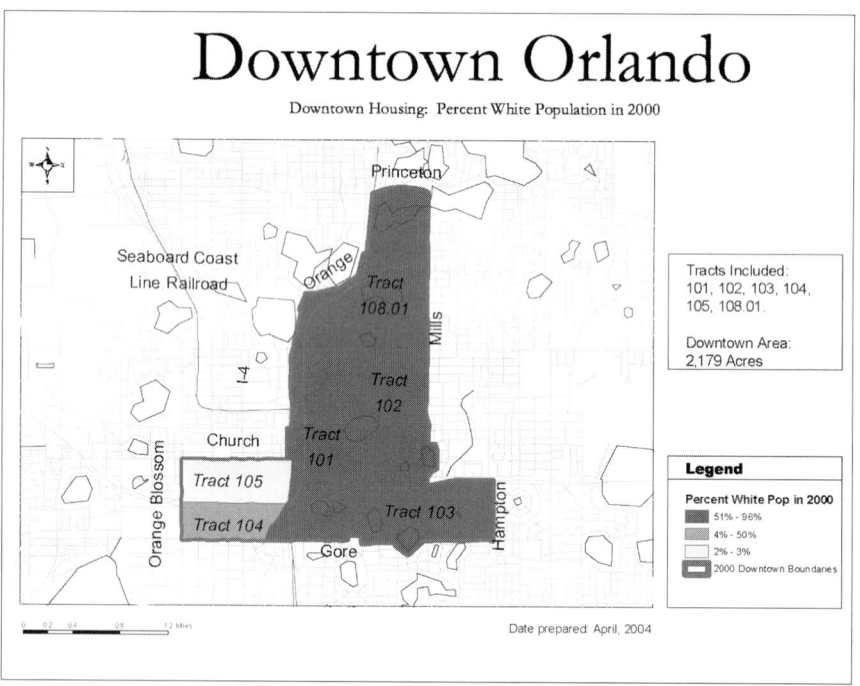

Figures 7.8a and b Downtown Orlando. *Downtown Orlando Median Income and Race, 2000*

Chapter 7: LIVING DOWNTOWN

Downtown Orlando
Downtown Housing: Percent Black Population in 2000

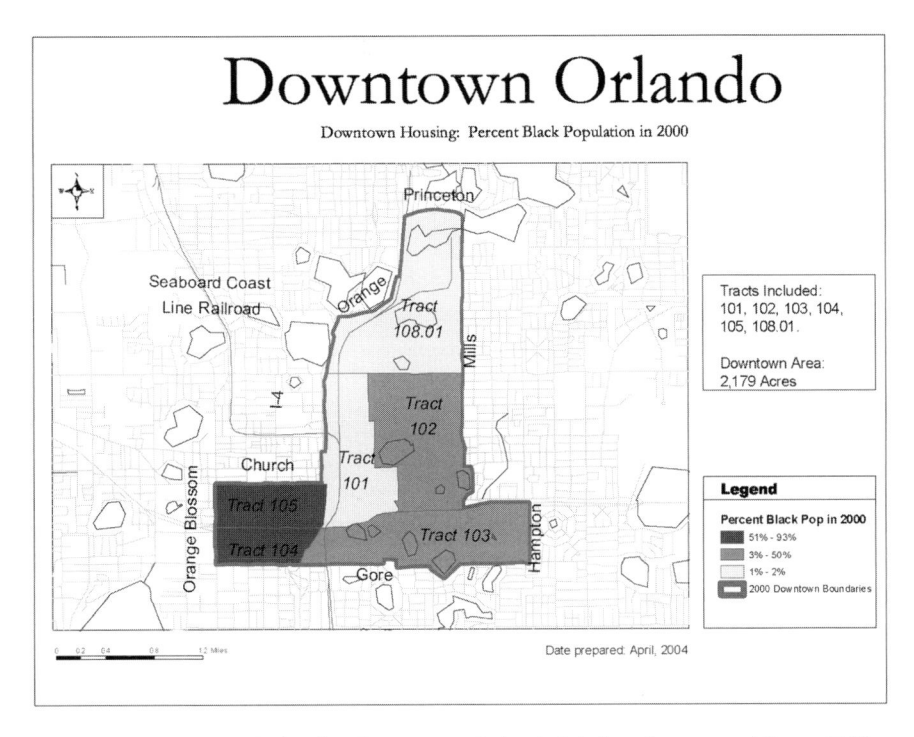

Tracts Included: 101, 102, 103, 104, 105, 108.01.

Downtown Area: 2,179 Acres

Legend
Percent Black Pop in 2000
51% - 93%
3% - 50%
1% - 2%
2000 Downtown Boundaries

Date prepared: April, 2004

Figure 7.8c Downtown Orlando. *Downtown Orlando Median Income and Race, 2000*

array, the median is $28,206. The range between the highest and lowest tracts is $34,000. Two-thirds of the Orlando tracts are 91 percent or more White. The remaining third, accounting for 22 percent of the households, is 92 percent or more African-American.

Dimensions of Downtown Median Incomes and Other Characteristics

Mapping downtown median incomes and other characteristics provides a physical dimension to the variations discussed earlier. The high-end Philadelphia and Milwaukee households, whose median incomes are greater than both the national and their own city and MSA medians, are each concentrated in one large tract in highly amenable locations, adjacent to attractive water bodies. And in both cases, the dominant racial group is White. In contrast, Los Angeles stands out as having a high percentage (30 percent) of its households living in three tracts with median incomes under $10,000, much lower than the national, city, and MSA median incomes. Here, the dominant population is African-American.

The meaning of affluence and poverty varies from downtown to downtown. In Philadelphia, about 4,000 households (9 percent of the total) live in the highest median income tracts, where the high ranges from $72,625 to $87,027, while in Los Angeles, about 4,000 households (30 percent) live in the highest income tracts but the high is only $25,000. Philadelphia and Orlando have approximately the same median income ($9,620 to $9,800) at the lowest level but different household proportions in the category: 2 percent (or about

149

450 total households) for Philadelphia and 11 percent (or 750 households) for Orlando. In Los Angeles, the bottom level median incomes ($6,250 to $8,250) are much lower and encompass a much higher percentage of households (30 percent). Comparisons for race, ethnicity, age, and educational levels yield similar variation.

Downtown Density

In addition to variation among income and race, other differences also exist. An important distinction among downtowns is density. Downtowns in the Northeastern United States tend to have the highest densities, with up to 76 people per acre, while those of the South and West are lower-density places, with lows of only 2 people per acre. Naturally, the downtowns with the greater number of housing units (10,000 or more) are also the most dense, a phenomenon that holds for all but Dallas and Detroit.

More than half of the downtown households live in high density (20 or more people per acre) arrangements in eight cities primarily on the eastern seaboard. This downtown density is higher than the sample cities' (8 people per acre), their suburbs (0.6 people per acre), and the nation (0.12 people per acre). Thirteen percent of downtown residents live at very low density (fewer than five people per acre). Thirty percent of downtown households live in medium density districts (five to 19 people per acre).

Density is not evenly distributed in downtowns as Lower Manhattan (76 people per acre) and Philadelphia (33 people per acre) demonstrate. In Lower Manhattan, the range is between 10 and 260 people per acre, with the 10 being a former warehouse district and the 260 being large-scale apartments. In Philadelphia, the range is between 1 and 83, with 1 being a waterfront district currently under development, it had one new apartment building at the time of the census, and 83 being an older, densely built neighborhood of row houses and high-rise apartment buildings.

Conclusions and Some Remaining Issues Related to the Rise of Downtown Living

This chapter describes the rise of downtown living, quantifies this shift, and outlines its nature, including an assessment of today's downtown residents. It shows that the downtown housing trend began earlier than had previously been thought and accelerated in the 1990s. It resulted in the development of a niche market, concentrated in the amenity-filled cities of the Northeast, Midwest, and California coast, and has attracted young, diverse, childless, highly-educated, affluent renters who tend to be transient when they marry or look for ownership units. However, the record for individual downtowns varies considerably from the overall picture, with some barely maintaining a critical mass of households and others stimulating spots of gentrification. Additionally, almost half of the downtowns have experienced suburban-garden-apartment density. Further, analysis of downtown settlement patterns reveals important submarkets or districts defined by housing stock, income, and race and ethnicity. These findings give rise to several concerns of interest to public and private decision-makers that revolve around development issues, demographics, and market potential and density.

Chapter 7: **LIVING DOWNTOWN**

Development Issues

First, downtown residential development takes a long time, the most successful downtowns have sustained housing unit increases for two or three decades. Additionally, it requires an ambience that is conducive to urban life. This ambience is often encouraged by the presence of large numbers of supportive downtowners. Successful downtowns have jobs, amenities, and interesting physical features or architecture. A downtown residential strategy flounders in the absence of these other elements.

Second, land or property disposition issues can emerge. Development in a large, dense downtown may present gentrification problems in places where land and units are scarce, thus threatening any supply of affordable housing that may be in the area. These issues have arisen in Lower Manhattan, for example. Conversely, downtowns with significant land in parking lots or vacant parcels may have trouble attracting sufficient housing to provide the critical mass to support needed amenities and residential services.

Third, focusing on a limited dwelling unit product, rentals to the exclusion of ownership can threaten stability. This issue concerns all downtowns regardless of type. Despite the doubling of ownership rates between 1970 and 2000, the downtown stock is primarily rental, the highest ownership level of 41 percent pales in comparison to national suburban rates of 71 percent. As the predominant population group (25- to 34-year-olds) ages and/or makes an economic decision to leave the rental market, persuaded by the current low interest and cheap mortgage environment, they have few downtown options, forcing these residents to leave. Additionally, the emerging 25- to 34-year-old cohort is smaller than the current one, raising questions of who will fill the growing inventory of housing.

Demographic and Market Potential

First, high levels of transients and reliance on a single population group pose significant disadvantages for downtowns. Transients have minimal interest in their communities, make few home improvements, and generally have little stake in the future of places that they consider temporary stopping points. Dependence on a narrowly defined population cohort, tailoring housing to satisfy their tastes, can limit the transferability of downtown dwellings to other groups in the future.

Second, the focus on downtown housing has highlighted the young urban professionals who constitute half of the households and neglected the other half, those who do not fit the "yuppie" profile. Given this situation, public policy and development efforts may be tempted to take a "one-size-fits-all" approach, a move that could limit the success of downtown residential strategies.

Density

Density matters. In general, the downtowns that are more dense have had the greatest success in attracting downtown residents. While a city with a substantial amount of vacant or underutilized land might be tempted to allow low-density residential construction, this would be a mistake. Such a decision would undermine the concept of downtown housing, whose sole market advantage is its accessibility to jobs or city-based quality-of-life amenities. Producing low-density suburban models squanders the advantages of centrally-located real estate and limits the ability to support the very services, facilities, and amenities that determine downtown character. In addition, low-density development is wasteful with regard to utilization of existing infrastructure, streets, water, parks, transit systems, and others.

With the maturing of the downtown housing trend, city leaders will likely begin to confront these issues as they perceive the permanence of the conversion of their central business districts into important multi-use nodes. Nonetheless, the continued, monitoring of center city residential use that the author will undertake will provide helpful directions.

Notes

1. The author has written about this topic in the following: "Having Longer View on Downtown Living," *Journal of the American Planning Association* 68:1 (Winter 2002): 5–21; "Who Lives Downtown?" (Washington, DC: The Brookings Institution, 2005); "Who Lives Downtown Today (And Are They Any Different from the Downtowners of Thirty Years Ago?" Lincoln Institute of Land Policy Working Papers, 2005. "Changing Place in the New Downtown," in Jonathan R. Oakman, *The New Downtowns, The Future of Urban Centers*, Princeton: Policy Research Institute on the Region, (2006) and "Downtown in the 'New American City,'" *Annals of the American Academy of Political and Social Sciences* 626 (November 2009): 134–153.

2. Susanna McBee, *Downtown Development Handbook* (Second edition) (Washington, DC: Urban Land Institute, 1992).

3. Hamilton, Rabinowitz and Altschuler, Inc. *Downtown New York: A Community Comes of Age* (New York, Alliance for Downtown, 2001); Leland Consulting Group, *Boise Downtown Housing Analysis* (Portland, Oregon, 2003).

4. William Fulton made this same observation in "Living the Niche of Life," *Governing*, August, 2004 (accessed on line August 11, 2004 at http://www.governing.com/articles/8econ.com.htm).

5. In Edward L. Glaeser and Jesse M. Shapiro, "Urban Growth in the 1990s: Is City Living Back?" *Journal of Regional Science* 43:1 (2003): 139–165, the authors discuss their methodology arguing "The return to city living is really about downtowns not big metropolitan regions, so cities make more sense as units of analysis (145)." They used data for cities of 100,000 or more to test whether various characteristics (density, weather, auto-dependence, human capital, poverty rates) were determining factors in city population increases. They concluded that for *cities* (not downtowns) human capital, weather and auto-dependence were positively correlated with growth. This study provides a valuable foundation for my study.

6. Recent examples include articles ranging from the effects of the current credit crises: Jennifer S. Forsyth and Jonathan Karp, "Woes in the Condo Market Build as New Supply Floods Cities," *Wall Street Journal*, March 22–23, 2008 pp. 1, A-8 to reports on new construction: Cynthia L. Kemper, "Art on View, A Complex Public Private Condominium Project in Denver, Colorado leverages Culture and World Class Architecture," *Urban Land,* May, 2007 pp. 108-111; Patricia Kirk, "Changing Places, Growing Demand for Housing in Urban Cores is Prompting Some Developers to Recognize Older Buildings," *Urban Land*, November–December, 2007, pp. 100–105.

Chapter 7: **LIVING DOWNTOWN**

7   The Brookings Institution and the Fannie Mae Foundation, *A Rise in Downtown Living* (Washington DC: authors, 1998); John Eckberg, "More People Calling Cincinnati's Downtown Home," *New York Times*, July 30, 2000, p. 5; "Downtowns Make Cities Winners," *USA Today*, May 7, 2001, p. 2. Rebecca R. Sohmer and Robert E. Lang, Downtown Rebound (Fannie Mae Foundation Census Note 03) (Washington, DC: Fannie Mae Foundation and Brookings Center on Urban and Metropolitan Policy, May 2001); and Eugénie L. Birch, "Having Longer View"; "Who Lives Downtown?"; "Who Lives Downtown Today (And Are They Any Different?"; and "Changing Place in the New Downtown."

8   Central Philadelphia Development Corporation, *Residential Development 2009, Riding Out the Storm, Confidence and Continued Demand* (Philadelphia 2009) http://www.centercityphila.org/docs/CCR09_Residential_FINAL.pdf

9   See for example, Christopher Leinberger, *The Option of Urbanism, Investing in a New American Dream* (Washington, DC: Island Press, 2007).

10   Richard Florida, *The Rise of the Creative Class And How it is Transforming Work, Leisure, Community and Everyday Life* (New York: Basic Books, 2002); Charles Landry, *The Creative City: A Toolkit for Urban Innovators* (London: Earthscan, 2000).

11   Gerald William Breese, The Daytime Population of the Central Business District of Chicago (Chicago: University of Chicago Press: 1949); John Rannells, *The Core of the City, A Pilot Study of Changing Land Uses in Central Business Districts* (New York: Columbia University Press, 1956); Raymond E. Murphy, *The Central Business District* (New York: Aldine-Atherton, 1972).

12   Robert Fogelson, *Downtown: Its Rise and Fall, 1880–1950* (New Haven, Yale University Press, 2001). See also Alison Isenberg, *Downtown America: A History of the Place and the People Who Made It* (Chicago: University of Chicago Press, 2004).

13   Robert E. Lang, *Edgeless Cities: Exploring the Elusive Metropolis* (Washington, DC: 2003).

14   Louis G. Redstone, *The New Downtowns, Rebuilding Business Districts* (New York: McGraw Hill, 1976).

15   Bernard Friedan and Lynne B. Sagalyn, *Downtown Inc.: How America Rebuilds Cities* (Cambridge, MA: MIT Press, 1989); Alexander Garvin, *The American City, What Works, What Doesn't* (New York: John Wiley and Sons, 2002); Roberta Gratz and Norman Mintz, *Cities Back from the Edge* (New York: John Wiley and Sons, 1998).

16   See for example, Herbert Gans, *The Urban Villagers* (New York: The Free Press, 1982); Chester Hartman, *City for Sale* (Berkeley, CA: University of California Press, 1993); Jane Jacobs, *The Death and Life of the Great American City* (New York: Random House, 1961).

17   Center City District, *Office Market, 2008* accessed at http://www.centercityphila.org/docs/SOCC-2008-Office.pdf August 12, 2008.

18   David A. Wallace, personal communication, April, 2002; Gratz and Mintz, *Cities, Back from the Edge*, Chapter 13.

19   Due to size, historical development and internal geography, she assigned two downtowns to New York City, Lower Manhattan and Midtown.

20   Downtown Preservation Council, *The Boundaries of Downtown: A Study of 48 Major US Cities* (Fairhope, Alabama: author, June, 2003); Raymond E. Murphy, *Central Business District*, US Census Bureau.

21 The author appreciates that this method defines each city's 2000 downtown, whose area may have been different (most likely smaller) thirty years ago. However, she is interested in tracking changes in the space now considered as that city's downtown and thus made this choice.

22 She also cross-referenced it with the Downtown Preservation Council's recently issued study noted above. This study focused on 48 downtowns, 31 of which are in this Brookings-sponsored research project. The Downtown Preservation Council method is more fine-grained, delineating the downtown boundaries in blocks. As the Brookings-sponsored study is longitudinal, assembling a database from 1970 to the present, it was beyond the data collection capacities to collect block data. Instead, the investigator tracked the data of the 2000 census tract *boundaries* backward, making adjustments where required for changes in tract boundaries. Thus the Brookings report is based on an assessment of the changes to the 2000 downtown.

23 The sample represents MSAs containing 59 percent of the nation's urban population and 70 percent of the nation's suburban inhabitants.

24 Center City District, *State of Center City, 2008*; Center City Development Corporation, *2008 Downtown Living Guide*; Downtown DC Business Improvement District, State of Downtown, 2006; and *Alliance for Downtown, State of Lower Manhattan, 2007*.

25 In the 1970s five experienced precipitous drops (St. Louis, 55 percent; Shreveport, 50 percent; Austin, 43 percent; Albuquerque, 42 percent; Columbus, Ohio, 42 percent) but a bright spot in this grim picture was the growth surge in five downtowns (Los Angeles, 46 percent; Des Moines, 41 percent; Lower Manhattan, 20 percent; Indianapolis, 20 percent; Midtown Manhattan 15 percent).

26 In the 1980s five lost 25 percent or more of their residents: Indianapolis, 55 percent; Des Moines, 52 percent; Albuquerque, 30 percent; Columbus, GA 30 percent and Chattanooga, 25 percent. Of the 25 downtowns (or 54 percent of the sample) that gained population, seven increased by 25 percent or more (Norfolk, 98 percent; Cincinnati, 52 percent; San Diego, 46 percent; Shreveport, 43 percent; Memphis, 32 percent; Austin, 26 percent and Lafayette, 26 percent).

27 In the 1990s Columbus, GA, 24 percent; St Louis, 18 percent, Cincinnati, 17 percent and Minneapolis, 17 percent experienced the highest percent losses while Seattle, 77 percent; Houston, 69 percent; Denver, 51 percent; Colorado Springs, 48 percent and Albuquerque, 45 percent had the greatest percent gain.

28 Seven downtowns, Columbus, GA, Detroit, Jackson, Orlando, Phoenix, San Antonio and St. Louis, had losses in all three decades while Lower Manhattan, Los Angeles, Midtown Manhattan, San Diego and Seattle had gains in the three decades.

29 Eight downtowns having gains of 25 percent or more are Houston, Norfolk, Cincinnati, San Diego, Shreveport, Memphis, Austin, and Lafayette. Only San Diego did not lose population in the previous decade.

30 Many cities view their downtowns as repositories for locally unwanted land uses, notably prisons, homeless shelters, group homes for delinquents and drug treatment facilities. They make these location decisions for a variety of reasons, often responding to a perceived need to avoid community opposition to unpopular activities. In the case of jails, their siting may also be related to the location of the courts, generally found downtown. Between 1970 and 2000, the downtown prison population increased 86 percent with the greatest change (+43 percent) occurring in the 1980s, the decade following the rapid decline in the number of downtown

residents. Although in 2000, prisoners were only 6 percent of all downtowners, some places have greater proportions of this population than others. Twenty cities (40 percent of the sample) had 1,000 or more prisoners in their downtowns. For some, such as Boston, Minneapolis and Lower Manhattan, this number represented less that 4 percent of their downtowners. For others, the prison population was much more significant, constituting 25 percent or more of those living downtown. They are Houston (81 percent), Norfolk (46 percent), Pittsburgh (34 percent) and Memphis (26 percent).

In some cases, the presence of the incarcerated dramatically affects the data on population size and growth rates. For example, between 1970 and 2000, Houston (+209 percent) and Norfolk (+97 percent) posted the highest growth rates of the sample. Removal of prisoners yields far different results with Houston losing almost a third of its population (–32 percent) and Norfolk growing more slowly (+40 percent). The distortions caused by the incarcerated disappear in the household data because the US Census does not include prisoners in that count. Nonetheless, since Houston had such a high proportion of prisoners, the following discussion of population change in individual cities will exclude that city.

31   Household data also eliminate the distortion caused by the institutionalized groups encompassed in population figures.
32   This phenomenon is seen beyond the top and bottom ten as exemplified by Charlotte (population down –31 percent, households up +1 percent), Memphis (–10 percent population; +7 percent households) and New Orleans (–15 percent population; +17 percent households) had the same experience.
33   The remainder (0.6 percent) would be male heads of household with children.
34   Paul Levy, "Positioned for Growth, State of Center City Report Released," *Center City Digest*, Spring 2008. Accessed at http://www.centercityphila.org/docs/CCdigestSpring08.pdf August 12, 2008.
35   Birch, "Downtown in the New American City," p. 150.

References

Birch, Eugénie L., "Having Longer View on Downtown Living," *Journal of the American Planning Association* 68 (1): 5–21, 2002.
Birch, Eugénie L., "Who Lives Downtown?," Washington, DC: The Brookings Institution, 2005.
Birch, Eugénie L., "Who Lives Downtown Today (And Are They Any Different from the Downtowners of Thirty Years Ago?" Lincoln Institute of Land Policy Working Papers, 2005.
Birch, Eugénie L., "Changing Place in the New Downtown," in Jonathan R. Oakman, *The New Downtowns, The Future of Urban Centers,* Princeton, NJ: Policy Research Institute on the Region, 2006.
Birch, Eugénie L., "Downtown in the New American City," *Annals of the American Academy of Political and Social Sciences* 626: 124–153, 2009.
Breese, Gerald William, *The Daytime Population of the Central Business District of Chicago*, Chicago: University of Chicago Press, 1949.
Brookings Institution and the Fannie Mae Foundation, *A Rise in Downtown Living*, Washington, DC: Brookings Institution and the Fannie Mac Foundation, 1998.

Center City Development Corporation, "Downtown Living Guide," accessed at http://www.ccdc.com/ August 12, 2008.

Center City District, "State of Center City, 2008," accessed at http://www.centercityphila.org/ August 12, 2008.

Downtown Alliance, "State of Lower Manhattan, 2007," accessed at http://www.downtownny.com/research/current/ August 12, 2008.

Downtown DC Business Improvement District, State of Downtown, 2006, accessed at http://www.downtowndc.org/ August 12, 2008.

Downtown Preservation Council, *The Boundaries of Downtown: A Study of 48 Major US Cities*, Fairhope, AL: Downtown Preservation Council, June, 2003.

Eckberg, John, "More People Calling Cincinnati's Downtown Home," *New York Times*, July 30, 2000, p. 5.

El Nasser, Haya, "Downtowns Make Cities Winners," *USA Today*, May 7, 2001, p. 2.

Florida, Richard, *The Rise of the Creative Class And How it is Transforming Work, Leisure, Community and Everyday Life*, New York: Basic Books, 2002.

Forsyth, Jennifer S. and Jonathan Karp, "Woes in the Condo Market Build as New Supply Floods Cities," *Wall Street Journal*, March 22–23, 2008, pp. 1, A-8.

Friedan, Bernard and Lynne B. Sagalyn, *Downtown Inc.: How America Rebuilds Cities,* Cambridge, MA: MIT Press, 1989.

Fulton, William, "Living the Niche of Life," *Governing*, August, 2004, accessed at http://www.governing.com/articles/8econ.com.htm, August 11, 2004.

Gans, Herbert, *The Urban Villagers*, New York: The Free Press, 1982.

Garvin, Alexander, *The American City, What Works, What Doesn't*, New York: John Wiley and Sons, 2002.

Glaeser, Edward L. Glaeser and Jesse M. Shapiro, "Urban Growth in the 1990s: Is City Living Back?" *Journal of Regional Science* 43 (1): 139–165, 2003.

Gratz, Roberta and Norman Mintz, *Cities Back from the Edge*, New York: John Wiley and Sons, 1998.

Hamilton, Rabinowitz and Altschuler, Inc. *Downtown New York: A Community Comes of Age*, New York: Alliance for Downtown, 2001.

Hartman, Chester, *City for Sale*, Berkeley, CA: University of California Press, 1993.

Jacobs, Jane, *The Death and Life of the Great American City*, New York: Random House, 1961.

Kemper, Cynthia L., "Art on View, A Complex Public Private Condominium Project in Denver, Colorado Leverages Culture and World Class Architecture," *Urban Land*, 108–111, November–December 2007.

Kirk, Patricia, "Changing Places, Growing Demand for Housing in Urban Cores is Prompting Some Developers to Recognize Older Buildings," *Urban Land*, 100–105, November–December, 2007.

Landry, Charles, *The Creative City: A Toolkit for Urban Innovators*, London: Earthscan, 2000.

Lang, Robert E., *Edgeless Cities Exploring the Elusive Metropolis*, Washington, DC: Brookings Institution, 2003.

Leland Consulting Group, *Boise Downtown Housing Analysis*, Portland, OR: Leland Consulting Group, 2003.

Leinberger, Christopher, *The Option of Urbanism, Investing in a New American Dream*, Washington DC: Island Press, 2007.

Chapter 7: **LIVING DOWNTOWN**

Levy, Paul, "Positioned for Growth, State of Center City Report Released," *Center City Digest*, Spring 2008. Accessed at http://www.centercityphila.org/docs/CCdigestSpring08.pdf August 12, 2008.

McBee, Susannah, *Downtown Development Handbook*, second edition, Washington, DC: Urban Land Institute, 1992.

Murphy, Raymond E., *The Central Business District*, New York: Aldine-Atherton, 1972.

Rannells, John, *The Core of the City, A Pilot Study of Changing Land Uses in Central Business Districts*, New York: Columbia University Press, 1956.

Redstone, Louis G., *The New Downtowns, Rebuilding Business Districts*, New York: McGraw Hill, 1976.

Shapiro, Jesse M. "Urban Growth in the 1990s: Is City Living Back?" *Journal of Regional Science* 43 (1): 139–165, 2003.

Sohmer, Rebecca R. and Robert E. Lang, *Downtown Rebound* (Fannie Mae Foundation Census Note 03), Washington DC: Fannie Mae Foundation and Brookings Center on Urban and Metropolitan Policy, May 2001.

Wallace, David A., Personal communication, April, 2002.

Chapter 8

THE CULTURAL COMPONENT OF LIVABILITY: LOSS AND RECOVERY IN POST-KATRINA NEW ORLEANS

Jane S. Brooks
Professor and Department Chair, Department of Planning and Urban Studies
University of New Orleans

Rebecca Houtman
2010 of M.S. Graduate in Urban Studies, Department of Planning and Urban Studies
University of New Orleans

Introduction to Livability in Post-Katrina New Orleans

Nothing brings the question of what contributes to a community's livability into sharp focus like the sudden loss of the most basic living requirements altogether. Since September 2005, citizens of New Orleans have been engaged in an urgent, ongoing, and often heated debate about what the post-hurricane city should offer. No aspect of life in New Orleans, good or bad, could be taken for granted – neither that the pre-existing serious detractors from the city's quality of life would necessarily resume as before, nor that New Orleans' unique pleasures would reemerge unchanged. New Orleanians have learned not only that "you don't know what you've got 'til it's gone," but that you don't know what you've got until you have to decide whether it is worth restoring it. Encouraging the survival of cultural traditions is a high recovery priority in the minds of New Orleanians, and additionally, culture has been a powerful influence on the course of the overall recovery effort. The impact of every restored cultural event and institution on citizens' faith in New Orleans' prospects is hard to overestimate. From the largest events, like the first post-Katrina Mardi Gras or the reopening of the Superdome and return of the Saints football team, to the opening of the smallest neighborhood hole-in-the-wall, every resumption of a local tradition is an indicator of both the economic viability of the city and its neighborhoods and also of just what the essential character of a "new" New Orleans is to be.

With tens of thousands of citizens having spent weeks, months, or even years in evacuation, New Orleanians have had ample time to discover what it is they have missed the most about

Chapter 8: **POST-KATRINA NEW ORLEANS**

their city and their neighborhoods. Many have had the same opportunity, though, to experience the standards of livability that dozens of other communities across the country have to offer. There are many hazards in choosing to return to a radically destabilized city, hazards that are too great for some to bear relative to the assets they have found in their new homes. Still, the city's population has grown somewhat faster than expected,[1] and the returnees and newcomers alike who have decided that life in New Orleans, however uncertain at present, is preferable to life elsewhere are bringing sensibilities shaped by stays in other towns and cities.

Among the questions that New Orleanians have had to pose to themselves is whether their investment of time, money, and energy in rebuilding their homes and businesses will be matched by a collective investment in restoring everything that formerly made New Orleans uniquely livable to them, while improving on what did not. The "2006 South Louisiana Recovery Survey" commissioned by Louisiana Speaks (the long-range planning element of the Louisiana Recovery Authority, or LRA), found that one of respondents' "Highest Hopes, Key Themes, and Values" going forward was the preservation of cultural integrity. "Perhaps nowhere in America is the longing for cultural continuity stronger than in South Louisiana. And citizens are not just talking about culture as it is known in New Orleans, but Cajun culture and all the other micro-cultures that exist throughout the region. Art, music, and food play a central role but culture here also refers to shared history and a deep connection to family roots" (Louisiana Speaks 2006: 6). New Orleans is itself a collection of diverse micro-cultures and histories, many based in individual neighborhoods, at risk of being lost or substantially changed if those neighborhoods do not recover successfully. At the same time that respondents rated Louisiana's traditions so highly, however, "when asked what they liked most about their new locations, displaced citizens most frequently mention that it is clean, safe, quiet, and peaceful, that the government seems more competent, and there are better job opportunities" (Louisiana Speaks 2006: 10).

In many respects, the recovery process has been seen as an opportunity to undo some of New Orleans' worst problems, a "silver lining" even while the streets were still inundated. No one could hope for a return to the same failing public schools, shocking rates of violent crimes, poor health, or depths of poverty of August 2005. And yet, between the vast physical destruction that would necessitate extensive rebuilding from scratch and the dispersal of people that would inevitably mean an at least somewhat smaller population of a changed demographic composition, concerns arose just as early in Katrina's aftermath about what conception of "New Orleans" it would be that would ultimately recover and occupy roughly the same spot on the crescent of the Mississippi River. Rebuilding after disaster can have unanticipated consequences; the ways in which even the most urgent survival needs are met may impact lifestyles and livability for years to come. After the December 2004 Indian Ocean tsunami, concerns arose about the cultural impact of housing solutions in the fishing communities of Tamil Nadu – most NGOs assisting villages with reconstruction opted for "modern" concrete homes for nuclear families, failing to consider not only religious and social rituals involved in home-building, but such material considerations as how local self-building traditions accommodated a family's growth over the years, and how ample verandas mitigate heat (Barenstein 2008). New Orleans, for all its uniqueness, is still a typical American city in most respects. The new housing that is being built will never exactly duplicate the styles of what it is replacing, but the risk of drastic misunderstandings of household sizes or religious custom is less dire than in Tamil Nadu. Still, looking at the changes entire neighborhoods may undergo, there have been serious questions about how the rebuilt environment will influence New Orleans' culture. What would become of the hard-to-measure cultural qualities of life never exactly duplicated elsewhere? What, for instance, would the future hold for the food and music customs that have so often originated in and been maintained by the most modest neighborhoods, now among the most devastated? What would become of the Social Aid and Pleasure Clubs (originators of the "second line" musical and parading styles), the Mardi Gras Indians (elaborately costumed paraders and musicians commemorating the ties between slaves, freedmen, and Native Americans going back to colonial Louisiana), and the innumerable other social organizations, formal and informal, with their members scattered and deep losses sustained, their gathering places in ruins, and the parading streetscapes themselves virtually emptied of residents and possibly beyond repair? And in what ways have these and other cultural qualities contributed not only to making life more enjoyable, but also to other elements of livability like employment and social capital building?

While planners, scholars, policy makers, and neighborhood groups examine best practices in urban livability from around the world for their application in the rebuilding of New Orleans, they have not been operating on a "blank slate" swept clean by the levee breaches. The inundation of 80 percent of the land area of New Orleans did not wash away the intricate cultural mixture that has made the city unique in the American experience. Founded by the French and Spanish nearly three centuries ago, the Afro-Caribbean culture that came to this city as a result of the slave trade and the city's position as one of the busiest ports in the world has influenced almost every aspect of New Orleans. A philosophy of valuing cultural aspects of life over many other more "progressive" indices has played a significant role in the city's history; that philosophy has also steered the city's recovery and priorities for a better future. The pursuit of cultural values need not necessarily be divorced from progressive urban concerns going ahead. New Orleanians are engaged in applying their considerable cultural assets to solve the problems of recovery as well as the problems that pre-date the disaster. The largest city in a state whose second-highest employment sector is "cultural industries" (Louisiana Department of Culture, Recreation and Tourism 2007: 5), Louisiana's Department of Culture, Recreation and Tourism describes the cultural economy as "a sustainable, natural resource that cannot be outsourced" (Louisiana Department of Culture, Recreation and Tourism 2007: 3). Regarding culture as an "industry" alone, culture-based businesses and workers are helping to fuel the economic recovery of the region. But as critical as culture's contribution to a healthy local economy is, New Orleans' cultural natural resources also afford its citizens the places, events, recreations, and pastimes to bring them together for mutual support, much-deserved periods of relief, and a sense of common purpose. Volunteers have devoted untold hours and energy in recovery projects not just out of an abstract sense of philanthropy, but because of a sense of a shared stake in the preservation of something whose importance rivals their personal health and security. That sense of common purpose does not always extend citywide or statewide. Political, social, and racial divisions still run deep. But at the neighborhood and micro-culture levels, where so much of New Orleans culture is rooted, the inspirational impact of culture can be powerfully evident. One neighborhood among the many that could be chosen to exemplify New Orleans' recovery experiences for this chapter is Mid-City, which, as the name suggests, was once the geographical center of the city, a sort of connective tissue between Uptown and Downtown, river and lake.

Chapter 8: **POST-KATRINA NEW ORLEANS**

Mid-City's Physical Development and Cultural Composition

From the advent of modern drainage systems around the turn of the twentieth century until the aggressive development of New Orleans East began in the 1950s and 1960s, Mid-City was, as its neighborhood organization proclaims, "The Heart of New Orleans." By the 1890s, post-Civil War population growth pressed the limits of the high ground along the Mississippi River's natural levee, and at the same time, the growing recognition that New Orleans' infamous epidemics of malaria and yellow fever could be mitigated by mosquito control added urgency to the latest in a series of attempts to innovate in drainage. The Sewerage and Water Board was formed in 1899, and by 1905 it had

> completed forty miles of canals (mostly lined and covered), many more miles of pipelines and drains, and six operating pumping stations on the east bank [of the Mississippi River], draining an area of 22,000 acres with a maximum capacity of 5,000 cubic feet per second.
> (Campanella 2002: 60)

The cypress swamp known as "Back of Town" began receding, the mortality rate began declining, and in 1913 the invention and construction of the Wood Screw Pump by New Orleans native Albert Baldwin Wood lent even more security to life on the reclaimed land that would eventually reach all the way to Lake Pontchartrain. Back of Town became a number of new neighborhoods, Mid-City one of the first.

Most of the official Mid-City neighborhood coincides with two National Register Historic Districts: Mid-City, also known as Upper Canal, and Parkview. The supporting documents for both indicate that the great majority of building was completed prior to 1943, with very low rates of subsequent intrusion (below 15 percent and 8 percent, respectively). Although twentieth-century through and through, the architectural character of Mid-City's residential blocks is of a piece with most of "old" New Orleans. The same population pressure that pushed the city limits into the swamps was increasing the density of the earlier streetcar suburbs and semi-rural stretches between formerly independent towns in Orleans Parish, with variations on shotgun houses in the same array of styles proliferating all over, knitting together a common urban fabric.

In Mid-City, early development extended along Canal Street, the "Main Street" of New Orleans which, at the river, divides the Creole Vieux Carré from the original American sector. As it runs lakeward, the surroundings lose their Creole/Anglo distinction and become simply New Orleanian. Canal crosses Carrollton Avenue in Mid-City, which is the main traffic artery of the former town of Carrollton, annexed by New Orleans in 1975. Canal and Carrollton are two of the primary spokes in the street pattern that fans out within the portion of New Orleans that sits within the crescent formed by the Mississippi. Another historic transport lane influenced the development of Mid-City: Bayou Saint John and the Carondelet Canal. The founders of New Orleans selected its future site for its proximity to the portage Bayou Saint John afforded from Lake Pontchartrain to the Mississippi. Navigating the mouth of the Mississippi was treacherous at that time; connecting the Gulf of Mexico to the thousands of miles of the Mississippi River system via the lake, the bayou, and a short portage dramatically reduced shipping risks (Campanella 2000: 20). The inland tip of Bayou Saint John penetrates

Mid-City, and from the late eighteenth century until it was filled in 1938 and replaced for a time by a railway, the canal ran from the end of the bayou to Basin Street behind the French Quarter, further facilitating passage between the river and the gulf. The waterways left little impact on the architecture along their banks, apart from a few French plantation-style houses still extant just outside Mid-City. Industrial uses, though, still flank the abandoned rail corridor that runs along present-day Lafitte Street. One of the initiatives underway in Mid-City's rebuilding is the conversion of the Lafitte Corridor into a greenway with bicycle and pedestrian paths for the benefit of the several neighborhoods it touches.

The shotgun houses that make up around 50 percent of Mid-City tended to be built speculatively as rentals. Mid-City prior to Hurricane Katrina retained a rental-dominated character, with 72.1 percent of its households rented, according to the 2000 Census (GNOCDC 2008). The neighborhood had a racial composition comparable to Orleans Parish as a whole, with one significant exception: while Mid-City's African-American population, at 64.3 percent, was just below the parish's of 66.6 percent, and its 23.2 percent non-Hispanic White population was close to the parish's 26.6 percent, Mid-City's Latino population was 10.0 percent, compared to the parish-wide 3.1 percent. Beginning around the turn of the twentieth century, tropical fruit importers based in New Orleans had extensive influence in parts of Central America, particularly Honduras. One of the largest concentrations of Hondurans outside Honduras itself is in New Orleans, particularly Mid-City. Post-Katrina, Latino numbers in New Orleans have probably at least doubled, according to Census estimates, possibly more, given the number of undocumented workers who have come seeking employment in rebuilding. Signs of more Spanish speakers are evident all over, in faces and voices on the street, Spanish-language billboards, taco trucks, and more visible Latin American-oriented businesses (Bahr 2007). Not surprisingly, Mid-City thoroughfares like Carrollton Avenue and Jefferson Davis Parkway are home to several reopened, relocated, and new Latino businesses. Another prominent immigrant group to leave a lasting impression on the neighborhood was the Sicilians. A wave of Sicilian immigration in the late nineteenth century spread throughout the city (making St. Joseph's Day as prominent a holiday on the local calendar as St. Patrick's), moving into new affordable territory opened up by the drainage projects – their mark in Mid-City is still felt in the culinary landmarks of Mandina's and Liuzza's restaurants, and Angelo Brocato's Ice Cream Parlor.

Cultural Recovery and the Endymion Parade Mardi Gras Tradition in Mid-City

By August 31, 2005, most of Mid-City was under 2 to 7 feet of water. A few areas running along natural ridges saw scarcely any flooding, and here and there, depths exceeding seven feet could be found. In all, 23,651 housing units out of 35,582 in the greater Mid-City area were flooded by at least two feet (United States Department of Housing and Urban Development 2005: 1). Mid-City's moderate flooding relative to harder-hit areas like the Ninth Ward, Gentilly, New Orleans East, and Lakeview, combined with its high retention rate of historic buildings usually elevated a couple feet above street level, gave it somewhat of an advantage over neighborhoods where entire houses were subsumed, but the damage was considerable nevertheless.

Like several other areas with strong neighborhood organizations, Mid-City began its own independent planning process even before participating in the City- and State-recognized

Chapter 8: **POST-KATRINA NEW ORLEANS**

exercises, the New Orleans Neighborhoods Rebuilding Plan (NOLANRP, or "The Lambert Plan") and Unified New Orleans Plan (UNOP). The Mid-City neighborhood plan owes something to the flourishing of Internet resources and online New Orleans communities. Its first draft debuted on a resident's personal blog (Everson, "Mid-City"), and its third and final draft resides on the New Orleans Wiki. The plan recommends many of the touchstones of livability today: neighborhood-based health clinics, multi-function community assets, like a library branch doubling as a community center, remediation of blighted properties as affordable housing (emphasizing increased opportunities for home ownership, a departure from Mid-City's pre-Katrina status), commercial development along public transportation routes, with an emphasis on support for locally-owned businesses and on a variety of goods and services to meet most needs within the neighborhood, pedestrian- and bicycle-friendly development, and ample, safe recreation space. A high priority is also placed on preserving the historic character in general of Mid-City, from its architecture to its existing "Main Street" commercial corridors. Much of the recipe for an improved Mid-City, according to the ideals expressed in its plan, is already present in its historic structure.

The most dramatic event in Mid-City's recent history occurred on Saturday, February 2, 2008: the enormous Krewe of Endymion resumed its customary parade route through Mid-City for the first time since Katrina. The Saturday parade represented a victory for the Krewe, the neighborhood, and the entire city, after fears beginning in 2006 that a Mid-City parade would never again be supportable by a city strapped for the money and manpower to police a Mardi Gras on a pre-Katrina scale.

Heir to the centuries-old pre-Lenten festivities of Europe, New Orleans' Carnival season runs from the Feast of the Epiphany to the eve of Ash Wednesday – Mardi Gras, or "Fat Tuesday" – itself. Although small, private celebrations are held throughout the Carnival season, it is in the two weeks or so leading to Mardi Gras day that celebrating takes on a distinctly public quality, with enormous parades overtaking major streets in New Orleans and surrounding suburbs and towns. These large parades, composed of massive and elaborately decorated floats, marching bands, and other entertainments, running several miles and usually taking several hours from beginning to end, are produced by members-only organizations usually dubbed "Krewes." Since the elite, exclusive, and secretive "Mistick Krewe of Comus" was formed in 1857 and held the first formal Mardi Gras parade, "krewe" has been the appellation of most large parading groups, and even some of the smaller marching troupes, or "walking krewes." Besides staging parades, most krewes hold elaborate balls for their members and their invited guests, the oldest and most elite of which are still the focal point of the local debutante season. The krewes are at once the most private and most public faces of New Orleans' Mardi Gras. Although most of today's actively parading krewes have considerably more open membership policies than the oldest groups, annual dues of hundreds or thousands of dollars alone are enough to put joining a high-profile krewe out of reach for most of the tens of thousands who line the streets to watch the parades, even for those krewes that do not have additional requirements, like referral by a member. *Pro bono publico* is the motto of the venerable Rex, another of the elite krewes dating back to the nineteenth century – for the good of the public, enormous shows are conducted in the city streets, but by (mostly) masked men privy to a lavish private celebration afterward and association with exclusive social circles year-round.

Mardi Gras parading has experienced shifts and transformations throughout its history. Krewes have come and gone, routes have changed, elitism has waned (but not disappeared), segregation has been confronted (but not eliminated), the demand for elaborate floats and throws has burgeoned. Mardi Gras parade-goers do not merely stand on the sidelines and watch, but clamor for plastic beads, aluminum doubloons stamped with krewe insignia, plastic cups, and other favors. Endymion itself was once a brash newcomer that helped change the face of Carnival. Rolling for the first time in 1967, it went from its fifty-or-so original members to become one of the "super krewes"[2] with the floats and balls to accommodate them. Like the super krewe of Bacchus, formed in the same period, Endymion's founding was influenced at least in part by the perception of a declining interest in Mardi Gras. Already important to the local economy as a tourist attraction, Mardi Gras attendance was in danger with hotel occupancy in the 1960s at only 60 percent during the peak of Carnival season (Endymion 2008). Bacchus and Endymion ushered in a new level of spectacle, with celebrity guests, mega-floats with ever-escalating design and technological features, and generous throws. They also introduced a new level of accessibility to the parading experience. The oldest parading krewes are elite and secretive, impenetrable even to most native New Orleanians. Small neighborhood krewes afforded locals chances to participate, albeit not on the level that the super krewes would; so long as you could pay your dues – and were white and male (in the early years) – you could join.

Endymion is the last krewe to parade through Mid-City; even the eponymous Krewe of Mid-City, founded in the 1930s by men from the Mid-City Civic Organization (Krewe of Mid-City 2008) left the area in 2002. Krewe of Mid-City, along with other formerly neighborhood-based krewes, has joined the Uptown route, which, with few deviations, has become the standard for almost every East Bank parade in Orleans Parish. Pre-Katrina Endymion was not, however, any desperate holdout clinging to its roots while slowly losing attendance to the centralized attractions Uptown. Endymion was, and still is, one of the most popular parades, with immense attendance along its entire route. Moving from the official concerns expressed by police superintendent Warren Riley that "the Mid-City area with all of the blight, and with the abandoned houses, makes it a lot harder to control what's going on" (Lee 2006: 2), to the resolution passed by City Council supporting a Mid-City route for Endymion "going forward in perpetuity" (Reckdahl 2008) marks both a faith in Mid-City's future, and a recognition of its recovery progress.

Ironically for Mid-City, the rise of super krewes has been a contributing factor to the decline of neighborhood-based krewes and parade routes. A former king of the Krewe of Mid-City said of their decision to move to the St. Charles Avenue route,

> many people who once lived in the Mid-City neighborhood had moved out to the suburbs, the people who once came to the parade were going to see bigger parades, the children of the people who once rode in our parade were now riding in super krewes, and the new people who moved to Mid-City wouldn't accept an invitation to ride.
>
> (DuBos 2008)

Most former neighborhood krewes keep their "den" (where meetings are held and floats stored) in its original location, but have weakened connections to their old homes. The Krewe of Mid-City presently has only two members who live in Mid-City – they joined in 2007

Chapter 8: **POST-KATRINA NEW ORLEANS**

(Finch 2006). The Krewe of Carrollton, started in 1924 by Oak Street business owners, left the Carrollton neighborhood in the 1970s, traveling a Mid-City route among others before settling on the standard Uptown path in 1995 (Krewe of Carrollton 2008). The Krewe of Okeanos was similarly civic-minded when it formed in the late 1940s. A handful of the original members, who were drawn from business owners on and around St. Claude Avenue who wanted to bring a parade experience to the Upper Ninth Ward, still belong. After roadwork forced Okeanos from the Ninth Ward, the parade never returned there, moving first to Mid-City and eventually succumbing to the pull of Uptown (DuBos 2008).

Besides Endymion, whose super krewe popularity helps moor it in the vicinity of founder Ed Muniz's childhood home, only a couple other Orleans Parish parades have held on to nonstandard routes. The Krewe of Thoth joins the standard Napoleon Avenue-to-St. Charles Avenue path only after winding through the narrower streets farther uptown. Its route was deliberately designed in 1950 to pass 14 institutions that serve the severely ill, the handicapped, and the elderly, including Children's Hospital. The krewe has real pride, not only in keeping its upper-Uptown roots, but also in its nickname, "The Krewe of Shut-Ins." Zulu Social Aid and Pleasure Club, the famous African-American Carnival organization that had its origins at the beginning of the twentieth century in the Tramps club, first gained fame outside Black neighborhoods when its King satirized the pompous Rex parade. But for years, it could only be seen on the segregated "back streets" (Becknell *et al.* 2008). Today, Zulu joins the St. Charles route midway, after first traveling through heavily African-American Central City. Returning, after Katrina, to routes that reflect a critical feature of their identity was a challenge to each of these groups as it was to Endymion, on top of the immediate challenges of ruined floats and members spread across America.

Although as a super krewe Endymion has a somewhat different relationship with Mid-City than more traditional neighborhood krewes, its environs have shaped a parade experience quite distinct from other routes. Its specific launching point has been at Orleans Avenue where it meets City Park since 1981 (Endymion 2008). Orleans Avenue's "neutral ground" (as New Orleanians call broad, grassy medians) is 150 feet wide at that point. Over the years of Endymion's existence, Mid-City parade-goers have availed themselves of the Orleans neutral ground, and the narrower neutral grounds of Carrollton and Canal, to stake out parade-watching territory as early as the Thursday and Friday before the Saturday evening parade. Friends and family members take turns guarding their "turf" overnight, and the watchmen are joined in such force on Saturday morning that the police have taken to closing off Orleans and surrounding streets by 11:00 am. In 1997, the Krewe of Endymion inaugurated a "Samedi Gras" festival. A series of local bands play in Orleans all afternoon, and krewe members are encouraged to join the crowd before boarding their floats. In 2006 and 2007, no Samedi Gras was held, but Uptowners were treated to a somewhat different Mardi Gras streetscape than they were accustomed to. Seasoned Mid-City Endymion fans brought their early turf-staking to St. Charles, where streetcar tracks had formerly prevented Uptowners from forming similar habits (most of the St. Charles streetcar line was not operating in 2006 or 2007). Although it cannot be said that Uptown parade-goers are completely unterritorial, "campers" who blocked off entire sections of neutral ground through the Friday night and Saturday morning parades made for a different Mardi Gras weekend experience. It was not entirely for the benefits it posed to Mid-City that some Uptown residents were glad to see the parade go home in 2008.

In addition to the psychological boost Endymion's return gave to Mid-City, a parade of its size has incredible economic impact, even for just one day a year. In preparation for City Council deliberations on reestablishing Endymion's route "in perpetuity," the Mid-City Neighborhood Organization (MCNO) prepared an economic impact survey. Although Mid-City is not a major tourist destination, the businesses surveyed reported from two to eight times their ordinary Saturday revenue (Winkler-Schmidt 2008). The extension of a new streetcar line along Carrollton Avenue in 2003 had forced Endymion Uptown once before, and Mid-City business owners were acutely sensitive to the value of that annual shot in the arm, having seen their most profitable day turn into their least so recently. Some business owners also cited the prospect Endymion provides for both repeat tourists and locals outside the neighborhood to discover Mid-City amenities and build their pools of regulars, and to remind everyone that Mid-City was not all lost to the flooding (Winkler-Schmidt 2008).

MCNO pled its case for the return of Endymion to City Council and the broader public for a variety of reasons: "the economic need, the emotional need, the family nature of the event, the impact on the community, and so forth" (Everson 2006a). An MCNO member who attended the City Council meeting noted that, prior to Mid-City's turn on the agenda, a presentation on the recovery of Kobe, Japan after its earthquake emphasized the role of a comprehensive approach to disaster-struck neighborhoods' community-building. "Specifically, that giving neighborhoods 'wins,' things residents want but aren't necessarily easy to provide or obvious parts of the recovery is important" (Everson 2006a). The neighborhood's sense of its "win" was evident on February 2, in banners and signs welcoming Endymion back. Businesses, new and old, along with churches and informal entrepreneurs, hawked food and drinks to-go, clean bathroom privileges, and parade-watching accessories. The crowds and the floats did, however, pass some pockets of persistent ruins. One Canal Street watcher said from the sidelines, "it used to be, you couldn't see any green," referring to the grass on the neutral ground between her and the parade: bodies, scaffolding, and tents spread across its whole extent, but not so tightly that the ground could not be seen. One "win" cannot make the recovery of a neighborhood, but Endymion 2008 was an exceptionally visible and emotional mark on the Mid-City scorecard.

Cultural and Economic Impacts of New Orleans' Mardi Gras Traditions

Despite the absence of Endymion on its usual route, the 2006 Mardi Gras was an emotional and economic victory for the city as a whole. The University of New Orleans' Division of Business and Economic Research estimated Mardi Gras attendance at only 350,000 compared to the pre-Katrina average of 1 million, but holding a public Mardi Gras at all just six months after the hurricane was a feat, and given the reduced hotel capacity and the widespread perception of a city still in utter ruins, the approximately $839 a piece spent by visitors was a shot in the arm to the tourism industry. One of the most intriguing findings of the DBER study was that 9.8 percent of surveyed participants who identified themselves as coming from the Greater New Orleans area were attending Mardi Gras parades for the first time. At 40.5 percent, "sense of tradition" was the highest-rated motivation for New Orleans residents attending Mardi Gras (CityBusiness 2006). Perhaps for some of those 9.8 percent watching parades in their own city for the first time, that sense elevated the importance of what in other years had seemed to be merely a nuisance interrupting traffic and everyday business.

Chapter 8: **POST-KATRINA NEW ORLEANS**

In the course of coming together at nearly the six-month mark after Katrina, having something to celebrate, reconnecting with friends and neighbors, and restimulating tourism, the 2006 Carnival gave New Orleanians another important opportunity: for all its changes from its medieval roots, the New Orleans Mardi Gras has never entirely lost its satirical element. Krewe du Vieux, an amalgamation of smaller "walking krewes" (krewes that do not ride in floats), is the best known for its bitingly satirical (and often raucous and lewd) themes, and was the first major parade of the season. Even more staid krewes, which normally choose mythological or popular culture themes for their parades, were rarely without at least some reference to Katrina-related politics or the chaotic nature of life in the city's early stage of recovery. Floats and costumes were dedicated to such subjects as the "blue roofs" (the tarps protecting storm-damaged homes while waiting for roofers), the spoiled refrigerators left on the curbsides that became magnets for political graffiti while they waited weeks for pick-up, levee breaches, and even the spray-painted marks left on homes by rescue workers searching for survivors and bodies. Political figures and agencies at every level of government were pilloried with papier-mâché caricatures: President Bush, Governor Blanco, FEMA director Michael Brown, and Mayor Nagin were particular favorites. For a short space, the deep anger and frustrations at the tragically bungled rescue efforts and confused, tumultuous recovery living conditions were recast as a somewhat bitter in-joke.

Meanwhile, the spaces between floats that in normal years are filled by the city's middle- and high- school marching bands were noticeably reduced, underscoring the extent of the devastation and how much work was yet to be done, but also some small hope. Most schools had not reopened, and for those that had managed to resume educating, it had only been a matter of weeks since readmitting students – hardly enough time to muster a band out of the new mixes of students enrolling in whatever schools they could find that could accept them, and with instruments and uniforms lost. For students, parents, teachers, alumni, and parade-goers accustomed to years of seeing the same groups perform, each year's progress in restoring New Orleans' high school bands and dance troupes is closely watched. One of the highlights of the 2006 Carnival was the MAX band. Neither the illustrious "Purple Knights" of the historic African-American Catholic boys' school St. Augustine, nor the bands of the African-American Catholic girls' schools, St. Mary's Academy and Xavier University Preparatory School, were prepared to march on their own. To stay afloat, the three schools and their bands united in 2006 until each could resume functioning independently.

Musical Roots of the City's Culture and Rebirth

Music is probably New Orleans' best-known tradition, notwithstanding the renown of its cuisine or architecture. The Birthplace of Jazz is known the world over, and not surprisingly, tributes to New Orleans' musical heritage along with musical benefits for New Orleans' citizens exploded while the extent of Katrina's devastation was still unfolding. Many people saw the setting of international legend Fats Domino's home, the Lower Ninth Ward, for the first time in the unrelenting series of shocking images exposing the depths of America's "hidden" poverty. Plenty more musicians with less spectacular fame than Fats Domino lived in such neighborhoods, well beyond the iconic French Quarter but at least as culturally critical. Usually predominantly African-American and lower income (but sometimes, as in the case of the Lower Ninth Ward, also enjoying higher rates of home-ownership than the citywide average), these neighborhoods have been the home to New Orleans' musical traditions, where boys and girls learn their instruments from relatives, neighbors, and school band programs, and where Mardi Gras Indian and Second Line customs keep New Orleans music vital and evolving. Their affordability also made the typical musician's career, sometimes just surviving from gig to gig, more plausible. Even while demand for New Orleans musicians surged and Blues, Jazz, Brass Band, Hip-Hop, and Bounce artists became the city's primary ambassadors to the world, the questions hung heavily of where they would live, where they would play locally, and how a next generation of musicians would one day join their ranks if flooded neighborhoods – like the Ninth Ward, Gert Town, Tremé, or others – did not recover.

Housing for its culture-bearers, especially musicians, is a need the city is still struggling with. Recognition of its importance came early: two of New Orleans' most successful and recognized musicians, Harry Connick, Jr. and Branford Marsalis, helped launch the Musicians' Village program with Habitat for Humanity in December 2005 – a development that would offer both affordable home-ownership, and the Ellis Marsalis Center for Music for education and community-building. En route to its implementation, however, the Musicians' Village plan faced the daunting obstacle that all low-income housing initiatives experience: many of its applicants were not sufficiently credit-worthy, particularly the musicians who were intended to be its primary (although not exclusive) beneficiaries. "I always say, creative people are creative 24/7. They pay their bills creatively too," Cherice Harrison-Nelson, counsel queen for the Mardi Gras Indian tribe, Guardians of the Flame, told the Times-Picayune (Reckdahl 2007). Harrison-Nelson qualified for a Musicians' Village home, but many of her fellows did not, and still struggle to bring their social and artistic communities back into physical proximity amidst the escalating post-Katrina rents and rebuilding costs.

Musicians' Village is, of course, not the only initiative to help New Orleans musicians with housing, nor is housing the only issue facing the music community. Richard Webster of New Orleans CityBusiness offers a brief list of just some of the organizations and services directed at musicians: "The New Orleans Musicians Clinic offers affordable medical care; the Entertainment Law and Legal Assistance Project provides free counsel; Sweet Home New Orleans offers housing assistance; Renew Our Music, formerly known as the Hurricane Relief Fund, subsidizes live performances; Music Rising replaces lost or damaged instruments; and Music Cares provides substance abuse recovery programs." Storm-ruined venues in a city whose live music clubs are not limited to an entertainment district or two, but dispersed through neighborhoods all over the city including the most flooded areas, have limited the opportunities for performers attempting to return permanently to New Orleans, as have reduced convention and special event bookings. Even clubs that were capable of reopening quickly operated drastically reduced schedules for months after the city reopened to residents: historic music venues like Preservation Hall and Tipitina's went from between five to seven shows a week to only one or two (Spera 2006), Preservation Hall is poised to finally return to a seven-night week on September 1, 2008, and Tipitina's calendar now has bookings three to five nights more weeks than not.

The New Orleans music scene immediately post-Katrina and beyond has not been universally grim. In fact, the returns of performers, venues, and events have been anything but grim. Of early shows following Katrina, Tipitina's music director Adam Shipley told the

Chapter 8: **POST-KATRINA NEW ORLEANS**

Times-Picayune, "Everything that was taken for granted was suddenly not available. When people came back, they were like, 'We've got to go see this stuff'" (Spera 2006). In Mid-City, one of the inaugural events of the neighborhood's commercial recovery was the reopening of Mid-City Lanes Rock 'n' Bowl – an 18 lane bowling alley featuring live music and dancing four or five nights a week – in December 2005, with surrounding streets still eerily dark. By April 2006, Mid-City was hosting the annual Jazz and Heritage Festival, despite early concerns that the ravaged Fair Grounds Race Track where the Jazz Fest is held would not be ready, and worse fears that the thousands of music fans who travel to New Orleans every year for the festival would not trust the city itself to be ready for such an event.

African-American Mardi Gras Indian and Second Line Parading Traditions

Inseparable from New Orleans' musical traditions are its African-American parading traditions, whose musical stylings have always informed the recording artists coming out of the city. Many of New Orleans' cultural traditions run deep, appearing almost unchanged over decades. For as much continuity as New Orleans culture has exhibited though, customs have always adapted to new times in order to remain vital. Naysayers predicted the end of Carnival in 1992, when an ordinance was passed denying parade permits to Mardi Gras Krewes that discriminated on the basis of race or religion. Instead, new, more inclusive organizations formed to fill the spots left by the few Krewes who refused to comply, and the parade schedule in the weeks leading up to Fat Tuesday is as vibrant as ever. Marching brass bands, virtually a metonym for the city itself, struggled to find paying gigs in the 1970s, but revived beginning in the 1980s thanks to innovators like the Dirty Dozen Brass Band who freely experimented with funk and bebop additions to the traditional sound. The challenges to custom posed by Katrina are more than changing tastes and mores, which, of course, continue to evolve as always. Every neighborhood-based club, band, krewe, or congregation is facing both the dispersal of its members and the still unfolding changes to the physical landscape itself.

The term "Super Sunday" in New Orleans does not evoke a football championship – it is the annual date of one of the city's most exuberantly colorful African-American traditions. Mardi Gras Indians, "tribes" of mostly men (although women and children have been increasingly involved over the years) masking in lavishly detailed, handmade feathered and beaded suits sometimes weighing as much as 150 pounds, parade on two major occasions every year: Mardi Gras day, and a Sunday (or Sundays, as Uptown and Downtown Indians sometimes parade on different weekends) close to St. Joseph's Day in March. Downtown Indians start their Super Sunday in Mid-City, where Orleans Avenue crosses Bayou St. John. "Masking Indian" in 2006 posed special challenges: not only were tribe members still dispersed, but volumes of colored feathers, beads, sequins, and fabric had been utterly ruined in the floodwaters, along with several months' labor on the construction of the suits, which are made anew each year. Commitment to masking is passionate, and even with so many members displaced there will continue to be a concerted effort to keep the music, costume design, and parading alive.

Similarly, a few dozen Social Aid and Pleasure Clubs keep up another parading custom dating to the nineteenth century, the Second Line, in which a main line composed of a Grand Marshall or other leader, hired band, and club members parade through neighborhood streets followed by a "second line" drawn from parade-goers along the route. Neither the Social Aid and Pleasure Clubs nor the Mardi Gras Indians normally parade along major thoroughfares, as the grander Mardi Gras Krewes usually do. As Times-Picayune columnist and regular commentator on Second Line culture has noted, "there are no second lines outside the older sections of the city. This is true despite the fact that many musicians have moved to these areas in recent decades." Even with musicians and members moving away from the groups' neighborhoods of origin, community roots have been maintained in other ways, especially the choice of parade routes. The urban form of old New Orleans is itself a critical component of the parade experience. Low vehicular traffic along the narrow side streets combined with densely populated, close-set rows of cottages and shotgun houses, and in some cases, the city's older public housing projects, have provided a participatory experience unimaginable in a more suburban-style setting. Two-and-a half years later after Katrina, though, it is still hard to tell what shape many of the historic lower-income neighborhoods that are the base of New Orleans' parading traditions will take. Recovery of private homes and apartments has been an uneven process, varying from neighborhood to neighborhood, and block-to-block, hampered by the presence of blight pre-dating the floods. At the same time, four large public housing projects, formerly home to plenty of tribe and club members and parade goers alike, as well as the "coming out" spots of some tribes, are undergoing demolition and redevelopment as HOPE-VI projects. Controversies have raged over the demolition and rebuilding plans – New Orleans' public housing was badly in need of reform of some sort, but feelings are deeply divided over what direction that reform should have taken. One consequence of the decision to demolish, whether it is ultimately for the better or worse, is that when parades follow their traditional routes, they will pass through relatively low-populated regions for some time to come. At present, staging parades along traditional routes, even if they pass through sparsely repopulated areas, is a powerful sign of resilience and hope, and sometimes also a memorial and a protest, even for people who are not currently living in their New Orleans homes. "When we had the big parade in January [2006], people came back for the culture. You know, the mayor couldn't bring people back, but a second line brought them back to the city," Lady Buckjumpers Social Aid and Pleasure Club president, Linda Porter, told a WWOZ radio interviewer in Spring of 2006.

Obstacles Faced in Protecting the Second Line Tradition

The January 2006, the All-Star second line Porter refers to was also, sadly, the occasion of three shootings within blocks of the parade route. Although Social Aid and Pleasure Club leaders and members have been among the most tireless anti-crime activists, their parades have been marred frequently enough by violence in the crowds or nearby that police protection is mandatory and expensive. Following the All-Star parade, second line parade permit fees for police staffing were raised from $1,200 to $4,445 (by contrast, the fees charged to the Mardi Gras Krewes that put on enormous, multi-hour parades are limited by a city ordinance to $750). The nascent Social Aid and Pleasure Club Task Force, representing 27 of the 39 actively parading Social Aid and Pleasure Clubs of New Orleans, grew from the defunct pre-Katrina Second Line Cultural Tradition Task Force in the course of organizing the All-Star parade of at least 30 individual clubs, combating the fee increase (which was successfully reduced to

Chapter 8: **POST-KATRINA NEW ORLEANS**

$1,985 in an April 2007 compromise between the police department and the clubs, ending a lawsuit filed by the ACLU on behalf of the clubs). The organizers of the All-Star parade have proven to be effective in other sorts of organizing as well, and the "social aid" aspect of second lining has not only taken the fore again after Katrina, it has taken directions entirely new in second line history.

New Orleans' Social Aid and Pleasure Clubs have been a critical source of social capital for the city's low- and moderate-income African American neighborhoods throughout their existence, harnessing that capital for tangible material benefit in some eras, and always maintaining strong neighborhood ties. Traditional Social Aid and Pleasure Clubs grew out of African-American mutual aid societies of the nineteenth century, providing such services to members as burial insurance, lending pools, and training in skilled trades. As private insurance, banking, and other opportunities began to open to African-Americans in the latter half of the twentieth century, the social aid element of second line culture began to wane, apart from the community-building and tradition-bearing performed by the continuation of the "pleasure" aspect: holding annual parades. Post-Katrina, a new form that mutual aid is taking is mutual aid between the clubs themselves, with the Task Force assisting not only in the lawsuit to reduce parade permit fees, but in guiding the member clubs through the complicated permitting process itself, liaising with the police and city agencies to improve relations, and educating city officials and the general public alike on the history and importance of second line traditions. Today's social aid is not all mutual, however, or at least not mutual exclusively within the clubs' memberships. Tamara Jackson, president of both the Task Force, and of the VIP Ladies and Kids Social Aid and Pleasure Club is adamant that the well-being and morale of the city as a whole are the concern of the clubs. "There are clubs in every part of the city, even the West Bank," Jackson says, in the course describing some of the activities the clubs perform citywide. Annual school uniform and supply drives, holiday toy drives, and referral services for housing, schools, and children's summer camps are some of the Task Force's regular activities on behalf of their wider community, and for the first time ever, the Task Force and its members are partnering with other non-profits like Sweet Home New Orleans, Silence Is Violence (a local anti-crime organization), Fotos for Humanity (offering volunteer photography services to non-profits and community groups), and health organizations including the New Orleans AIDS Task Force and LSU's TigerCare. Jackson envisions a not-too-distant future when the Task Force can obtain and remediate a blighted building to serve as both its permanent headquarters and a resource center for youth and elderly, possibly the first of several such centers. Meanwhile, Social Aid and Pleasure Clubs and their members contend with their own hurricane losses and recovery hurdles (the Bring New Orleans Back Commission's Cultural Committee estimated the financial losses of Social Aid and Pleasure Clubs, Mardi Gras Indians, and other second lining groups at over $3 million, conservatively (9)).

Challenges to Restaurants and Foodways as Cultural Icons

Not unlike the musical or parading communities, one of the most significant blows to the restaurant industry as a whole in New Orleans was the loss of employees due to the scarcity of affordable housing. Even the iconic dining institutions of the French Quarter that weathered Katrina with little physical damage have had to contend with a drastically reduced workforce.

The first Mardi Gras post-Katrina saw lower tourism than previous years (estimated at around 70 percent of average attendance), but met those crowds with an even lower level of staff. The Louisiana Restaurant Association reported a drop from around 70,000 employees to 20,000 in March of 2006 (Duncan 2006: 2–3). Some restaurateurs have scrambled to secure temporary housing for employees who lost apartments: Mother's Restaurant, a favorite of tourists and locals in the Central Business District, is just one of the businesses that set up trailers in a parking lot for its staff.

The loss of staff was acutely felt in the locally owned, generations-old restaurants in flooded and unflooded areas alike – despite the food service industry's famously high turnover rate, many family-run businesses in New Orleans have had family-like relationships with their cooks, waiters, bartenders, and busboys who have made long-term careers with them and become like family to regular patrons as well. The management of Mandina's, a third-generation, family owned restaurant in Mid-City, has fielded complaints from customers "who can't understand why the waiter who has served them for decades has been replaced by someone they don't recognize" (Anderson 2007b: 3). Lack of housing is not the only constraint restaurants and their staff have faced. While higher wages have been a considerable boon to the restaurant workers in short supply, those costs added to renovation expenses and other higher costs to doing business post-Katrina have required higher prices and new attention to the bottom line. The Louisiana tradition of adding a little lagniappe, or "something extra" (whether for goodwill or in hopes of a higher tip) is less tenable in new circumstances, and Mandina's is one instance where some long-tenured staff did return, but could not survive the newly stringent working conditions (Anderson 2007b: 3).

Over time, though, New Orleans dining in general has rebounded considerably. By the beginning of August 2008, local food journalist Tom Fitzmorris's "Restaurant Index" counted 952 open restaurants in the Greater New Orleans area, not including "fast-food restaurants, most national chains, bars and coffeehouses," compared to 809 before Katrina. Twenty-four of the restaurants listed are in Mid-City, including the cultural landmarks Mandina's, Liuzza's, and Angelo Brocato's. Even within a year of the hurricane, Times-Picayune's restaurant critic, Brett Anderson, found that the city's "highest achieving" restaurants were performing at or near their pre-Katrina levels of quality food and service. Still, Anderson held off publishing a formal review of any New Orleans restaurant for three years after his July 2005 assessment of an Uptown French bistro – "I was . . . uncomfortable with what the critical analysis of food and service could imply: that things were back to normal when they so clearly were not" (Anderson 2008b).[3]

Changing Food Traditions in the Post-Katrina Landscape

"Back to normal *and* clearly not" is an apt characterization of reopened historic eateries, not to mention those entire neighborhoods with little enough flood damage to have rebounded quickly population-wise and commercially. New Orleans' storm-damaged historic dining institutions have been in the throes of meeting twenty-first-century restaurant standards while retaining generations-old expectations of character as the city as a whole has been attempting to reconcile its historic culture with modern urban ideals. While critic Brett Anderson abstained from restaurant reviewing, reporting on culinary culture recovery took the fore for him instead,

Chapter 8: POST-KATRINA NEW ORLEANS

including a five-part series on a blow-by-blow account of the restoration of Mid-City's Sicilian jewel, Mandina's Restaurant. Mandina's reopening staffing woes, above, were only the closing chapter in the chronicle of a local institution's pangs of rebirth. Like so much of the city, Mandina's and other iconic eateries were a combination of charming anachronism and ad hoc renovations, now compelled to meet increasingly modern demands, posed both by customers and by lost grandfathered exemptions from code compliance. As the city as a whole has dealt with the agonizing dilemmas of how to preserve its cherished traditions while bringing its residents the ideal amenities of twenty-first-century urbanity, with some proposals calling for demolition and reconstruction of vast tracts of the cityscape in the service of better flood protection and access to amenities, the decisions of individual businesses have mirrored the citywide processes: starting entirely anew, buying the idea that Katrina presented a "blank slate," is profoundly inspiring in some ways, and by some calculations, more cost-efficient. But at the same time, appeal to tradition is not mere nostalgia. From a dollars-and-cents perspective, as well as from a community-building stance, New Orleans and its cultural landmarks, one by one, must weigh the relative merits of evolution and preservation. At the same time that Mandina's architect, John Montgomery, counseled planning for increased capacity during the rebuilding process rather than later, he also told the family, "You want people to feel like they're in Mandina's." "I've seen this," Montgomery said, "where you change the physical structure of a business and the business disappears" (Anderson 2007a: 3–4). Mandina's ultimately reopened to enormous popular acclaim, altered, but with recognizable continuity with its past. Other restaurants, small businesses, schools, clinics, entire neighborhoods, and institutions of all kinds throughout the city have engaged in, or are still engaged in hammering out the right balance between preservation and innovation to make people feel like they are "in New Orleans," and simultaneously, that New Orleans is a vital, promising place keeping pace with the best of modernity.

Communities all over the nation have recognized the economic, social, and environmental merits of supporting local businesses. New Orleans has its share, like any city, of national chains and branch offices; it has also keenly felt the effects of capital mobility (the impact of the collapse of oil prices on New Orleans' energy industry in the 1980s is still palpable). Envisioning a renewed New Orleans that is sustainable in every sense has entailed a great deal of attention to what sorts of industries – small and large – to foster, from supporting the existing tourism, port, and shipbuilding activities to cultivating a world-class biomedical district based on local hospitals and university programs (an effort predating Katrina). Attending to the recovery and growth needs of small businesses and local producers of all sorts, an interest that also predates Katrina, is another keen interest of New Orleanians.

A region renowned for its distinct culture has an advantage in this respect: there is often simply no acceptable alternative to locally made products. This is especially, but not exclusively, apparent where food is concerned. In addition to the myriad beloved local restaurants, the return of suppliers of those eateries and of supermarkets has been keenly anticipated and celebrated. The po'boy sandwich is served on a local variation on French bread – not a traditional baguette, but an airier loaf rarely reproduced outside the metro area. As a major coffee port, resumption of local processing and roasting was critical, and the city's taste for coffee and chicory blends made the fates of local coffee companies a matter that touched households entirely unconnected to the coffee trade. Many varieties of hot sausages and cured meats inspire fierce loyalties, and several sausage companies were still located in hard-hit neighborhoods like the Ninth Ward and Mid-City when Katrina hit.

Slightly farther afield than the city itself, regional crops of all sorts, including crawfish and Gulf shrimp, were dealt devastating blows. Besides the loss of a year's yields, the futures of the harvesters themselves were sometimes very much in doubt. Shrimpers in particular were faced with enormous losses in their fleets and refrigerated dock facilities; farmers and fishers in general all had to contend with not only damaged equipment and buildings, but survive through a season's lost income and speculate on when or whether their primary market would return to South Louisiana. Imports have long had a foothold in Louisiana markets: Asian shrimp and crawfish tails are never hard to find in supermarket seafood coolers; California strawberries and Florida citrus sit alongside their Louisiana counterparts even in their peak seasons. Although imports would probably never fully suffice the Louisiana palette in either taste or principal, how crippled industries would compete with larger-scale producers and exporters was and is a troubling question.

There is some real promise, however, for local food producers' futures: Louisianans' fidelity to unique local flavors, combined with concerns shared nationwide for health, energy efficiency, and local economies, have bolstered farmers' market initiatives and efforts to promote local products on supermarket shelves. Indeed, the creation of new "Mobile Markets" and support for existing farmers markets is a key feature of New Orleans' Office of Recovery and Development Administration's (ORDA) Healthy Communities plan. The Mobile Markets address yet another facet of the city's problems that were exacerbated by disaster: supermarkets were unevenly distributed before the storm – some neighborhoods, like the Ninth Ward, had none at all – and have been slow to reopen in the hardest hit areas. New ORDA-sponsored Mobile Markets are being operated by the French Market Corporation, also operator of the nation's oldest city market, the eponymous French Market. The ORDA markets join preexisting initiatives like the Crescent City Farmers Markets, launched in 1995. Local food and urban farming activists whose efforts predate Katrina have seen a surge of interest in community gardening and markets; gardening and urban farming combine interest in healthier eating, income supplementation, and the beneficial reuse of some of the city's many vacant tracts, while the markets provide both neighborhood-level access to local products and afford a reason for interested consumers to visit different neighborhoods, as most of the markets are held weekly or monthly. Many of the markets are situated in the small "Main Street"-style neighborhood commercial districts and incorporate local arts and crafts, workshops, and events, integrating neighborhood-based efforts to restore and reinvigorate their communities over all. Bridging organizations, like marketumbrella.org, which operates the Crescent City Farmers Markets (among other initiatives) and Stay Local!, which supports locally owned businesses of all sorts through comprehensive neighborhood- and category-based listings and general advocacy, operate citywide.

Beyond the city limits, the thousands of evacuees settling into long-term or permanent homes elsewhere have brought their tastes with them. Plenty of New Orleanians are happy to have found new homes with less crime, better jobs, and better schools that balance or even outweigh the positive elements of New Orleans culture they have left behind, but one's comfort foods are hard to give up entirely. Relatives back in Louisiana are often relied on to send care packages of those products that can be packaged to survive the trip, and in areas like East

Chapter 8: POST-KATRINA NEW ORLEANS

Texas, where the proportion of evacuees is high, some New Orleans-made products are finding a spot on supermarket shelves. The Fiesta supermarket chain in Houston, for instance, has garnered a reputation as one of the best places to go for a good selection of New Orleans products. A number of the producers themselves have had to relocate, at least temporarily, in order to keep their businesses alive while waiting to rebuild – or to see whether it would be worth rebuilding. Finding a temporary home at a plant in Georgia, the Wheats – of Mrs. Wheat's Foods, which makes locally famous meat- and crawfish-pies – discovered that Georgians had a taste for their wares as well, and that enough demand exists to warrant keeping up service to their newly expanded territory. Some local producers had exclusively in-state operations prior to Katrina, with no federal inspections or certification to permit interstate trade. When Patton's Hot Sausage rented space in a federally inspected plant in Bogalusa, it opened the possibility of a regional market for their meats for the first time (Walker). New Orleans-based food brands may not sweep the nation quite like the Cajun craze of the 1980s, but for a few local businesses, exposure to a wider market may have secured a stronger future despite the heavy losses at home. Successes are inspiring, but tenuous while the fates of surrounding neighborhoods are still uncertain and the long-term sustainability of new markets is hard to gauge.

Strength of Cultural Traditions in Anchoring the Post-Katrina Recovery

"I live in the neighborhood, but I didn't really start working on my house until I knew for sure that Mandina's was coming back," a patron told New Orleans food journalist, Tom Fitzmorris while waiting for a table at the Mid-City restaurant's reopening. It would surely be an overstatement for most New Orleanians to say that the status of a favorite restaurant was the deciding factor in their rebuilding plans, but the impact of New Orleans' cultural recovery on the city's general recovery is hard to underestimate. As evidenced by the many polls, surveys, and participatory planning exercises that have taken place since Katrina, preservation of local culture (while not always consistently defined) is one of the highest recovery priorities among citizens, one of the critical indices of what makes New Orleans livable. Rather than a blank slate, post-Katrina New Orleans is left with a rough template from which to work, based on its most valued traditions. Innovation for enhanced livability is greatly desired in many areas: safety from both future disasters and from crime, improved education, better economic opportunities, wider access to health care, and neighborhood-based goods and services. Not least of the neighborhood-based services desired by New Orleanians is the continued presence of the "third places" and public events where informal civic life occurs. Large-scale public projects like better levees, new school systems, and the re-envisioning of public health care provision are all critical factors in individual decisions regarding the long-term desirability of reinvesting in a life in New Orleans, but while those public projects remain slow, cumbersome, and sometimes contentious, the most immediate gauge available for the viability of New Orleans' neighborhoods remains the actions and opinions of the neighbors themselves. Cultural institutions and events are not only valuable for the occasions they provide for citizens to meet and exchange news and views on recovery, but their presence is a recovery indicator in itself. Every reopened small business, like the family-run Mandina's, and every club, krewe, or band whose members carry on their traditions despite commutes from other cities and full-time rebuilding work of their own is evidence of a shared commitment to New Orleans' future and raising its quality of life (along with its foundations).

While New Orleans' remarkable retention of traditional cultures lends itself in many ways to recovery and enhanced livability – from the built environment of Mid-City and neighborhoods like it, already amenable to Main Street-style commerce and community-based resources, to the gathering places and events that promote a civic life outside the political sphere – New Orleans' culture has never been entirely static, and the template it provides for recovery priorities is seldom completely clear. The evolution of local culture has frequently been a positive influence on the city's livability, as with the reconstitution of the meaning of "Social Aid" among New Orleans' pleasure clubs, the city's and state's decision to deliberately cultivate cultural occupations as a "sustainable natural resource," the involvement of arts and music organizations in matters like housing and health, and even the somewhat faltering steps toward a more inclusive Mardi Gras. The course of local culture's evolution through the long years of recovery ahead, and in what ways it will continue to contribute to a locally valued quality of life, is sensitive to other recovery decisions, both public and private. Scarce resources have entailed the concentration of public recovery activities in prioritized target zones, but no one can say for certain now how non-target zones will fare without special attention, or how deeply those neighborhoods contributed to cultural vitality citywide. The continued scarcity of affordable housing, a severely circumscribed public health sector, and a public school system still redefining itself all raise serious questions about who will be able to return to and thrive in New Orleans over the years to come. Despite the certainty of cultural changes, the sense of public spirit based in commitment to New Orleans' cultures is one of the most vital elements of the recovery effort, and one of the most visible signs of progress. It would be a stretch to say that the entire city is unified behind a sense of common culture, or that there is widespread agreement on just what value to place on all of New Orleans' micro-cultures and their features, but publicly and privately debating "what it means to miss New Orleans" and determining how to keep those values integral to defining and rebuilding a more livable city have underlain the entire recovery process.

Notes

1   Estimating New Orleans' repopulation is difficult. A US Census report estimated Orleans Parish's population (contiguous with the City of New Orleans) at 239,124 as of July 1, 2007 (a drop from an estimated 454,863 in July 2005), a figure contested by prominent local demographers GCR and Associates, and the Greater New Orleans Community Data Center (Plyer and Rigamer).

    GCR and Associates reported an estimated 60 percent of New Orleans' July 2005 population returned by July 2007 (GCR and Associates, Inc. 1), a figure GCR had anticipated as a moderate- to high-repopulation scenario for 2008 when they provided the Unified New Orleans Plan with repopulation estimates (UNOP 2006: 29). Using US Postal Data, the Greater New Orleans Community Data Center estimates that 72 percent of New Orleans' pre-Katrina population was actively receiving mail by May 2008 (GNOCDC 2008: 1).

2   Organizations with over 500 members. Endymion presently has more than 2,000.

3   Anderson awarded the Brennan family's Mr. B's Bistro three beans (in lieu of stars), or a rating of "very good" on July 24, 2008.

Chapter 8: POST-KATRINA NEW ORLEANS

References

Anderson, Brett (2007a). "Hell's kitchen." *The Times-Picayune* 2 Sept. 2007: LIVING.

Anderson, Brett (2007b). "It's still Mandina's: eighteen months after Hurricane Katrina, old customers get a taste of a renewed New Orleans institution." *The Times-Picayune* 5 Sept. 2007: LIVING.

Anderson, Brett (2008a). "Mr. B's Bistro earns three beans." *The Times-Picayune* 24 July 2008. NOLA.com http://blog.nola.com/brettanderson/2008/07/mr_bs_is_back.html.

Anderson, Brett (2008b). "Time to review New Orleans restaurants again." *The Times-Picayune* 24 July 2008. NOLA.com http://blog.nola.com/brettanderson/2008/07/what_took_me_so_long.html.

Associated Press (2005). "Plenty of help wanted in New Orleans." Associated Press. *CBS News* 28 Nov. 2005. http://www.cbsnews.com/stories/2005/11/28/ap/national/mainD8E5L71G0.shtml.

Barenstein, Jennifer Duyne (2006). "Challenges and risks in post-tsunami housing reconstruction in Tamil Nadu." *Humanitarian Practice Network*. http://www.odihpn.org/report.asp?id=2798 (accessed May 1, 2008).

Bahr, Emilie (2007). "Business cater to growing Hispanic population." *New Orleans CityBusiness* 12 July 2007. http://www.neworleanscitybusiness.com/viewFeature.cfm?recID=806.

Becknell, Clarence A., Thomas Price, and Don Short. "History of the Zulu social aid and pleasure club." *Zulu Social Aid and Pleasure Club*. http://www.kreweofzulu.com/krewe-of-zulu/history-of-the-zulu-social-aid-&-pleasure-club.html (accessed May 1, 2008).

Campanella, Richard (2002). *Time and Place in New Orleans: Past Geographies in the Present Day*. Boston, MA: Pelican Company, Inc., 2002.

Cangelosi, Robert J. (1993a). "Mid-City historic district." Louisiana Division of Historic Preservation, 10 Dec. 1993. http://www.crt.state.la.us/hp/nhl/document2.asp?name=36066001.pdf&title=Mid%2DCity+Historic+District.

Cangelosi, Robert J. (1993b). "Parkview historic district." Louisiana Division of Historic Preservation, 10 Dec. 1993. http://www.crt.state.la.us/hp/nhl/document2.asp?name=36076001.pdf&title=Parkview+Historic+District.

City of New Orleans, Office of Recovery and Development Administration (2008). "City of New Orleans launches mobile food markets." Press release. 30 May 2008. http://www.cityofno.com/pg-1-66-press-releases.aspx?pressid=4852.

CityBusiness (2006). Staff Report "University of New Orleans report: Mardi Gras, Jazz Fest and FQF all." *New Orleans CityBusiness*. Sep 5, 2006. FindArticles.com. http://findarticles.com/p/articles/mi_qn4200/is_20060905/ai_n16706378.

Collective Strength (2006). "2006 South Louisiana recovery survey: citizen and civic leader research summary of findings." Louisiana Speaks. http://www.louisianaspeaks.org/redir.html?id=315&url=http%3A%2F%2Fwww.louisianaspeaks.org%2Fcache%2Fdocuments%2F3%2F315.pdf June 2006.

DuBos, Clancy (2008). "Krewe to their roots." *The Gambit Weekly* 22 Jan. 2008 The *Best of New Orleans*. http://www.bestofneworleans.com/dispatch/2008-01-22/news_feat3.php.

Duncan, Jeff (2006). "The good times roll again in New Orleans, as Carnival is deemed a critical success." *The Times-Picayune* 2 Mar. 2006: NATIONAL.

Elie, Lolis Eric (2008). "Our music, architecture are linked." *The Times-Picayune* 16 Apr. 2008. http://www.nola.com/news/t-p/elie/index.ssf?%2Fbase%2Fnews-0%2F1208323471243710.xml&coll=1.

Endymion. "History." http://www.endymion.org/history/tabid/6058/default.aspx.

Endymion (2008). "Samedi Gras." http://www.endymion.org/samedigras.php (accessed May 1, 2008).

Everson, Bart (2006a). "Endymion update." *Mid-City Neighborhood Organization*. 15 Dec. 2006. http://mcno.org/2006/12/15/endymion-update/.

Everson, Bart (2006b). "Mid-City needs a plan." *B.rox*. 31 May 2006. http://b.rox.com/2006/05/31/mid-city-needs-a-plan/.

Finch, Susan (2006). "By living in Mid-City, krewe couple unique." *The Times-Picayune* 6 Jan. 2006. NOLA.com http://www.nola.com/news/t-p/metro/index.ssf?/base/news-26/1199600461164240.xml&coll=1.

Fitzmorris, Tom (2007). "Commentary: Mandina's return fills gaping Mid-City gap." *New Orleans CityBusiness* 14 May 2007.

Fitzmorris, Tom (2008). "Restaurant index." *The New Orleans Menu*. 5 Aug. 2008. http://www.nomenu.com/restaurantsopen.html.

GCR and Associates, Inc. (2007). "GCR releases population estimate for July 2007." Press release. July 2007. http://www.gcr1.com/images/gcrpop072007.pdf.

Greater New Orleans Community Data Center (GNOCDC) (2006). "Mid-City neighborhood: housing and housing costs." 25 June 2006. http://gnocdc.org/orleans/4/45/housing.html.

Greater New Orleans Community Data Center (GNOCDC) (2008). "May 2008 population estimates confirm decelerated growth in first quarter 2008." Press release. 26 June 2008. http://gnocdc.org/media/gnocdcjun30-08.pdf.

Jackson, Tamara (2008). Telephone interview. 3 July 2008. Interview conducted by the author.

Krewe of Carrollton, The (2008). "About." http://www.kreweofcarrollton.com/about (accessed May 1, 2008).

Krewe of Mid-City, The (2008). "History of the krewe of Mid-City." http://www.kreweofmid-city.org/krewe%20history.htm (accessed May 1, 2008).

Lee, Trymaine (2006). "NO parade routes limited for 2nd year." *The Times-Picayune* 11 Nov. 2006. NOLA.com. http://www.nola.com/news/t-p/frontpage/index.ssf?/base/news-7/116322851624040.xml&coll=1&thispage=1.

Louisiana Department of Culture, Recreation and Tourism (CRT) (2007). "Louisiana: Where culture means business." Mt. Auburn Associates. 2 Feb. 2007.

New Orleans Wiki (2006). "Mid-City recovery plan." *New Orleans Wiki*. Oct. 2006. http://thinknola.com/wiki/mid-city_recovery_plan.

Plyer, Allison and Greg Rigamer (2008). "For census challenge, solid grounds." *The Times-Picayune* 24 Mar. 2008. NOLA.com. http://www.nola.com/timespic/stories/index.ssf?/base/news-0/1206336024175050.xml&coll=1.

Porter, Linda, Tamara Jackson, and Gerie Thompson (2006). "Second line fee increase." Interview with Eve Troeh. *WWOZ Street Talk*. WWOZ, New Orleans. 1 Apr. 2006.

Reckdahl, Katy (2007). "Sour note." *The Times-Picayune*. 2 Jan. 2007. http://www.nola.com/frontpage/t-p/index.ssf?/base/news-7/1167720179104140.xml.

Reckdahl, Katy (2008). "Endymion makes colorful return to Mid-City." *The Times-Picayune*. 1 Feb. 2008. http://www.nola.com/mardigras/index.ssf/2008/02/endymion_makes_colorful_

return.html.

Report of the Cultural Committee (2006). "Bring New Orleans Back Commission (BNOB)." Cultural Committee. 17 Jan. 2006.

Spera, Keith (2006). "The beat goes on: local musicians make surprising progress post-Katrina but the music scene faces uncertainty." *The Times-Picayune* 6 Aug. 2006: NATIONAL.

Unified New Orleans Plan (UNOP) (2006). "Citywide strategic recovery and rebuilding plan." April 2006. http://www.unifiedneworleansplan.com/uploads/UNOP-FINAL-PLAN-April-2007-15744.pdf.

United States Department of Housing and Urban Development (HUD) (2005). "Extent and depth of flooding August 31, 2005 Orleans Parish, LA." Office of Policy Development and Research. http://www.huduser.org/maps/district_map_with_flood.pdf.

US Census Bureau (2004) Statistical Abstract of the United States: 2004–2005. 124th ed. Washington, DC: GPO.

Walker, Judy (2006). "Local flavor: slowly but surely, New Orleans favorites are returning to their rightful places in stores, restaurants and pantries." *The Times-Picayune* 5 Jan. 2006: LIVING.

Webster, Richard A. (2007). "Band of Benevolence." *New Orleans CityBusiness* 17 Sept. 2007. http://www.preservationhall.com/press/content-nolacb091707.htm.

Winkler-Schmidt, David (2008). "Samedi Gras." *The Gambit Weekly* 29 Jan. 2008 *Best of New Orleans* http://www.bestofneworleans.com/dispatch/2008-01-29/cover_story.php.

SECTION III

SPECIFIC INTERVENTIONS

Chapter 9

PUBLIC PARTICIPATION IN NEIGHBORHOOD PLANNING, A NEGLECTED ASPECT OF COMMUNITY LIVABILITY: THE CASE OF SEATTLE

Hilda Blanco

Research Professor, Interim Director of the Center for Sustainable Cities
University of Southern California

Introduction

Livability, like sustainability, is a nebulous concept with various facets. Most often it is identified with certain quality of life aspects of the physical city: compactness of form, diverse modes of transportation, mixed housing types, adequate open spaces, and so forth (Corbett and Velazquez 1994; Godschalk 2004). However, very often, the concept is identified not just as a physical set of characteristics, but also with certain social aspects, e.g. diversity in population, economic opportunities, a sense of identity or belonging in a place (Partners for Livable Communities 2002). The various aspects of the concept of livable communities can be interpreted as comprising a set of normative criteria for good city design, similar to Kevin Lynch's performance dimensions for good urban form (1981). As part of this social set of characteristics, community livability should also include a measure of community involvement in the planning process at the neighborhood scale. The Ahwahnee Principles developed by leaders in the new urbanism movement and which are often associated with livable cities do promote an open participatory process of community design (Calthorpe *et al.* 1991). Such an open process, however, could call for designer-led charrettes or other episodic community involvement in design processes rather than the municipally-sponsored neighborhood planning processes that I argue here as vital for livable communities.

City-wide issues have dominated the field of urban planning, but in the past few decades, municipally sponsored neighborhood planning is being practiced in a growing number of cities (Rohe and Gates 1985; Martz 1995; Rohe 2009). The neighborhood scale enables the planning process to focus on many aspects of livability beyond zoning, including pedestrian amenities, mixed use, mixed housing types, neighborhood scale open spaces, and neighborhood character in general. Neighborhood planning, in addition, provides an opportunity for community engagement at a scale where issues are widely familiar, and likely to engage more residents, unlike city-wide issues which may require more technical understanding. Participation in a neighborhood planning process is an indicator of an important social aspect of livability, the extent to which people who live and work in a neighborhood have the ability to influence the characteristics and future development of their community. This is a primary democratic process. As Dewey put it, "Democracy must have a home, and its home is the neighborly community" (Dewey 1927: 213). Participatory processes in neighborhood planning can also ensure that communities are inclusive of diversity. Participation in community planning provides a sense of control, or empowerment, and of identity with a place that enhances democracy, and social cohesion (Berry *et al.* 1993).

The concept of social capital in the community development literature is another theoretical lens that lends support to the inclusion of neighborhood planning as an important aspect of livability. Participatory neighborhood planning can be interpreted as a key means for developing social capital in cities. Putnam (2000) distinguishes between two types of social capital, bonding and bridging. Bonding social capital refers to practices that develop ties that bond members in a community, typically among people who share certain interests or values, while bridging social capital refers to practices that connect people with different socio-demographic characteristics. Woolcock (1998) identifies a third type of social capital, linking social capital, by which he means the capital of individuals or communities to leverage resources, ideas or information from formal institutions.[1] Participatory neighborhood planning provides opportunities for building these three types of social capital. Individuals involved in neighborhood planning develop bonds with other participants. If the process is inclusive, participants also form links across their own networks that bridge demographic and social differences. In addition, through a municipally sponsored neighborhood planning process, such neighborhoods can successfully leverage resources, ideas and information from city-wide institutions.

Participation in a neighborhood planning process can also enhance a person's identity with a community. From a social psychology perspective, community identity can be characterized as a combination of two components, sense of community, a more socially-oriented concept, and place-attachment, a more spatially-oriented concept (Puddifoot 1996; Pretty 2002). Empirical research also indicates a strong correlation between the two (Korpela 1989; Long and Perkins 2007). Participatory neighborhood planning can enhance both a sense of community, and place-attachment. By providing a bonding practice, through the planning process, it can enhance a sense of community; and by planning future changes or enhancements for a place-based community, it can enhance place-attachment. Some researchers also argue that sense of community, a central concept in community psychology, is one of four dimensions of social capital, along with collective efficacy, or sense of empowerment, neighboring behavior, such as informal mutual assistance and information sharing, and formal citizen participation (Perkins and Long 2002; Long and Perkins 2007).

These three theoretical perspectives on participatory neighborhood planning, i.e. local democracy, social capital, and community psychology lend support to the value of neighborhood planning and its inclusion in the concept of livable communities. The various aspects of participatory neighborhood planning, i.e. democratic processes at a familiar scale, its potential for inclusiveness, empowerment, sense of identity with and belonging to a community provide strong support for incorporating it as a vital aspect of livability.

Chapter 9: **THE CASE OF SEATTLE**

Prompted by Washington State's Growth Management Act (1990), which required cities to prepare comprehensive plans to accommodate their urban growth allocations, the City of Seattle recently undertook (1995 to 1999) an extensive neighborhood planning process, which has been recognized as a successful model for participatory neighborhood planning (Sirianni 2007). The framework of the neighborhood planning process was the City's Comprehensive Plan (1994). Seattle's comprehensive plan adopted a strategy of concentrating new growth in a set of centers, from downtown to neighborhood centers. Seattle developed an innovative way of getting neighborhoods to buy into the growth allocations – it left it up the neighborhoods to organize themselves for planning, while providing them with guidelines, some technical assistance, and funds for hiring consultants. The City estimates that over 20,000 people participated in the neighborhood planning process that produced 38 neighborhood plans. Also, Seattle established a distinctive way of reviewing plans for incorporation into the comprehensive plan, and for implementing such plans.

This chapter, after providing a brief account of neighborhood planning in the US, uses the Seattle neighborhood planning experience to elicit important aspects of participatory neighborhood planning using the distinction developed by Berry *et al.* (1993) that sets out various aspects of the breadth and the depth of participatory democracy, as well as other criteria more focused on the process of planning (Martz 1995). To assess the extent of participation, this chapter relies on a review of city documents, including planning and budget documents, as well as a review of the literature on Seattle's experience, concluding with exploratory findings on how Seattle's neighborhood planning process met the criteria identified. The final section links these findings to the three theoretical perspectives discussed above to articulate the benefits of incorporating participatory neighborhood planning as a crucial aspect of community livability.

Neighborhood Planning in the United States

While urban planning developed as a city-wide practice, the idea of neighborhood plans or designs goes back to Clarence Perry's neighborhood planning unit, which was incorporated in the regional plan for New York (1929). Rohe (2009) traces the history of neighborhood planning in the US from Clarence Perry's neighborhood planning unit through urban renewal, community action, municipal neighborhood planning, community economic development planning, and new urbanism's traditional neighborhood design. Although not all cities include municipal neighborhood planning programs, comprehensive plans have often included more specific or area plans for special neighborhoods or districts, e.g. for example, San Francisco's 1970s General Plan included a plan element on Chinatown. Several cities, such as Raleigh, North Carolina and Portland, Oregon began to establish neighborhood planning processes in the 1970s and 1980s (Martz 1995). These processes had two objectives: the participatory, to involve residents in planning for their neighborhood; and the substantive, to develop more precise or detailed plans for neighborhoods.

Substantively, neighborhood planning expands planning beyond zoning into design and land use-transportation and other community issues. In this way, neighborhood planning is a major means for developing and implementing a broader place-based livability agenda.

185

The participatory objective dates back to the 1960s and 1970s, prompted by federal requirements for public participation in plans for redevelopment projects that received federal funding, and by citizen movements reacting to the urban renewal and highway projects of the 1950s and 1960s. New York City, for example, formally established community planning boards in 1963. These boards, currently 59 boards, have had a role in advising the City's Planning Commission on major projects and Borough Presidents, the Mayor's Office and the City Council on budget priorities within their districts. New York City's 1975 city charter revisions allowed the development of community or neighborhood plans, but such plans were slow in developing, due to the undefined process for adopting such plans, and the lack of dedicated staff or funds to assist communities in their planning. Due to these problems, only ten community-board initiated plans had been approved by the City Council as of 2008 and the first one for Bronx was approved in 1992 (PlanNYC 2008). Seattle itself, before the 1995–1999 neighborhood planning process had a history of neighborhood planning dating back to the 1960s, developed in response to federal requirements for planning for areas with high poverty rates. But Seattle had a long tradition of community involvement with neighborhood clubs dating back to the early part of the twentieth century (Diers 2004).

Seattle's Neighborhood Planning Process

The Larger Context of Seattle's Neighborhood Planning Process

Seattle's neighborhood planning process was developed in the context of a state-wide urban growth management plan and the City's response to the State's urban growth allocation in the form of its Comprehensive Plan. Washington's state-wide Growth Management Act (1990) required that each county with high growth rates prepare a plan that would include an Urban Growth Area, in effect an urban growth boundary (UGB), which could accommodate urban growth for the next twenty years. Counties under GMA rely on state projections for growth, and allocate to cities and rural growth their "fair share" of urban growth. In addition, each municipality in growing counties was required to prepare a comprehensive plan consistent with countywide policies that included a future land use map (FLUM) and to adhere to concurrency requirements, in effect, the requirement that urban development not be allowed unless it could be served by adequate public facilities within a reasonable period.

King County's urban growth area included all of Seattle, and the city was allocated its fair share of growth both in terms of new households and of employment.

Seattle had a growth allocation of from 50,000 to 60,000 households and 140,000 jobs by 2014 (Diers 2004).[2] Although Seattle had some infill opportunities, the city in general was fully urbanized, and so meeting its allocation required some densification. To meet the requirements of GMA, the City prepared a Comprehensive Plan, adopted in 1994. Responding to negative responses to densification from the by-and-large low density residential neighborhoods in the city, the city introduced a neighborhood planning process, which was subsequently incorporated into the Comprehensive Plan. The neighborhood planning process included financial incentives for the neighborhoods to participate in the effort. The process allowed residents to decide how they would densify their neighborhoods, and by how much.

Chapter 9: **THE CASE OF SEATTLE**

Seattle's 1994 Comprehensive Plan

The major strategy of *Seattle's Comprehensive Plan, Towards a Sustainable Seattle* (adopted in 1994) for accommodating population and employment growth was its urban village strategy. The strategy allocated population to various neighborhoods in the city based on willingness and zoning capacity. The urban village strategy targeted growth to a set of centers, ranging from urban centers such as downtown, hub urban villages, e.g. Fremont, and residential urban villages, e.g. Madison Valley. See Figure 9.1 for the City's future land use map that sets out the various types of centers. Thirty-seven areas were targeted for growth under the plan, and all participated in the neighborhood planning program.[3] Urban centers were designated as the densest areas, with the widest range of land uses. These centers were not to exceed one-and-a half square miles, and their boundaries were set in the comprehensive plan. Hub urban villages were designated as the next level of urban intensity, with lower densities than urban centers, and a broad mix of uses. Residential urban villages were meant to describe centers with low to moderate densities of residential development and compatible support services and employment.

The neighborhood planning process was meant to refine and turn into reality the vision of the plan. The process the City set out for developing neighborhood plans required consistency between neighborhood plans and the comprehensive plan, an inclusive planning process and provisions to ensure that urban centers, urban villages and manufacturing/industrial centers were included in neighborhood plans. The boundaries for the centers set out in FLUM, as well as preliminary growth targets for these centers, could be amended through the neighborhood planning process.

The Neighborhood Planning Program

A new office, the Neighborhood Planning Office, under the Mayor's supervision was created to provide technical assistance to organizing neighborhood planning groups and to be dissolved at the end of the process. The City's Department of Neighborhoods already had a set of district offices, which provided outreach, community gardens, and an innovative Matching Fund program which fostered neighborhood-initiated projects. Although Seattle had many types of community organizations in place in 1995, including community councils, district councils, advisory councils for park districts, and Community Development Corporations, new groups were encouraged to organize to undertake the planning process.

Technical assistance to neighborhood planning groups was provided by the new neighborhood planning office, which consisted mainly of ten project managers. These project managers were primarily community organizers, rather than professional planners. In addition, the City developed and made available to neighborhood planning groups a community profile which included a standard set of maps and data, as well as a toolbox of regulations, programs, and examples.

In addition to technical assistance, the City provided financial support to groups undertaking neighborhood planning. The neighborhood planning process in Seattle was divided into two phases. The first phase included organizing, outreach, issue identification, community vision statement, and the preparation of the scope of work for Phase II. During the second

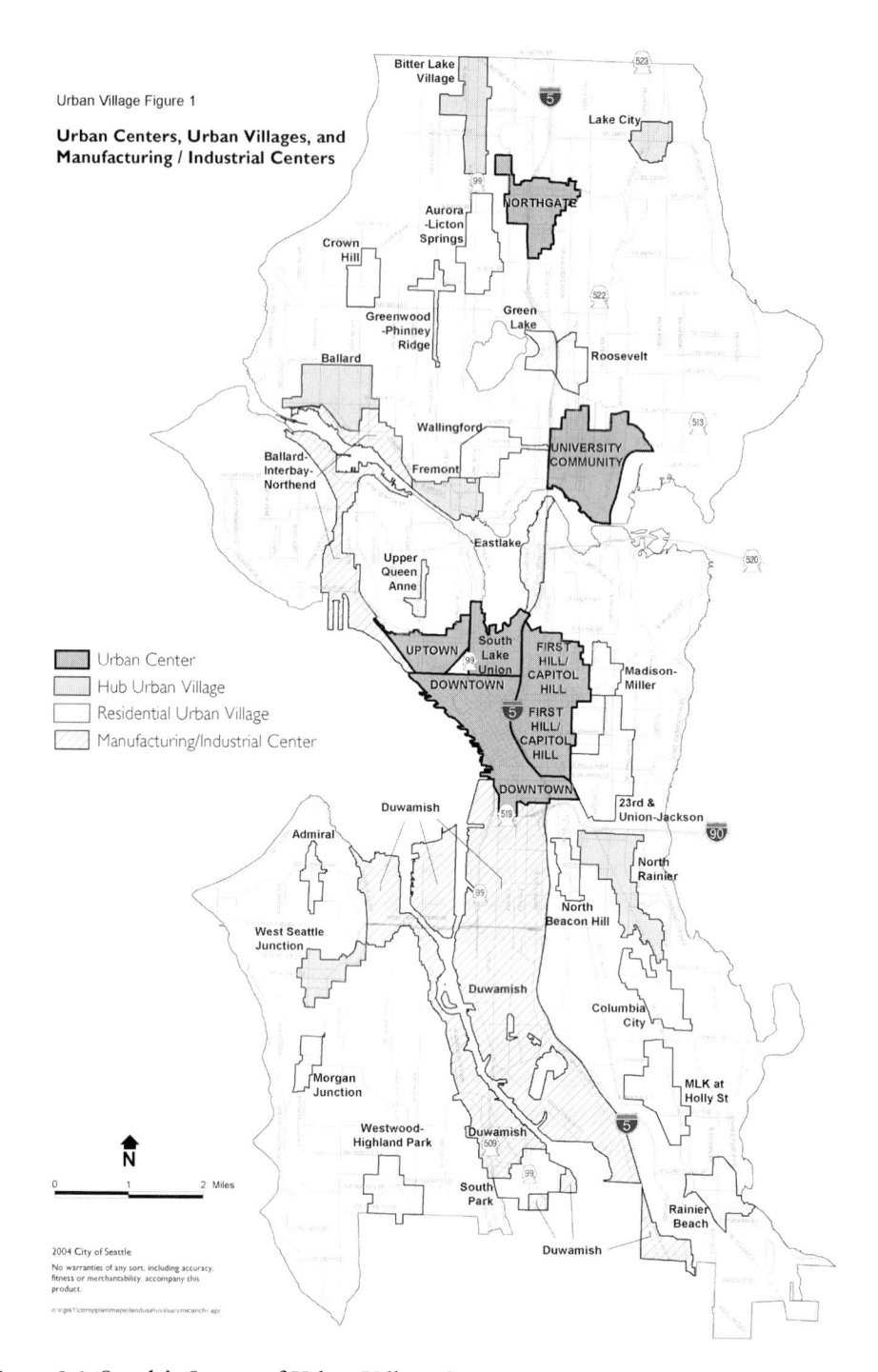

Figure 9.1 Seattle's System of Urban Village Centers.

Source: Seattle's Comprehensive Plan, Urban Village Element. January 2005, p. 1.8. Online. http://www.seattle.gov/DPD/static/Urban%20Village%20element_LatestReleased_DPDP016169.pdf

Chapter 9: **THE CASE OF SEATTLE**

phase, the Planning Committee for the neighborhood was formed, and the committee entered into a planning agreement with the city. Ongoing outreach and preparation of the draft plan for community validation also occurred during this phase. At the end of the phase, the City Council was to deliberate, approve and adopt the neighborhood plan, which was then incorporated into the Comprehensive Plan for the City. After plan approval, planning committees were to disband, as well as the Neighborhood Planning Office, and thus, the plan made no provisions for ongoing neighborhood monitoring or stewardship (the word that official city documents employ) of plan implementation. Neighborhood groups were eligible for up to $10,000 in funding for the first phase of the process, which included engaging the community and developing a vision for the area. The objective of inclusiveness was thus incorporated into the planning process. Altogether, including the second phase of the process, urban center villages, and manufacturing and industrial areas were eligible for planning grants of between $80–100,000; residential urban villages for grants between $60–80,000; and distressed areas were also eligible for planning funds (Seattle Neighborhood Planning Office 1996a–e).

Assessing Participation in Neighborhood Planning

In contrast to public administration, city planning has had a uniquely active engagement with the communities with which it plans. The type of engagement, however, varies. Often it does not go beyond public hearings and citizen task forces, the kind of strategies that Sherry Arnstein in an influential article (1969) identified as forms of tokenism. Arnstein used as the criterion for characterizing different techniques of citizen participation the degree to which citizens actually control policy decisions, ranging from no control to complete. A more recent and productive framework for analyzing citizen involvement in public policy and planning was developed in a Brookings Institution study, *The Rebirth of Urban Democracy* (Berry *et al.* 1993). The authors of the study argued, based on their application of Dahl's criteria for representative democracy (1956) to participatory democracy, that efforts to involve citizens in government can be gauged in two dimensions: their breadth and their depth.

An advantage of this approach is that it can be applied to any situation and not just, as Arnstein's theory, to disadvantaged communities. Breadth refers to the "extent to which an opportunity is offered to every community member to participate at every stage of the policymaking process" (Berry *et al.* 1993: 54). Gauging for breadth leads us to inquire into the outreach functions of citizen participation structures, including access to agendas, the extensiveness of information to citizens about alternatives, and the rates of participation among the population. Depth, on the other hand, refers to "the extent to which citizens who choose to participate have the opportunity to determine the final policy outcome by means of the participatory process" (55). Gauging for depth leads to an analysis of the mechanics of participation, and includes the extent of opportunities for face-to-face discussion, setting agendas, and consensus formation, and, most important, the outcome of participatory processes.

Neighborhood planning is a specific form of participatory democracy with formal links to representative democratic processes in local government. To take into account the key distinguishing features of neighborhood planning, this chapter relies on the features identified in Martz's (1995) study of five neighborhood planning cases. Martz identifies the following key features of a neighborhood planning effort: the purpose or legal status of the plans; who initiates and controls the process; who controls or has resources; what is the planning timeframe; special planning tools; and the scope of the planning process.

The purpose or legal status of neighborhood plans is crucial for the eventual outcome of such plans. If such plans are advisory, they may not be implemented. If such plans legally amend the comprehensive plan, then they are as important as the comprehensive plan in amending zoning and public infrastructure and services. Who initiates the plan and controls the process, whether it is the city or the neighborhood planning group, is key to the sense of neighborhood empowerment, and the extent to which participants identify with the plan. Who controls resources for neighborhood planning and how they are distributed will partially determine the quality of such plans, and the sense of empowerment of participants in the process. Resources are needed since preparing community plans are based on studies with technical aspects that require professional work, e.g. traffic studies, marketing studies, financing, etc. Without resources, the planning process can be delayed, and participants may lose interest. Is there a specific framework for preparing the plan? Is it a long- or short-time frame? Too long a time frame may result in leadership turnover, or community burnout. Are there special zoning techniques or tools that the city encourages – such as Seattle's urban village strategy? Such special techniques or concepts can aid participants in identifying with a plan, making such a plan more memorable. Is the scope of a plan clear? Although there may be core issues, such as land use that all neighborhood plans need to address, to what extent do neighborhood groups have flexibility in determining the scope of the plan? Here, again, this feature of neighborhood planning can enhance the sense of control or empowerment.

Many of these features relate to control of the planning process, and are very consonant with Arnstein's concept of community participation. The primary focus in Arnstein's approach is who controls the process, although it is clear that for Arnstein the pinnacle of community empowerment was the actual outcome of these processes. But there are some issues that cannot be neatly understood as control issues. Issues relating to the level of participation, and of how representative participants are of the neighborhood population are not clearly related to control, but to another attribute of the democratic process – the extent or breadth of participation. Control issues are clearly related to the depth of participation, but we can distinguish between control of the planning process and the implementation or outcomes of the process, since implementation requires the resources and approvals of citywide elected and appointed officials. There may be other dimensions to participation as well, the time frame of the planning effort, for example, is not so much an issue of control between citizens and government as a psychological factor, important for maintaining enthusiasm among volunteers and avoiding burnout. The Brookings Study provides us with a broader theoretical framework, while Martz's features are more specific to neighborhood planning, and relate to a large extent to a dimension of control of the neighborhood planning process. Combining the two can provide a set of dimensions and measurable criteria or questions uniquely sensitive to neighborhood planning embedded in a broader theoretical framework.

Table 9.1 relates various features of neighborhood planning and relates them to the three criteria or dimensions of participatory democracy identified above: breadth, control, and depth. Note that in this scheme, the criterion of depth that the Brookings study introduced is split into two criteria, *control* focused on control of the process, and *depth*, focused directly on ultimate outcomes or implementation, although these concepts can overlap. Note also other

Chapter 9: **THE CASE OF SEATTLE**

Table 9.1 How features of neighborhood planning relate to criteria of participatory democracy

Features of Neighborhood Planning	Criteria or Dimensions of Participatory Democracy			
	Breadth	Control	Depth	Other
Legal status		•	•	
Who initiates		•		
Who controls process		•		
Neighborhood role		•		
Resources available		•		
Scope of plan			•	
Length of process				Psychological
Special techniques for neighborhoods implementation			•	Facilitates
% of people who participate	•			
Representativeness of participants	•			
Adoption of neighborhood plans			•	
Relation of neighborhood plans to city budget process			•	
Monitoring and evaluation			•	
Other institutional changes related to planning effort			•	Service delivery restructuring

features of neighborhood planning not discussed by Martz related to implementation, i.e. relation to budgeting processes, monitoring and evaluation, and institutional changes.

Review of Key Features of Seattle's Neighborhood Planning Process

This section provides a brief review of how Seattle's neighborhood planning efforts measure up to the key features identified above. With respect to the status of the plans, Seattle's neighborhood planning process was first set out by a City Council Resolution in late 1994, and later incorporated in its Comprehensive Plan, which conferred legal status to plans once reviewed and approved by the City Council (City Auditor Report 2007). This is very important for the implementation of neighborhood plans, since with the passage of Washington State's GMA, plans and regulations were required to be consistent with each other. This consistency requirement meant that land use changes incorporated in plans would need to be followed up with zoning changes, a major way of implementing neighborhood plans.

On the issue of who initiated planning and controlled the process, the City of Seattle, through its Comprehensive Plan and the neighborhood groups undertaking planning shared responsibilities. The City in its Comprehensive Plan identified neighborhoods eligible for neighborhood planning funding, but neighborhood groups organized themselves and applied to the city for undertaking the task. The City established the framework, but the process of constituting the planning committees through the preparation of the plan was controlled by the neighborhood planning groups. The adoption and implementation process was controlled by the city. This ensured that city-wide issues would be addressed in a consistent way, and provided for some measure of quality control.

In the case of Seattle, the neighborhood role was substantive and extensive. Groups of participants organized themselves, provided outreach to other members and groups within their neighborhood, negotiated with staff from the City's Neighborhood Planning Office, hired technical and process consultants, determined the scope of work for the plans, as well as participated actively in the preparation of plans.

The resources that Seattle made available to planning committees were substantial, as indicated, ranging from $60,000 to $100,000 per neighborhood. It was up to each neighborhood planning committee to determine how to spend these resources on planning and community engagement processes. In addition, Seattle through its Neighborhood Planning Office provided ten planning coordinators who provided technical and organizational assistance the neighborhood planning groups and served as liaisons to city departments.

The neighborhoods had considerable flexibility in the focus of their plans, although all needed to deal with several basic elements, such as land use and transportation. Some neighborhoods were very focused on economic development, or safety issues while others focused on design issues.

The length of the process varied from two to four years. Four years is on the long-side of a community planning process. It is likely that the length of the process led to community exhaustion, contributing to a neglect of concern for stewardship of the implementation of the plans. The 2007 Auditor's report on implementation confirms this by indicating that some citizen participants who had been active in the process for ten years or more were experiencing burnout (31).

The urban village concept was a special technique that benefited the neighborhood planning process in Seattle. It was a flexible enough concept enabling each neighborhood to develop its own version. At the same time, it provided a memorable, overall synthesizing concept to enhance the quality of life of existing neighborhoods, and provide lively centers of activity.

Over 20,000 people are estimated to have participated in some aspect of the neighborhood planning process. The city's population at that time was over 563,000, with over 475,000 residents over eighteen years old. Thus, 4.2 percent of the population over eighteen participated in the neighborhood planning process.[4]

One of three original goals of the neighborhood planning process in Seattle was community building, in terms of bridging across social and demographic differences. Seattle recognized the difficulty of creating inclusive neighborhood planning processes and developed several strategies to promote this. The first phase of the neighborhood planning process was by and large devoted to ensuring broad community participation in developing the initial neighborhood vision to guide the subsequent plan. The City provided grants of $10,000 to help neighborhoods do appropriate outreach to groups that do not normally get involved in planning processes. Neighborhoods had to show the Neighborhood Planning Office an Outreach Plan for involving a full diversity of residents and interests, including minority groups, renters, youth, the disabled, and affected businesses and institutions. The approach was more qualitative than quantitative, with NPO encouraging surveys for small businesses, or homeless people. In addition, the amount of funds for Phase II could be reduced, if the neighborhood excluded any major group (Seattle Office of City Auditor 2007; Sirianni 2007, 2009). There is no formal study on the inclusiveness of the process, but Sirianni in a comment on the 2007 City Auditor's report on implementation notes that he "doesn't know any department of neighborhoods that is doing a better job than Seattle's" in reaching out to underrepresented groups.

Since neighborhood plans were to be incorporated into the City's Comprehensive Plan, neighborhood plans, once completed and validated by the community, were reviewed by planning staff and adopted by the City Council through Comprehensive Plan Ordinances. The process took fifteen months, from 1998 to 1999. By the mid-2000s, over thirteen of the thirty-eight plans had land use changes to the City's future land use map and zoning.

One of the most impressive achievements of Seattle's neighborhood planning process was the implementation of these plans through special bond measures as well as through the City's regular budget process facilitated by a restructuring of city agencies to respond better to neighborhood plans. Over 4,200 specific recommendations were included by the neighborhood plans to be implemented by 2014. The innovative Matching Fund Program of the Department of Neighborhoods provided small grants for community projects to be matched with neighborhood resources. These grants were often for small community projects, such as traffic circles. The annual allocation for the program was $1.5 million and in 1998 to 1999, Mayor Schell increased the allocation to $4.5 million to enable the funding of more small- and medium-sized projects incorporated in the neighborhood plans. Also, during Mayor Schell's administration (1998 to 2002), many of the neighborhood recommendations were incorporation into budget priorities by the city departments. Diers, who served as director of the Department of Neighborhoods during the planning process and was instrumental in shaping the neighborhood planning process, estimates that this strategy accounted for "tens of millions of dollars' worth of transportation improvements, pedestrian lighting, affordable housing, community gardens, neighborhood-specific design guidelines, public art, human service programs, and public safety enhancements in accordance with neighborhood plans" (2004: 139). Most substantial was the passage of special bond issues by voters in 1998 to 2000. Three bond issues provided an overall total of $430 million to fund neighborhood libraries, community centers and parks and open space called for in the plans. In addition, a low-income housing levy of $86 million was passed in 2002. The passage of these bond issues was to a large extent due to the broad participation in the neighborhood planning process that generated a wide community consensus on the need for these public facilities (Diers 2004; Sirianni 2007, 2009).

Planning is an ongoing process, and monitoring and evaluation of plans and their implementation are recognized aspects of the planning process. Countywide policies required monitoring of how city plans were meeting growth targets, but monitoring and evaluation of the neighborhood plans was not incorporated into the Seattle neighborhood planning process. As a result, after the approval of the plans by the city, neighborhood stewardship of the plans or citizen involvement has been very uneven. By 2002, the city had identified stewardship groups for most communities that prepared plans, but few of these groups included neighborhood planning groups. The city itself has not supported these stewardship groups with staff or financial resources. According to the recent City Auditor report on neighborhood plan implementation, when the City Auditor contacted people listed as stewards in the Department of Neighborhoods website, "some did not understand their role or had become disconnected from the process" (2007: 28). In addition, the same report notes that there had been no regular reporting on plan accomplishments by the City (30) and that the City had reduced its staff support for plan implementation, eliminating by 2004 the six sector manager positions that directly provided stewardship assistance to the neighborhood groups (17–18). On the other hand, the City has published several reports on how the city is meeting its growth targets, as required by GMA, and the recent City Auditor report is evidence of ongoing evaluation of the process.

After the adoption of the neighborhood plans, Mayor Schell decentralized some city services into six districts to respond better to neighborhood concerns and recommendations of the neighborhood plans. City agencies contributed representatives to interdepartmental teams for each of the six districts. Six sector managers were hired to facilitate coordination between interdepartmental teams and the stewardship groups within each district. These sector managers were vital for the early implementation of the plans until their positions were eliminated in 2004. While it lasted, this restructuring provided an unprecedented level of coordination and responsiveness of city services within districts and neighborhoods, as well as facilitated the incorporation of neighborhood plan recommendations into city agency budgets (Diers 2004; Sirianni 2007).

Overall, Seattle's experience with neighborhood planning rates very high in all but one feature of neighborhood planning, i.e. community involvement in monitoring the implementation of plans. On the other hand, the implementation of the neighborhood plans has been outstanding. As part of the 2007 City Auditor's report, over 800 people participated in a survey on the implementation of the neighborhood planning effort, and over 93 percent indicated that the process produced positive impacts in their neighborhoods. The study also found "a high level of accomplishment for plan recommendations" (9).

Conclusion: Connecting the Seattle Findings to the Concept of Livability

Neighborhood planning in Seattle contributed the following to the livability of the City:

- It produced actual plans for more livable neighborhoods, thirty-eight plans to be exact.
- It empowered thousands of residents to plan for their neighborhoods through a planning process that gave participants much control over the process, thus increasing the breadth of the process.

Chapter 9: **THE CASE OF SEATTLE**

- It reached out to various typically underrepresented groups in planning, improving the inclusiveness, the breadth of participation, and increasing opportunities for bridging social capital development.
- It resulted in robust implementation of the plan recommendations through zoning, city budget allocations and bond issues, providing great depth to the participatory process, evidence of linking social capital.

This chapter examined three important dimensions of participation in neighborhood planning: breadth, control, and depth. The livability of communities is a concept defined from the human perspective. Neighborhood planning, as illustrated in Seattle's process, represents important aspects of livability. The process itself can enhance place attachment and a sense of community, twin components of community identity. If the process has adequate breadth, it forges bonds among participants in the process and the community it builds is inclusive. Institutional aspects of the planning process can determine the amount of control over planning provided to neighborhoods within the city-wide context. This is an important ingredient in community empowerment. If the neighborhood process has depth, that is, if it leads to successful implementation of plans, it builds a strong sense of citizen empowerment. In addition, neighborhood planning is a major means for ensuring that the physical and socio-economic aspects of community are livable. From such a perspective, neighborhood planning provides indispensable elements of livability: inclusive and empowering community building.

Notes

1   Blanco and Campbell (2006) provide illustrations of horizontal assistance among cities that exemplify the concept of linking social capital.
2   These growth targets are modified on a periodic basis, for example, in 2000, Seattle was estimated to have 258,500 households, and its 2000–2022 growth target under GMA was 51,510 new households (Puget Sound Regional Council 2005).
3   One more neighborhood was subsequently identified as a center, and thus thirty-eight neighborhood plans have been developed.
4   Seattle's overall rate of participation in community affairs for those years was much greater, since in addition to the neighborhood planning process, Seattle had many voluntary community-based organizations.

References

Arnstein, S. (1969) "A ladder of citizen participation," *Journal of the American Institute of Planners* 35, 216–244.

Berry, J.M., Portney, K.E. and Thompson, K. (1993) *The Rebirth of Urban Democracy*, Washington, DC: The Brookings Institution.

Blanco, H. and Campbell, T. (2006) "Social capital of cities: emerging networks of horizontal assistance," *Technology in Society* 28, 169–181.

Calthorpe, P., Corbett, M., Duany, A. Moule, E., Plater-Zyberk, E., and Polyzoides, S; with editors: Katz, P., Corbett, J. and Weissman, S. (1991) *Ahwahnee Principles for Resource-Efficient*

Communities, Sacramento, CA: Local Government Commission. http://www.lgc.org/ahwahnee/ahwahnee_principles.pdf.
Corbett, J. and Velasquez, J. (1994) "The Ahwahnee principles. Towards more livable communities," *Western City Magazine*.
Dahl, R.A. (1956) *A Preface to Democratic Theory*, Chicago, IL: University of Chicago Press.
Dewey, J. (1927) *The Public and Its Problems*, New York: Henry Holt and Company.
Diers, J. (2004) *Neighbor Power. Building Community the Seattle Way*, Seattle, WA: University of Washington Press.
Godschalk, D.R. (2004) "Land use planning challenges. Coping with conflicts in visions of sustainable development and livable communities," *Journal of the American Planning Association* 70, 1: 5–13.
Korpela, K.M. (1989) "Place-identity as a product of environmental self-regulation," *Journal of Environmental Psychology* 9, 3: 241–256.
Long, D.A. and Perkins, D.D. (2007) "Community social and place predictors of sense of community: a multilevel and longitudinal analysis," *Journal of Community Psychology* 35, 5: 563–581.
Lynch, K. (1981) *A Theory of Good City Form*, Cambridge, MA: MIT Press.
Martz, W.A. (1995) *Neighborhood-Based Planning: Five Case Studies,* Planning Advisory Report # 455. Chicago, IL: American Planning Association.
Partners for Livable Communities (2000) *The Livable City. Revitalizing Urban Communities*, New York: McGraw-Hill.
Perkins, D.D. and Long, D.A. (2002) "Neighborhood sense of community and social capital: a multi-level analysis," in A.T. Fisher and C.C. Son (eds.) *Psychological Sense of Community: Research, Applications, and Implications*, New York: Kluwer Academic/Plenum Publishers, pp. 291–318.
Perry, C.A. (1929) *A Plan for New York and Its Environs*, Volume 7. New York: New York Regional Planning Association.
PlanNYC (2008) "197 a Plans" Furman Center for Real Estate and Urban Policy, New York University, last updated November 15, 2008. Online. Available HTTP: http://www.plannyc.org/taxonomy/term/44, accessed July 22, 2009.
Pretty, G.M.H. (2002) "Young people's development of the community-minded self: considering community identity, community attachment and sense of community," in A.T. Fischer and C.C. Sonn (eds.) *Psychological Sense of Community: Research, Applications, and Implications* 1, New York: Kluwer Academic/Plenum Publishers, pp. 83–2003.
Puddifoot, J.E. (1996) "Some initial considerations in the measurement of community identity," *Journal of Community Psychology* 24, 4: 327–336.
Puget Sound Regional Council (2005) *Growth Management by the Numbers: Population, Households, and Employment Growth Targets in the Central Puget Sound Region*, Seattle, WA: Puget Sound Regional Council.
Putnam, R. (2000) *Bowling Alone. The Collapse and Revival of American Community*, New York: Simon and Schuster.
Rohe, W.M. (2009) "From local to global. One hundred years of neighborhood planning," *Journal of the American Planning Association* 75, 2: 209–230.
Rohe, W.M. and Gates, L.B. (1985) *Planning with Neighborhoods,* Chapel Hill, NC: University of North Carolina Press.

Chapter 9: **THE CASE OF SEATTLE**

City of Seattle (1994) *Seattle Comprehensive Plan. Towards a Sustainable Seattle,* Seattle, WA: City of Seattle.

Seattle Neighborhood Planning Office (1996a) "Phase I – organizing/outreach/issue identification," March 21, 1996. Seattle: Seattle Neighborhood Planning Office.

Seattle Neighborhood Planning Office (1996b) "Phase II guidelines," December, 1996, Seattle: Seattle Neighborhood Planning Office.

Seattle Neighborhood Planning Office (1996c) "Phase II – planning," March 21, 1996, Seattle: Seattle Neighborhood Planning Office.

Seattle Neighborhood Planning Office (1996d) "Preapplication," March 21, 1996, Seattle: Seattle Neighborhood Planning Office.

Seattle Neighborhood Planning Office (1996e) "Seattle Neighborhood Planning Guidelines," March 21, 1996, Seattle: Seattle Neighborhood Planning Office.

Seattle Office of the City Auditor (2007) "Time to revisit neighborhood planning implementation," Sept. 2007, Seattle: Seattle Neighborhood Planning Office.

Sirianni, C. (2007) "Neighborhood planning as collaborative democratic design. The Case of Seattle," *Journal of the American Planning Association* 73, 4: 373–387.

Sirianni, C. (2009) *Investing in Democracy: Engaging Citizens in Collaborative Governance,* Washington, DC: Brookings Institution.

Washington State (2009) "Chapter 36.70A RCW growth management – planning by selected counties and cities," Revised Code of Washington (RCW). Online. Available HTTP: http://apps.leg.wa.gov/RCW/default.aspx?cite=36.70A, accessed August, 12 2009.

Woolcock, M. (1998) "Social capital and economic development: toward a theoretical synthesis and policy framework," *Theory and Society* 27: 151–208.

Chapter 10

ENVISIONING A CITY'S GREEN INFRASTRUCTURE FOR COMMUNITY LIVABILITY

Nancy D. Rottle
Associate Professor, Landscape Architecture
University of Washington

Brice Maryman
Lecturer, Landscape Architecture
University of Washington

Introduction

The history of American city-making is rooted in a dialectic between natural and cultural forces. From John Winthrop's "city on a hill," to the rise of Olmstedian pastoralism as a counterpoint to the city, American urbanists have set their vision of the ideal city in counterpoint to a caricatured natural world. However, a more sophisticated, complicated, and ultimately rich version of human settlement has begun to emerge, fostering a fused ecology of green infrastructure that benefits both ecological and cultural concerns.

Just like the visions of Olmsted and Winthrop, these ideas are emerging from broader cultural undercurrents. For contemporary urbanists, re-envisioning how we design, build and live has become imperative as we begin to perceive and experience the impacts of climate change, peak oil consumption, global food crises, and an increasingly well-documented decline in human health. These pressures add to a litany of pressing environmental concerns including declining watershed health, diminished biodiversity, and a loss of functioning farm and forest land that is proximate to urban centers.

Especially in the sprawling metropolitan regions of North America, planners have recently advocated high-density urbanism as one of the most powerful tools to begin to redress these past mistakes. Embedded in zoning codes and comprehensive plans is the supposition that dense urban nodes are magnets for growth that attract populations away from outward-creeping suburbs and back to city cores, thereby decreasing pressure on rural resource lands, preserving aquatic integrity, supporting mass transit, and decreasing automobile CO_2 emissions.

Chapter 10: **ENVISIONING GREEN INFRASTRUCTURE**

However, creating compact communities will not, by itself, solve the ills listed above. In fact, urban density strategies may only be successful if cities are satisfying places to live, providing the same infrastructure for livability that sells buyers on the promises of the suburbs. As has been well-documented, robust civic, recreational and social space, and opportunities to experience nature are high on this requisite list of urban livability amenities. A bevy of evidence indicates that urban open spaces provide opportunities for human activity and health, restorative benefits, positive conditions for child development and learning, deep knowledge, economic robustness and social conviviality (Kaplan 1998; Harnik 1999; Frank *et al.* 2003; Childs 2004; Kellert 2005; Louv 2005).

In fact, urban open space is considered a primary factor in community livability ratings systems: The UN-sponsored International Award for Livable Communities criteria emphasize landscape enhancement, environmentally sensitive practices, "community sustainability" and "healthy lifestyles" as four of its six criteria.[1] Likewise, one of the six criteria of the Mercer Company's livability rating system is recreation.[2] Monacle magazine's awards for the most livable city consider access to nature, the amount of green space and key environmental initiatives within their overall evaluation criteria.[3]

Yet, all too often, municipal planning has been conducted in a way that promotes intensified development, yet neglects consideration of multi-use public spaces or ecological infrastructures that support quality of life. This void seems particularly apparent as we consider the host of new infrastructural systems and open space types that have been successfully implemented to address contemporary and future urban needs while promoting the environmental quality necessary to support human health and biodiversity (Thompson 2002; Wenk 2002; Schneekloth 2003; Cranz and Boland 2004). However, if human and natural systems are to mutually benefit from their reciprocal utility then we need to re-imagine the way we plan, permit, incentivize and regulate community development patterns. In doing so, we may begin to imagine a development matrix that grows from a hybrid ecology of cultural and natural concerns – a built environment that we will see as a "new normal" for a changing planet.

To illustrate these principles, we will explore a 2005 grassroots visioning effort from Seattle to suggest how this "green infrastructure" approach to urban planning might work for other cities. This citizen-university effort allowed for planning outside the traditional municipal structures and focused on reshaping the spaces between buildings and the potential interconnected green and blue spaces of the city. Using this "void-based" approach, citizens looked at ways to maximize the uses and benefits of the public realm in ways that not only benefited human and economic health, but also, importantly, environmental health.

Urban Green Infrastructure

What, exactly, is green infrastructure? While the term is fast becoming part of the planner's lexicon, it has multiple definitions and connotations, all which are useful but – not unlike its counterpart of traditional or "gray" infrastructure – refer to various systems at diverse scales and in rural, urbanizing, and urban contexts.

The most widely embraced definition for green infrastructure in the US comes from the conservation planning movement. Speaking from this vantage, Mark Benedict and Ed McMahon define green infrastructure as "the interconnected network of natural areas and other open spaces that conserves natural ecosystem values and functions, sustains clean air and water, and provides a wide array of benefits to people and wildlife" (2006, 1). In this context, the authors are primarily considering greenway development and conservation of landscapes in rural and urbanizing greenfield contexts, in contrast to the gray infrastructure of human settlements. Beginning with the Trust for Public Land's on-line document *Building Green Infrastructure: Land Conservation as a Watershed Protection Strategy* (2000) the concept has grown from a land and water conservation strategy to one that also recognizes landscape protection for community benefit.

So, too, urban foresters – eager to elevate status of the often-overlooked vegetation in the city – have used the concept of "green infrastructure" for at least a decade to describe the multiple ecological services provided by forests and natural systems in the developed landscape. In addition to the aesthetic benefits of urban forests, numerous studies have verified the stormwater-mitigating benefits of trees and shrubs that slow runoff and return moisture to the atmosphere via evapotranspiration, reducing flooding and the deleterious effects of rapid runoff on wetlands and streams.[4] Similarly, the tremendous cooling and climate-related benefits of trees and vegetation in the urban environment are well documented, reducing local "heat island" effects through evapotranspiration processes and direct shading of thermal retentive materials such as concrete. In the era of climate change, trees are also being looked to in order to reduce greenhouse gases by reducing the need for fossil fuel-powered air conditioning, and the entirety of urban forests – including soils – are valued as carbon sinks (McPherson *et al.* 1994; Nowak 2000; Nowak and Crane 2002). To assess the value of urban forests, the USDA Forest Service has established a partnership of working groups to examine forests' contributions to environmental and human well-being in various contexts and scales, applied not only to woodlands surrounding urban areas, but also to street trees and vegetation in city parks and urban open spaces. Likewise, the National Urban and Community Forestry Advisory Council, affiliated with the USDA Forest Service, offers matching grants to advance research and education for the "green infrastructure" of urban forests.

While each of the definitions above refer to natural systems and the value of ecosystem services to the human species, other definitions have emerged that are more culturally based. For example, bicycle and pedestrian linkages found in vegetated corridors, or greenways, are also considered part of a green infrastructure. Although bicycle lanes, sidewalks and trails are "gray" hardscapes, various authors have described them as "green" because they provide the armature for low-impact mobility that promotes non-polluting travel modes and human health.

In their book *Skinny Streets and Green Neighborhoods*, Cynthia Girling and Ron Kellett (2005) acknowledge these complementary meanings in a broad definition of green infrastructure that marries a community's ecological structure – its green networks – and the greening of its traditionally gray infrastructure, to incorporate "the entirety of urban green spaces" that "performs a multitude of vital environmental services in cities" (59). Such environmental services are the same that Benedict and McMahon cite in terms of large-scale landscapes such as flood control and maintenance of air and water quality, but also include the services traditionally provided by gray urban infrastructure systems such as water conveyance and urban mobility.

Internationally, the term *green infrastructure* has found broad resonance and has been studied and further developed through academic research. A 2007 European literature review

Chapter 10: ENVISIONING GREEN INFRASTRUCTURE

of green infrastructure publications proposes an encompassing, comprehensive urban and rural-based concept for green infrastructure, "considered to comprise of all natural, semi-natural and artificial networks of multi-functional ecological systems within, around and between urban areas, at all spatial scales" (Tzoulas *et al.* 2007, 167–78).

While green infrastructure itself has a variety of definitions, it is important to note that there are several related concepts that should be considered simultaneously. These include *low impact development*,[5] *high performance infrastructure* (New York 2005) and *sustainable urban infrastructure* (Lahti *et al.* 2007). Low impact development is an approach to development that focuses on practices and structures that mimic the hydrological cycle of a particular area. Through minimizing site disturbance, protecting native vegetation and using techniques like green roofs and walls, porous paving systems, "rain gardens" and other localized stormwater detention structures, low impact development aims to control stormwater at its source in order to protect a larger watershed.

Running parallel to low impact development, high performance infrastructure includes many of the same techniques but places an additional emphasis on the concomitant benefits of livability. So while low impact development may promote narrower streets for the sake of reducing stormwater runoff, high performance infrastructure also values the traffic-calming and aesthetic benefits of that street. Used interchangeably with "high performance," *sustainable urban infrastructure* also includes community-scale facilities designed to provide traditional transportation, energy and waste management services using renewable and regenerative methods. Contemporary examples are biogas digesters, windfarms, and geothermal heating approaches. Both "high performance" and "sustainable" infrastructure recognize the value of integrated solutions that reduce or eliminate environmental impacts, enhance local ecologies and promote community livability.

Synthesizing these definitions, we employ the following definition for green infrastructure in this chapter: "All natural, semi-natural and artificial networks of multi-functional ecological and low-impact systems within, around and between urban areas that provide services while promoting the health of humans and their related environments."

While not a requirement for green infrastructure, the quality of multi-functionalism creates higher value urban green infrastructure systems. Boston's post-Civil War planners, for example, were able to secure funding for the "Emerald Necklace" because of its many benefits. From a purely infrastructural perspective, the connected parks were designed for flood water control. However, multiple constituencies became excited about the project because of its many subsidiary benefits including park and recreational uses, a transit corridor for bicyclists and pedestrians, and an opportunity to improve public health through contact with a vivifying nature.

Five Overlapping Systems of Urban Green Infrastructure

The elegance of green infrastructure is its ability to benefit human and natural systems while simultaneously providing multiple human and ecological services. Yet it is challenging to conceptualize and convey these overlapping services to the public. For communication and planning purposes it helps to consider the multiple layers as discrete yet interconnected systems. Just as early scientists sought to understand the infinite complexity of the natural world by categorizing taxonomic and chemical orders, so too should green infrastructure systems be understood as five distinct "natural, semi-natural and artificial networks of multi-functional ecological and low-impact human systems" comprising a city's green infrastructure. These systems are community open space, low-impact mobility, water, habitat, and metabolism. Within these green infrastructure systems are individual components and typologies – e.g. bike lanes, rain gardens, and parks.

Since these systems are integrated and interrelated, usually several green infrastructure elements simultaneously serve to enhance multiple systems (e.g. urban forests provide habitat while also helping to control stormwater, reduce energy use and mitigate warming city climates). We describe these five green infrastructure systems below.

Community Open Spaces

A diverse spectrum of urban open spaces comprise this system, which together can significantly improve urban livability. These are the spaces that foster connections between community members and the people and places where they live. Traditional parks and playgrounds are part of this system, as are squares, sidewalks and plazas, outdoor theaters, dog parks, farmers markets, public art installations and urban agriculture gardens. Community open spaces bring people together as they recreate, grow food, celebrate cultural traditions, enjoy performances, meet for coffee or a meal, shop, and publicly express their civic views. These spaces also offer opportunities for individuals to find mental restoration and spiritual renewal.

Low-Impact Mobility

Locomotion is an integral part of the human experience. We move to explore, learn, exercise and pursue our daily objectives. However, much of the infrastructure that we've built has neither brought us closer together, nor has it helped us connect to the natural world. Our increased awareness of the deleterious impacts of roads and vehicles – especially in CO_2 emissions, water pollution and disruption of habitat corridors – indicates that low-impact mobility systems are critical to environmental health. We need to find better ways to move that not only bring us to our destinations but that do so in a profoundly more ecologically responsible way. In this definition, we include bikeways, bike boulevards, sidewalks, trails, and pedestrian-priority environments such as walking streets and woonerfs. Research indicates that the presence of these systems also may improve human health by affording regular opportunities for physical activity.

Designing streets and urban land use patterns so that communities are "walkable" and enticing to pedestrians also encourages low-impact mobility. Incorporating amenities at the human scale contributes to overall livability while also supporting walking and biking as viable transport systems.

Water

In nature, every drop of water is used, recycled and used again in the hydrologic cycle. Within urban systems, green infrastructure provides the opportunity to closely mimic these natural

Chapter 10: **ENVISIONING GREEN INFRASTRUCTURE**

systems while also removing contaminants that run off of the many pollution-generating surfaces within the city. Such water systems aim to work with the entirety of the water cycle, e.g. collecting, purifying and re-using water for irrigation, household and building functions; infiltrating stormwater so that it recharges local groundwater; and detaining and cleaning runoff so that overland flows do not pollute or degrade streams, lakes and other receiving water bodies. Examples of water system green infrastructure elements include cisterns, green roofs, bioretention swales, rain gardens, and stormwater planters. Often these features are used together in a continuous "treatment train" to achieve complete filtration.

While these elements have been implemented as prototype projects or, at their most extensive, as part of larger-scale redevelopment projects, the systemic implementation of water infrastructure has not been accomplished in the United States. Though many of these technologies were pioneered in the Mid-Atlantic, it is not surprising that the wet climate of the Pacific Northwest has allowed these elements to flourish. Seattle's High Point redevelopment, Portland's Stephen Epler dormitories, and Victoria, British Columbia's Dockside Green are pioneering examples of these types of developments.

Habitat

Many urban areas were developed in places that ecologists today would identify as critical habitat areas. For early urban settlers, the streams of Chicago, the estuaries of Galveston, Texas, and the swamps of New Orleans each represented un-perfected lands to be tamed in the interest of commerce, trade or land speculation. Today, habitat enhancement has become an increasingly important and valued intervention in urban areas with millions funneled into stream and wetland restoration and the protection of salmon habitat in urban areas of the West Coast. While the wholesale restoration of an indigenous habitat is unlikely, it is possible to craft urban infrastructure systems that promote and accommodate insects, birds, butterflies and other urban wildlife. Urban forests provide the canopies for avian species to nest, forage and rest during their migration. Habitat system elements include wetlands, riparian corridors, urban forests, shorelines, and green roofs and walls that address urban biodiversity needs. Habitat is closely linked with the quality and quantity of urban stormwater and its potential deleterious impacts on streams and rivers, which in the Pacific Northwest particularly affect juvenile and spawning salmon. In a synergistic relationship, it should be noted that urban water features intended to control pollution such as natural drainage swales may provide important habitat for amphibians, insects and birds.

Metabolism

Across the world, in places as diverse as China and Texas, Dubai and London, people are realizing that the energy sources that we have been using are no longer safe for the planet. While some look toward increased, cleaner production of coal power or flirt with nuclear energy as new fuels to continue centralized energy production, others are looking to partner with nature to reduce energy consumption and increase energy production. In many urban areas, this means planting more street trees, installing green walls and planting green roofs to naturally mediate the temperature of buildings and cities, thereby reducing CO_2 outputs from heating and cooling and mitigating the urban heat island effect. In some regions, the natural assets of solar, wind, geothermal, biomass and even wave power are potential green infrastructure systems.

While some of the power sources above relate to large-scale harvesting installations, increasingly smaller scale opportunities are finding their way into the urban environment. Much like the distributed, at-the-source philosophy of "low impact development," such small-scale sources can reduce peak demands on the power grid, and even feed power into the grid to be used by others. Examples are integrated solar-power, skyscrapers with wind turbines, and sensors that use the friction and weight of pedestrian footsteps to generate power. In Oregon's Pringle Creek housing development, for example, heat is taken from groundwater wells that are also used for irrigation.

We include in this system the local production and distribution of food, which provides calories for human energy. The typical production and transporting of our food over long distances consumes unfathomable amounts of fossil fuels, even though in many regions such as the Pacific Northwest local food production is possible throughout most of the year. Farmers' markets for locally-grown food support agricultural land preservation, "green collar" jobs and community cohesiveness while reducing the carbon footprint of our food consumption.

Planning For Green Infrastructure – A Process Case Study: Open Space Seattle 2100

Background

Having identified the components that make up the various green systems of the city, how does one plan for this infrastructure? Can existing urbanized areas patch together cohesive, connected systems? What processes can be used to promote adoption of green infrastructure methods and materials, and to advance visioning and support for the programs, policies and funding that are required to shift our reliance on single-purpose gray infrastructure?

This chapter describes a grassroots green infrastructure planning process that took place in the City of Seattle over the course of a year, and the continuing citizen and governmental accomplishments furthering the City's integrated green infrastructure systems.

The Seattle Context

In 1903, the Olmsted Brothers' landscape architecture firm laid the foundation for Seattle's open space system with a proposal for a connected system of parks and boulevards. Similar to strategies used in Boston, Philadelphia, Portland, Minneapolis and Chicago (Harnik 2000), John Charles Olmsted relied heavily on municipal investments in public space to achieve his vision. The primary plans took the form of a rough figure-eight that connected existing municipal parks, proposed acquisition of shoreline open spaces, and encompassed the major ridgelines with their spectacular views.

Seattle's plan was designed for a city of a million and a half, a population figure that the city has now exceeded. The centennial of Seattle's Olmsted Parks and Boulevards Plan catalyzed a series of new long-range planning initiatives to preserve and create open space.

Chapter 10: **ENVISIONING GREEN INFRASTRUCTURE**

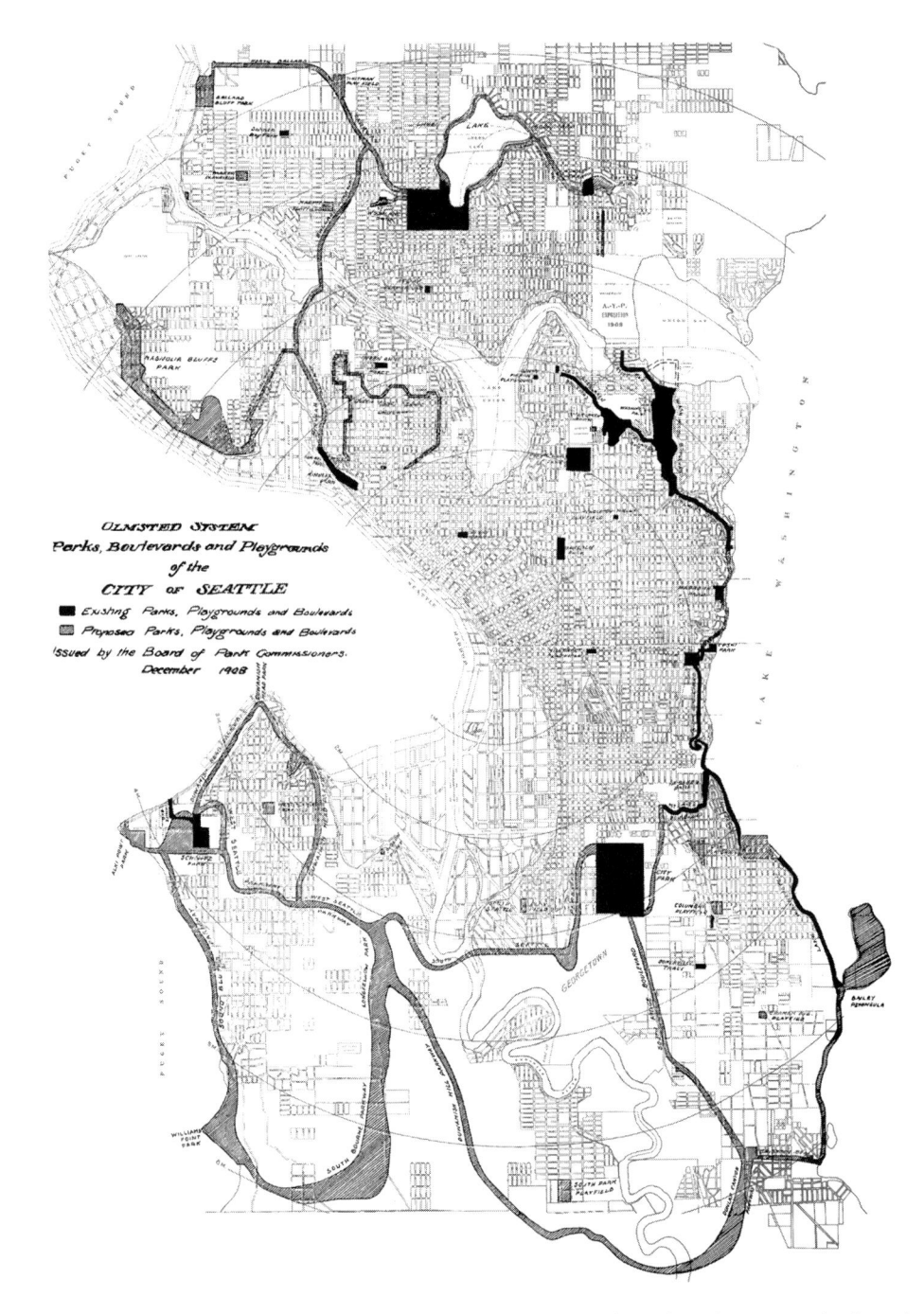

Figure 10.1 1908 Olmsted Plan for Seattle Parks and Boulevards. *The renowned Olmsted Brothers Landscape Architecture firm proposed Seattle's first system of Parks and Boulevards in 1903, revised as shown here in 1908.*

Source: Seattle Department of Parks and Recreation and Friends of Seattle's Olmsted Parks

These included the regionally-focused Cascade Agenda, aimed at preserving farm and forest lands in the four counties surrounding Seattle through concentration of growth in existing cities, and King County's Greenprint, which targeted conservation priorities for the immediate metropolitan area.

Building on these efforts, in 2005 Open Space Seattle 2100 (OSS2100) was formed, challenging citizens to create a new vision for the city's connected, integrated, ecological open space system for the ensuing hundred years, while accommodating an anticipated doubling of the city's population over the same period. OSS2100 leaders at the University of Washington coordinated a year-long process that featured a two-day, citywide "Green Futures Charrette."[6] The process provoked professionals, civic leaders, citizens and students to grapple with complex and challenging questions about the future of the city and the region. It aimed to create a pedagogical context where students, civic leaders and the broader public would learn about future probabilities, exemplary urban open space models and contemporary research, which they would collaboratively apply to envisage new urban environments.[7]

Led by the authors of this chapter, Open Space Seattle 2100 built upon the Northwest's tradition of design charrettes (Condon 1996, 1999; Kelbaugh 1997; Maryman and Maggio 2004), combining expert and populist approaches by encouraging professionals, academics, city leaders and neighborhood activists to collaboratively develop what University of British Columbia Professor Patrick Condon described in his keynote lecture as "improbable solutions to impossible problems in an impossibly short amount of time." The extra-bureaucratic process allowed participants to move beyond current community stalemates and wrestle with larger issues that would "illuminate the connection between open space, density, livability and sustainability" (Open Space Seattle 2100 Charrette Brief 2005). The project also aimed to establish a group of committed open space advocates from multiple sectors who would guide the process, contribute informed creativity, and invest in implementation of the visions well after the two-day event finished. We describe our year-long process below, and present our outcomes to date in the next section.

The Open Space Seattle 2100 Process

Establishing Leaders, Issues and Goals

The OSS2100 process was initiated by conducting group interviews with business, government, professional and non-profit leaders to garner insight into issues, resources, ideal processes and critical players. We broke these groups into five thematic orientations, allowing allied organizations to express themselves in an unrestrained manner regarding environmental concerns, low-impact transportation methods, "green" planning and design, parks advocacy and real estate development. Taking what we learned to heart, we invited representatives from these same sectors and from neighborhood organizations to join the Open Space Seattle 2100 coalition, and to serve on its advisory committees. Our Executive Committee of twenty included agency heads and NGO leaders, while the Guidance Committee of almost eighty represented planning and design firms and organizations, e.g. American Society of Landscape Architects (ASLA), American Planning Association (APA); City agencies (Parks and Recreation, Transportation, Utilities, Sustainability and Neighborhoods); community and non-profit organizations; and the University of Washington. We met four times in as many months to develop the goals, principles, methods and future scenarios that would guide the charrette teams.

The resulting overarching goal was stated as: "To create a bold integrated Open Space Plan with implementation strategies for Seattle's next hundred years which will enhance the health and well-being of both our cultural and natural environments. This vision of a regenerative green infrastructure will strive to create a healthy, beautiful Seattle while maximizing our economic, social and ecological sustainability" (Open Space 2005).

In addition, the set of eight guiding principles expressed that an exemplary open space system should include the following qualities:

- regionally responsive to Seattle's context;
- integrated and multi-functional, incorporating all types of open spaces and layering functions within single places;
- equally accessible to all persons, with a variety of open spaces in each neighborhood and especially giving access to water;
- connected, linking between neighborhoods and communities;
- possessing quality, beauty, identity and rootedness, building on intrinsic qualities and inspiring a deep connection to place;
- promoting high ecological function and integrity, resilience and biodiversity in the face of climate change;
- supporting health and safety; and
- feasible, flexible and inspiring ongoing stewardship.

(Open Space Seattle 2100, 2005)

Informing the Process and Public

As we were meeting with coalition representatives, we began to build knowledge and resources that could be used by the public in the upcoming charrette. In a graduate seminar at the University of Washington our students who would serve as charrette team leaders explored texts on urban landscape ecology, open space benefits, relationships between density, sprawl and sustainability, and impending future challenges such as global climate change. To prepare for the charrette, students conducted case study research on exemplary open space systems, developed green infrastructure typologies, and explored potential implementation mechanisms. Additionally, students conducted a collaborative session with members of under-represented populations within the city, investigated needs of user groups such as the elderly, youth, ethnic minorities and the homeless, and researched questions relating to landscape ecology and predicted future scenarios for the city. They compiled resource bibliographies for existing maps and plans, which were critical resources that we used later in directly preparing for the charrette.

We took an innovative approach to dividing the city into planning units for the charrette. Rather than using the traditional neighborhood boundaries, we delineated the city by its topography and drainage, dividing it into seventeen watershed-based study areas. This act served to mix future participants between neighborhoods, and retained their focus on the primacy of water as a connective element for both its concurrent open space benefits and for considering continual downstream impacts.

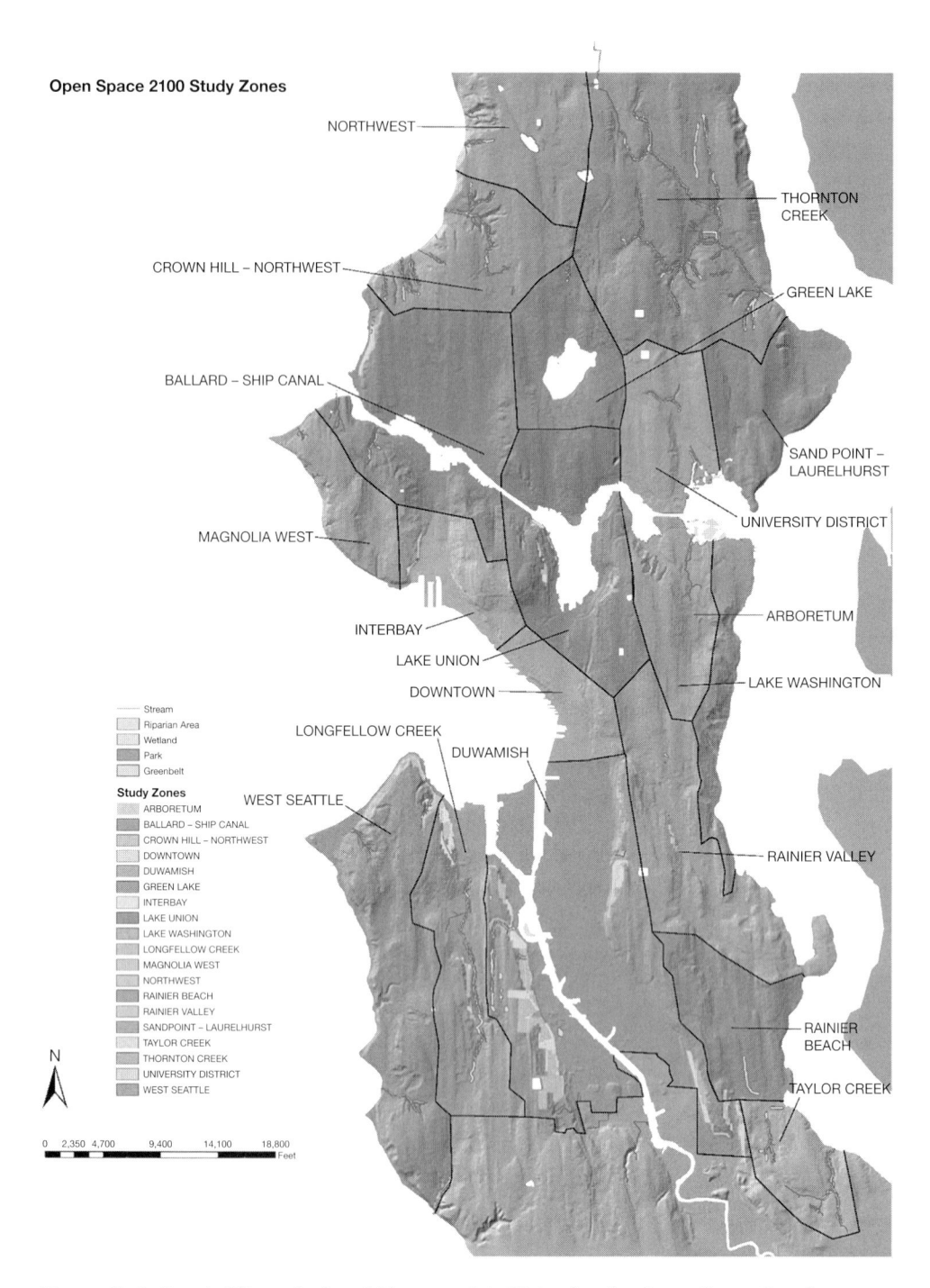

Figure 10.2 Seattle Watershed and Topographic Units for the Open Space Seattle 2100.
For the Open Space Seattle 2100 process we partitioned the city into watershed planning units and assigned at least one charrette team to focus on each of these topographically defined areas.

Chapter 10: **ENVISIONING GREEN INFRASTRUCTURE**

Students presented the illustrated case study and research findings to our advisory committees to build common knowledge among them. We then posted the students' informative, easy-to-read documents on our website (www.open2100.org) to advance public education and awareness, where they remain accessible to the general public. We also compiled these studies into a "Green Futures Toolkit" that was given to each charrette team to inspire participants during the event.

Beginning three months before the charrette, we co-sponsored public lectures that brought a diverse range of outside perspectives to how different communities value open space. Mark Childs from University of New Mexico presented research on civic open space, arguing for multiple-use public works, rather than myopic infrastructure expenditures; Mike Houck of Portland State's Urban Greenspaces Institute relayed his city's strategies for urban ecology and livability; and Robert Garcia from the Los Angeles City Project addressed the often-present issue of economic inequality in the distribution of and access to urban open space. Additionally, a panel of seven local researchers and professionals spoke to the particularities of Seattle issues, including considerations for aquatic and terrestrial wildlife habitat, historic open space planning, global climate change implications, transportation needs and sustainable building. On the eve of the charrette, Patrick Condon from the University of British Columbia gave the keynote lecture on Green Urban Infrastructure, presenting strategies that he and his students have used to design dense, hydrologically-stable communities in British Columbia.

Preparing for the Charrette

Our students continued to play key roles throughout the OSS2100 process. In combined graduate and undergraduate landscape architecture studios, student pairs selected study areas which they then documented by creating GIS (Geographic Information System) maps and building community "dossiers" to understand an area's history, prior plans, and demographic information. The GIS maps represented four layers of green infrastructure: Water and Drainage; Habitat; Community Open Spaces and Facilities; and Low-Impact Circulation. These maps also showed hazard and sensitive areas such as steep slopes, earthquake hazard zones, inundation and liquifaction zones that might offer future open space, and planned urban growth centers. Some student teams further synthesized the data into "Opportunity" and "Need" maps for the charrette, adding to this information the City's park gap analyses and vacant parcels. Prior to the charrette, students worked with their citizen and professional team leaders to create and lead study area tours for their charrette teams.

The public lectures and coalition of organizations represented on our advisory boards cultivated rich ground to solicit charrette participation from professional, government and citizen community members. We set up our website for registration, displaying the map of Seattle's eighteen watersheds, and asked potential participants to express their top choices for which areas they would like to work on. We also encouraged teams to form on their own, leaving space for additions, and actively recruited team leaders with charrette experience. Leaders tended to be design and planning professionals, many with graphic skills, with whom students served as co-leaders. The combined experience, skill and demeanor of leaders were critical to the success of each team.

The Green Futures Charrette

In February 2006, the two-day Green Futures charrette engaged over 350 participants, working on 23 teams composed of professionals, citizens, and students. We asked each group to produce illustrated 100-year and twenty-year plans for its study area, to coordinate with adjacent areas for maximum connectivity, and to suggest priorities and near-term actions. We gave each participant a "Charrette Brief" containing our principles, requirements, and future scenarios developed with the Guidance Committee. We also supplied each team with the pre-prepared base maps and dossiers to provide specific information on their study areas; an "ecological scorecard" to guide and evaluate their work; and the students' case studies and research bound into the *Green Futures Toolkit* to use as a reference and inspiration over the two days. Teams followed the requirements outlined in the brief, such as planning for a doubling of the city's population and higher water elevations in Puget Sound by the end of the century. Some assumed that a catastrophic earthquake – predicted for Seattle – would open opportunities on the steep slopes and along ground faults located over fill soils.

Each team produced thoughtful yet visionary scenarios that accounted for community space, stormwater and shorelines, habitat networks and pedestrian and bicycle circulation. Common patterns were concentration of population in urban nodes, fed by interconnected networks of green and blue spaces. We displayed all teams' drawings at a Saturday night celebration attended by over 400 participants and guests and addressed by City Council member Richard Conlin, who gave hope that the visions might actually make a difference in the City's planning.

Post Charrette: Making Sense of it All

After the charrette, our students digitized and refined their teams' drawings using GIS, after which we combined the GIS databases of each team's study area to create overall visions for Seattle's Green Network in 2020 and 2100.

Telescoping further down in scale, students then further developed particular sites or prototype tools for the city to use in implementing green infrastructure principles. Two students evaluated the potential stormwater and habitat outcomes of their teams' plans, learning that combined sewer overflows could be eliminated and connected habitat could be established if the plans for their study areas were followed.

Sharing the Results

We then presented these refined and synthesized plans to our advisory committee and the public, exhibited them at City Hall and at the UW, posted them to the project website, and documented the ideas in an extensively illustrated, 230-page report titled *Envisioning Seattle's Green Future: Visions and Strategies from the Green Futures Charrette*. We produced an Executive Summary of the report and distributed over a thousand copies in the community (Rottle and Maryman 2006a, 2006b). The project website continues to be a digital distribution source of these documents and the resources developed for the charrette. We have presented the Open Space Seattle 2100 process and its results to numerous community groups as well as to national

Chapter 10: **ENVISIONING GREEN INFRASTRUCTURE**

Figure 10.3 Photo of the Green Futures Charrette. *In the two day Green Futures Charrette, over 350 professionals, students, and citizens participated on twenty-three teams to envision Seattle's green infrastructure for the years 2020 and 2100.*

Source: Nancy Rottle

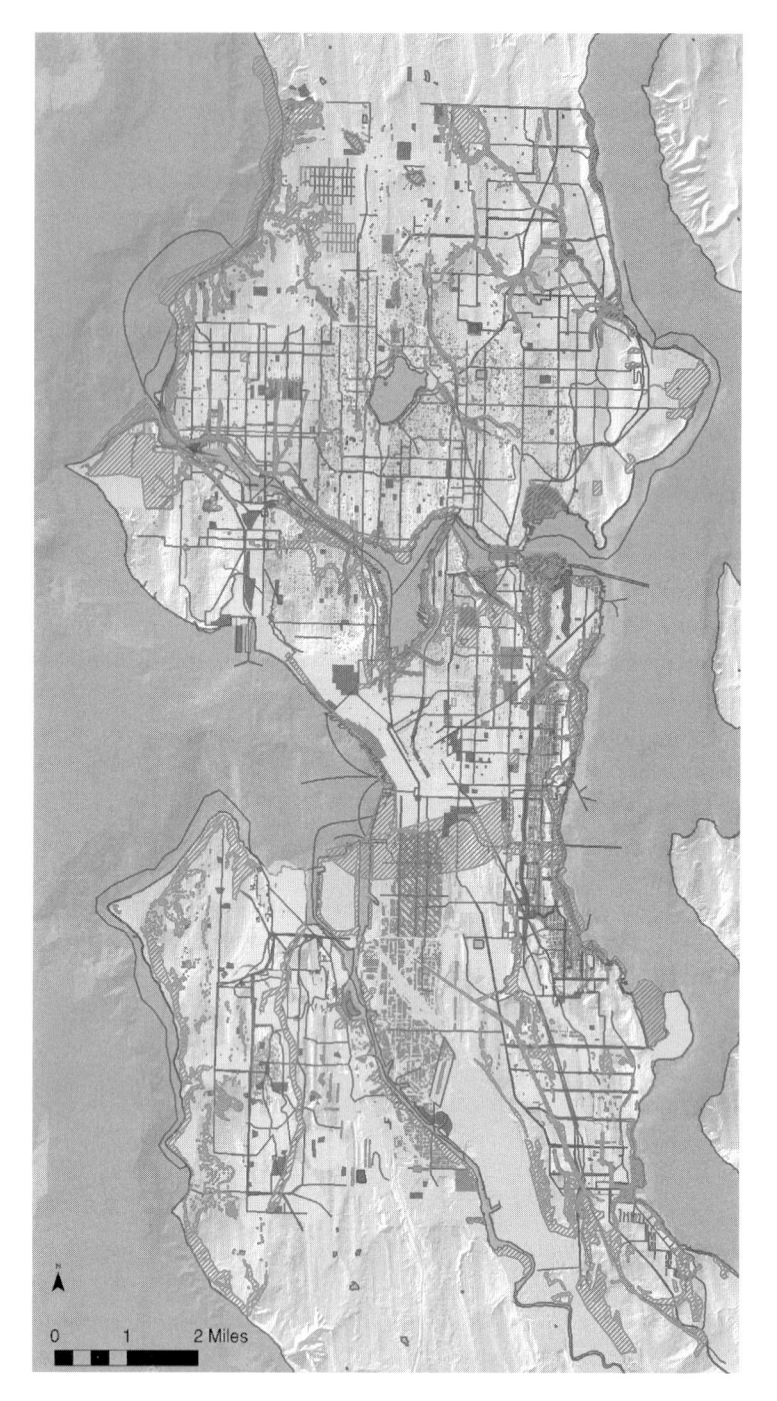

Figure 10.4a Visions for Seattle's Green Infrastructure, 2025 and 2100. *Each team's plans from the charrette were digitized in GIS and then joined to form layered whole-city green infrastructure visions for 2020 and 2100. The plans can be viewed at www.open2100.org.*

Source: Open Space Seattle 2100

Chapter 10: **ENVISIONING GREEN INFRASTRUCTURE**

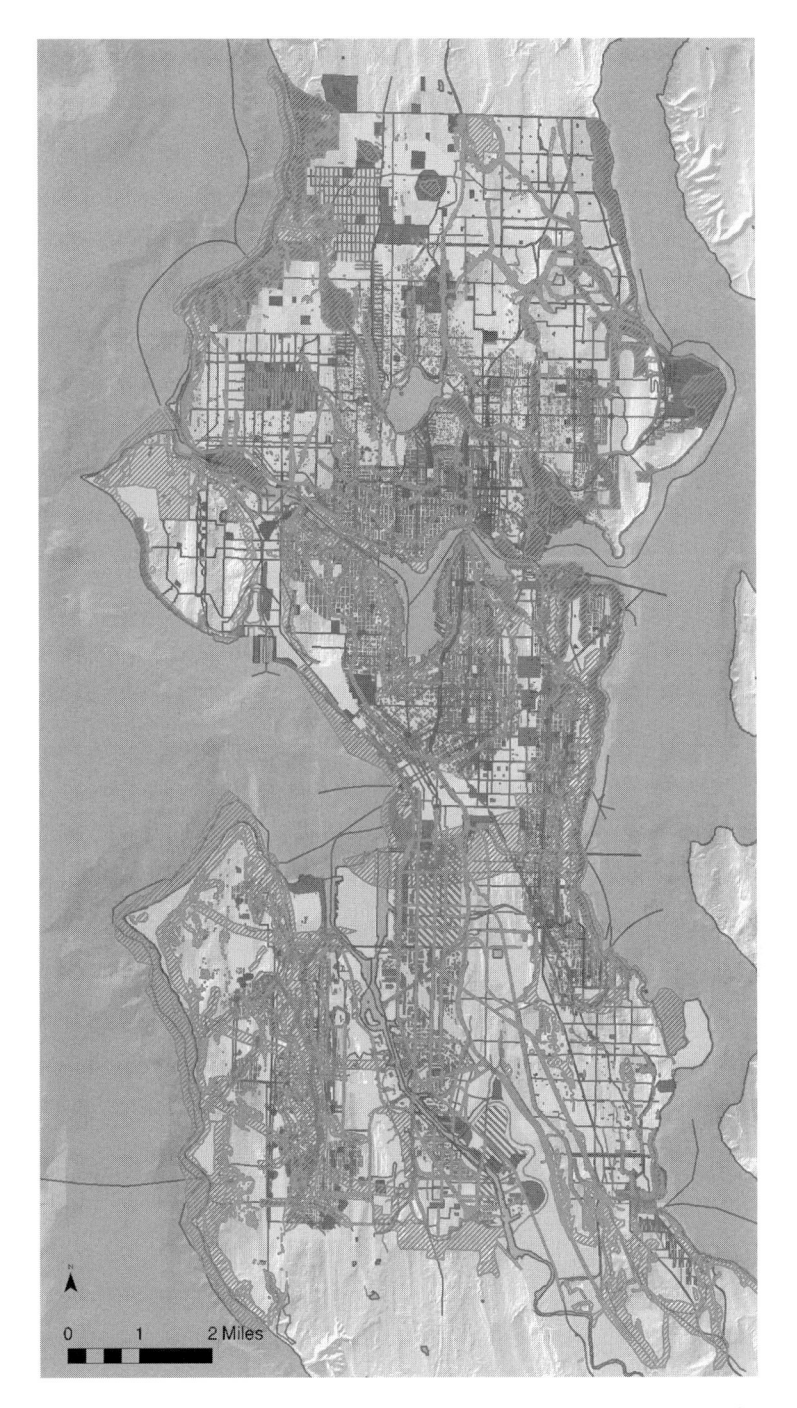

Figure 10.4b Visions for Seattle's Green Infrastructure, 2025 and 2100. *Each team's plans from the charrette were digitized in GIS and then joined to form layered whole-city green infrastructure visions for 2020 and 2100. The plans can be viewed at www.open2100.org.*

Source: Open Space Seattle 2100

and international audiences and published papers and articles in academic proceedings and a professional journal (Rottle 2006; Rottle and Maryman 2006c, 2007).

What Difference Has It Made?

While the boldness of this vision may be daunting, the City has taken several tangible steps toward implementing the themes and ideas of the Green Futures charrette participants. In the Executive branch, the Mayor's office convened a Sustainability and Environment sub-cabinet level team to coordinate environmental functions across various agencies including the city's parks, transportation, drainage utility, and planning administrators. Aided by continued work in the UW's Department of Landscape Architecture, the City's public utilities department proposed a program to encourage residents to rethink their streetside planting strips so that they better function as ecological infrastructure.[8]

At the City Council, our goal and eight guiding open space principles were unanimously endorsed through an official proclamation. A subsequent lobbying effort to secure funds to further conduct long-range green infrastructure planning came up short in a year where public safety expenditures were of primary importance. However, the Council directed planning and development staff to begin working on ways that an integrated approach to green expenditures could be fostered in the city and to include the public in that discussion. One promising result was the establishment of a city-wide interdepartmental asset management system that would apply triple bottom line evaluation of municipal expenditures for green infrastructure investments. Another was garnering support for a change in the open space code requirements for new development in Commercial and Neighborhood Commercial districts via an innovative "green area factor." This "Seattle Green Factor" (SGF) is a flexible regulatory system that aims to improve ecological function as well as provide public amenity. Initial evaluation of the system shows it to be working, and a refined version has now been expanded from areas zoned Commercial to also influence Multi-Family zoning areas of the city.

The process of the charrette itself appeared to advance participants' visionary thinking and has inspired interest and action by the citizenry. One long-time open space advocate wrote, "life is not the same after being asked to envision what open space should be in Seattle in 2100." Numerous participants on the Green Futures teams intended to advance ideas generated in the charrette through reconvening, taking proposals to their neighborhood councils, and seeking City funding toward implementation.

This coalescing of the public imagination and groundswell of caring reformulated in the Green Legacy Coalition, a group convened to secure continued investment for Seattle's green infrastructure. That story is told later.

Creating a City's Green Infrastructure: Green Infrastructure Lessons from the OSS2100 work

Recognizing that the ideas generated in the Green Futures charrette offered rich fodder for finding transferable wisdom, the authors mined the twenty-three teams' plans to identify lessons for creating a city's green infrastructure, seeking common themes and diverse strategies. Our conclusions for creating a healthy, humanistic and ecological open space system include four major concepts, with a complement of strategies for each. They are:

Chapter 10: **ENVISIONING GREEN INFRASTRUCTURE**

Theme 1: Create an Integrated Green Infrastructure

Strategies:

- *Aggregate Open Space to Create Connections and Urban Greenways*, forming loops, connecting uplands to shorelines, linking backyards, and connecting to regional trails.
- *Create Multi-functional Open Space* that maximizes the uses and benefits of every parcel. For example, multiple use of the street-rights-of-way could include transit, water purification, stream corridors, and recreation.
- *Redefine Transportation Corridors* to include more green spaces and ecosystem functions in the rights-of-way. Lid freeways to create new urban space and reconnect neighborhoods.
- *Recreate Natural Drainage to Restore Our Waters,* using pervious surfaces, rain gardens, restored wetlands and bioswales that can clean and detain water before entering streams, lakes and other collector water bodies.

Theme 2: Promote Ecological Open Space

Strategies:

- *Understand the City as Watersheds* to repair water-based ecological corridors and to connect neighborhoods.
- *Respect Underlying Natural Conditions* to honor the existing ecology and minimize damage from natural disasters.
- *Re-establish Historic Streams* that are now buried in pipes by bringing water to the surface and restoring riparian corridors to support aquatic habitat.
- *Restore Shorelines for Habitat.* Coastal cities, many which are located in estuaries, have typically displaced critical habitat. Vegetated shorelines supply shade, food and refuge for fish, and rising waters from global climate change provide opportunities to reclaim waterfronts for habitat.
- *Establish and Protect Greenbelts and Habitat Networks* to extend existing urban forests, with potential wildlife, forestry and recreational uses.

Theme 3: Balance Density and Community

Strategies:

- *Focus Development in the Urban Core* to protect outlying resource and farmlands, support public transportation, and reduce the impacts of sprawl to lakes and streams, climate and air.
- *Create New Urban Villages with Civic Hearts* that are walkable with mixed residential, commercial, public amenities and civic gathering spaces. Locate these urban villages outside sensitive lands, such as on ridgelines where residents can enjoy the views.
- *Employ Green Roofs and Walls* on residential and commercial buildings to reduce the city's heat island effects, detain stormwater, create habitat and provide green relief.

- *Encourage Decentralized Self-sufficiency* with localized power generation, water treatment, and agriculture to reduce dependency and impacts on outside resources.

Theme 4: Provide Democratic Access and Use

Strategies:

- *Provide Equality in Accessibility* to open space for all citizens, addressing diverse cultural needs and environmental justice.
- *Give Increased Access to Water* from every neighborhood with waterfront acreages through public and private incentives.
- *Use Open Space for Education and Schools for Open Space* by incorporating schoolyards as community open space, and creating learning spaces such as gardens, views, interpretive trails and eco-revelatory features.
- *Provide a Hierarchy and Variety of Open Spaces* including natural areas, large parks, playgrounds, community gardens, trails and pocket parks.

After the Stone, the Green Infrastructure Ripples

While the Green Futures Charrette was a catalyzing event, the changes that it helped foster have come echoing back. The efforts by the Seattle community to align ecological functions with zoning, regulatory and policy objectives have been noticeable, and while not all of these efforts could be directly attributed to the Open Space Seattle 2100 process, the frequency with which the charrette process is invoked within these discussions confirms its influence as a potent moment in the city's history.

One of the criticisms that could be aimed at the Open Space Seattle 2100 process was that there was no identified organization that would continue to move the process forward. Rather, the coordinators proposed to have the charrette experience act as a re-conceptualization of the very structure of the city, and in that reimagining the Open Space Seattle 2100 process would foster a new type of civic activism oriented toward cultural and natural collusion. Like a pebble dropped in a pond, this moment would ripple across various neighborhoods to effect change throughout the city.

Beyond the various neighborhood-level interventions, several city-wide initiatives have been developed since the charrette, both from the grassroots and from the political leadership. For example, we briefly described the Seattle Green Factor above. The most direct offshoot grown from the Open Space Seattle 2100 process proceeded from the recognition that without continuation of the Pro-Parks Levy, a $198 million, eight-year property tax that was instituted in 2000, many of the projects identified in the Open Space Seattle 2100 process would have little chance of coming to fruition. With the levy set to expire in 2008, and the Mayor and City Council either hostile toward or unwilling to act on behalf of further green space investments, a grassroots coalition consisting of many of the same organizations that had coalesced around the Open Space Seattle 2100 process formed to advocate for continuation of this important funding source.

Called the Green Legacy Coalition, this group of twenty-five organizations was the brainchild of an organization that had taken the messages of the Open Space Seattle 2100

Chapter 10: ENVISIONING GREEN INFRASTRUCTURE

process and folded them into its newly formed mission. Dubbed the Seattle Great City Initiative (Great City), this member driven organization was founded on the heels of the Open Space Seattle 2100 process. Great City was founded to bring together a diverse constituency of businesses, environmentalists and neighborhood activists to create a great, livable city as part of the larger regional visioning of the Cascade Land Conservancy's Cascade Agenda.

Among the organization's three priorities was a continuation in investments in the City's green infrastructure. Starting in late spring of 2007, Seattle Great City Initiative identified a Green Infrastructure Committee that was tasked with catalyzing an effort to place a ballot measure in the November 2008 election to replace the expiring levy.

Though Seattleites had overwhelmingly supported park-focused ballot measures that benefited the entire city in the past, the hurdles that would need to be overcome to bring this levy package to voters were not inconsiderable. The Mayor had stated, and continued to state until Election Day, a preference for not renewing the levy, and the City Council's Parks Committee was reluctant to step forward to begin the process of engaging citizens to make a new levy package to put to voters. From the outset, it was clear that a broad coalition of organizations would be needed to surmount these barriers.

Inviting participation from a variety of organizations, the Green Legacy Coalition was quickly able to gather a constituency of groups invested in making a new levy a reality. Consisting of neighborhood business organizations, environmental groups like the Sierra Club and Audubon Society, non-motorized transportation advocates like the Cascade Bicycle Club and FeetFirst – much as in the Open Space Seattle 2100 process – the coalition's breadth would become one of its great strengths.

Over the ensuing months, this coalition lobbied the Mayor's office and City Council to take the necessary steps to make a ballot measure possible. Instrumental in these efforts was the early involvement and lobbying from the Trust for Public Lands. Though they would eventually need to step away from the larger campaign, their early efforts in making the case for a 2008 levy were significant in wearing away Council reluctance.

Another significant event happened during the City Council election of 2007 when a new Council Parks Committee Chair was appointed in the person of Tom Rasmussen. Councilor Rasmussen, with the support and assistance of Council President Richard Conlin and Councilor Tim Burgess, commissioned a poll of Seattle voters in early 2008. With more than 67 percent of Seattle voters either favoring or strongly favoring a renewal of the Pro Parks Levy, both the Council and the Coalition felt strongly that the time to act was coming on quickly.

In short order, a twenty-eight-person citizen's committee was assembled and began holding hearings and deliberations. Using a variety of previous plans and reports, over 500 potential projects were identified for inclusion in a new levy, and from this master list approximately fifty discrete projects were finally included in a recommended package to City Council. In addition to the standard "parks" projects, several projects that speak toward the goals of the Open Space Seattle 2100 process were also recommended, including:

- funding for a number of hiker-biker trails;
- a $15 million "Opportunity Fund" for citizens to use to make unforeseen projects come to fruition;
- monies for community gardens;

- environmental restoration monies for shorelines, riparian zones and urban forests; and
- $26 million in money to acquire additional park land in the areas of Seattle that are targeted to receive the most growth.

In August of 2008, the City Council voted to approve the ballot measure for the November 2008 ballot. Despite the stressed economic climate, in November 2008 the Parks and Green Spaces Levy passed with nearly 60 percent of the vote, providing six years of continued parks and expanded green infrastructure funding.

Reflections

While the establishment of green spaces in ex-urban environments has been the focus of much of the environmental community in the last forty years, there is an increasing focus on creating great urban places – ones that are livable, equitable and well-designed – as the most ecologically and economically responsible choice as we consider impending challenges to sustaining human and environmental health. The bifurcation of natural and cultural motivators and interventions is being replaced by urban infrastructure solutions that address the real world needs of both constituencies. Visions of an integrated green infrastructure as both an armature for and an addition to a densified urbanity will begin to break down these centuries old divisions.

But talking about these places and showing these places are two very different propositions. The great strength of a visioning process like Open Space Seattle 2100, then, is that it cannot only serve the gestational purpose of defining a vision, it can also conjure what that place looks and feels like. In this collective process, communities are given the tools to empower themselves by giving them the opportunity to incorporate fact-based spatial and research data about current and future conditions. Over the long-run, those community members become, or remain, engaged in the active re-shaping of their city.

The overlapping green infrastructure layers presented in this chapter – community space, habitat, water, mobility and metabolism – form a heuristic for thinking about urban systems that not only address cultural interests, but that also speak to other, interrelated concerns impacting human systems which are all too often overlooked in the making and remaking of our built environments.

Additionally, if we attempt to shape environments that exist as localized emergences of broader networks of the five systems described above then we are not just creating a better world for our future, but we are also tapping into larger American narratives of stewardship, self-sufficiency, and community. For the scholar and student, engaged scholarship approaches like Open Space Seattle 2100 bring cutting edge research and exemplary built-projects to academic and civic audiences, challenging these communities to imagine and implement new design practices that may lead to more ecologically, socially and economically healthy metropolitan regions. In the process, citizens' environmental literacy may be enhanced; in an informed charrette experience, participants learn from the places to which they are connected, and may perceive their inherent qualities and potentialities in new and inspiring ways. Such learning and resulting commitment to change may be necessary to create "magnet" urban environments effective in protecting air, water, and biodiversity and reducing pressure on forests and prime agricultural lands. A resulting city rich in ecological and open space opportunities may be self-perpetuating (a "virtuous cycle")

Chapter 10: ENVISIONING GREEN INFRASTRUCTURE

where daily contact with nature continually fosters experiential education and promotes the caring and stewardship needed to maintain both human and non-human organisms and communities.

Change on bureaucratic municipal scales typically occurs at a snail's pace. However, the threats facing American metropolitan regions and the planet as a whole demand a radical shift in reconsidering the way we conceive our infrastructures, not only at the local level, but from regional and national leadership as well. From anticipated threats of climate disturbance to the loss of America's social capital to the public health crisis borne, in part, from the auto-centrism of our current infrastructure solutions, it is apparent that we need to begin to develop new, innovative ways of shaping our cityscapes so that they are simultaneously livable and low-impact.

Indeed, we might take a broad, high-performance, low-impact approach to the multiple environmental systems that provide urban services, much as we are beginning to expect from "high performance" or "green" buildings. At the forefront of that movement, the US Green Building Council (USGBC) "promotes a whole-building approach to sustainability by recognizing performance in five key areas of human and environmental health: sustainable site development, water savings, energy efficiency, materials selection, and indoor environmental quality" (USGBC 2007). Similarly, the efforts of the participants in the Green Futures Charrette point toward a "whole-city" approach to sustainability by recognizing five key areas of human and environmental health: open spaces and community, replication of the natural hydrologic cycle, creation of low-impact transportation networks, restoration of ecological function and the shortening of a city's metabolic functions.

This approach suggests a radical rethinking of the ways in which American municipalities approach their capital expenditures. Typical civic bureaucracies compartmentalize infrastructure expenditures, and are thus measured via a single-bottom line, providing one service (water, transportation, etc.) as efficiently as possible. However, by encouraging high-level municipal integration and using triple bottom-line budget metrics, communities can begin to transform the means and methods of urban infrastructure expenditures. Directing these expenditures to green infrastructure systems may not only provide profound efficiencies, but may also produce truly livable cities.

Fundamental to the Open Space Seattle 2100 process were the authors' convictions that each community has the power to evoke a compelling, sustainable vision from within its own ranks, based upon a realistic assessment of both current realities and future challenges. Engaging the public in such a process may indeed empower citizenries to take an active role in re-orienting investments in public infrastructures from grey to green.

Authors' Note

This chapter is an extension of papers previously published in Conference Proceedings of the Council of Educators in Landscape Architecture (2006) and the Fabos Greenway Symposium (2007).

Notes

1   www.livcomawards.com/2008-awards/whole-city-awards.htm. Judging criteria includes: (1) Enhancement of the Landscape, including "protection of the natural heritage and of ecologically

important sites, biodiversity and introduction of vegetation in more difficult environments" (2) Environmentally Sensitive Practices, such as "efforts to apply sustainable development and to promote best practices that lead to the development, conservation and preservation of the environment . . ." (3) Community Sustainability, including "ongoing involvement of individuals, groups and Organisations in the planning, development and management of the local community . . ." (4) Healthy Lifestyles "both through the provision of appropriate facilities, and the promotion of active participation . . ." (5) Heritage Management and (6) Planning for the Future.

2   www.mercer.com/qualityofliving. This global human resources consulting firm conducts a quality of living survey of thirty-nine world cities annually, applying the criteria of safety, education, hygiene, recreation, political-economic stability and public transportation.

3   www.monacle.com. Monacle magazine rates the "components and forces that make a city . . . truly livable."

4   See http://www.americanforests.org/resources/urbanforests/naturevalue.php as a starting point.

5   See the Low Impact Development website at: www.lowimpactdevelopment.org. Several jurisdictions have adopted Low-Impact Development guidelines and requirements, such as King County, WA.

6   Lennertz and Lutzenhiser define "charrette" as "a multiple-day, collaborative planning workshop" (2006: xi). Applying the term to urban design, Condon describes it as a "time-limited, multi-party design event organized to generate a collaboratively produced plan for a sustainable community" (2008: 1).

7   www.open2100.org

8   See Seattle Public Utilities and Rottle *et al.*, *Re-Imagining Seattle Streets: Planting Strips and Street Edge Treatments for Urban Green Infrastructure* at http://www.seattle.gov/util/About_SPU/Yard_System/Reports/SPU01_003278.asp

References

Benedict, M. and McMahon, E. 2006. *Green Infrastructure, Linking Landscapes and Communities*. Washington, DC: Island Press.

City of New York and Design Trust for Public Space. 2003. High performance infrastructure: best practices for public rights of ways. New York: City of New York. Accessed 3/07/07 at: http://www.nyc.gov/html/ddc/html/ddcgreen/reports.html.

Childs, M. 2004. *Squares: A Public Place Design Guide for Urbanists*. Albuquerque, NM: University of New Mexico Press.

Condon, P., ed. 1996. *Sustainable Urban Landscapes: The Surrey Design Charrette*. Vancouver, BC: University of British Columbia, James Taylor Chair in Landscape and Liveable Environments: Distributed by the University of British Columbia Press.

Condon, P.M. 2008 *Design Charrettes for the Sustainable Community*. Washington, DC: Island Press.

Condon, P. and Proft, J., eds. 1999. *Sustainable Urban Landscapes: The Brentwood Design Charrette*. Vancouver: University of British Columbia, James Taylor Chair in Landscape and Liveable Environments, Distributed by the University of British Columbia Press.

Chapter 10: ENVISIONING GREEN INFRASTRUCTURE

Cranz, G. and Boland, M. 2004. Defining the sustainable park: a fifth model for urban parks. *Landscape Journal* 23: 2–4.

Frank, L., Engelke, P., and Schmid. 2003. *Health and Community Design*. Washington, DC: Island Press.

Girling, C. and Kellett, R. 2005. *Skinny Streets and Green Neighborhoods*. Washington, DC: Island Press.

Harnik, P. 1999. *Economic Benefits of Open Space*. Trust for Public Land. Accessed at: http://www.tpl.org/tier3_cd.cfm?content_item_id=1195&folder_id=727.

Harnik, P. 2000. *Inside City Parks*. Washington, DC: ULI-the Urban Land Institute: Trust for Public Land.

Kaplan, R., Kaplan, S., and Ryan, R. 1998. *With People in Mind*. Washington, DC: Island Press, pp. 67–77.

Kelbaugh, D. 1997. *Common Place: Toward Neighborhood and Regional Design*. Seattle, WA: University of Washington Press.

Kellert, S. 2005. *Building for Life: Designing and Understanding the Human-nature Connection*. Washington, DC: Island Press.

Lahti P. *et al.* 2006. *Towards Sustainable Urban Infrastructure. Assessment, Tools and Good Practice*. Helsinki: European Science Foundation ESF/COST.

Lennertz, B., Luzenhiser, A., and The National Charrette Institute. 2006. *The Charrette Handbook*. Chicago: APA Press.

Louv, R. 2005. *Last Child in the Woods: Saving Our Children from Nature-deficit Disorder*, Chapel Hill, NC: Algonquin Books.

McPherson, E.G., Nowak, D.J., and Rowntree, R.A. 1994. *Chicago's Urban Forest Ecosystem: Results of the Chicago Urban Forest Climate Project*. Gen. Tech. Rep. NE-186. Radnor, PA: US Department of Agriculture, Forest Service, Northeastern Forest Experiment Station, pp. 83–94.

Maryman, B. and Maggio, C. 2004. In Seattle, the Mother of All Charrettes. *Landscape Architecture Magazine*, 94/8 (August 2004), 64, 66–70, 72–75.

Nowak, D.J. 2000. The interactions between urban forests and global climate change. In Abdollahi, Kamran K., Ning, Zhu H., Appeaning, Alexander (eds.) *Global Climate Change and The Urban forest*. Baton Rouge, LA: Gulf Coast Regional Climate Change Council and Franklin Press, Inc., pp. 31–44.

Nowak, D.J. and Crane, D.E. 2002. Carbon storage and sequestration by urban trees in the USA. *Environmental Pollution*, 116, 3, 381–389.

Open Space Seattle 2100 Charrette Brief, accessed at www.open2100.org.

Rottle, N. 2006. Collaborative visioning for the new normal: designing Seattle's open space for the next century. *Council of Educators in Landscape Architecture Proceedings* (CELA). Vancouver, BC: University of British Columbia.

Rottle, N. and Maryman, B. 2006a. *Envisioning Seattle's Green Future: Visions and Strategies from The Green Futures Charrette*. Seattle, University of Washington.

Rottle, N. and Maryman, B. 2006b. *Executive Summary: Envisioning Seattle's Green Future: Visions and Strategies from the Green Futures Charrette*. Seattle, University of Washington.

Rottle, N. and Maryman, B. 2006c. Strategies for a greener future. *Landscape Architecture Magazine*, November.

Rottle, N. and Maryman, B. 2007. Designing Seattle's green infrastructure for the next century. *Proceedings of the 2007 Fabos Greenway Symposium.* Amherst, MA, University of Massachusetts.

Schneekloth, L. 2003. Urban green infrastructure. In D. Watson, A. Plattus and R. Shibley (eds.) *Time-Saver Standards for Urban* Design, New York: McGraw-Hill, Chapter 7, 4–1.

Thompson, C. 2002. Urban open space in the 21st century. *Landscape and Urban Planning* 60, 59–72.

Tzoulas, K., Korpela, K., Venn, S., Yli-Pelkonen, V., Kazmierczak, A., Niemlea, J., and James, P. Promoting ecosystem and human health in urban areas using green infrastructure: a literature review. *Landscape and Urban Planning* 81, 3, 167–178.

USGBC. 2007. Leadership in energy and environmental Design. Accessed 12 March, 2007 at http://www.usgbc.org/DisplayPage.aspx?CategoryID=19

Wenk, William E. 2002. Toward an inclusive concept of infrastructure. In B. Johnson and K. Hill (eds.) *Ecology and Design.* Washington, DC: Island Press.

Chapter 11

DOES LAND USE AND TRANSPORTATION COORDINATION REALLY MAKE A DIFFERENCE IN CREATING LIVABLE COMMUNITIES?

Ruth L. Steiner

Associate Professor, Department of Urban and Regional Planning
University of Florida

Introduction

Historically, transportation has been the driving force behind the urban form of our cities. As transportation technology has evolved, cities have changed shape to accommodate new modes and faster speeds. Newman and Kenworthy (1995) define three classifications for cities based on chronological age: the walking city, the transit city, and the automobile city. Each of these is distinguished not only by optimal travel mode, but also by associated characteristics of urban form and land uses. The traditional walking city, exemplified in pre-1850 European cities, is characterized by high residential densities, mixed land uses, narrow streets, and organic street patterns that fit the landscape. The transit city originated during the industrial age and was prominent from 1850 to 1940. As rail and trams increased in popularity, city boundaries expanded. Tram and rail-based suburbs were developed around railway and tram stations, resulting in medium-density, and mixed use areas – much like the walking city only further from the center. Automobile cities, the dominant city form since World War II, disperse development in all directions, resulting in low residential densities. In addition, a trend toward separation of uses through zoning encouraged the decentralization of cities. The street pattern of the automobile city is characterized by an arterial grid, curvilinear streets, and disconnected *culs de sac*. More recently, Garreau (1991) defined what is known as an edge city: growth centers formed away from the downtown of an established city consisting of large multipurpose core areas surrounded by low-density residential suburbia. The formation of such cities relies on convenient freeway and interstate automobile transportation. An edge city is a job center for the suburban population living beyond its borders, generally consisting of mid- to large-scale commercial, industrial, office, restaurant, and hotel uses (Garreau 1991).

When first introduced, the automobile and its necessary infrastructure seemed to offer freedom from transportation-related constraints. With a car, which allows fast access to all destinations, a person is much less restricted in residential location choice. As automobile cities have grown popular and aged over the past half-century, however, it has become clear that they introduce a variety of problems and shortcomings that manifest themselves in the forms of mobility and accessibility. Low public transit ridership and a failure to sufficiently plan for the pedestrian and bicyclist contribute to traffic and parking nightmares. In addition, studies have shown that automobile dependence may result in reduced physical activity, a lack of economic and social equity among income groups and ethnic groups, and negative environmental consequences, among other outcomes (Litman 2002; Frank *et al.* 2004).

Research has shown that better coordination of land use and transportation can combat such problems. A wider range of studies have shown that characteristics of the built environment can constrain or facilitate use of transportation modes other than the automobile. A diverse mix of land uses and higher residential densities contribute to positive transportation-related outcomes such as greater mode shift toward active modes of transportation like walking and bicycling, decreased vehicle miles traveled per person, and fewer single occupant automobile trips.

In addition to economic, social, and environmental qualities, travel behavior and transportation mode choice are contributing factors in determining whether a city is livable. A car-owner living in a typical modern-day automobile-oriented city has a substantial amount of freedom in residential location choice. Unrestricted individual behavior, however, is often in conflict with socially optimal behavior (Vuchic 1999). For example, if an auto-oriented city does not support alternative transportation modes or if there is a lack of available affordable housing near employment centers, low-income workers will be disproportionately adversely affected. Absent programs such as carpooling or car-sharing, traffic would be problematic even if we assume everyone in the city has access to an automobile. For these reasons, among others, mode-bias in transportation planning may be detrimental to a city's livability.

Multimodal transportation planning, in which all transportation modes are considered in the planning process, has been shown to have potential positive environmental, health, economic, and social outcomes, and thus is important in planning for a livable city (Belzer and Autler 2002; Dittmar and Ohland 2004; Brown *et al.* 2008). Because a multimodal transportation system requires certain land use elements such as density, mix of uses, and street network connectivity, a successful multimodal transportation system requires coordination with land use planning (Steiner *et al.* 2003). In examining the elements of land-use transportation coordination, multimodal transportation planning is a unifying element. Its influence on mode choice and travel behavior is explored throughout this chapter.

Basic Concepts of Land Use-Transportation Coordination

In order to understand the complexity of land use and transportation coordination it is useful to consider some of the fundamental underlying concepts that characterize this relationship. These concepts include: accessibility versus mobility, the scale of analysis, and the context of travel. The importance of these concepts in understanding this relationship is first explored. Then various methods and measures involved in implementing land use and transportation

Chapter 11: LAND USE AND TRANSPORTATION

coordination are described below. They include: traditional neighborhood development, transit-oriented development, location efficiency, the jobs-housing balance, spatial mismatch, and transportation concurrency.

Accessibility vs. Mobility

The concept of accessibility refers to the connection between people and the activities of daily living, while mobility refers to the ability to move around to get to the destinations where these activities take place. A highly accessible neighborhood incorporates most of the activities of daily living in close proximity to residences. Another related concept is regional versus local accessibility. Local accessibility is the ability to get around to activities in a neighborhood while regional accessibility relates to the ability to move around within a region. Where there is limited transportation choice in a region, mobility is generally equated to regional accessibility (Handy 1992). The transportation network needs to be designed to support the economic activities of the community. However, this approach will favor investments in regional accessibility. Too frequently these improvements are limited to regional highway infrastructure rather than facilities for public transit, bicycling and walking. In this way, as Handy (1992) argues, these investments favor regional over local accessibility and mobility for the automobile over mobility using other modes.

Scale of Analysis and Context of Travel

The coordination of land use and transportation takes place at multiple scales of development from the site scale to the neighborhood, regional, statewide and national scales. At the site level, connections between modes are made: a driver walks from a parking place to a grocery, a transit user walks from a transit stop to his office, and a bicyclist walks from a bike rack to her office. At the neighborhood scale, connections between land uses create environments to support transportation choice. Thus, the density, diversity and design matter (Bernick and Cervero 1996). Density or intensity of development, mix of land uses and connectivity between land uses become most important. If these components are all present, the opportunity for access to a diversity of services is possible. To understand the importance of these components, it is useful to consider each of them separately. Density without a mix of land uses means that residents have few destinations and low accessibility; they may need to drive or use transit in order to go about the activities of daily living available to them. A mix of land uses without density or connectivity means that people cannot easily walk from their residence to other non-residential land uses. Good street connectivity with a single land use or with low-density residential affords few opportunities for interaction between people. These concepts will differ depending upon whether the development is located in an urban, suburban or rural context (see Duany 2002 for a discussion of the Transect).

Overview of Land Use-Transportation Coordination

Over the last few decades, different methods and measures have been developed to assess the coordination between land use and transportation. While these planning tools are somewhat distinct, they share some aspects in common: (1) they suggest that the coordination of land use and transportation makes a difference in individuals' travel in some places and contexts; (2) they are based on a series of research projects that define the context in which they may be applicable; and (3) they assume the availability of multiple choices of transportation. These methods and measures include: (1) traditional neighborhood development; (2) transit-oriented development; (3) location efficiency; (4) jobs-housing balance; (5) spatial mismatch; and (6) transportation concurrency.

Traditional neighborhood development, which is sometimes called neo-traditional development or design, incorporates many of the concepts that are incorporated into New Urbanism. Traditional neighborhood development includes high-density, mixed land uses and an interconnected grid street network that supports all modes of travel. Transit-oriented development is a narrower term that refers to design of neighborhoods to take advantage of public investments in transit, particularly fixed rail and light rail transit.

Over the last decade many of the concepts discussed in this chapter have been incorporated into a broader concept called location efficiency. Location efficiency incorporates the concept of matching transportation characteristics to the surrounding land uses and to considering the combined cost of housing and transportation. Jobs-housing balance refers to the concept of spatially matching housing to employment as a means to reduce overall travel to employment. A jobs-housing balance can be seen in bedroom communities that provide expensive housing for people who want to live in an exclusive community and commute to another, or in bedroom communities that support affordable housing for nearby major urban areas where residents "drive to qualify" for mortgages. The spatial mismatch hypothesis, which was put forward by John Kain in the 1960s, postulated that the loss of jobs in the inner city was due to the increase in jobs in suburban communities. The spatial mismatch can be seen in the jobs-housing imbalance in inner-city neighborhoods where jobs for low-income residents had moved to the suburbs and low-paid workers had to travel long distances for work. Later the spatial mismatch hypothesis was extended to include the travel of other categories of low-income workers who may or may not live in the central city (Ihlanfeldt and Sjoquist 1998).

Transportation concurrency is a mandate that transportation infrastructure be available concurrent with the impact of development. Concurrency, which is implemented as an adequate public facilities ordinance, has been employed by individual communities, often suburban ones, which use it as a part of suburban exclusion of low-income projects. Two states, Washington and Florida, require concurrency as a part of the implementation of growth management by local governments participating in statewide growth management.

Traditional Neighborhood Development

Traditional Neighborhood Development (TND) focuses on the residential neighborhood as a social, convenient, walkable, community-oriented environment. It is distinct from conventional suburbs in several respects. Whereas conventional suburbs are characterized by low-street connectivity and separation of land uses, TND exhibits higher density residential uses, mixed uses, an interconnected grid-patterned street network, access to public transportation, and pedestrian and bicyclist accommodations. This combination of characteristics contributes to the potential of TND to break from the auto-dependency of conventional suburbs.

Chapter 11: **LAND USE AND TRANSPORTATION**

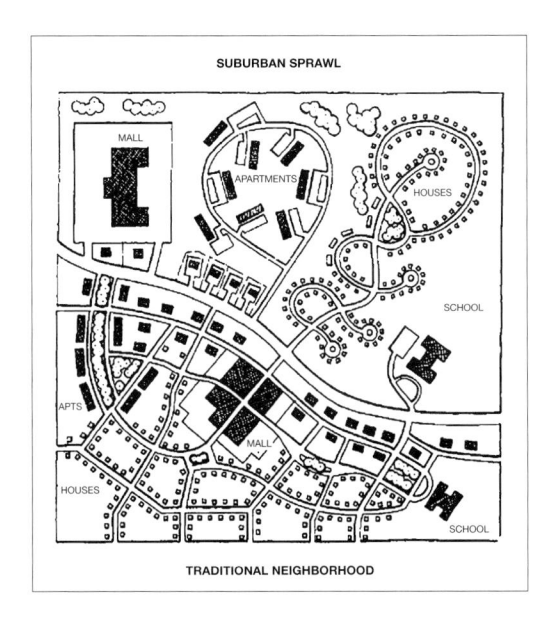

Figure 11.1 Conventional Suburban Development versus TND.

Source: Spielberg 1989: 17

The concept of traditional neighborhood development is incorporated into the New Urbanism, whose charter defines the structure of cities at three scales: the regional (the metropolis, city and town; the neighborhood; the district and corridor; and the block) the street and the building (Congress for the New Urbanism [CNU] 2001). At each scale, the social, economic and political aspects are incorporated into the design. Metropolitan regions should have well-structured cities, towns with well-defined neighborhoods with centers and edges. The physical organization of the region should support transportation alternatives to maximize access and mobility throughout the region. Neighborhoods should be designed to support bicycling and walking by incorporating a grid street network, appropriate density and intensity of development, and a mix of land uses. Transit corridors should be designed to connect a string of transit-oriented centers together to organize the metropolitan structure and to revitalize urban centers. At the block level, the Charter of the New Urbanism emphasizes the physical definition of the street and public spaces and the use of civic buildings and public gathering places to reinforce community identity and the culture of democracy (Katz 1994; CNU 2001; Ellis 2002).

Transit-Oriented Development

Transit-oriented development (TOD), a sub-category of TND, is a neighborhood incorporating a mix of land uses centered around a transit station (Calthorpe 1993). As in TND, these land uses include a mélange of high-density residential, retail, office, and open space uses. At the core, intensity of use is at its height. Within a short walk of the core, residents have easy access to stores and other services. Areas beyond a ten-minute walk from the core are reserved for lower intensity uses, such as single-family housing, schools, or parks. In addition to stressing the affordability of TOD, Calthorpe (1990) emphasizes its function by stating that

> the location, mix, and configuration of land uses in TODs are designed to encourage convenient alternatives to the auto, to provide a model of efficient land utilization, to better serve the needs of [. . .] diverse households, and to create more identifiable, livable communities.
>
> (Calthorpe Associates 1990: 2)

By allowing convenient access to other transportation modes in addition to the automobile, TOD has the potential to reduce the number of auto trips and vehicle miles traveled.

Belzer and Autler (2002) make a distinction between *transit-related* development and *transit-oriented* development. In the past, development around transit stations was mainly a joint initiative between the federal government and transit agencies as a way to capitalize on increased land values in those areas. Such financially-oriented projects were planned without consideration of how transit might interact with adjacent land uses and development. Belzer and Autler (2002: 12) outline several measures of livability that relate to TOD, including:

- positive environmental effects in the form of reduced gasoline consumption and the resultant improved air quality;
- increased transportation mode choices through increased walkability and access to public transportation;
- decreased traffic congestion;
- more convenient access to services and activities, such as retail, recreational, and cultural opportunities;
- more convenient access to public spaces; and
- positive health outcomes.

The Built Environment and TOD

Bernick and Cervero (1996) outline three necessities for the success of TOD: density, diversity, and design. Densities lower than ten to fifteen dwelling units per acre preclude a thriving TOD due to lack of transit ridership. However, lower densities in secondary areas may support transit by allowing convenient access to transit by bicycle along an interconnected street network. Diversity refers to the mix of uses at the TOD's core, allowing convenient access to services and activities. Design incorporates block length, street pattern, and pedestrian amenities, among other design-related elements that encourage walking and transit ridership. It is important to note that the density requirement narrows the focus of TOD to that subset of development which has adequate density to support transit. Based upon Calthorpe's early work (1992), regional destinations are also necessary to ensure success of TODs. In a successful TOD, these four elements are put together at three different scales: (1) downtown; (2) urban; and (3) neighborhood. These scales go from the highest density and intensity of development, the greatest mix of uses, employment, offices, and residential, and the highest level of transportation services with frequent service on a fixed rail system in the downtown, to the lowest density and intensity of development, a lesser

Chapter 11: **LAND USE AND TRANSPORTATION**

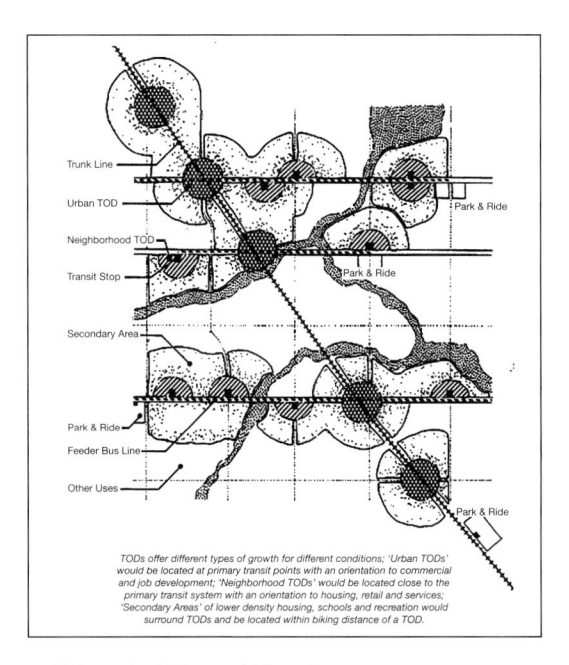

Figure 11.2 Context of Transit Oriented Development.

Source: Calthorpe Associates 1990: 4

mix of land uses, retail, small offices, and residential, and less frequent transit service to urban centers in the neighborhood centers. The urban centers have characteristics at these two scales (see Figure 11.2 for a graphical representation of this relationship).

Location Efficiency and Transportation Choice

The concept of location efficiency – the proximity of homes to transit systems – is central to TOD. Dittmar and Ohland (2004) identify three key components of location efficiency:

- density: a sufficient number of customers must exist to support the transit system, as discussed above under *The Built Environment and TOD*;
- transit accessibility: conveniently-located transit stations; and
- pedestrian friendliness: interconnected streets with pedestrian-scale elements.

When an automobile is no longer a necessary expense, as may be the case when one lives so close to transit, more lower- and middle-income Americans are better able to afford homes and thus participate more fully in the economy (Dittmar and Ohland 2004). The concept of location-efficiency has been incorporated into location-efficient mortgages in Seattle, Chicago, Los Angeles, and the San Francisco Bay. These mortgages are set up to allow residents of neighborhoods to amortize the savings associated with reducing the number of vehicles in the household into a larger mortgage (Center for Neighborhood Technology 2004; Krizek 2005). Research by Holtzclaw *et al.* (2002) showed a significant correlation between urban design and transportation infrastructure and auto ownership and distance driven. Neighborhoods in San Francisco, Los Angeles, and Chicago with fewer households per residential acre exhibit greater annual vehicle miles traveled (VMT) per household than neighborhoods with higher residential density. These differences of over 3:1 variations in VMT per household for a constant level of income and household size may be explained not only by density, but also by greater choice of transportation mode leading to a shift away from single-occupant driving.

Assessment of the Potential Mode Shift Associated with TND and TOD

The potential for reduced transportation impacts with TOD and TND are several. Within TOD, there is an opportunity to reduce the use of single-occupant vehicles in several ways: (1) reduced automobile trip generation; (2) higher rate of internal capture; (3) more trips by alternative modes of travel; (4) reduced trip length; and (5) more chaining of a series of trips together resulting in a different activity pattern. In assessing the impacts of TND and TOD, it is important to understand the scale at which trips occur and needs of users of specific modes of transportation. Pedestrians generally travel shorter distances than any other users of the transportation system. Many advocates of TND suggest that people are not willing to walk more than a quarter of a mile, while other studies suggest that people may walk farther for some activities (e.g. recreation and in connection with transit trips) (see Steiner 1994). Bicyclists are willing to travel longer distances but are sensitive to the volume and speed of traffic and presence of trucks when riding on roadways. Transit users will also go longer distances but they will be sensitive to some of the same factors as pedestrians with respect to access to transit. In assessing impacts, it is important to make a distinction between TND and TOD. TND principles apply to neighborhoods even where transit is not available, while TOD requires that transit be available. Thus, a well-designed neighborhood that facilitates walking and bicycling could be considered a TND but that same neighborhood would require transit to be a TOD.

Several studies have been completed to understand the connection between density, diversity, and design and regional destinations. They consistently show a pattern of reduced travel in locations with the characteristics of TND. Ewing and Cervero (2001) summarize a series of studies that consistently show a reduction in travel associated with high-density, mixed use, and transit-oriented development. Similarly, a study by the Transportation Research Board and the Institute of Medicine (TRB/IOM 2005) to understand the connections between the built environment and walking and bicycling summarizes a series of studies that found that higher rates of walking and bicycling typically exist in places with land uses that include density, diversity and grid street network. The study found that "certain neighborhood types, traditional, transit-served, and walkable, are positively correlated with walking and nonmotorized travel" (TRB/IOM 2005: 154). Studies have also shown that TND is associated with increased physical activity, an important consideration in an age of increasing concern for health issues such as obesity and diabetes (Brown *et al.* 2008).

Potential for Mode Shift from Single-Occupant Driving

In their 2008 study, Brown *et al.* compare the body mass indices[1] (BMI) as a measure of the level of health outcomes and travel behaviors of residents of conventional suburban neighborhoods to those of residents of comparable New Urbanist neighborhoods. A large New Urbanist neighborhood near Chapel Hill, North Carolina was selected in addition to five contiguous suburban neighborhoods in the same area. Results showed that household heads of the New Urbanist neighborhood made 0.76 fewer motorized trips per day than residents of the suburban neighborhoods (for single family households). Walking and bicycling trips were significantly higher for New Urbanist household heads compared to household heads in conventional neighborhoods. Examining all walking and bicycling trips, New Urbanist heads of household made 3.1 more utilitarian, as opposed to recreational, physical activity trips than their suburban counterparts. These trips were associated with reduced BMI, suggesting a causal relationship between the number of utilitarian physical activity trips made and BMI. In addition to important health outcomes, this research shows potential for mode shift to walking and bicycling within New Urbanist developments.

Alternatives to Trip Generation

In another study, Khattak and Rodriguez (2005) again compared a New Urbanist neighborhood and a conventional suburban neighborhood in Chapel Hill, North Carolina to determine the difference in travel patterns. They found that households in both neighborhoods made similar numbers of trips, but residents of traditional neighborhoods made fewer external trips, and they traveled fewer miles than households in the conventional neighborhood, even after controlling for demographic characteristics and for residential self-selection. The authors concluded that households in New Urbanist developments substitute driving trips with walking trips. This study shows that TND may contribute to reduced overall trip generation as compared to conventional suburban development.

Jobs-Housing Balance

The theory of jobs-housing balance posits that by balancing job and housing growth, in other words, matching the locations of jobs and residences, positive transportation-related outcomes will result, such as shorter commute distances, greater mode shift away from the automobile, and reduced traffic congestion (Cervero 1989). These outcomes are accompanied by benefits in the areas of health, the environment, and the economy in the respective forms of increased physical activity due to greater potential for walking and bicycling, decreased energy consumption and pollution caused by reduced vehicle emissions, and increased residential opportunities for the working class through the provision of affordable housing near job centers.

There is some debate as to the effects of jobs-housing balance. Levine (1998) argues that jobs-housing balance wrongly assumes that workers will necessarily choose housing close to their job locations if it is affordable; rather, the decision of home location is affected by many variables including density preferences and other individual valuations. In addition, jobs-housing balance does not address non-work trips, which account for a majority of trips (Guiliano 1991), and thus may not result in a decrease in overall traffic congestion. Instead, its main effects are in the area of transportation and land use choices. Jobs-housing balance allows households a greater range of transportation and land use options (Levine 1998).

Achieving a Jobs-Housing Balance

The literature generally identifies governmental regulation as a necessity for jobs-housing balance. Comprehensive plans and zoning regulations can be designed to provide for mixed land uses and for the simultaneous development of residences and employment centers. Other specific ways a local government might work toward jobs-housing balance include encouraging planned unit developments, home-occupation regulations (home-work arrangements), inclusionary zoning, linkage programs in which employers must secure or provide housing for a portion of their employees, and development incentives such as density bonuses (Weitz 2003). Local government interventions, however, are often blamed as the cause of job-housing mismatches. Levine (1998) identifies this paradox in which policy is seen as both the source of and the cure for jobs-housing imbalance, and he recommends less restrictive land controls as a way to increase households' residence and transportation choices.

The Spatial Mismatch Hypothesis and Social Equity

The spatial mismatch hypothesis (Kain 1968) in part attributes high unemployment rates among minorities to a deficiency in jobs-housing balance. The hypothesis suggests a correlation between the movement of jobs from the city to the suburbs and the lack of residential choice among low-income urban minorities. Lower-income city dwellers are effectively priced out of growing suburban employment opportunities because suburban housing is prohibitively expensive, automobile travel to the suburbs is also prohibitively expensive, and transit is often inadequate or inconvenient. More recent research by Ong and Blumenberg (1998) and Pugh (1998) has explored a similar situation among welfare recipients.

In addition to economic outcomes associated with jobs-housing balance, Cervero (1989) suggests that by spatially matching affordable housing and job sites, positive social outcomes may result in the form of reduced housing discrimination and greater economic participation by lower- and middle-income groups, a theory similar to the one advanced by Dittmar and Ohland (2004) regarding the expense of owning an automobile. The spatial mismatch hypothesis is a significant component of the debate within New Urbanism over its effect on transportation equity, housing equity, and, more broadly, social equity. In theory, TND provides for the availability of affordable housing near employment centers and prevents the concentration of poverty by providing such housing throughout a region (Talen 2002), but some research has suggested that in practice some TND may exclude or displace lower-income groups (Day 2003). Other studies have refuted this claim, maintaining that when implemented correctly, smart growth strategies such as TND and TOD increase housing affordability and overall affordability of living expenses (Litman 2007).

Concurrency

Transportation concurrency takes its name from the requirement that infrastructure be made available concurrent with the impact of development. Concurrency, sometimes implemented using adequate public facilities ordinances (APFO), requires that infrastructure be made concurrent with the impact of development. One major distinction can be made between the

Chapter 11: LAND USE AND TRANSPORTATION

use of concurrency by a single community as a part of a local growth control strategy and the requirement by the states of Florida and Washington that local governments develop a concurrency management system.

At its core, concurrency attempts to coordinate land development with investments in infrastructure including transportation. In contrast to other forms of land use transportation coordination, concurrency incorporates planning with ongoing monitoring as a part of implementation. At a most basic level, concurrency attempts to link development with the provision of infrastructure, as White and Paster (2003) describe in these seven major objectives of an APFO or concurrency system:

1. To link the provision of key public facilities and services with the type, amount, location, density, rate and timing of new development.
2. To properly manage new growth and development so that it does not outpace the ability of service providers to accommodate the development at the established LOS (level of service) standards.
3. To coordinate public facility and service capacity with the demands created by new development.
4. To discourage sprawl and leapfrog development patterns and to promote more infill development and redevelopment.
5. To encourage types of development patterns that use infrastructure more efficiently, such as New Urbanism or Transit-Oriented Development.
6. To require that the provision of public facilities and service to new development does not cause a reduction in the levels of service provided to the existing residents.
7. To provide an approach for providing necessary infrastructure for new residents.

The essence of these objectives is to provide a link between the various elements of the comprehensive plan – capital improvements, transportation and land use – and to have a financially feasible plan for implementation (Steiner 2001; Delaware Valley Regional Planning Commission 2002). The land use plan shows the location of future growth and the transportation plan specifies the necessary infrastructure to achieve the desired development pattern. Thus, the land use, transportation, and capital improvements elements are consistent with each other and the plans should be financially feasible. The third element of concurrency involves timing because concurrency requires that public facilities are available concurrent with the impact of development.

Statewide Approaches to Concurrency

To more fully understand how land use and transportation are coordinated under concurrency, it is useful to understand the context of the implementation of concurrency and APFOs in the states in which these policies have been enacted. Florida and Washington are the only two states that incorporate concurrency into their growth management framework for all counties that participate in statewide growth management programs. Until recent changes in its growth management legislation, Florida required concurrency of all local governments while Washington only requires concurrency in counties with high populations, or high rates of growth or counties that opt into the growth management program. Once a county opts into growth management in Washington, they are required to follow the state requirements for concurrency. Even though both states require concurrency, the context for implementation differs. Florida's Growth Management has been characterized as being top-down, while Washington's is characterized as being a fusion between state and local governments (Bollens 1992). The differences between the approaches taken by these states includes the use of exception areas, the establishment of level of service (LOS) standards and their measurement, the coordination of concurrency review with environmental review, the LOS standards on State Highways, and the use of urban growth boundaries and interregional cooperation.

The state of Florida has provided significant guidance to local governments on how to meet the requirements of concurrency. The legislation mandating concurrency was passed in 1985 and began to be implemented in the late 1980s. The transportation concurrency system has been evolving from a system that was based almost exclusively on the use of LOS standards based on a volume to capacity ratio to a multimodal planning system for communities that choose to have greater flexibility than a capacity-based system affords.

Beginning in 1992, the state incorporated area-wide and project-specific exceptions into the concurrency framework. Project-specific exceptions include: (1) urban redevelopment projects (FSA 163.3180 (8)); (2) *de minimis* projects (FSA 163.3180 (6)); (3) projects that promote public transportation (FSA 163.3180 (5) (b) and 9J-5.0057 (7)); (4) part-time projects (FSA 163.3180 (5) ©); and (5) projects for which private contributions are made (FSA 163.3180 (11) ©). Areawide exceptions include: (1) transportation concurrency management areas (TCMAs) (FSA 163.3180 (7)); (2) long-term concurrency management systems (LTCMS) (FSA 163.3180 (7)); (3) transportation concurrency exception areas (TCEAs) (FSA 163.3180 (5)); and (4) multimodal transportation districts (MMTDs) (FSA 163.3180 (15) (a)). The purpose of a TCMA is to "promote infill development or redevelopment within selected portions of urban areas in a manner that supports the provision of more efficient mobility alternatives, including public transit (FAC 9J-5.50055)." The TCMA may be established in "a compact geographic area with an existing network of roads where multiple, viable alternative travel paths or modes are available for common trips (FSA Sec. 163.3180 (7))." LTCMS are established in areas with existing deficiencies. To eliminate the backlog, a comprehensive plan is established that identifies the improvements to be made over a ten-year period or, in exceptional circumstances, over a fifteen-year period (FAC 9J-5.0055 (4)). The situations under which TCEAs are allowed have become more complex with recent legislation. Under SB 360 (2009) (The Community Renewal Act) communities that meet the following conditions are eligible to be designated as "dense urban land areas" (DULAs) and as such are exempt from transportation concurrency: a municipality that has an average of at least 1,000 people per square mile of land area and a minimum total population of at least 5,000; a county, including the municipalities located therein, which has an average of at least 1,000 people per square mile of land area; or, a county, including the municipalities located therein, which has a population of at least 1 million (FDCA 2010). Prior to the recent legislative changes, the purpose of a TCEA was to "reduce the adverse impact transportation concurrency may have on urban infill and redevelopment and the achievement of other goals and policies of the state comprehensive plan, such as promoting the development of public transportation (FAC 9J-5.0055 (7) and FSA Sec. 163.3180 (5) (b))." A TCEA could be established to meet one of four purposes: (1) promotion of urban infill development, (2) urban redevelopment, (3) promotion of downtown revitalization, or (4) urban infill and redevelopment. Guidelines published by the Florida

Chapter 11: LAND USE AND TRANSPORTATION

Department of Transportation (2003) recommend (however, the Florida Statutes do not require) that an MMTD have at least 5,000 in residential population, a minimum of population to jobs ratio of 2:1, an appropriate mix of land use (including residential, educational, recreational, and cultural uses), and an interconnected network of streets designed to encourage walking and bicycling. Furthermore, it should use traffic calming, appropriate densities and intensities of land uses within walking distance of transit stops, and a pattern of land uses that promotes transit, bicycle and pedestrian travel, including good intermodal connections. In MMTDs, the roadway LOS is relaxed and higher pedestrian, bicycle, and transit LOSs are required. In 2005, the state passed legislation that requires TCEAs to incorporate the characteristics of MMTDs into districts even as local governments are permitted to continue to allow development, even if they are not required to meet established roadway level of service standards.

In sharp contrast to Florida's complex set of transportation concurrency regulations, Washington is seen as providing significant flexibility in how to implement concurrency. The Growth Management Act in Washington directs local governments to establish LOS standards for their transportation systems and use them as a baseline for determining whether new development can be accommodated. The Act "only requires jurisdictions to adopt ordinances that establish a concurrency *measurement* system for transportation. As a result, the ability of the transportation system to support new development has become the primary test for whether development and infrastructure are 'concurrent'" (Hallenbeck *et al.* 2003: ix; emphasis in original). Local governments in the State of Washington have used a variety of approaches to measure concurrency including: (1) travel delay system, (2) average vehicle operating speed, (3) LOS at a screen line rather than intersection or a link LOS, (4) arterials that serve a new development are required to meet certain construction standards, (5) person throughput or person carrying capacity, and (6) certain transportation facilities (streets, intersections, or both) that are built out are not included in concurrency calculation (Trohimovich 2001).

A second difference between the two states lies in the development review process. Local governments in Washington are required to conduct a review of all development impacts, including the impacts on the transportation system, under the State Environmental Policy Act (SEPA). In Florida, local governments conduct such comprehensive reviews on a narrower set of projects. Large-scale development projects that are expected to have an impact on more than one county are required to complete a review for Developments of Regional Impact (DRI). The DRI review process takes place instead of, rather than in addition to, the concurrency review process (FDOT 1998).[2] Concurrency review is completed on projects that are larger than the *de minimis* standard and smaller in size than a DRI. Small projects are thus often exempted from transportation concurrency, yet research has shown that cumulatively these smaller projects may generate more new trips than DRIs or other planned unit developments. In her research on transportation concurrency mitigation in the Tallahassee area, Simmons (2008) argues that larger projects pay a disproportionate share of the cost of transportation facilities as a result of the *de minimis* concurrency exemption (Simmons 2008).

The third area of major difference between the states is that Florida has established a Strategic Intermodal System that includes all roadways on the Florida Intrastate Highway System (FIHS). Since the roadways on the FIHS are intended for travel between regions in Florida, the FDOT protects the LOS on these roadways. In Washington, the highways of statewide significance are specifically exempted from concurrency.

One other major area of difference is the approach taken to intergovernmental coordination and urban growth boundaries. Although both states' legislation includes the use of urban growth boundaries, Florida's laws are less strictly enforced and Florida lacks a solid framework for intergovernmental cooperation. In contrast Washington's laws include Regional Transportation Planning Organizations (RTPOs).

In examining the concept of regional versus local impacts of a given development project, Montgomery County, Maryland, serves as a unique case study. Montgomery County has had an adequate public facilities system since 1974 (Levinson 1997). The system was established with a requirement that all development proposals pass two tests of transportation facilities adequacy (Delaware Valley Regional Planning Commission (DVRPC) 2002). The first of these, the Policy Area Transportation Review, analyzed the effect of growth on overall road system of the twenty-two policy areas in the community. If the growth in population or jobs could be accommodated with existing roadway capacity, programmed roadway capacity or programmed bus, rail, or other forms of mass transportation, the development could be permitted. The second test is the Local Area Transportation Review, which measures levels of service at local intersections, and requires certain standards to be met before development is approved. The standards are lower in areas with better transit service and ensure that nearby intersections will not be overwhelmed. In 2005, the Policy Area Transportation Review was eliminated from the process. Much of the structure of the Policy Area Review was retained but the process was simplified (Montgomery County Planning Department 2008). The success of the Montgomery County APFO system can be measured by the length of time that it has been in place. Yet, the program is generally seen as not being transferable because it is too complex (DVRPC 2002). Additionally, concerns have been raised about whether traffic congestion is worse in the county because adjacent counties have not used such strict growth controls and they have allowed development that uses the roads in Montgomery County (Levinson 1997). In all, the program is noteworthy in that it recognizes the importance of assessing the regional impacts of development as opposed to only local impacts.

Assessment of Methods of Coordinating Land Use and Transportation

The results from the various methods of coordination of land use and transportation suggest a great deal of complexity related to their successful use in communities. In the following sections, a framework is developed for understanding the relationships between land use and transportation and implementing them in communities throughout the country. Within this framework, the critiques of the methods of coordinating land use and transportation are assessed.

The critique of the coordination of land use and transportation needs to be understood within the context of the broader debate over growth management, compact development and "smart growth." The debate over sprawl has generated a significant literature and the coordination of land use and transportation is one aspect of the overall discussion (see, for example, Cervero 2000). Similarly, it is one aspect of the goals of New Urbanism. New Urbanism incorporates cultural, social, political and economic aspects into its design philosophy. While transit-oriented development, jobs-housing balance and spatial mismatch largely focus on the relationship between residences and the activities of daily living, e.g. work and shopping, the success of any of these methods of land use-transportation coordination ultimately depends upon the behavior of

Chapter 11: **LAND USE AND TRANSPORTATION**

people in a specific community and political and economic decisions of a wide variety of actors in the development process. Thus, in order to ensure the success of approaches to land use transportation coordination, it is necessary to understand the broader context in which they are being implemented. Land use coordination should not be limited to TND, TOD, jobs-housing balance, location efficiency and concurrency. To be successful it needs to be reinforced by other policies promoting a healthy market for land-use decisions and that support the goals and vision of the community.

In order to understand the broader context of local coordination of land use and transportation and the associated travel behavior, it is useful to consider a conceptual diagram adapted from a study of the Transportation Research Board and the Institute of Medicine (2005) on the choice to engage in active modes of travel, bicycling and walking (see Figure 11.3). Within the context of understanding land use and transportation, the goal is to encourage the use of alternatives to single-occupant vehicles. How individuals travel in their community is constrained or facilitated by the built environment. The built environment is, in turn, determined by the social environment of the community, including the society values, the public policies and professional norms, and economic and market factors.

Figure 11.3 shows that individual travel behavior is influenced by the various characteristics of that individual including their households and lifestyle characteristics, preferences, culture, genetic factors, biological dimensions and time allocation. These factors interact with the built environment with an associated set of land use, transportation, and design elements. At the core of the strategies outlined in this chapter is an assumption that if we develop an urban form that coordinates land use and transportation better through high density, mixed-use, grid-street pattern and transit-oriented design, people who live in these places will travel differently. If this assumption is correct, congestion in the area will be minimized. However, if residents use automobiles at the same rate as residents of typical suburban neighborhoods, traffic congestion will be increased (Steiner 1994). Similarly, if a person is not able to drive due to physical, cognitive, age, income, or other limitations, they may be limited in how they can get around in their community. If

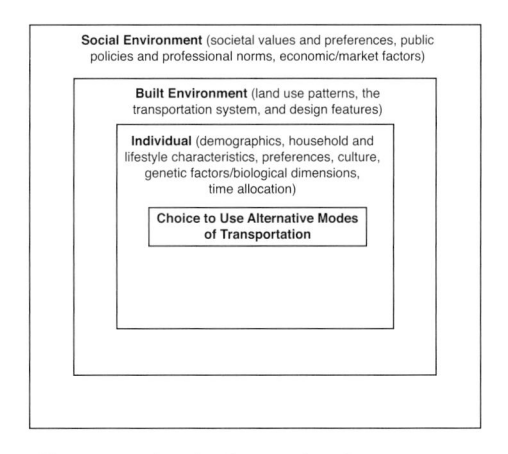

Figure 11.3 Variables Affecting Individual Travel Behavior.

Source: Adapted from TRB/IOM 2005: 22

their neighborhood does not offer a safe way to travel except by automobile, they will either depend upon others to drive them to their activities, or travel by transit, bicycle or walking and put their personal safety and security at risk or they will be prevented from participating in activities of daily living. Travel choice is also influenced by people's attitudes towards various modes of travel. Mohktarian and Schwanen (2005) used travel diaries to understand individual's travel behavior in San Francisco and measured their preferences for urban environments. They found that people with urban values drove less than people with suburban values irrespective of whether they lived in an urban or suburban environment. Similarly, Karash *et al.* (2008) found that attitude towards transit use strongly influenced both residential location and use of transit. They identified a market segment that was transit-oriented; transit-oriented individuals are less likely to own an automobile and more likely to live in compact neighborhoods and to walk more than others.

The social environment in which land use and transportation coordination takes place is even more complex. This complexity can be seen by examining the goals of various actors involved in local land use and transportation decisions. Land use and transportation decisions can involve multiple levels of government, including local, regional, state, and federal, that may have similar or conflicting goals. Within a community, property owners, developers, lenders, neighborhood residents and transit users also may have conflicting goals. The state government may have one set of goals for the movement of traffic through a community while the community may have a different goal. The regional agency may want local governments to provide transit-oriented development but the local government may respond to opposition from the neighborhood to any changes in the density and intensity of development around the transit station. A local government may want to increase the density in a neighborhood to support a higher level of transit service while the residents of the neighborhood may resist any change in density in the neighborhood.

Within each of these groups the goals may also conflict. A local government may want to change the land use in a neighborhood to higher density and mixed land use to support public investments in transit, but an adjacent city may oppose this project because they may bear the impact of greater traffic from non-residents who are riders of the transit system. The city may want transit-oriented development but the developer may not be able to get lenders to support the project or she may prefer to build a less complex project.

The social environment can be assessed from the perspective of the actions that are necessary to successfully implement coordinated land use and transportation solutions. Using the example of a region that plans to bring in a light-rail system it is easy to see the complexity of the social environment. The justification for receiving federal funding to match local funding for a light rail system would include a requirement that land use be coordinated with the transit investment. Even if the citizens of the community have a preference for light rail, they may not support the necessary land uses to support that investment. Beyond a preference for transit-oriented development, they will need to make a long-term commitment to the changes necessary to increase the density near transit stations. They will need to elect local officials who share their commitment to this goal. They will need to ensure that they have written inter-local agreements between the regional transit agency, the local government who will benefit directly from the investment in transit and adjacent jurisdictions, who will bear the costs of increased traffic near transit stations. They will need to have local comprehensive plans that implement the regional plan and local ordinances that are consistent with the comprehensive

Chapter 11: LAND USE AND TRANSPORTATION

Table 11.1 Actors in the Process of Coordinating Land Use and Transportation

Actor	Possible Goals
Local Government	– Maximize tax revenue – Support economic development – Please constituents – Redevelop underutilized land
Regional Government	– Efficient use of federal and state funding sources – Minimize conflicts between adjacent local governments
State Government	– Protect state resources – Minimize conflicts between adjacent local governments
Federal Government	– Protect "public interest" and set limits on how federally-funded investments can be used
Developer/Lender	– Maximize return on investment – Minimize risk, complexity – Ensure long-term value of investment
Transit Agency	– Maximize monetary return on land – Maximize ridership – Capture value of land in the long-term
Riders	– Create/maintain high level of parking – Improve transit service and station access – Increase mobility choices – Develop convenient mix of uses near station
Neighbors	– Maintain/increase property values – Minimize traffic impacts – Increase mobility choices – Improve access to transit, services, jobs – Enhance neighborhood livability – Foster redevelopment

Source: Adapted from Belzer and Aulter 2002: 20

plan. In summary, successful implementation requires a political environment that is supportive of the plan in the long-term and an ongoing commitment from elected officials, citizens and legal and judicial support for the overall plan.

Critique of Methods of Land Use and Transportation Coordination

The critiques of the various forms of land use and transportation coordination have been extensive and frequently related to issues other than the functionality of the various methods of coordination. In this section, the critiques limited to land use and transportation will be presented. Then they will be assessed within the framework concepts developed throughout this chapter. In organizing this critique, it is important to highlight the differences between these concepts. The scale of comparison is one such difference. Jobs-housing balance and spatial mismatch focus on the journey to work and travel by transit especially within the regional context. In contrast, traditional neighborhood development focuses on travel within a single neighborhood and travel by bicycling or walking. As such, jobs-housing balance and spatial mismatch focus on broader regional land use-transportation relationships, while traditional neighborhood development may focus on access to local services and, where transit is available, on access to other destinations within the region. Jobs-housing balance thus becomes a way of measuring spatial mismatch. These two concepts, jobs-housing balance and traditional neighborhood development, come together in the regional organization of transit-oriented development as advocated by New Urbanists at three scales: neighborhood, urban and regional. Where transit is available on a frequent basis and connected to a high-frequency transit, residents have access to services not only in their own neighborhood but also throughout the broader region.

Jobs-Housing Balance

Jobs-housing balance comes out of the tradition of matching homeplace to workplace. It is based on simple land economics, which suggests that if you increase the supply of housing near employment centers, people will move to be closer to where they work. The major policy rationale for jobs-housing balance is that it would reduce the distance people travel to work and reduce the need for long-distance commuting, particularly for low to moderate income households (Levine 1998). As such it would represent location efficiency and would reduce the overall cost of travel, especially to suburban employment locations. With the reduced travel, there should be a reduction in congestion near suburban office locations.

While simple in concept, jobs-housing balance has some inherent difficulties in the concept. By definition, regions have a balance between the number of jobs and the number of residents, but at smaller units of analysis – census blocks and neighborhoods – they are not balanced. Thus, it is difficult to determine the proper scale of analysis and the level at which a geographic area is out of balance (Guiliano 1991). The workforce participation and household size can vary across a region; thus, a simple concept becomes more complex and it becomes difficult to determine what the ratio represents. Jobs-housing balance attempts to characterize the level of spatial mismatch within a region but the lack of a consistent method of measuring it undermines its effectiveness as a measure.

Jobs-housing balance makes assumptions about the dynamics shaping residential choice. People are assumed to choose to live close to where they work (Giuliano 1991). Such an assumption overlooks the complexity of how people choose where they live and work. In the United States, households with a wide range of housing choices have tended to seek lower residential densities at increasing distances from work (Levine 1998). This overall trend may be changing for certain segments of the population, who are moving to more central locations to reduce their cost of travel. However, households with children may place greater importance on school quality and other activities for their children than proximity to work (see, for example, Wachs *et al.* 1993). Over the last few decades, two trends in employment undermine the concept of a closer geographic relationship between workplace and homeplace, two-worker households and higher rates of job turnover (Levine 1998). Finally, jobs-housing balance will require changes in land use regulations

Chapter 11: LAND USE AND TRANSPORTATION

in suburban communities, where residents and elected officials are often opposed to high-density residential development. Even if developers are willing to develop at a higher density, they are prevented from doing so by the local land use regulations.

New Urbanism, Traditional Neighborhood Development, and Transit Oriented Development

As policies to coordinate land use and transportation, New Urbanism, traditional neighborhood development and transit-oriented development share many of the same concerns when attempting to implement them. New Urbanism incorporates most of the concepts incorporated into traditional neighborhood development and transit-oriented development by considering the scale and context of projects within a broader regional context. The Transect (Duany 2002) shows the diversity of infrastructure and urban form that should be incorporated into different development contexts. TND focuses largely on the neighborhood in which activities are likely to take place. By definition, TOD takes place where transit is available. In contrast, New Urbanism and TND may incorporate walking and bicycling into its design even where transit is not available. At the heart of each of these solutions to coordinating land use and transportation is high density residential development located in close proximity to a mix of land uses and a connected network of transportation facilities. This critique focuses on a variety of concerns related to the relationships between the residents who live in these neighborhoods, their travel behavior once they live in the neighborhood, the types of land uses available to them and the difficulties associated with designing transit service. These solutions can be more or less effective depending upon the context in which they are implemented. TND and New Urbanism are designed for different contexts, while TOD requires reasonable transit service.

The question of who lives in New Urban (NU) developments has received a limited amount of attention. In part this is related to the context in which NU developments have been built. These projects are generally presumed to be built as new suburban development, but many are built on urban sites or previously developed suburban sites (Ellis 2002 citing *New Urban News*). The issue differs in these two contexts. In the suburban context, there is a question of whether the housing in NU communities is affordable even if it includes a variety of housing types. In infill projects, the question of how they relate to adjacent land uses is of great significance. Like most infill projects, projects that bring new transportation infrastructure into an already developed community will frequently face neighborhood opposition (Cervero and Landis 1997). Residents may fear increases in the density and mix of uses because they believe it will harm the character of the neighborhood or it will depress property values (Belzer and Aulter 2002). Redevelopment projects may also face resistance from developers who perceive of mixed-use and TOD projects as involving higher costs and being more difficult to finance and thus higher risk (Belzer and Aulter 2002).

Studies have shown that homebuyers are willing to pay a premium of as much as 25 percent to live in New Urban communities (Eppli and Tu 1999). Sander (2002: 229) explains that "this price premium may be a short-term trend, as interest in New Urbanism exceeds the available supply, or it may be longer-term market validation that potential residents believe a New Urbanist town is a more livable community." NU developments must continue to be studied over time in order to determine true consumer opinions and preferences regarding them.

The premium that homeowners pay in New Urban communities will have implications for housing affordability among residents of the neighborhood. For new development this may continue the pattern of the surrounding development. In the case of infill projects, this may lead to displacement of low-income residents who can take advantage of the availability of transit in more urban neighborhoods. From a transportation efficiency and equity perspective, low-income residents who can least afford higher costs for transportation may be pushed out to neighborhoods that have more affordable housing but less transportation choice and higher transportation costs.

While TODs and TNDs are developed in a manner to facilitate the use of modes of transportation other than the automobile, they may not achieve the change in travel behavior that is claimed. Crane and Boarnet (2001) suggest that improvements in access to goods and services may induce additional travel by automobile. Studies from the 1980s show higher use of transit and lower levels of driving alone to work in suburban activity centers with a mix of uses (Cervero 1991). Many studies have shown lower levels of driving in traditional neighborhood developments compared to conventional suburban developments (see Ewing and Cervero 2001 for a summary of these studies). But these studies are criticized for being only cross-sectional and for not taking into account the self-selection of residents into specific neighborhood types. More recent studies have attempted to control for the characteristics of the population and self-selection and overall they confirm the advantages of residents having diversity of choice in travel mode. The process of choosing where to live is a complex process in which people are balancing the characteristics of the neighborhood with the quality of the schools, the rate of crime and other social disorder, and characteristics of the housing unit itself. Thus, some people may choose to move to TODs or TNDs for reasons other than the transportation choice they afford.

In addition to the marketability of residences within a New Urban development, there is also the issue of retail marketing. Gyourko and Rybczynski (2000) discuss several problematic aspects of small-scale retail components within NU developments. For example, NU retail projects are associated with high perceived risk by financiers due to a lack of a population base at the completion of construction, and competition with suburban strip retail. Many industry practitioners from the development and finance fields interviewed by Gyourko and Rybczynski felt that in order to be successful, retail must serve a market area much broader than a NU development. If the retail attracts from a larger area than the surrounding neighborhood, the development will need to provide high levels of parking that may detract from the pedestrian and transit-friendliness of the development (Steiner 1994, 1998).

Concurrency

Transportation concurrency represents an attempt by state governments to coordinate infrastructure investments with new development. As such, it explicitly ties land use to transportation. However, it has been criticized in several ways. The initial set of concerns include questions about

> how to establish level of service standards on the state highway system, the standards used for roadway concurrency, the long lead time for transportation projects, the backlog of

Chapter 11: LAND USE AND TRANSPORTATION

transportation projects, the meaning of the requirement that facilities be 'available concurrent with development', how to measure concurrency, . . . concurrency was causing sprawl.

(Nicholas and Steiner 2000)

"Concurrency can't work because you can't build your way out of congestion (Downs 2003), and it does not work at a regional level" (Calthorpe and Fulton 2001).

Many of the problems with concurrency as a method of coordinating land use and transportation stem from the fact that the measures of concurrency have generally been based upon conventional measurements of roadway capacity rather than multimodal measures of transportation capacity (Hallenbeck *et al.* 2006; Steiner 2007). If the measure of concurrency is roadway capacity then a solution to a shortage of capacity is to expand highways. Thus, there is merit in the concern that concurrency may have contributed to sprawl since the least expensive place to build additional highway capacity is usually at the edge of the community. However, this criticism does not consider other factors affecting land markets in a region. Concurrency is only one of many interventions into the land market. If, for example, firm growth boundaries are incorporated into the local land use regulation, concurrency may be effective. If other measures of concurrency or multimodal transportation planning techniques are used, concurrency can be more effective at coordinating land use and transportation.

The lessons from the implementation of transportation concurrency in the states of Washington and Florida are numerous. At its core, concurrency attempts to address the relationships between the state government and the local government with respect to the coordination of land development with investments in transportation infrastructure. The role of the state is to establish a framework through which local governments can develop their community based upon a vision for what they would like their community to be. Thus, one of the major characteristics of a state's framework for concurrency is the flexibility for local governments to implement concurrency in a manner that is consistent with their community vision. Both states allow local governments flexibility in their implementation of concurrency. Florida accomplishes this with the transportation concurrency exception areas, transportation concurrency management areas, long-term concurrency management systems and the multimodal transportation districts. Washington provides flexibility by letting local governments establish their own measures of the level of service (Puget Sound Regional Council 2003). Even though the state laws and regulations allow the development of multimodal transportation systems, local governments ultimately have responsibility for determining how concurrency is implemented. Some local governments have used the multimodal transportation tools to create multimodal environments while others have not (see Florida Department of Community Affairs 2005).

Conclusion

Coordination of land use and transportation is an important aspect of building a livable community, but this coordination will remain an ongoing challenge for most communities. The transportation system provides access to the activities of daily activities. At the same time, it also provides for the movement of goods between communities throughout sub-state regions and states and multistate regions. The needs of the transportation system vary depending upon the scale of analysis and, at times, can be in conflict with each other. At the regional scale the rapid movement of goods can be more important than ensuring that individuals can safely walk across the street to go to the grocery store. A community without a well-coordinated land use-transportation system may provide an efficient means of moving traffic through the community without providing convenient access for residents to engage in the activities of daily living.

Each of the methods and measures of land use and transportation coordination – traditional neighborhood development, transit-oriented development, New Urbanism, jobs-housing balance, spatial mismatch, and concurrency management – contribute to our understanding of how to coordinate land use and transportation to build a livable community. Traditional neighborhood development emphasizes the importance of providing access to goods and service to residents of a neighborhood. The jobs-housing balance and spatial mismatch highlight the importance of providing affordable housing in close proximity to employment and the need to reduce the amount of travel at the sub-regional level for work. Transit-oriented development refers to the coordination of land uses around transit stations at both in the neighborhood and around employment and retail sites. Concurrency is a much broader concept through which coordinated land use and transportation can be planned and implemented by local governments.

At the core of each of these methods for coordinating land use and transportation is the need to ensure location efficiency and multimodal planning. Location efficiency ensures that people can get around a neighborhood or an activity center without needing to use an automobile. In order for communities to be livable, residents should have choice about their transportation mode, convenient access to the activities of daily living, and choice of the type of neighborhood in which they live.

Coordinated land use and transportation planning have an impact on community livability in a variety of ways. The components contributing to community livability – or the perceived environmental and social quality of an area (Victoria Transport Policy Institute 2008) – include a neighborhood's accessibility, environmental quality, and social variables, among others. Coordinated land use and transportation planning affect each of these livability factors. Studies have shown that the coordinated land use and transportation seen in traditional neighborhood development and transit-oriented development encourages increased physical activity and reduced BMI (Brown *et al.* 2008). Increased zero-emissions modes of travel, due to decreased vehicle miles traveled associated with location efficiency and multimodal planning, positively impacts the environment through decreased levels of pollution and energy consumption. Positive economic and social outcomes of coordinated land use and transportation planning can be seen in the provision of equal access to employment centers regardless of income status. In sum, if people live close enough to their job and other necessities to walk there, the community and individuals within it are sure to benefit in the form of positive health, environmental, economic, and social outcomes. Measurement and implementation difficulties associated with the coordination of land use and transportation planning continue to exist, but research shows that in many instances such coordination makes a difference regardless. Thus, land use and transportation coordination, with careful consideration of the context and scale of development, do make a difference in creating livable communities.

Chapter 11: **LAND USE AND TRANSPORTATION**

Notes

1. Body Mass Index (BMI), as defined by the Centers for Disease Control and Prevention, is a number calculated from a person's weight and height used to screen for weight categories – overweight, obese – that may lead to health problems.
2. Under the Community Renewal Act of 2009, DRIs are no long reviewed in dense urban land areas.

References

Belzer D. and Autler, G. (2002). Transit oriented development: moving from rhetoric to reality. Discussion paper prepared for the Brookings Institution Center on Urban and Metropolitan Policy and the Great American Station Foundation. Available: http://www.ocs.polito.it/biblioteca/mobilita/TOD.pdf.

Bernick, M. and Cervero, R. (1996). *Transit Villages in the 21st Century.* New York: McGraw-Hill.

Bollens, S. A. (1992). State growth management: Intergovernmental frameworks and policy objectives. *Journal of the American Planning Association*, 58(4), 454–466.

Brown, A. L., Khattak, A. J. and Rodriguez, D. A. (2008). Neighborhood types, travel and body mass: a study of new urbanist and suburban neighborhoods in the US. *Urban Studies*, 45(4), 963–988.

Calthorpe Associates with Mintier and Associates (1990). *Transit-Oriented Development Design Guidelines.* Sacramento County Planning and Community Development Department. Available: http://library.ceres.ca.gov/cgi-bin/doc_home?elib_id=2027.

Calthorpe, P. (1993). *The Next American Metropolis: Ecology, Community, and the American Dream.* New York: Princeton Architectural Press.

Calthorpe, P. and Fulton, W. (2001). *The Regional City: Planning for The End of Sprawl.* Washington, DC: Island Press.

Center for Neighborhood Technology (CNU). (2004). *Making the Case for Mixed-income and Mixed-use Communities.* Prepared by the Center for Neighborhood Technology for Atlanta Neighborhood Development Partnership, Inc. and the Mixed-Income Communities Initiative.

Cervero, R. (1989). Jobs-housing balance and regional mobility. *Journal of the American Planning Association*, 55(2), 136–150.

Cervero, R. (1991). Land uses and travel at suburban activity centers. *Transportation Quarterly*, 45(4), 479–491.

Cervero, R. (2000). Transport and Land Use: Key Issues in Metropolitan Planning and Smart Growth. Berkeley, CA: The University of California Transportation Center.

Cervero, R. and Landis, J. (1997). Twenty years of the Bay Area Rapid Transit system: land use and development impacts. *Transportation Research Record* A, 31(4), 309–333.

Congress for the New Urbanism. (2001). Charter of the new urbanism. Available: http://cnu.org/sites/files/charter_english.pdf.

Crane, R. and Boarnet, M. (2001). *Travel by Design: The Influence of Urban Form on Travel.* New York: Oxford University Press.

Day, K. (2003). New urbanism and the challenges of designing for diversity. *Journal of Planning Education and Research*, 23, 83–95.

Delaware Valley Regional Planning Commission [DVRPC]. (2002). *Managing Growth: Infrastructure Concurrency Implementation Barriers and Ways to Overcome Them*. Philadelphia, PA: DVRPC.

Dittmar, H. and Ohland, G. (eds.) (2004). *The New Transit Town*. Washington, DC: Island Press.

Downs, A. (2003). Why Florida's concurrency principles (for controlling new development by regulating road construction) do not – and cannot – work effectively. *Transportation Quarterly*, 57(1), 13–18.

Duany, A. (2002). The transect. *Journal of Urban Design*, 7(3), 251–261.

Ellis, C. (2002). The new urbanism: critiques and rebuttals. *Journal of Urban Design*, 7(3), 261–291.

Eppli, M. and Tu, C. (1999). *Valuing the New Urbanism*. Washington, DC: Urban Land Institute.

Ewing, R. and Cervero, R. (2001). Travel and the built environment: a synthesis. *Transportation Research Record*, 1780, 87–114.

Fan, Y., A. J. Khattak, and Rodríguez, D. A. (2007). Household excess travel and neighborhood characteristics: associations and trade-offs. *Transportation Research Part A: Policy and Practice*.

Florida Department of Community Affairs (FDCA). (2005). *A Guide for the Creation and Evaluation of Transportation Concurrency Exception Areas*. Tallahassee, FL: Florida Department of Community Affairs.

Florida Department of Community Affairs (FDCA). (2010). 2009 list of local governments qualifying as dense urban land areas. Available: http://www.dca.state.fl.us/fdcp/dcp/Legislation/2009/CountiesMunicipalities.cfm.

Florida Department of Transportation, Systems Planning Office (FDOT). (1998). *1998 Level of Service Handbook*. Tallahassee, FL: Florida Department of Transportation Systems Planning Office.

Florida Department of Transportation, Systems Planning Office (FDOT). (2003). *Multimodal Transportation Districts and Areawide Quality of Service Handbook*. Tallahassee, FL: Florida Department of Transportation Systems Planning Office.

Frank, L., Andresen, M., and Schmid, T. (2004). Obesity relationships with community design, physical activity, and time spent in cars. *American Journal of Preventive Medicine*, 27(2), 87–96.

Garreau, J. (1991). *Edge City: Life on The New Frontier*. New York: Anchor Books.

Giuliano, G. (1991). Is jobs-housing balance a transportation issue? *Transportation Research Record* 1305, 305–312.

Gyourko, J. E. and Rybczynski, W. (2000). Financing new urbanism projects: obstacles and solutions. *Housing Policy Debate*, 11(3), 733–750.

Hallenbeck, M. E., Carlson, D., and Simmons, J. (2003). The possibilities of transportation concurrency: Proposal and evaluation of measurement alternatives. Final report. Washington State Transportation Center, University of Washington, Seattle.

Hallenbeck, M. E., Carlson, D., Ganey, K., Moudon, A. V., de Montigny, L., and Steiner, R. L. (2006). Options for making concurrency more multimodal. Final Report. Washington State Transportation Center, University of Washington, Seattle.

Handy, S. L. (1992). Regional versus local accessibility: neotraditional development and its implications for non-work travel. *Built Environment*, 18(4), 253–267.

Hotzclaw, J., Clear, R., Dittmar, H., Goldstein, D., and Haas, P. (2002). Location efficiency: neighborhood and socioeconomic characteristics determine auto ownership and use – Studies in Chicago, Los Angeles, and San Francisco. *Transportation Planning and Technology*, 25(1), 1–27.

Chapter 11: LAND USE AND TRANSPORTATION

Ihlenfeldt, K. and Sjoquist, D. (1998) The spatial mismatch hypothesis: a review of recent studies and their implications for welfare reform, *Housing Policy Debate*, 9(4), pp. 849–892.

Kain, J. (1968). Housing segregation, negro employment, and metropolitan decentralization. *Quarterly Journal of Economics*, 82(2), 175–197.

Karash, K. H., Coogan, M. A., Adler, T., Cluett, C., Shaheen, S. A., Aizen, I., and Simon, M. (2008). Understanding how individuals make travel and location decisions: implications for public transportation. Transit Cooperative Research Program Report 123.

Kattak, A. J. and Rodgriguez, D. (2005). Travel behavior in neo-traditional neighborhood developments: a case study in the USA. *Transportation Research Part A: Policy and Practice* 39(6), 481–500.

Katz, P. (1994). *The New Urbanism: Toward an Architecture of Community.* New York: McGraw-Hill.

Krizek, K. J. (2005). User perspectives on location efficient mortgages and car sharing. Final Report: Minnesota Department of Transportation.

Levine, J. (1998). Rethinking accessibility and jobs-housing balance. *Journal of the American Planning Association*, 64(2), 133–149.

Levinson, D. (1997). The limits to growth management: development regulation in Montgomery County, Maryland. *Environment and Planning B: Planning and Design*, 24, 689–707.

Litman, T. (2002). The costs of automobile dependency and the benefits of balanced transportation. Victoria Transport Policy Institute. Available: http://www.vtpi.org/autodep.pdf.

Litman, T. (2007). Evaluating criticism of smart growth. Victoria Transport Policy Institute. Available: http://www.vtpi.org/sgcritics.pdf.

Montgomery County Planning Department. (2008). *History of Montgomery County's Growth Policy.* Silver Spring, MD: Montgomery County Planning Department. Available: http://www.mcparkandplanning.org/development/agp/documents/HistoryoftheGrowthPolicy.pdf.

Mokhtarian, P. L. and Schwanen, T. (2005). What affects commute mode choice: neighborhood physical structure or preferences toward neighborhoods? *Journal of Transport Geography*, 13, 83–99.

Newman, P. W. G. and Kenworthy, J. R. (1995). The land use-transport connection: an overview. *Land Use Policy*, 13(1), 1–22.

Nicholas, J. C. and Steiner, R. L. (2000). Smart growth and sustainable development in Florida. *Wake Forest Law Review*, 35(3), 645–670.

Ong, P. and Blumenberg, E. (1998). Job access, commute and travel burden among welfare recipients. *Urban Studies,* 35(1), 77.

Puget Sound Regional Council. (2003). *Assessing the Effectiveness of Concurrency: Final Report*. Seattle, WA: Puget Sound Regional Council.

Pugh, M. (1998). *Barriers to Work: The Spatial Divide between Jobs and Welfare Recipients in Metropolitan Areas*. Washington, DC: Brookings Institution.

Sander, T. H. (2002). Social capital and new urbanism: leading a civic horse to water? *National Civic Review*, 91(3), 213–234.

Schwanen, T. and Mohktarian, P.L. (2005). What affects commute mode choice:neighbourhood physical structure or preference towards neighbourhoods? *Journal of Transport Geography*, 13, 83–99.

Simmons, M. (2008). Healthy communities program report: an analysis and critique of Tallahassee transportation funding by residential project size. Florida State University Healthy Communities Program.

Southworth, M. (1997). Walkable suburbs? An evaluation of neotraditional communities at the urban edge. *Journal of the American Planning Association*, 63(1), 27–44.

Spielberg, F. (1989). The traditional neighborhood development: how will traffic engineers respond? *Institute of Transportation Engineers Journal*, 59(9), 17–18.

Steiner, R. L. (1994). Residential density and travel patterns: Review of the literature. *Transportation Research Record*, 1466, 37–43.

Steiner, R. L. (1998). Trip generation and parking requirements in traditional shopping districts. *Transportation Research Record*, 1617, 28–37.

Steiner, R. L. (2001). Florida's transportation concurrency: are the current tools adequate to meet the needs for coordinated land use and transportation? *University of Florida Journal of Law and Public Policy*, 12(2), 269–297.

Steiner, R. L. (2007). Transportation concurrency: an idea before its time? In Connerly, C., Chapin, T., and Higgins, H. (Eds.) *Growth Management in Florida: Planning for Paradise*. Aldershot: Ashgate Publishing, Chapter 13.

Steiner, R. L., Li, I., Shad, P., and Brown, M. (2003). Multimodal trade-off analysis in traffic impact studies. Final Report: Florida Department of Transportation, Office of Systems Planning.

Talen, E. (2002). The social goals of New Urbanism. *Housing Policy Debate*, 13(1), 165–188.

Transportation Research Board and Institute of Medicine. (2005). *Does the Built Environment Influence Physical Activity? Examining the Evidence.* Committee on Physical Activity, Health, Transportation, and Land Use, Transportation Research Board, Institute of Medicine of the National Academies.

Trohimovich, T. (2001). Current issues in growth management/land use and transportation: The "new cities" experience. 1000 Friends of Washington. Available: depts.washington.edu/trac/concurrency/pdf/trohimovich-b.pdf.

Victoria Transport Policy Institute. (2010). Online Transportation Demand Management Encyclopedia. Available: http://www.vtpi.org/tdm/tdm12.htm.

Vuchic, V. R. (1999). *Transportation for Livable Cities*. New Brunswick, NJ: Center for Urban Policy Research.

Wachs, M., Taylor, B. D., Levine, N., and Ong, P. (1993). The changing commute: a case-study of the jobs-housing relationship over time. *Urban Studies,* 30(10), 1711–29.

Weitz, J. (2003). Jobs-housing balance. *PAS Memo*, Report 516. Available: http://www.planning.org/affordablereader/pasreports/PAS516integrating.pdf.

White, S. M. and Paster, E. L. (2003). Creating effective land use regulations through concurrency. *Natural Resources Journal*, 43(3), 753–779.

Chapter 12

LIVABILITY, HEALTH, AND COMMUNITY DESIGN

Sarah Heaton Kennedy
Principal, Designing 4 Health LLC, Atlanta, Georgia
Former Public Health Analyst for the Healthy Community Design Initiative, Centers for Disease Control and Prevention (CDC)

Andrew L. Dannenberg
Affiliate Professor, Environmental and Occupational Health Sciences and Urban Design and Planning, University of Washington

A Historical Perspective on Land-Use and Development in the Modern Age

Over the last few generations, cities and towns in the United States have evolved in a historically unprecedented way, featuring geographic expansion over large areas, low-density development, separation of different land uses, low connectivity among places, and heavy reliance on the automobile for travel. This pattern has typically been referred to as urban sprawl.

A Twentieth Century American Dream

Following World War II, a new American Dream was being marketed. With a booming birthrate, home loan guarantee programs for veterans, the rise of the personal automobile, and the construction of the interstate highway system – the new American Dream looked a lot like what we now refer to as suburbia; a house, a yard, a car in the garage, and a white picket fence. And, for millions of people across the country, this dream became a reality.

New approaches to land use and transportation planning became the norm. Farmland and forest at the urban edge was converted to residential use. Standard housing densities began to decline from five to ten homes per acre to one or two households per acre. Local zoning laws began to separate land uses which had once been mixed into residential, commercial, educational and recreational lands.

Such features came to define twentieth-century community design. Zoning aimed at the separation of land uses, initially intended to protect people from harmful industrial exposures, now more commonly began to distance residential neighborhoods from sources of employment and common services as well as segregate populations by income. As investment and economic opportunity in the outlying areas skyrocketed, the central cities languished. Disinvestment in the urban core left those who could not afford to move to the new suburbs with decreasing opportunity for employment, substandard housing, and a deteriorating social structure leading to patterns of social inequity and injustice (Kennedy and Leonard 2001; ICCMA 2005). Auto-centric transportation systems and development (e.g. multilane freeways, drive through eateries, and ever expanding parking lots) became expected as pedestrian infrastructure such as sidewalks, parks, and plazas began to disappear in new roadway and development planning. With longer distances between destinations, decreased density, and urban flight, active transportation modes such as walking, bicycling, and mass transit became less practical. Transportation planners estimate a housing density of at least twelve dwelling units per acre is needed to support rapid rail service and seven units per acre to support local bus service every half hour (Booth *et al.* 2002) and the average person will only walk one-quarter to one-half mile, or bike up to a couple miles, to reach a destination. In the newly developing suburbs, housing was being built at densities much too low to support such services.

Looking at Community Design and our Health

In recent years, the consequences of such development patterns have become better understood. While some of the consequences are economic in nature, think "housing bubble," others are directly related to livability and, more specifically, our health. The effects on health operate through the physical activity people get, the injury risks they sustain, the air they breathe, the food they eat, the noise they hear, and even the ways they interact with each other. Those who design and build communities, urban planners, developers, transportation engineers, and others, are increasingly working with health professionals to achieve healthy, safe, livable communities.

When discussing livability, community design, and health, it is important to take into consideration the various people groups that make up our communities. Specifically, potential impacts to vulnerable populations ought to be considered first and foremost in community design decision making. These populations include individuals who are the youngest (children) as well as the older adults living in our communities; individuals with mobility, vision, hearing, or cognitive impairments; communities living at a lower socio-economic level (income, education); those with chronic health conditions; as well as communities or individuals isolated from the majority by race or ethnicity. Historically such communities have borne an unequal burden of negative environmental and/or health impacts associated with the built environment. With each redevelopment, new development, or other project, there is an opportunity to remedy injustice by increasing equity and well-being for such communities. When designing and planning built environments, our common spaces, or our community places, planners and developers will often find that the solutions to vulnerabilities for one group will act to benefit many groups, including the broadest of populations.

Physical Activity and Obesity

A growing evidence base tells us that community design practices of the last century have had major impacts on physical activity levels. Over 50 percent of American adults are physically

Chapter 12: LIVABILITY, HEALTH, COMMUNITY DESIGN

inactive on a regular basis, and over one quarter of Americans report no regular leisure-time physical activity (Macera *et al.* 2003). An inactive or sedentary lifestyle increases the risk of cardiovascular disease, stroke, and all-cause mortality, while physical activity prolongs life (Wannamethee *et al.* 1998; Wannamethee *et al.* 1998; Lee and Paffenbarger 2000). Physical activity also appears to protect against cancers of the breast, colon, and other organs (Kampert *et al.* 1996; Lee 2003; Bauman 2004).

Physical inactivity is also a factor for weight gain. Overweight (defined as a body mass index [BMI][1] between 25 and 30) and obesity (BMI of 30 or more) have become one of the most widespread and costly public health issues in the United States. In 1960, one in four Americans was overweight (Kuczmarski *et al.* 1994); by 2003–4, that proportion had increased to two in three (Ogden *et al.* 2006). Similarly, obesity prevalence has followed suit. By 2009, the US Centers for Disease Control and Prevention reported, thirty-three states had obesity prevalence equal to or over 25 percent and in nine states over 30 percent of the population was obese (CDC 2011) (Figure 12.1). Children as well as adults are suffering, and disproportionately affected are poor and minority communities. Overweight and obesity are risk factors for some of our nation's primary health threats including cardiovascular disease, diabetes, hypertension, and depression.

The societal and medical-related costs attributed to overweight and obesity-related disease and disability have been on the rise as Americans have become larger. An analysis of overweight and obesity-related medical costs found that 9.1 percent of health-care dollars in the US are spent on these largely preventable conditions (Finkelstein *et al.* 2003). Other unforeseen societal

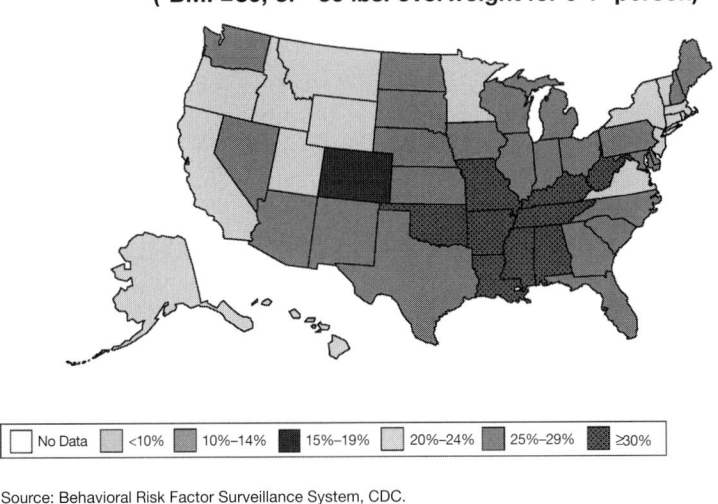

Figure 12.1 Obesity in adults in the US, 2009.

Source: Centers for Disease Control and Prevention, Behavioral Risk Factor Surveillance System, 2009

costs of rising obesity have ranged from increased fuel costs for airlines as the average weight of their passengers has increased (Dannenberg 2004) to a need for larger beds in hospitals (Rundle 2002), increased load capacity for consumer automobiles (Woodyard 2008) and even the necessity of newly engineered rides and seats at major theme parks to accommodate the larger park-goers (Pedicini and Clark 2010).

Community Design for Physical Activity

Physical activity levels in a community are affected by multiple factors including community design (Cervero and Kockelman 1997). The mix of land uses in an area is associated with physical activity (TRB 2005). When common destinations such as homes, schools, retail, and employment centers are closer together, this enables people living in the community to walk or bike from place to place instead of having to drive. When using an active form of transportation for your daily commute or regular errands becomes the norm, then sustaining health-promoting physical activity levels are easier to attain.

Other important features of community design, such as connectivity in the street network and the presence of safe pedestrian and bike facilities are also associated with increased physical activity through walking and bicycling (TRB 2005). Developments that provide a mix of destinations without convenient pedestrian connectivity will discourage active transportation and may be unsafe for pedestrians. Unlike the grid-like street network of many urban areas, most suburban neighborhoods feature low connectivity, with design features such as culs-de-sac and long block lengths. Retrofitting such areas to increase pedestrian connectivity and bicycling infrastructure is important to consider when seeking to enhance livability in such areas.

Between 1991 and 2010, the City of Portland, Oregon increased its established bikeways from seventy-nine to 325 miles, and otherwise improved bicycle-related infrastructure (Figure 12.2). The number of daily bicycle trips across Portland's four main bridges has steadily increased from 2,850 trips in 1991 to 17,576 trips in 2010, and the bicycle mode-share as a percent of all vehicles on those bridges has increased from 2 percent in 1991 to 14 percent in 2010. There has also been a 5 percent reduction in the number of automobiles traveling over these bridges during this time despite a 40 percent increase in the Portland metropolitan population since 1990 (Portland Bureau of Transportation 2010).

Other community design features such as shade, scenery, and safety are also associated with increased walking trips (TRB 2005). In addition, perceptions of neighborhood safety and crime affect decisions about outdoor activity, including walking (Frank and Engelke 2000).

Injury Risk and Community Design

Community design has considerable influence on injury risk, primarily on transportation-related injuries. Since the first recorded motor vehicle collision in 1896 in New York City (USDOT 2006), motor vehicle crashes and fatalities have increased, peaking in the 1970s and 1980s. They are a major contributor to the toll of unintentional injuries, which represent one of the top five causes of premature death in the United States (Foege 2006). Approaches to reducing fatal and nonfatal motor vehicle injuries have included interventions in vehicle design, driver behavior,

Chapter 12: LIVABILITY, HEALTH, COMMUNITY DESIGN

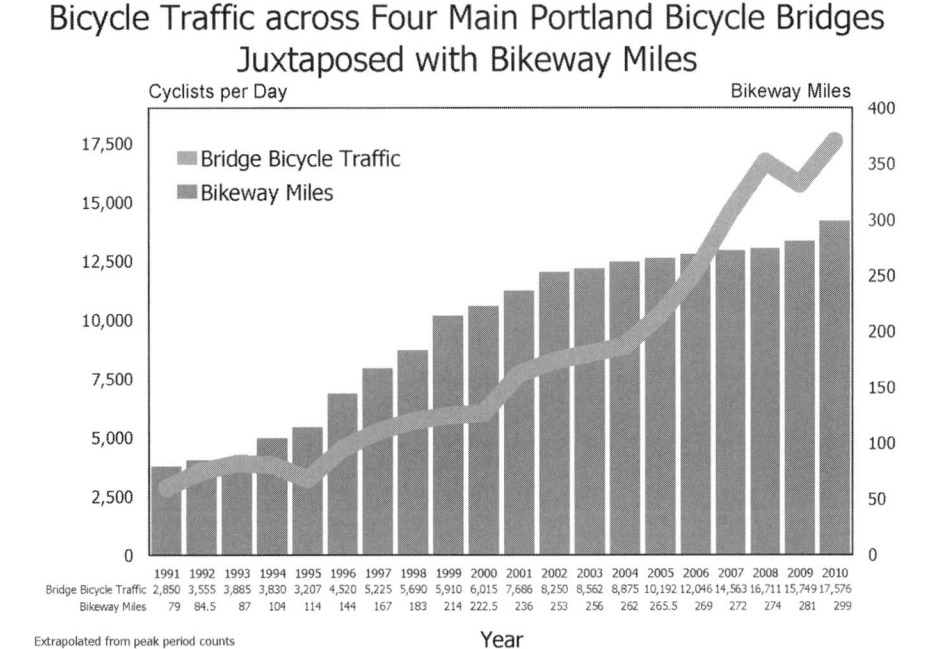

Bicycle Traffic across Four Main Portland Bicycle Bridges Juxtaposed with Bikeway Miles

Year	1991	1992	1993	1994	1995	1996	1997	1998	1999	2000	2001	2002	2003	2004	2005	2006	2007	2008	2009	2010
Bridge Bicycle Traffic	2,850	3,555	3,885	3,830	3,207	4,520	5,225	5,690	5,910	6,015	7,686	8,250	8,562	8,875	10,192	12,046	14,563	16,711	15,749	17,576
Bikeway Miles	79	84.5	87	104	114	144	167	183	214	222.5	236	253	256	262	265.5	269	272	274	281	299

Extrapolated from peak period counts

Figure 12.2 Bike traffic and bikeway miles in Portland, OR.
Source: Courtesy of the Portland Bureau of Transportation

and the environment. Such approaches have grown in effectiveness, helping to reduce motor vehicle fatality rates by 75 percent over the last forty years (USDOT 2008c). Further reducing fatality rates, including those to pedestrians, require these and other interventions.

Motor vehicle collisions: The form of the built environment plays a considerable role in the number and severity of motor vehicle collisions. The sprawling communities that characterize American cities encourage automobile use and higher speed roadways. Approaches to prevention include a focus on the design of roadways. Interstate highways incorporate design features such as limited access interchanges and center medians that give them a relatively low rate of fatalities per vehicle miles traveled (VMT). Local roadway design uses traffic-calming techniques such as roundabouts, one-way streets, and speed bumps to alter driver behavior and reduce crash likelihood and severity. On average these measures reduce traffic crashes by 15 percent and related injuries by 11 percent (Elvik 2001; Bunn *et al.* 2003). Modern roundabouts reduce injury crashes at intersections by 76 percent and fatal or incapacitating crashes by 90 percent (Retting *et al.* 2001).

Pedestrian and bicyclist injuries: More than 10 percent of those killed in motor vehicle crashes are pedestrians (USDOT 2008c), and bicyclists account for roughly 2 percent of fatal and nonfatal motor vehicle crash injuries (USDOT 2008b). Community design can influence both how much people walk and their risk of pedestrian injury. Pedestrian-friendly street designs that include crosswalks and sidewalks reduce injury risk. Evidence from the Federal Highway Agency states that the presence of a sidewalk or pathway on both sides of the street corresponds to approximately an 88 percent reduction in collisions associated with pedestrians walking along a road (FHWA 2010). Risk factors for bicyclist fatalities are also well characterized; they are more likely in non-intersection locations, in urban areas, and between the hours of 6:00 and 9:00 PM (USDOT 2008b). Research shows that increasing the number of pedestrians and bicyclists can contribute to safety, possibly because drivers become more aware of and more careful around pedestrians and bicyclists as their numbers increase. Doubling the number of pedestrians and bicyclists appears to reduce an individual's risk of being struck by approximately 66 percent (Jacobsen 2003). Such evidence can influence community design policies and standards that not only increase livability but improve community health outcomes. The concept of *Complete Streets* and similar policies address this issue with a focus on multimodal accessibility and safety for all users, including pedestrians and bicyclists (McCann 2005). According to the National Complete Streets Coalition (2011) such policies encourage transportation agencies and communities to change their approach to transportation by "directing their transportation planners and engineers to routinely design and operate the entire right of way to enable safe access for all users, regardless of age, ability, or mode of transportation."

Air Quality

Human exposures to air pollution can increase the risk of premature death, asthma, cardiovascular disease, cancer, and other conditions. The risk varies with duration of exposure and proximity to pollution sources. Modern patterns of urbanization and transportation, features of community design, have emerged as primary determinants of local, regional and global air pollution. In cities, the evolution of larger roads and escalating levels of traffic explains why the roadways themselves seem to represent the "source" of air pollutants. Pollution from cars and trucks is most marked near transportation corridors with high traffic density, leading to *hot spots*, or small areas with particularly high air pollution levels. Accordingly, people at higher risk include those living, working, or attending school within 150 meters of a busy road (Venn *et al.* 2001; Schikowski *et al.* 2005; Kim *et al.* 2008). The association between traffic-related air pollution and childhood asthma is particularly well-documented and may account for some of the dramatic increase in asthma over the last two decades (Brauer *et al.* 2002; McConnell *et al.* 2006; Delfino *et al.* 2008). Transportation-related air toxics and diesel particulates appear to contribute to the development of lung cancer among people who live near roadways, increasing their risk up to 40 percent (Nyberg *et al.* 2000; Vineis *et al.* 2006). Exposure to traffic-related air pollutants is also associated with premature mortality, particularly from cardiovascular causes (Hoek *et al.* 2002; Finkelstein *et al.* 2004; Maynard *et al.* 2007). Many of these hot spots are in low-income neighborhoods that face other environmental and social threats to health.

In the 1950s, the State of California first officially recognized this issue of transportation-related air pollution and instigated motor vehicle emissions regulations. Other states followed suit. Since then, technological advances have reduced vehicle pollutant emissions by over 90 percent per mile driven, although increasing vehicle miles traveled (VMT) have partially offset these gains (USDOT 2002). Reducing VMT in single-occupancy vehicles is a primary way to reduce air pollution and the resulting health consequences in both the local and global environments. This underscores the need for alternative modes of dependable and safe transportation as a goal for livability, community design, and transportation planning.

Chapter 12: LIVABILITY, HEALTH, COMMUNITY DESIGN

Parks and Greenspace

Parks, public lands, greenspace, and other open spaces often provide places for respite, to get away from the noise of our daily lives, to be physically active, to play, and to enjoy contact with nature and with other people (Cohen *et al.* 2007). Parks and greenspace add value to a city or neighborhood in various ways, through increased property values and general quality of life and also through improved community health. Think of how different New York City might be without Central Park, San Francisco without Golden Gate Park, Atlanta without Piedmont Park or Chicago without Grant Park; it's hard to imagine. You might be from a city that has been designed with a great park as one of its central features, or perhaps your city or town has added smaller parks through urban redevelopment efforts; these parks are built to make a city more livable for those residing and visiting there, and such features impact our health and well-being.

In a 2006 report, *The Health Benefits of Parks*, published by the Trust for Public Land (TPL), Erica Gies provides a clear picture of the primary ways in which parks and greenspace can benefit the health of communities. With the overwhelming costs of physical inactivity and obesity-related disease in the United States, parks can offer a safe place for hiking, biking, walking, or playing. Aside from this, parks and greenspace can also function to mitigate air pollution and reduce urban heat, which can improve health conditions, such as asthma or heat stroke, which are associated with such factors. The psychological and social health impacts of parks and greenways are also considered in the TPL report. Access and exposure to nature and natural settings has been shown to improve psychological health, attention deficit disorder, coping mechanisms, social contact, and even cognitive development in children (Gies 2006).

Unfortunately for many people, parks and greenspace are not always accessible. Most notably are the lack of parks in poor communities and communities of color (Gies 2006). A commonly used benchmark for city planners recommends 10 acres of parkland per 1000 population (Cohen *et al.* 2007). People use parks more when they are conveniently located, especially when they are within safe walking distance of their homes, usually within one-quarter to one-half mile. Other features such as recreational facilities (play structures, walking trails), lighting, public toilets and water fountains, and park maintenance also affect park use (Gies 2006).

Programs and efforts such as *Rails-to-Trails (R2T)* and brownfield restoration can increase access to parks and greenspace. Rails-to-Trails projects give new life to former railroad lines by repurposing them as trail corridors and multi-use pathways through urban, suburban and rural areas (Rails-to-Trails Conservancy 2011). Many examples of R2T projects can be found on the Rails-to-Trails Conservancy website. According to the US Environmental Protection Agency (2011), "brownfields are real property . . . complicated by the presence or potential presence of a hazardous substance, pollutant, or contaminant. Cleaning up and reinvesting in these properties protects the environment, reduces blight, and takes development pressures off greenspaces and working lands." One impressive example of brownfields redevelopment is Fresh Kills Park in New York City. This brownfield restoration project is the outcome of a community effort to transform what was formerly the world's largest landfill into New York City's largest park. Fresh Kills Park, once fully redeveloped, will provide over 2,000 acres of greenspace and recreational areas to the residents and visitors of New York City (New York City Department of City Planning 2011).

Healthy Food Environments

In an age of auto-centric development and drive-thru culture, we have also witnessed a changing "foodscape" across the US. The retail food environment, both at the community level (e.g. presence and location of food stores or other retail outlets) and the consumer level (e.g. healthful, affordable foods at these locations) affect American dietary choices (Glanz *et al.* 2005). In the modern age, dietary patterns among Americans have moved away from whole foods and home cooking and increasingly toward processed, pre-packaged, and purchased meals. Such patterns impact multiple health outcomes in communities, including those related to overweight and obesity, as well as cardiovascular disease and some types of cancer (IOM and NRC 2009). Zoning, transportation decisions, community development initiatives, public infrastructure development, and other land-use decisions and policies may encourage or discourage development of a healthy food environment and therefore affect health outcomes in affected communities.

Healthy eating is a central strategy in improving community health by reducing obesity and chronic diseases. However, changes in diet require access to healthy foods in addition to education and motivation. Low-income and predominately minority communities often have limited access to grocery and retail stores that sell high quality fruits and vegetables (Horowitz 2004; Zenk *et al.* 2006; Powell *et al.* 2007) and have a disproportionate number of unhealthful fast-food outlets (Block *et al.* 2004).

Examples of strategies to improve the food environment include providing incentives for grocery store and supermarket development, restricting fast food retail store density (Mair *et al.* 2005), and encouraging community supported agriculture programs, farmers markets, street carts with fruit and vegetables, and community gardens (Figure 12.3). Land-use policy and environmental changes are emerging as important and potentially modifiable targets for interventions to improve the food environment and community livability (Story *et al.* 2008).

Noise

Unwanted noise from neighbors, industrial and commercial activities, vehicles, and aircraft have long been associated with urban living. While much of the noise we hear does not negatively affect our health, some noise exposure (and/or duration of noise exposure) contributes to hearing loss, increased blood pressure, heart disease, changes in hormonal levels, and circulatory problems (Passchier-Vermeer and Passchier 2000). Although few communities face dangerous levels of exposure, some residents and workers in close proximity to urban traffic experience varying degrees of noise-related health impacts (Leong and Laortanakul 2003; Barbosa and Cardoso 2005).

Evidence supports a relationship between transportation-related noise exposure and cardiovascular health effects, from hypertension to myocardial infarction (Spreng 2000). Noise exposure has also been associated with adverse psychological, performance, and sleep impacts (Stansfeld and Matheson 2003; Jakovljević *et al.* 2006). And aircraft noise near schools has led to poorer reading comprehension, decreased recognition memory, and heightened annoyance in school children (Matheson *et al.* 2003; Stansfeld *et al.* 2005).

There are several ways to reduce community exposure to transportation noise: reduce the amount of noise produced per vehicle, reduce the number and/or speed of vehicles driving past communities, construct sound barriers around large highways and other major noise sources,

Chapter 12: **LIVABILITY, HEALTH, COMMUNITY DESIGN**

Figure 12.3 Access to healthy eating. Farmers' markets, such as this one in Coppell, Texas, contribute to healthy nutrition and social capital.

Courtesy of Coppell Farmers Market, Coppell, Texas

and route new or expanded highways through less densely populated areas (FHA 2006). Aircraft noise in surrounding communities can similarly be reduced by changes in runway use or flight path location, compatible land use zoning, and sound insulation of buildings (FAA 1999).

Social Capital and Mental Health

The social networks and resources within a community as well as the norms of reciprocity and social benefit that arise from them are often referred to as social capital. Such resources and networks can include the level of community involvement in local organizations, community centers, churches, and locally-focused philanthropic organizations, as well as support systems to insure disadvantaged community members have access to food, shelter, and health care (Minkler and Wallerstein 2005; Campbell 2006). Social capital is associated with a wide range of health benefits including improved mental health (Kweon *et al.* 1998). Indicators of low social capital such as social isolation and income inequality are associated with higher mortality (House *et al.* 1988; Kawachi *et al.* 1997; Kawachi 1999; Lynch *et al.* 2000).

Many features of the built environment facilitate different opportunities for social interactions and thereby act to protect or improve mental health and overall well-being (Cannuscio *et al.* 2003). Informal interactions such as bumping into your neighbor while out jogging, conversations while at the playground with your children, or seeing your friend while walking the dog are made more likely by components and features in the built environment including the layout of streets, the presence of greenspace or parks, even the width of sidewalks or the placement of water fountains (Jacobs 1961; Wood *et al.* 2005). Formal interactions such as a community barbecue, adult soccer league, or a children's summer camp can happen only when places for them to occur are incorporated into community design. Such places in a community are also features that can promote mental well-being for those living nearby. Access to nature, greenspace, and safe places for physical activity, or simply having well-maintained sidewalks, all support positive psychological health (Evans *et al.* 2001; Kaplan 2001; Galea *et al.* 2005; Berke *et al.* 2007).

Housing type and mix also affects social capital, mental health, and general well-being. Many neighborhoods have been built in which the homes are simply a randomized placement of homes with slightly different floor plans, square footage, and lot size. While there is variation, the differences may be more related to aesthetics than anything else. Such neighborhoods are often appropriate for specific populations, but not others (e.g. suitable for growing families but not for "empty nesters" or for elders who can no longer drive). Without real variation in housing mix within the same community, people often must move away from their neighborhood when life-circumstances change, depriving them of the opportunity for "aging in place" and disrupting community networks formed over many years (Fried *et al.* 1997; Alley *et al.* 2007). Mental health and well-being are significantly higher in aging populations when such social ties are maintained (Kweon *et al.* 1998).

Community design that is aimed at supporting social capital and overall livability includes the presence of "great good places" – the "cafés, coffee shops, bookstores, bars, hair salons, and other hangouts at the heart of a community" where people may gather to socialize (Oldenburg 1989). Communities with an ample stock of such places may provide more opportunities for social interchange and improved psychological well-being.

Livability: Current Conversations and Approaches to Community Design

In 1926, the US Supreme Court validated local governments' authority to regulate land use through zoning in a decision on the case *Village of Euclid v. Ambler Realty*. As part of its justification, the Court cited the protection of public health. Over time the professional fields of planning and public health seemed to drift apart. But, in recent years, urban planners, transportation engineers, and related professionals have rediscovered their professional links to public health, and likewise, public health professionals have rediscovered the importance of community design in promoting health (Hoehner *et al.* 2003; Corburn 2004; Kochtitzky *et al.* 2006; Malizia 2006). From these efforts have arisen many insights into the unintended health consequences of contemporary land use and transportation, and many strategies for promoting livability and health through community design.

Many of these strategies are found in an approach known as *Smart Growth*. Features of Smart Growth often include mixed land uses; diverse housing types; multi-modal transportation choices; activity centers such as traditional downtown squares or plazas; *universal design*; and an emphasis on parks, greenspace, and public spaces (Center for Universal Design 1997; Geller 2003). Smart Growth principles are implemented through a combination of market forces, social marketing, and deliberate policy-making, often with the active participation of public health professionals (Perdue, Stone and Gostin 2003; Bragg *et al.* 2003; De Ville and Sparrow 2008).

Chapter 12: LIVABILITY, HEALTH, COMMUNITY DESIGN

Other terms and professional movements overlap with Smart Growth. *New Urbanism* is an architectural and planning movement whose principles similarly include walkable neighborhoods, a range of housing choices, mixed land uses, participatory planning, and revitalization of urban neighborhoods (http://www.cnu.org). *Brownfield redevelopment* often incorporates mixed-use walkable community design while focusing on cleaning up and re-using contaminated urban areas that had been allowed to fall into decay (http://www.epa.gov/brownfields). *Traditional Neighborhood Development* (TND) is focused on compact, mixed-use, transit-oriented, pedestrian-friendly communities that were common before World War II. *Transit-Oriented Development* (TOD) follows similar principles while highlighting easy access to public transit.

Emerging tools and resources for livability: a number of tools and resources are available to facilitate community design that incorporates Smart Growth and other Smart Growth-like principles. Two examples are LEED for Neighborhood Development (LEED-ND) and Health impact assessment (HIA). Created by the US Green Building Council, LEED-ND is a set of prerequisites and credits based on energy efficiency, sustainability, and health promotion characteristics. HIA is a framework that can be used by public health professionals and others to examine prospectively the health impacts of a proposed project or policy and recommend ways to promote the positive health impacts and mitigate the adverse health consequences of the proposal.

Professional development resources are also emerging both in the academic realm and in planning and public health agencies and organizations around the country. According to University of Virginia planning Professor Nisha Botchwey's *Built Environment and Health Curriculum* website (www.bephc.com), over fifty universities are now offering access to faculty expertise, courses, certificates and/or joint degrees in planning and public health. Botchwey has also developed a model curriculum for graduate level courses on the topic (Botchwey 2009).

BOX 12.1 Principles of Smart Growth

- *Mixed Land Uses*: Smart growth supports the integration of mixed land uses into communities as a critical component of achieving better places to live.
- *Create Walkable Neighborhoods*: Walkable communities are desirable places to live, work, learn, worship and play, and therefore a key component of smart growth.
- *Provide a Variety of Transportation Choices*: Providing people with more choices in housing, shopping, communities, and transportation is a key aim of smart growth.
- *Preserve Open Space, Farmland, Natural Beauty, and Critical Environmental Areas*: Open space preservation supports smart growth goals by bolstering local economies, preserving critical environmental areas, improving our communities' quality of life, and guiding new growth into existing communities.
- *Create a Range of Housing Opportunities and Choices*: Providing quality housing for people of all income levels is an integral component in any smart growth strategy.
- *Foster Distinctive, Attractive Communities with a Strong Sense of Place*: Smart growth encourages communities to craft a vision and set standards for development and

construction which respond to community values of architectural beauty and distinctiveness, as well as expanded choices in housing and transportation.
- *Encourage Community and Stakeholder Collaboration*: Growth can create great places to live, work and play – if it responds to a community's own sense of how and where it wants to grow.
- *Strengthen and Direct Development Towards Existing Communities*: Smart growth directs development towards existing communities already served by infrastructure, seeking to utilize the resources that existing neighborhoods offer, and conserve open space and irreplaceable natural resources on the urban fringe.
- *Take Advantage of Compact Building Design*: Smart growth provides a means for communities to incorporate more compact building design as an alternative to conventional, land consumptive development.
- *Make Development Decisions Predictable, Fair, and Cost Effective*: For a community to be successful in implementing smart growth, it must be embraced by the private sector.

Source: Smart Growth Network. Principles of Smart Growth. Available at: http://www.smartgrowth.org/about/principles/default.asp

---

BOX 12.2 Principles of Universal Design

The Principles of Universal Design promote the concept that the design of products and environments should be usable by all people, to the greatest extent possible, without the need for adaptation or specialized design.

1. *Equitable Use*: The design is useful and marketable to people with diverse abilities.
2. *Flexibility in Use*: The design accommodates a wide range of individual preferences and abilities.
3. *Simple and Intuitive Use*: Use of the design is easy to understand, regardless of the user's experience, knowledge, language skills, or current concentration level.
4. *Perceptible Information*: The design communicates necessary information effectively to the user, regardless of ambient conditions or the user's sensory abilities.
5. *Tolerance for Error*: The design minimizes hazards and the adverse consequences of accidental or unintended actions.
6. *Low Physical Effort*: The design can be used efficiently and comfortably and with a minimum of fatigue.
7. *Size and Space for Approach and Use*: Appropriate size and space are provided for approach, reach, manipulation, and use regardless of user's body size, posture, or mobility.

Source: The Center for Universal Design (1997). The Principles of Universal Design, Version 2.0. Raleigh, NC: North Carolina State University. Available at: http://design.ncsu.edu/cud/about_ud/udprinciplestext.htm

Chapter 12: **LIVABILITY, HEALTH, COMMUNITY DESIGN**

BOX 12.3 LEED for Neighborhood Development (LEED-ND)

LEED (Leadership in Energy and Environmental Design) is a third-party certification program managed by the US Green Building Council (USGBC). Under the LEED system, building designers, builders, owners, and operators can benchmark their performance through a series of measurable indicators in five areas: sustainable site development, water savings, energy efficiency, materials selection, and indoor environmental quality. In 2008, the USGBC introduced LEED for Neighborhood Development (LEED-ND), in collaboration with the Congress for the New Urbanism and the Natural Resources Defense Council. The current version of LEED-ND includes 12 prerequisites. Examples include:

A   Smart location: Encourages development within and near existing communities or public transportation infrastructure. Reduces vehicle trips and miles traveled and supports walking as a transportation choice.

B   Compact development: Conserves land, promotes livability, walkability and transportation efficiency including reduced vehicle miles traveled.

C   Minimum building energy efficiency: Encourages the design and construction of energy efficient buildings to reduce air, water, and land pollution and environmental impacts from energy production and consumption.

The current version of LEED-ND offers over 40 credits, some of which offer multiple points; the number of credit points determines the level of LEED-ND certification achieved (Silver, Gold, or Platinum). Examples of credits include:

A   Neighborhood schools: Promotes community interaction and engagement and reduced risk of chronic diseases by encouraging daily physical activity associated with alternative modes of transportation, such as walking or biking.

B   Bicycle network: Encourages use of bicycles for transportation and decreased automobile dependency, thereby encouraging regular physical activity and reduced risk of chronic diseases.

C   Mixed-income diverse communities: Promotes socially equitable and socially engaging communities by enabling citizens from a wide range of economic levels, household sizes, and age groups to live within a community.

D   Access to public spaces: Provides a variety of open spaces close to home and work to encourage walking and other physical activities and time spent outdoors.

Source: US Green Building Council. LEED for Neighborhood Development. Available at: http://www.usgbc.org/DisplayPage.aspx?CMSPageID=148

BOX 12.4 Health Impact Assessment: A Tool for Land Use and Transportation Decision-making

Health impact assessment (HIA) is a tool that focuses on the health consequences of decisions in non-health sectors, including community design (CDC Healthy Places website n.d.). HIA can be used to evaluate the potential health effects of a project or policy *before* it is built or implemented. It can provide recommendations to increase positive and minimize adverse health outcomes. A major benefit of the HIA process is that it brings public health issues to the attention of people who make decisions outside traditional public health arenas, such as transportation or land use. An HIA is defined as "a combination of procedures, methods, and tools by which a policy, program, or project may be judged as to its potential effects on the health of a population and the distribution of those effects within the population" (European Centre for Health Policy 1999). For example, if planners are considering whether to invest in a highway widening project, bicycle trail network, or a trolley system, the health department might carry out an HIA to clarify the health consequences of each option.

The major steps in conducting an HIA include:

- *Screening*: Identify projects or policies for which an HIA would be useful.
- *Scoping*: Identify which health effects to consider.
- *Assessing risks and benefits*: Identify which people may be affected and how they may be affected.
- *Developing recommendations*: Suggest changes to proposal to promote positive or mitigate adverse health effects.
- *Reporting*: Present the results to decision-makers.
- *Evaluating and monitoring*: Determine the effect of the HIA on the decision process.

HIAs are similar in some ways to environmental impact assessments (EIAs), which are mandated analyses of environmental outcomes such as air and water quality. EIAs can incorporate health impacts under existing laws but seldom do (Bhatia 2008). Unlike EIAs, HIAs can be voluntary or regulatory processes that focus on health outcomes such as obesity, physical inactivity, asthma, injuries, and social equity. An HIA encompasses a wide array of qualitative and quantitative methods and tools. HIAs can be completed in a few days or may take many months, depending on availability of time and resources.

Numerous HIAs have been performed in Europe, Canada, and elsewhere. Some countries have mandated HIA as part of a regulatory process; others use it on a voluntary basis. In the United States, interest in the topic is growing. US HIA work is currently being supported and utilized in various states and communities as well as by the Robert Wood Johnson Foundation and Pew Charitable Trusts' Health Impact Project, the University of California, Los Angeles, San Francisco Department of Public Health, and the US Centers for Disease Control and Prevention's National Center for Environmental Health.

(Dannenberg 2008; HIP 2011)

Chapter 12: LIVABILITY, HEALTH, COMMUNITY DESIGN

Likewise, professional organizations, such as the American Planning Association, are offering training opportunities for Health Impact Assessment as well as professional interest groups specifically geared toward health and built environment topics (APA 2010).

These and other resources are shown in the "For Further Information" section at the end of this chapter.

This chapter adapted in part from:

Heaton, S. *et al.* (2010) Healthy Communities. In Frumkin, H. (ed) *Environmental Health: From Global to Local.* John Wiley and Sons, San Francisco CA.

Note

1   Body mass index is calculated as weight in kilograms divided by height in meters squared.

References

Aboelata M. The built environment and health: 11 profiles of neighborhood transformation. Community coalition: closure of South Los Angeles liquor stores. Oakland CA: Prevention Institute. 2004. Available at: http://www.preventioninstitute.org/pdf/BE_South_Los_Angeles_CA.pdf.

Alley D, Liebig P, Pynoos J, Banerjee T, and Choi IH. Creating elder-friendly communities: preparations for an aging society. *Journal of Gerontological Social Work*. 2007; 49: 1–18.

American Planning Association (APA). Smart Growth Codes. 2006. Available at: http://www.planning.org/research/smartgrowth/

American Planning Association (APA). Planning and Community Health Research Center, 2010. Accessed May 3, 2011. Available at: http://www.planning.org/nationalcenters/health/index.htm

Aviation and the Environment: Impact of Aviation Noise on Communities Presents Challenges for Airport Operations and Future Growth of the National Airspace System: Testimony Before the Subcommittee on Aviation, Committee on Transportation and Infrastructure, House of Representatives. 110th Cong. (2007) (testimony of Gerald L. Dillingham). Available at: http://www.gao.gov/new.items/d08216t.pdf.

Babisch W. Road traffic noise and cardiovascular risk. *Noise and Health*. 2008 Jan–Mar; 10(38): 27–33.

Babisch W. Transportation noise and cardiovascular risk: updated review and synthesis of epidemiological studies indicate that the evidence has increased. *Noise and Health*. 2006 Jan–Mar; 8(30): 1–29.

Barbosa ASM and Cardoso MRA. Hearing loss among workers exposed to road traffic noise in the city of São Paulo in Brazil. *Auris, Nasus, Larynx*. 2005; 32: 17–21.

Bauman AE. Updating the evidence that physical activity is good for health: an epidemiological review 2000–2003. *Journal of Science and Medicine in Sport*. 2004; 7(1 suppl): 6–19.

Berke, EB, Gottlieb, LM, Moudon, AV, and Larson, EB Protective Association Between Neighborhood Walkability and Depression in Older Men. *Journal of the American Geriatrics Society*, 2007; 55(i): 526–533.

Besser LM, Marcus M, and Frumkin H. Commute time and social capital in the US. *American Journal of Public Health*. 2008; 34(3): 207–211.

Bhatia R and Wernham A. Integrating human health into environmental impact assessment: an unrealized opportunity for environmental health and justice. *Environmental Health Perspectives*. 2008; 116(8): 991–1000.

Blair SN, Horton E, Leon AS, Lee I, Drinkwater BL, Dishman RK, Mackey M, and Kienholz ML. Physical activity, nutrition, and chronic disease. *Medicine and Science in Sports and Exercise*. 1996; 28(3): 335–349.

Block JP, Scribner RA, and DeSalvo KB. Fast food, race/ethnicity, and income: a geographic analysis. *American Journal of Preventive Medicine*. 2004; 27(3): 211–217.

Boarnet MG, Anderson CL, Day K, McMillan T, and Alfonzo M. Evaluation of the California Safe Routes to School legislation: urban form changes and children's active transportation to school. *American Journal of Preventive Medicine*. 2005; 28(2 Suppl 2): 134–140.

Booth G, Leonard B, and Pawlukiewicz M. *Ten Principles for Reinventing America's Suburban Business Districts 2002*. Washington, DC: Urban Land Institute. Available at: www.smartgrowth.org/pdf/uli_Ten_Principles.pdf.

Botchwey ND, Hobson SE, Dannenberg AL, Mumford KG, Contant CK, McMillan TE, Jackson RJ, Lopez R, and Winkle C. A model built environment and public health course curriculum: training for an interdisciplinary workforce. *American Journal of Preventive Medicine*. 36(2 Suppl): S63–S71, 2009; see also www.bephc.com.

Bragg B, Galloway T, Spohn DB, and Trotter DE. Land use and zoning for the public's health. *Journal of Law, Medicine and Ethics*. 2003; 31(4): 78–80.

Brauer M, Hoek G, Van Vliet P, Meliefste K, Fischer PH, and Wijga A, *et al*. Air pollution from traffic and the development of respiratory infections and asthmatic and allergic symptoms in children. *American Journal of Respiratory and Critical Care Medicine*. 2002; 166(8): 1092–1098.

Bunn F, Collier T, Frost C, Ker K, Roberts I, and Wentz R. Traffic calming for the prevention of road traffic injuries: systematic review and meta-analysis. *Injury Prevention*. 2003; 9: 200–204.

Campbell JM. *Renewing Social Capital: The Role of Civil Dialogue*. In S. Schuman (Ed.), *Creating a Culture of Collaboration*. San Francisco: Jossey-Bass, 2006.

Cannuscio C, Block J, and Kawachi I. Social capital and successful aging: the role of senior housing. *Annals of Internal Medicine*. 2003: 139(5 Part 2): 395–399.

Center for Universal Design (1997). The principles of universal design, Version 2.0. Raleigh, NC: North Carolina State University. Available at: http://design.ncsu.edu/cud/about_ud/udprinciplestext.htm.

Centers for Disease Control and Prevention. Healthy places website: Health Impact Assessment. Available at: http://www.cdc.gov/healthyplaces/hia.htm.

Cervero R and Kockelman K. Travel demand and the three Ds: density, diversity, and design. *Transportation Research Record*. 1997; 2: 199–219.

Clark DE and Cushing BM. Rural and urban traffic fatalities, vehicle miles, and population density. *Accident Analysis and Prevention*. 2004; 36: 967–972.

Cohen DA, McKenzie TL, Sehgal A, Williamson S, Golinelli D, and Lurie N. Contribution of public parks to physical activity. *American Journal of Public Health*. 2007; 97: 509–514.

Corburn J. Confronting the challenges in reconnecting urban planning and public health. *American Journal of Public Health* 2004; 94: 541–546.

Dannenberg AL, Burton DC, and Jackson RJ. Economic and environmental costs of obesity: the impact on airlines (letter). *American Journal of Preventive Medicine*. 2004; 27: 264.

Chapter 12: LIVABILITY, HEALTH, COMMUNITY DESIGN

Dannenberg AL, Bhatia R, Cole BL, Heaton SK, Feldman JD, and Rutt CD. Use of health impact assessment in the US: 27 Case Studies, 1999–2007. *American Journal of Preventive Medicine*. 2008; 34(3): 241–256.

De Leeuw E. Global and local (glocal) health: the WHO Healthy Cities programme. *Global Change and Human Health*. 2001; 2(1): 34–45.

De Ville KA and Sparrow SE. Zoning, urban planning, and the public health practitioner. *Journal of Public Health Management and Practice*. 2008; 14: 313–316.

Delfino RJ, Staimer N, Tjoa T, Gillen D, Kleinman MT, Sioutas C, and Cooper D. Personal and ambient air pollution exposures and lung function decrements in children with asthma. *Environmental Health Perspectives*. 2008; 116(4): 550–558.

Duffy J. *The Sanitarians: A History of American Public Health*. Urbana, IL: University of Chicago Press, 1990.

Elvik R. 2001. Area-wide urban traffic calming schemes: a meta-analysis of safety effects. *Accident Analysis and Prevention*. 33: 327–336.

European Centre for Health Policy, World Health Organization Regional Office for Europe. Gothenburg Consensus Paper. Health impact assessment: main concepts and suggested approach. Brussels, 1999. Available at: http://www.euro.who.int/document/PAE/Gothenburg paper.pdf.

Evans GW. The built environment and mental health. *Journal of Urban Health*. 2003; 80: 536–555.

Ewing R, Schieber RA, and Zegeer CV. Urban sprawl as a risk factor in motor vehicle occupant and pedestrian fatalities. *American Journal of Public Health*. 2003; 93(9): 1541–1549.

Federal Aviation Authority. Land use compatibility and airports, a guide for effective land use planning. 1999. Available at: http://www.faa.gov/about/office_org/headquarters_offices/aep/planning_toolkit/.

Federal Highway Administration (FHWA). Highway traffic noise in the United States: problem and response. 2006. FHWA-HEP-06-020. US Department of Transportation. Available at: http://www.fhwa.dot.gov/environment/probresp.htm.

Federal Highway Administration. Guidance Memorandum on Consideration and Implementation of Proven Safety Countermeasures. 2010 July 10, 2008 [cited 2010 August 26]; Available from: http://safety.fhwa.dot.gov/policy/memo071008/#walkways.

Federal Interagency Committee on Aviation Noise. Findings of the FICAN pilot study on the relationship between aircraft noise reduction and changes in standardized test scores. 2007. Available at: http://www.fican.org/pages/findings.html.

Finkelstein EA, Fiebelkorn IC, and Wang G. National medical spending attributable to overweight and obesity: how much, and who's paying? *Health Affairs* Web Exclusive, May 14, 2003.

Finkelstein MM, Jerrett M, and Sears MR. Traffic air pollution and mortality rate advancement periods. *American Journal of Epidemiology*. 2004; 160(2): 173–177.

Flynn BC. Healthy cities: toward worldwide health promotion. *Annual Review of Public Health*. 1996; 17: 299–309.

Foege WH. CDC's 60th anniversary: director's perspective – William H. Foege, MD, MPH, 1977–1983. *Morbidity and Mortality Weekly Report*. 2006; 55(39); 1071–1074.

Frank L. and Engelke P. How land use and transportation systems impact public health. Centers for Disease Control. 2000. Available at: www.cdc.gov/nccdphp/dnpa/pdf/aces-workingpaper1.pdf.

Fried LP, Freedman M, Endres TE, and Wasik B. Building communities that promote successful aging. *Western Journal of Medicine.* 1997; 167: 216–19.

Galea, S, Ahern, J, Rudenstine, S, Wallace, Z, and Vlahov, D (2005). Urban built environment and depression: a multilevel analysis. *Journal of Epidemiology and Community Health.* 2005; 59: 822–827.

Geller AL. Smart growth: a prescription for livable cities. *American Journal of Public Health.* 2003; 93(9): 1410–1415.

Gies, E. *The Health Benefits of Parks: How Parks Help Keep Americans and Their Communities Fit and Healthy.* San Francisco, CA: The Trust for Public Land, 2006.

Glanz K, Sallis JF, Saelens BE, and Frank LD. Healthy nutrition environments: concepts and measures. *American Journal of Health Promotion.* 2005; 19(5): 330–333, ii.

Glasser J. Back to the future [transcript]. Presented at global public health: issues and strategies for Hawai'i and the Pacific, June 12–13 2002. Available at: http://www.hawaii.edu/global/projects_activities/Past/GlasserXscript2.pdf.

Halpern D. *Mental Health and the Built Environment.* London: Taylor and Francis, 1995.

Health Impact Project (HIP) website 2011. Available at: www.healthimpactproject.org

Hoehner CM, Brennan LK, Brownson RC, Handy SL, and Killingsworth R. Opportunities for integrating public health and urban planning approaches to promote active community environments. *American Journal of Health Promotion* 2003; 18: 14–20.

Hoek G, Brunekreef B, Goldbohm S, Fischer P, and van den Brandt PA. Association between mortality and indicators of traffic-related air pollution in the Netherlands: a cohort study. *Lancet.* 2002; 360(9341): 1203–1209.

Horowitz CR, Colson KA, Hebert PL, and Lancaster K. Barriers to buying healthy foods for people with diabetes: evidence of environmental disparities. *American Journal of Public Health.* 2004; 94: 1549–1554.

House JS, Landis KR, and Umberson D. Social relationships and health. *Science.* 1988; 241: 540–545.

ICLEI – Local governments for sustainability. Building sustainable cities. No date. Available at: http://www.iclei.org/index.php?id=801.

ICLEI – Local Governments for Sustainability (USA). STAR Community Index. No date. Available at: http://www.icleiusa.org/programs/sustainability/star-community-index/.

International City/County Management Association. Active living and social equity: creating healthy communities for all residents. A Guide for Local Governments. 2005. Available at: http://www.icma.org/upload/library/2005-02/{16565E96-721D-467D-9521-3694F918E5CE}.pdf.

Jackson KT. *Crabgrass Frontier: The Suburbanization of the United States.* New York: Oxford University Press, 1985.

Jacobs J. *The Death and Life of Great American Cities.* New York: Random House, 1961.

Jacobsen PL. Safety in numbers: more walkers and bicyclists, safer walking and bicycling. *Injury Prevention.* 2003; 9: 205–209.

Jakovljević B, Belojević G, Paunović K, and Stojanov V. Road traffic noise and sleep disturbances in an urban population: cross-sectional study. *Croatian Medical Journal.* 2006; 47: 125–133.

Jarup L, Babisch W, Houthuijs D, Pershagen G, Katsouyanni K, and Cadum E, *et al.* Hypertension and exposure to noise near airports: the HYENA Study. *Environmental Health Perspectives.* 2008; 116(3): 329–333.

Chapter 12: LIVABILITY, HEALTH, COMMUNITY DESIGN

Joint M. Road rage. In: *Aggressive Driving: Three Studies*. Washington, DC: AAA Foundation for Traffic Safety, March 1997. Available at: http://www.aaafoundation.org/pdf/agdr3study.pdf.

Kampert JB, Blair SN, Barlow CE, and Kohl HW. Physical activity, physical fitness, and all-cause and cancer mortality: a prospective study of men and women. *Annals of Epidemiology*. 1996; 6(5): 452–457.

Kaplan R. The nature of the view from home: Psychological benefits. *Environment and Behavior*. 2001; 33, 507–542.

Kawachi I. Social capital and community effects on population and individual health. *Annals of the New York Academy of Sciences*. 1999; 896: 120–130.

Kawachi I, Kennedy BP, Lochner K, and Prothrow-Stith D. Social capital, income inequality, and mortality. *American Journal of Public Health*. 1997; 87: 1491–1498.

Kennedy M and Leonard P. Dealing with neighborhood change: a primer on gentrification and policy choices. Discussion paper prepared for the Brookings Institution Center on Urban and Metropolitan Policy and PolicyLink. 2001. Available at: http://www.policylink.org/pdfs/BrookingsGentrification.pdf.

Kim JJ, Huen K, Adams S, Smorodinsky S, Hoats A, Malig B, Lipsett M, and Ostro B. Residential traffic and children's respiratory health. *Environmental Health Perspectives*. 2008; 116(9): 1274–1279.

Kochtitzky CS, Frumkin H, Rodriguez R, Dannenberg AL, Rayman J, Rose K, Gillig, R, and Kanter T. Urban planning and public health at CDC. *Morbid Mortal Weekly Report* 2006; 55 Suppl 2: 34–38.

Koslowsky M, Kluger AN, and Reich M. *Commuting Stress: Causes, Effects, and Methods of Coping*. New York: Plenum Press; 1995.

Kuczmarski RJ, Flegal KM, Campbell SM, and Johnson CL. Increasing prevalence of overweight among US adults: The National Health and Nutrition Examination Surveys, 1960 to 1991. *JAMA*. 1994; 272(3): 205–211.

Kunstler JH. *The Geography of Nowhere: The Rise and Decline of America's Man-Made Landscape*. New York: Simon and Schuster, 1993.

Kweon B, Sullivan WC, and Wiley AR. Green common spaces and the social integration of inner-city older adults. *Environment and Behavior*. 1998; 30(6), 832–858.

Lee IM. Physical activity and cancer prevention – data from epidemiologic studies. *Medicine and Science in Sports and Exercise*. 2003; 35(11): 1823–1827.

Lee IM and Paffenbarger RS Jr. Associations of light, moderate, and vigorous intensity physical activity with longevity. The Harvard Alumni Health Study. *American Journal of Epidemiology*. 2000; 151(3): 293–299.

Leong ST and Laortanakul P. Monitoring and assessment of daily exposure of roadside workers to traffic noise levels in an Asian city: a case study of Bangkok streets. *Environmental Monitoring and Assessment*. 2003; 85(1): 69–85.

Litsios S. Charles Dickens and the movement for sanitary reform. *Perspectives in Biology and Medicine*. 2003; 46(2): 183–199.

Lynch JW, Smith GD, Kaplan GA, and House JS. Income inequality and mortality: importance to health of individual income, psychosocial environment, or material conditions. *British Medical Journal*. 2000; 320: 1200–1204.

McCann B. Complete the Streets! *Planning*. May 2005: 18–23.

Macera CA, Jones DA, Yore MM, Ham SA, Kohl HW, Kimsey CD, and Buchner D. Prevalence of physical activity, including lifestyle physical activities among adults – United States, 2000–2001. *Morbidity and Mortality Weekly Report*. 2003; 52: 764–779.

Mair JS, Pierce MW, and Teret SP. The use of zoning to restrict fast food outlets: a potential strategy to combat obesity. The Center for Law and the Public's Health at Johns Hopkins and Georgetown Universities. 2005. Available at: http://www.publichealthlaw.net/Zoning%20Fast%20Food%20Outlets.pdf.

Malizia EE. Planning and public health: research options for an emerging field. *Journal of Planning Education and Research* 2006; 25: 428–432.

Matheson MP, Stansfeld SA, and Haines MM. The effects of chronic aircraft noise exposure on children's cognition and health: three field studies. *Noise and Health*. 2003; 5(19): 31–40.

Maynard D, Coull BA, Gryparis A, and Schwartz J. Mortality risk associated with short-term exposure to traffic particles and sulfates. *Environmental Health Perspectives*. 2007; 115(5): 751–755.

McConnell R, Berhane K, Yao L, Jerrett M, Lurmann F, Gilliland F, Kunzli N, Gauderman J, Avol E, Thomas D, and Peters J. Traffic, susceptibility and childhood asthma. *Environmental Health Perspectives*. 2006; 114(5): 766–772.

Melosi MV. *The Sanitary City: Urban Infrastructure in American from Colonial Times to the Present*. Baltimore: Johns Hopkins University Press, 2000.

Minkler M. and Wallerstein N. Improving health through community organization and community building: A health education perspective. In M. Minkler (Ed.), *Community Organizing and Community Building for Health (2nd Edition)*. Piscataway, NJ: Rutgers University Press, 2005.

Mokdad AH, Serdula MK, Dietz WH, Bowman BA, Marks JS, and Koplan JP. The spread of the obesity epidemic in the United States, 1991–1998. *Journal of the American Medical Association*. 1999; 282: 1519–1522.

National Complete Streets Coalition website. Complete streets fundamentals. 2011. Available at: http://www.completestreets.org/complete-streets-fundamentals/.

New York City Department of City Planning. Fresh Kills Park Project. 2011. Available at: http://www.nycgovparks.org/sub_your_park/fresh_kills_park/html/fresh_kills_park.html.

Novaco R, Stokols D, Campbell J, and Stoklols J. Transportation, stress, and community psychology. *American Journal of Community Psychology*. 1979; 7: 361–380.

Nyberg F, Gustavsson P, Jarup L, Bellander T, Berglind N, and Jakobsson R, *et al.* Urban air pollution and lung cancer in Stockholm. *Epidemiology*. 2000; 11(5): 487–495.

Ogden CL, Carroll MD, Curtin LR, McDowell MA, Tabak CJ, and Flegal KM. Prevalence of overweight and obesity in the United States, 1999–2004. *JAMA*. 2006; 295: 1549–1555.

Oldenburg R. *The Great Good Place: Cafés, Coffee Shops, Community Centers, Beauty Parlors, General Stores, Bars, Hangouts, and How They Get you Through the Day*. New York: Paragon House, 1989.

Olmsted FL. Basic Principles of City Planning. In *City Planning: A Series of Papers Presenting the Essential Elements of A City Plan*. In J Nolen (editor). New York: D. Appleton and Company, 1916: 1–18.

Passchier-Vermeer W, and Passchier WF. Noise exposure and public health. *Environmental Health Perspectives*. 2000; 108(supp l): 123–131.

Chapter 12: LIVABILITY, HEALTH, COMMUNITY DESIGN

Perdue WC, Stone LA, and Gostin LO. The built environment and its relationship to the public's health: the legal framework. *American Journal of Public Health* 2003; 93: 1390–1394.

Portland Bureau of Transportation. Portland Bicycle Count Report. 2010. City of Portland, Portland, Oregon. Available at: http://www.portlandonline.com/transportation/index.cfm?c=44671anda=327783

Powell LM, Auld C, Chaloupka FJ, O'Malley PM, and Johnston LD. Associations between access to food stores and adolescent body mass index. *American Journal of Preventive Medicine*. 2007; 33(suppl 4): S301–S307.

Pucher J and Dijkstra L. Promoting safe walking and cycling to improve public health: lessons from the Netherlands and Germany. *American Journal of Public Health*. 2003; 93(9): 1509–1516.

Putnam R. *Bowling Alone: The Collapse and Revival of American Community*. New York, NY: Simon and Schuster, 2000.

Rails-to-Trails Conservancy website, 2011. Available at: http://www.railstotrails.org/aboutUs/index.html.

Rathbone DB and Huckabee JC. *Controlling Road Rage: A Literature Review and Pilot Study*. Washington, DC: AAA Foundation for Traffic Safety; June 1999.

Retting RA, Persaud BN, Garder PE, and Lord D. Crash and injury reduction following installation of roundabouts in the United States. *American Journal of Public Health*. 2001; 91: 628–631.

Rundle, Rhonda L. "US's obesity woes put a strain on hospitals in unexpected ways." *The Wall Street Journal*. May 1, 2002.

Schikowski T, Sugiri D, Ranft U, Gehring U, Heinrich J, Wichmann HE, and Krämer U. Long-term air pollution exposure and living close to busy roads are associated with COPD in women. *Respiratory Research*. 2005; 6: 152.

Schilling J and Linton L. The public health roots of zoning: In search of active living's legal genealogy. *American Journal of Preventive Medicine*. 2005; 28(2S2): 96–104.

Spreng M. Possible health effects of noise induced cortisol increase. *Noise and Health*. 2000; 2(7): 59–64.

Stansfeld SA, Berglund B, Clark C, Lopez-Barrio I, Fischer P, and Öhrström E, et al. Aircraft and road traffic noise and children's cognition and health: a cross-national study. *Lancet* 2005; 365: 1942–1949.

Stansfeld SA and Matheson MP. Noise pollution: non-auditory effects on health. *British Medical Bulletin*. 2003; 68: 243–257.

Stokols D, Novaco R, Stokols J, and Campbell J. Traffic congestion, type A behavior, and stress. *Journal of Applied Psychology*. 1978; 63: 467–480.

Story M, Kaphingst KM, Robinson-O'Brien R, and Glanz K. Creating healthy food and eating environments: policy and environmental approaches. *Annual Review of Public Health*. 2008; 29: 253–272.

Surface Transportation Policy Project. Mean streets 2004. 2004. Available at: www.transact.org/library/reports_html/ms2004/pdf/final_mean_streets_2004_4.pdf.

Transportation Research Board, Institute of Medicine. *Does the Built Environment Influence Physical Activity? Examining the Evidence. TRB Special Report 282*. Committee on Physical Activity, Health, Transportation, and Land Use. Washington DC: National Academy of Sciences, 2005.

US Centers for Disease Control and Prevention (CDC). Overweight and obesity: US obesity trends. 2011. Available at: http://www.cdc.gov/obesity/data/trends.html.

US Department of Transportation. Vehicle miles traveled (VMT) and vehicle emissions. 2002. Available at: http://www.fhwa.dot.gov/environment/vmtems.htm.

US Department of Transportation. Traffic safety facts 2006: Bicyclists and other cyclists. 2006. Available at: http://www.nhtsa.dot.gov/portal/nhtsa_static_file_downloader.jsp?file=/staticfiles/DOT/NHTSA/Traffic Injury Control/Articles/Associated Files/TSF2006_810802.pdf.

US Department of Transportation. 2008a. Traffic safety facts: motor vehicle traffic crashes as a leading cause of death in the United States, 2005. Available at: http://www-nrd.nhtsa.dot.gov/Pubs/810936.PDF.

US Department of Transportation 2008b. Traffic safety facts: 2006. Available at: http://www-nrd.nhtsa.dot.gov/Pubs/TSF2006FE.PDF.

US Department of Transportation 2008c. Traffic safety facts: 2007. Traffic safety annual assessment – Highlights. Available at: http://www-nrd.nhtsa.dot.gov/Pubs/811017.PDF.

US Environmental Protection Agency. Travel and environmental implications of school siting. 2003. EPA report 231-R-03-004. Available at: http://www.epa.gov/dced/pdf/school_travel.pdf.

US Environmental Protection Agency. Brownfields and land revitalization. 2011. Available at: http://www.epa.gov/brownfields/.

US Environmental Protection Agency, Office of Transportation and Air Quality. Greenhouse gas emissions from the US Transportation Sector, 1990–2003. EPA 420 R 06 003. Washington: USEPA, March 2006. Available: http://www.epa.gov/oms/climate/420r06003.pdf.

Venn AJ, Lewis SA, Cooper M, Hubbard R, and Britton J. Living near a main road and the risk of wheezing illness in children. *American Journal of Respiratory and Critical Care Medicine*. 2001; 164(12): 2177–2180.

Vineis P, Hoek G, Krzyzanowski M, Vigna-Taglianti F, Veglia F, and Airoldi L, *et al*. Air pollution and risk of lung cancer in a prospective study in Europe. *International Journal of Cancer*. 2006; 119(1): 169–174.

Wahl HW and Weisman GD. Environmental gerontology at the beginning of the new millennium: reflections on its historical, empirical, and theoretical development. *Gerontologist* 2003; 43: 616–627.

Wannamethee SG, Shaper AG, and Walker M. Changes in physical activity, mortality, and incidence of coronary heart disease in older men. *Lancet*. 1998; 351(9116): 1603–1608.

Wannamethee SG, Shaper G, Walker M, and Ebrahim S. Lifestyle and 15-year survival free of heart attack, stroke, and diabetes in middle-aged British men. *Archives of Internal Medicine*. 1998; 158: 2433–2440.

Watson M, and Dannenberg AL. Investment in safe routes to school projects: public health benefits for the larger community. *Preventing Chronic Disease*. 2008; 5(3). Available at: www.cdc.gov/pcd/issues/2008/jul/07_0087.htm.

Wei M, Kampert JB, Barlow CE, Nichaman MZ, Gibbons LW, Paffenbarger RS, and Blair SN. Relationship between low cardiorespiratory fitness and mortality in normal-weight, overweight, and obese men. *Journal of the American Medical Association*. 1999; 282: 1547–1553.

Wood, L, Giles-Corti, B, and Bulsara, M The pet connection: Pets as a conduit for social capital? *Social Science and Medicine*. 2005, 61(6), 1159–1173.

Woodyard C. Car weight limits are a big, fat problem, *USA Today*. September 13, 2007. Available at: http://www.usatoday.com/money/autos/2007-09-13-overloaded-cars_N.htm?imw=Y.

Chapter 12: LIVABILITY, HEALTH, COMMUNITY DESIGN

World Health Organization Europe. Twenty steps for developing a Healthy Cities project. Copenhagen: WHO Europe, 1997. Available at: http://www.euro.who.int/document/e56270.pdf.

World Health Organization. Guidelines for community noise: adverse health effects of noise. No date. Available at: http://www.who.int/docstore/peh/noise/Comnoise3.htm.

Zenk SN, Schulz AJ, Israel BA, James SA, Bao SM, and Wilson ML. Fruit and vegetable access differs by community racial composition and socioeconomic position in Detroit, Michigan. *Ethnicity and Disease*. 2006; 16(1): 275–280.

For Further Information

US-based Resources

Active Living Research at the Robert Wood Johnson Foundation. http://www.activelivingresearch.org/.
Active Living Research, a national program of the Robert Wood Johnson Foundation, focuses on preventing childhood obesity including improvements in the built environment to encourage physical activity.

American Planning Association (APA): Planning for Healthy Places with Health Impact Assessment. http://professional.captus.com/Planning/hia/default.aspx
The American Planning Association is the professional association of planners; this website offers an on-line training course on the basics of health impact assessment.

Association of State and Territorial Health Officers (ASTHO): Built Environment.
http://www.astho.org/index.php?template=built_synthetic_environment.html
ASTHO is the professional association of state and territorial health officers; this website provides information on health and built environment relevant to state level policies and projects.

Congress for the New Urbanism. http://www.cnu.org
CNU efforts encourage the restoration of existing urban centers, reconfiguration of suburbs, conservation of natural environments, and preservation of the built legacy.

Health Impact Project. www.healthimpactproject.org
The Health Impact Project, a collaboration of the Robert Wood Johnson Foundation and the Pew Charitable Trusts, is a national initiative designed to promote the use of health impact assessments (HIAs) as a decision-making tool for policymakers.

ICLEI-Local Governments for Sustainability USA (ICLEI-USA). http://www.icleiusa.org
ICLEI USA is a network of 500 cities, towns and counties striving to reduce greenhouse gas emissions and create more sustainable communities.

Local Government Commission: Center for Livable Communities. http://www.lgc.org/clc/center.html
The Center for Livable Communities helps local governments and community leaders adopt programs and policies that lead to more livable and resource-efficient land use patterns. LGC sponsors the annual Smart Growth conference: www.newpartners.org.

National Association of County and City Health Officials (NACCHO): Community Design/Land Use Planning. http://www.naccho.org/topics/environmental/landuseplanning/index.cfm

NACCHO is the professional association of local state and territorial health officials; this website provides information on health and built environment relevant to local level policies and projects.

National Association of Local Boards of Health (NALBOH), http://www.nalboh.org/.

NALBOH supports local boards of health on many issues including improving the built environment.

Safe Routes to Schools National Partnership. http://www.saferoutespartnership.org/

The Safe Routes to School National Partnership is a network of nonprofit organizations, government agencies, schools, and professionals working to advance the SRTS movement in the United States.

San Francisco Department of Public Health: Health, Equity, and Sustainability Program. http://www.sfphes.org/.

The San Francisco Health, Equity, and Sustainability Program website provides tools, training, research, and other useful information for health impact assessment HIA practitioners.

Smart Growth America. http://www.smartgrowth.org/

Smart Growth Online is a web-based catalogue of Smart Growth related news, events, information and resources.

Thunderhead Alliance for Biking and Walking. http://www.thunderheadalliance.org

The Thunderhead Alliance for Biking and Walking is the national coalition of state and local bicycle and pedestrian advocacy organizations that working to promote bicycling and walking in North America.

UCLA School of Public Health: Health Impact Assessment (HIA) Project. http://www.ph.ucla.edu/hs/health-impact

The UCLA HIA project conducts research on HIA, provides links to many HIA resources, and is developing a database of completed HIAs.

US Centers for Disease Control and Prevention: Healthy Places. http://www.cdc.gov/healthyplaces

CDC's Healthy Places website offers information and key resources about the major health issues related to land use.

US Department of Transportation, Federal Highway Administration: National Center for Safe Routes to School. http://www.saferoutesinfo.org/

The Federal Highway Administration provides funding and guidance for the Safe Routes to School program.

US Environmental Protection Agency: Smart Growth. http://www.epa.gov/smartgrowth/

EPA's Smart Growth website provides information and key resources about Smart Growth.

Urban Land Institute (ULI). http://www.uli.org

ULI is a nonprofit research and educational institute whose mission is to provide responsible leadership in the use of land in order to enhance the total environment. ULI members span the entire spectrum of the land use and development disciplines.

Chapter 12: LIVABILITY, HEALTH, COMMUNITY DESIGN

Global Resources

Association of Public Health Observatories (APHO): HIA Gateway. http://www.hiagateway.org.uk
Based in England, the HIA Gateway website is the largest single collection of information, resources, and links about health impact assessment.

ICLEI – Local Governments for Sustainability. http://www.iclei.org/index.php?id=801.
Local Governments for Sustainability is an international association of local governments as well as national and regional local government organizations that have made a commitment to sustainable development.

International Healthy Cities Foundation. http://www.healthycities.org
This website allows persons interested in health and quality of life issues in their communities to share information.

Sustainable Cities Network. http://www.rec.org/REC/Programs/Sustainablecities/
This network facilitates communications among world's leading sustainable development organizations.

UN-Habitat: Sustainable Cities and Localizing Agenda 21. http://www.unhabitat.org/categories.asp?catid=540.
The United Nations Human Settlements Programme, UN-HABITAT, works to promote socially and environmentally sustainable towns and cities with the goal of providing adequate shelter for all.

World Health Organization (WHO): Health Impact Assessement (HIA). http://www.who.int/hia/en
WHO supports the use of HIA because of its ability to influence policies, programs and projects.

World Health Organization: Healthy Cities Programme. http://www.euro.who.int/healthy-cities
The WHO Healthy Cities program engages local governments in health development through a process of political commitment, institutional change, capacity building, partnership-based planning and innovative projects. It also strives to include health considerations in economic, regeneration and urban development efforts.

Chapter 13

FINAL THOUGHTS ON COMMUNITY LIVABILITY
Roger Caves and Fritz Wagner

The concept of "livable communities" is certainly not a new one. Any discussion of the topic cannot be confined to any state or nation. It is a global topic. However, we can agree on one thing that there is no single definition of a livable community. It is an expansive topic involving different segments of the population, different topics, and different levels of government, nonprofit organizations, and the private sector. There are social, cultural, environmental, economic, health, education, housing, transportation, physical design, infrastructure, recreation, etc. dimensions to any discussion. It has been in the minds of citizens, policy officials, and other individuals and groups for many years. The idea of a livable community may differ by segment of the population, elderly, low-income, culturally diverse, etc. These segments of the population may have special needs that need to be met.

Communities are clearly multi-faceted puzzles to most people. The essays in this book, written by scholars and practitioners, clearly illustrate the challenges and multiple dimensions of how we might view "livable communities." They offer real life examples of issues facing livable communities. They look at local, state, national, and global experiences. Each essay offers insights into the topic and provides ideas and thoughts for further research.

There is no denying that we must continue to study our communities. We cannot become complacent and simply rest on our laurels. There is a constant need to monitor and evaluate the happenings of our communities. Communities are not static. In some shape or fashion they are always changing. As such, it is imperative that we observe the temporal dimension of livable communities. Just because a community is deemed livable at one point in time does not guarantee it will remain livable. Situations occur that might change how we view our communities. The economic crisis facing many of our global communities has caused disastrous consequences: unemployment, increasing crime rates, cutting of public services like police and fire protection, closing or curtailing hours of operation for libraries, closing of schools, human resources, and recreational services. A community once known as a livable community may now be known as an unlivable community.

We must also be vigilant in developing policies and programs designed to create and maintain livable communities. The nature of cities does not afford us the luxury of developing one "shrink-wrapped" solution on how to develop and maintain a livable community. The one-size-fits-all mentality simply does not work. Policies and programs developed in Portland,

Chapter 13: **FINAL THOUGHTS**

Oregon may not work in Minneapolis, Minnesota. What works in San Diego, California may not work in Seattle, Washington. However, this doesn't mean we cannot develop best practices. There is nothing wrong with taking someone else's idea and tweaking it to make it work in your community.

The essays contained in this book have examined "livable communities" from a number of different vantage points. Each essay has provided practical insights into this topic. It is up to each of us to learn from these essays and to help develop our own livable communities.

INDEX

Note: Page numbers in *italics* refer to figures, those in **bold** type refer to tables. Page numbers followed by 'n' refer to end of chapter notes.

accessibility 216, 225
accessory dwellings 83, 86, 87, 94
Active Adult Retirement Communities 84
adequate public facilities ordinances (APFOs) 232, 233, 236
AdvantAge Initiative 92, 93
aesthetics 42; France 53–4; Spain 55
affordable housing: incentives 11, 12, 21, 37; jobs-housing balance 226, 231; New Urbanism 242; Rio de Janeiro 106
aging: challenges of 82–3; obstacles in the built environment 81, 83–5; *see also* elder friendly communities
Aging in Place Initiative 90–1
Ahwahnee Principles 183
air quality 254
Albuquerque: population growth 135
Alley, D. *et al.* 92, 93
American Association of Retired Persons (AARP) 83, 90, 93
American Planning Association 35, 101, 263
Anderson, B. and Holden, A. 72–3
Anderson, Brett 172
Appleyard, Donald 2
Arizona 88; Phoenix *132*
Arnstein, Sherry 189, 190
Atlanta Regional Planning Commission 92
Australia: land use regulation 41–4
automobiles: elderly drivers 84–5, 90; impact on cities 223–4; injury risk 252–3; location efficiency 229–30; potential changes in use 230–1, 237–8

Bassett, Edward 55
Belgium: land use regulation 49–50
Belzer, D. and Autler, G. 228
Benedict, M. and McMahon, E. 199–200
Bernick, M. and Cervero, R. 228
Berry, J.M. *et al.* 185, 189
Bettman, Alfred 55
bicyclists 230; community design for 252, *253*; injury risk 253, 254; New Urbanist neighborhoods 231
Boston 201
Boyle, R. and Powell, M. 87
Brower, S. 101, 104
Brown, A.L. *et al.* 230–1
brownfields redevelopment 255, 259
Burnsville Economic Development Authority (BEDA) 20
Burnsville, Minnesota 19–22, *21*, 26

California 36, 40, 57
Calthorpe, Peter 1, 26, 228
Canada: land use regulation 40–1
Cavallieri, F. and Oliveira, S. 106
Central Business Districts (CBDs) *see* downtown revitalization
Cervero, R. 232
CFAA program 92–3

INDEX

Chapel Hill, North Carolina 231
Chennai 47–8
Chicago 2
child care 71
Childs, Mark 209
China: land use regulation 38
City Beautiful movement 2
city boosterism 67, 72–4
climate-related benefits of vegetation 200
CODESCO 109–10
collaborative resource development 93
communities of place 102
community change 274
community design: and air quality 254; emerging tools and resources 259–63; and health 250; healthy food environments 256; and injury risk 252–4; noise exposure 256–7; parks and green spaces 255; physical activity and obesity 250–2, *251*; social capital and mental health 257–8; urban sprawl 249–50
community identity 184, 195
community open spaces 202; *see also* green infrastructure (GI)
community, sense of 102, 103; deterministic approach to 101; enhanced through participation 184; Mata Machado 118–19, 121; small town neighborhoods 104; varying perceptions of livability 100
Complete Streets 89, 254
comprehensive plans 36
concurrency 226, 232–6, 242–3
Condon, Patrick 206, 209
Congress for the New Urbanism 1, 101, 261
Connick, Harry Jr. 168
conservation areas in France 53–4
contractual land use control 37–8, 39
Costa, Lucio 107
Crane, R. and Boarnet, M. 242
creative cluster strategy 128, 129
crime and violence: Rio de Janeiro 106–7, 117
culture and regeneration: importance post-Katrina 158, 159–60, 175–6; Liverpool 72–4; Mardi Gras traditions 163–6, 169–70; musical roots and post-Katrina recovery 167–9; post-Katrina Mardi Gras 166–7, 170–1; restaurants and food in New Orleans 170–5

demographic change 81
deprivation: Liverpool 63, 66–7, 75; *see also* equity; favelas
Detroit 129, 135
Diers, J. 193
disability 82, *82*, 84, 88, 250
Dittmar, H. and Ohland, G. 229, 232
downtown revitalization 90; 20th century decline 129–30; age and educational levels 138–9; assessing residential trends 130–1; assets supporting residential use 127; characteristics of study sample 131; colonization by seniors 87–8; density 150, 151–2; development issues 151–2; household composition and homeownership 137–8, *137*; household growth 135–6, *136*; mapping median income and race 140, *141*–2, 143, *143*–5, 146, *146*–9, 149–50; median income of residents 139–40; population trends 133–5; real estate market 127–8; rise in residential uses 128–9, 130, 150; spatial definition of downtowns 131; variable growth 134
drug trafficking: Rio de Janeiro 106–7
Duany, Andrés 1
Dublin 45, 46
duplex housing 55–6

ecological services 200
elder friendly communities: characteristics 93, **94**; focus on the built environment 93–5; planning frameworks 90–3; planning principles 85–90
employment *see* jobs-housing balance
empowerment 184, 190, 195, 218, 219
Endymion Parade 163, 164, 165–6
energy: 1970s crisis 2; sources 203–4
engagement *see* public participation
England 39–40; *see also* Liverpool
environmental impact assessments (EIAs) 262
Environmental protection Agency (EPA): Building Healthy Communities for Active Aging National Recognition Program 90
environmental sustainability 103, 119
environmental transactions 100, 103–4
equity 224, 232, 250; and health 254, 256
European Capitals of Culture (ECoC) 67–8, 72–4

277

INDEX

European Union (EU) 49
Ewing, R. and Cervero, R. 230

farmers' markets 174, 204, *257*
favelas 104–7, 121–2; *see also* Mata Machado, Rio de Janeiro
floating zones 35
Floresta da Tijuca 107, 119
Florida: Communities for a Lifetime 91; concurrency 226, 233–6, 243; median incomes and race in Orlando 146, *148–9*, 149–50
food 256, *257*; cultural importance in New Orleans 171–5; production and distribution impacts 204
France: land use regulation 51–4, 57
Francescato, G. *et al.* 117
Freund, Ernst 56
funding sources: Seattle parks levy 216–18; Twin Cities region 9, 11, 25; *see also* Livable Communities Development Account (LCDA), Twin Cities

Gallent, N. and Wong, C. 64
Garcia, B. *et al.* 73, 74
Garcia, Robert 209
Garreau, J. 223
Geertz, C. 120
Germany: land use regulation 55–6
Gies, Erica 255
Girling, C. and Kellett, R. 200
Godschalk, D. 1, 100
green infrastructure (GI): background to concept 198–9; definitions 199–201; five overlapping systems 201–4; lessons from Open Space Seattle 214–16, 218–19; Liverpool 74–6; Mata Machado 107, 108, *108*, 110, *111*, 119; Open Space Seattle 206–10, *208*, *211–13*, 214, 216; planning for in Seattle 199, 204, *205*, 206; Seattle Green Legacy Coalition 216–18; value of parks and greenspace 255
Gyourko, J.E. and Rybczynski, W. 242

habitats 203, 210, 215
Haryana Urban Development Authority-HUDA 48
Hayek, F.A. 56

Health Impact Assessment (HIA) 259, 262
health and wellbeing: aging 82, *82*; air quality 254; food 256, *257*; injury risk 252–4; Liverpool 70–1, 75; mobility 200, 202; noise exposure 256–7; parks and greenspace 255; physical activity and obesity 85, 230–1, 251–2, *251*; planning for 250, 258, 259, 262; social capital and mental health 257–8
Hennepin Community Works (HCW) 9
Hibbing, Maine 88
high performance infrastructure 201
Holtzclaw, J. *et al.* 229–30
homeownership 138
Hong Kong: land use regulation 37–8, 47
Hoover, Herbert 55
Hope-VI projects, New Orleans 170
Houck, Mike 209
households: composition 137–8, *137*, 138; growth in numbers 135–6, *136*; homeownership 138
housing: conditions 70–1; for the elderly 82–4, 88
housing developments: Burnsville 21–2; low-impact 204; mid-20th century downtown 130; Musicians' Village, new Orleans 168; Robbinsdale 18, 19; St Louis Park 16; St Paul North Quadrant 23; successful downtowns 151–2; to accommodate aging 86, 87–8, 258; *see also* New Urbanism
housing incentives 11, 12, 21, 37
Houston: land use regulation 34, 38
Howard County, Maryland 88
Hyderabad Urban Development Authority-HUDA 49

inclusion 184; Seattle 189, 192–3
India: land use regulation 47–9; post-tsunami reconstruction 159
injury risk 252–4
Institute of Medicine 230, 237, *237*
International Award for Livable Communities 199
Ireland: land use regulation 44–6
Irvington, New York 88
Israel 37

Jackson, Tamara 171
Jacobs, Jane 2
jobs-housing balance 226, 231–2, 240–1

INDEX

Kain, John 226
Kansas: Lifelong Communities Program 91–2
Karash, K.H. *et al.* 238
Katrina (hurricane) 162
Khattack, A.J. and Rodriguez, D. 231
Kunzmann, K. 73

land use regulation 37–9, 57–8, 83; Australia 41–4; Belgium 49–50; Canada 40–1; England 39–40; France 51–4; Germany 55–6; Hong Kong 47; India 47–9; Ireland 44–6; for jobs-housing balance 232, 240–1; The Netherlands 50–1; Singapore 46–7; Spain 54–5; *see also* zoning in the US
land use and transportation 223–4, 243–4; associated travel behaviors 237–8, *237*; basic concepts 224–5; concurrency 232–6, 242–3; coordination 225–6, 236–7; jobs-housing balance 226, 231–2, 240–1; potential mode shift associated with TND and TOD 230–1; social environment for coordination 238–9, **239**; spatial mismatch hypothesis 226, 232, 240; traditional neighborhood development (TND) 226–7, 240, 241–2; transit-orientated development (TOD) 226, 227–30, 240, 241–2; urban sprawl 250
LEED for Neighborhood Development (LEED-ND) 259, 261
legal basis for regulation 30; Australia 43; UK 39–40
Levine, J. 231, 232
life cycle housing 11, 24
life expectancy rates 63, 70, 82
linkages 86, 200
livability: cultural variations in perceptions of 99–100; defining 1, 31–2, 101–3, 183; development of concept 2, 274; emergence of concept in UK 63–6; matrix 103, *103*; as a person-environment fit 103–4, 122
Livable Communities Development Account (LCDA), Twin Cities 11, 12; Burnsville applications 20–1; Mendota Heights applications 24–5; project evaluation 25–8; Robbinsdale applications 18–19; St Louis Park applications 14–15, 16–17; St Paul application 23

Liverpool 63, 66–8; achievements 70, 71; green infrastructure strategy 74, 75–6; Healthy Homes initiative 70–1; 'Liverpool First' LSP 68, 70; renaissance city 72–4; Sure Start Children's Centres 71–2; Sustainable Community Strategy (SCS) 68–70, *69*; sustaining transformation 76–7
Local Area Agreements (LAA) 64
Local Area Formation Commissions (LAFCOs) 57
local businesses: post-Katrina New Orleans 171–5
local government powers: Australia 42; France 53–4; Ireland 44, 45–6; UK 40; US 33, 34–5, 42, 83
localism in the UK 63, 65, 66
Local Strategic Partnerships (LSP) 64, 65; Liverpool First 67, 68–70; monitoring 70
location efficiency 226, 229–30, 240, 244
Los Angeles: median incomes and race 143, *143–5*, 149, 150
Louisiana Recovery Authority (LRA) 159
low impact development 201, 204
low-impact mobility 200, 202
Lynch, Kevin 183

McMillan, D. and Chavis, D. 118
Mandina's Restaurant, New Orleans 162, 172, 173, 175
Mardi Gras tradition 163–6; African American 169; cultural and economic impacts 166–7; Second Line 169–71
Marsalis, Branford 168
Martz, W.A. 185, 189–90
Mata Machado, Rio de Janeiro: community 110–12, *113*, *114*, 118–19; environmental sustainability 119; history of 107–10; housing 117; location 107, *108*, *109*, *111*; main *praça* 113–14, *113*, 115, *115*, *116*; residents' worldview 120–1; site plan and study area *112*; study conclusions 121–2; study method 113, 117; utilization of public spaces 113–17, 118
Mendota Heights, Minnesota 24–5
mental health 257–8; and aging 82, 258; Liverpool 75; value of green spaces 202, 255, 258
Mercer Company livability rating system 199
metabolism 203–4

279

INDEX

Michigan Community for a Lifetime 92
Mid-City Neighborhood Organization (MCNO) 166
Milwaukee: median incomes and race 146, *146–7*, 149
Minneapolis: Neighborhood Revitalization Program (NPR) 9
Minnesota: Livable Communities Act (LCA 1995) 9, 10–12; *see also* Livable Communities Development Account (LCDA), Twin Cities
Metropolitan Reorganization Act (1994) 10; *see also* Twin Cities region
mixed use 54, 86, 88, 103, 104
mobility: and accessibility 225; elderly people 84–5, 86; low-impact 200, 202
Mohktarian, P.L. and Schwanen, T. 238
Monacle magazine 199
Montgomery County, Maryland 236
Montgomery, John 173
mortgages: location-efficient 229
Moses, Robert 2
motor vehicle collisions 252–3
multi-functionalism 201, 215
multimodal transportation planning 224–6, 243, 244
Multiple Intensive Land use (MILU) system 47

National Association of Area Agencies on Aging (n4a) 90–1
National Urban and Community Forestry Advisory Council 200
natural areas 103, 216; *see also* green infrastructure (GI)
negative externalities 34, 39
neighborhood planning 185–6; *see also* participatory neighborhood planning; traditional neighborhood development (TND); transit-oriented development (TOD)
neighboring 102, 103
The Netherlands: land use regulation 37, 50–1
Neuwith, Robert 110
Newman, P.W.G. and Kenworthy, J.R. 223
New Orleans: cultural implications in reconstruction 158, 159–60, 175–6; impact of Katrina on Mid-City 162; local food producers 173–5; Mardi Gras traditions 163–5, 169–70; Mid-City 161–2, 163, 169, 172; musical roots and post-Katrina recovery 167–9; Office of Recovery and Development Administration (ORDA) 174; post-Katrina Mardi Gras 166–7, 170–1; restaurants 171–3; return of Endymion parade 163, 166; returning residents post-Katrina 158–9; Social Aid and Pleasure Clubs 169–71
New South Wales 42
New Urbanism 1, 89, 259; Ahwahnee Principles 183; issues faced by developments 241–2; land use and transportation 231, 236–7, 240; regulations 30, 35; small town neighborhoods 104; and social equity 232; spatial determinism 101; Traditional Neighborhood Development (TND) 226, 227; Twin Cities region 10, 12, 15, 20, 22–3, 25, 26
New York City: Fresh Kills Park 255; Lower Manhattan 150, 151; neighborhood planning 185, 186; work of Jane Jacobs 2; zoning 33
noise exposure 256–7

obesity 85, 250–2, *251*, 256
Olmstead, John Charles 204, *205*
Ontario 40–1
Open Space Seattle 206–10, *208*, *211–13*, 214, 216; Green Futures Charrette 209–10, *211–13*, 214; informing the process and public 207, 209; leaders, issues and goals 206–7; lessons from 214–16; watershed and topographic units 207, *208*
Orlando: median incomes and race 146, *148–9*, 149–50
overlay zones 35

parks 202, 216, 255; Twin Cities region 21, 23
participatory democracy criteria 189–91, **191**
participatory neighborhood planning 186; assessing involvement 189–91; contribution to livability 194–5; theoretical perspectives 183–4; *see also* Seattle
Partners for Livable Communities (Partners) 1, 2, 90–1
pedestrians 230; community design 252; elderly 84–5, 89; green infrastructure 202; injury

INDEX

risk 253–4; Mata Machado 119; New Urbanist neighborhoods 231; twin Cities region 17, 18, 20, 23–4, 25, 26
performance codes 56
Perlman, J. 106–7
Perry, Clarence 185
Philadelphia: density 150; downtown housing market 128; median incomes and race 140, *141–2*, 143, 149–50; population growth 135; size of downtown *132*
Phoenix, Arizona: size of downtown *132*
physical activity 85, 231, 250–2, 255
place-attachment 184; *see also* communities of place
place and place-making 62, 63; Capitals of Culture 67–8, 72–4; contribution of green infrastructure 74–6
planned unit development (PUD or PD) zones 35, 37, 57
Planning and Development Act (Ireland) 44
Plater-Zyberk, Elizabeth 1
political culture 38–9; corruption 39, 44–5, 46
pollution: environmental sustainability 103; Mata Machado 119, *120*; The Netherlands 51; vehicles 202, 254; water 203
population growth 133–4, *133*, 186, 249–50
Portland, Oregon 88, 252, *253*
preschool education 71
Pringle Creek, Oregon 204
prison populations 154–5n
private sector development 57–8
property rights 33–4, 38; Australia 42
property values 87
public participation: Liverpool 73, 74; Open Space Seattle 206, 209–10, 214; park design 23; planning for aging 85–6, 86–7, 93; Seattle Green Legacy Coalition 216–18; *see also* participatory neighborhood planning
public restrooms 89
Putnam, R. 184

quality of life: favelas 106; UK focus 31–2, 62, 66

race and ethnicity: downtown households 138; mapping median income and race 140, *141–2*, 143, 143–5, 146, *146–9*, 149–50; New Orleans 162, 170–1
Rails-to-Trails (R2T) projects 255

Rasmussen, Tom 217
real estate market 30, 34; downtown living 127–8; Rio de Janeiro 109; suburban 128
regional accessibility 225
regional planning: Canada 41; Twin Cities region 10–12, 27–8; US 34
regulatory tools *see* land use regulation; zoning in the US
residential development *see* housing developments
residential satisfaction 102, 117
residents associations: Mata Machado 109, 110, 115, 118
retail development: food 256; Mendota Heights 24–5; in New Urbanist developments 242; St Louis Park 16; St Paul North Quadrant 23
rights to the city 105
Rio de Janeiro: Favela-Bairro 110, 115; favelas 104–7, 109; *see also* Mata Machado, Rio de Janeiro
risk: planning for 53; transportation-related 252–4
Robbinsdale Economic Development Authority (REDA) 18
Robbinsdale, Minneapolis 17–19, 26–7
Rohe, W.M. 185
Rosenbloom, S. and Stahl, A. 84–5
Royal Town Planning Institute 62

Safe Routes to School 89
safety: and crime 102, 106–7, 117, 252; *see also* injury risk
St Louis Park Excelsior and Grand, Minnesota 14–17, *15*, 26
St Paul's North Quadrant, Minnesota 22–4
San Francisco: travel behaviors 238
Schell, Paul 193, 194
Seattle: Comprehensive Plan 185, 186–7, *188*, 189, 192, 193; funding neighborhood planning 189, 192, 193; Green Legacy Coalition 216–18; livability of the City 194–5; neighborhood planning history and context 186; neighborhood planning program 187, 189; Open Space Seattle 206–10, *208*, *211–13*, 214, 216; planning for green infrastructure 199, 204, *205*, 206; population trends 135; review of neighborhood planning process 191–4
Seattle Green Factor (SGF) 214, 216

281

INDEX

self-help: Mata Machado 110, 121; post-Kristina New Orleans 170–1
Simmons, M. 235
Singapore: land use regulation 46–7
Sirianni, C. 193
small town neighborhoods 104
Smart Growth 1–2, 88, 90, 258–60
Smart Growth Network 2, 101
Soares, F.F. 108, 110
Social Aid and Pleasure Club Task Force 170–1
social capital 32; and mental health 257–8; participatory neighborhood planning 184; Social Aid and Pleasure Clubs 171
socio-economic context of research 99–100
Spain: land use regulation 54–5
spatial determinism 101
spatial mismatch hypothesis 226, 232, 240
spatial planning 57; The Netherlands 50; UK 62, 76–7
spot zoning 56
Standard State Zoning Enabling Act (SZEA) 33, 55
state zoning enabling acts 33, 34–5
stormwater control 200, 201, 203, 210
Sure Start Children's Centres 71–2
sustainable communities 50, 63–4, 68, 74–6; Sustainable Communities for All Ages (CFAA) program 92–3
sustainable development 103
sustainable urban infrastructure 201

takings issue 34, 36, 56
Tamil Nadu 159
Texas: Aging Texas Well Initiative 92; land use control 34, 36, 38, 57–8
Toronto 2
Town Planning and Development Act (Western Australia) 43
traditional neighborhood development (TND) 226–7, *227*, 240, 259; assessment of 230, 231; critique of 241–2; social equity 232
transit-oriented development (TOD) 89, 226, 227–8, *229*, 240, 259; assessment of 230; and the built environment 228–9; critique of 241–2; location efficiency 229–30
transit-related development 228
transparency 38, 39
transportation: and aging 84–5, 89, 90; Burnsville 22; and city livability 224; impact on urban form 223–4; and injury risk 252–4; Mata Machado residents 119; noise exposure 256–7; pollution from 202, 254; redefining corridors 215; regional planning 27–8; Robbinsdale 18, 19; St Louis Park 16–17; St Paul's North Quadrant 27; sustainable 103, 200; *see also* land use and transportation
Transportation Research Board 230, 237, *237*
travel behaviors 84–5, 230–1, 237–8, *237*, 242; community design 252, 253–4, *253*
Trust for Public Land 200
Twin Cities region 9; Burnsville 19–22, *21*, 26; downtown Robbinsdale 17–19, 26–7; Excelsior and Grand, St Louis Park 14–17, *15*, 26; LCA projects 12, **13**, *14*; Mendota Heights 24–5; Metropolitan Council 10–12, 25, 27; St Paul's North Quadrant 22–4, 27

UNESCO World Heritage Sites 72
United Kingdom (UK): Big Society 66; efficiency in service delivery 65–6; focus on quality of life 62–3, 66; land use regulation 39–40, 57; livability concept 63–4; Sustainable Development Strategy 64–5; *see also* Liverpool
Universal Design 86, 88, 93, 258, 260
urban density strategies 198–9, 215–16
urban forests 200, 203, 215
urban open space *see* green infrastructure (GI)
Urban Redevelopment Authority (URA) (Singapore) 46
urban sprawl 249–50
urban village concept: Seattle 187, *188*, 192
US Constitution 32–3
USDA Forest Service 200
US Green Building Council (USGBC) 219, 261

vehicle miles traveled (VMT) and residential density 230
visitability 88

Washington DC 2
Washington (state): concurrency 226, 233–4, 235–6, 243; Growth Management Act (1990) 185, 186, 191–2, 235; *see also* Seattle
water 200, 202–3, 215, 216

INDEX

Western Australia 43
White, S.M. and Paster, E.L. 233
Whyte, William H. 2
Wise Use Movement 36
Wood, Albert Baldwin 161
Woodlands, Texas 38, 57–8
Woolcock, M. 184
worldview 120–1

Zaluar, Alba 106
zoning *see* land use regulation; zoning in the US
zoning in the US 55–6, 57–8, 223, 249–50; changing practices 87–8; definition 32; interpretation by the courts 35–6; legal framework 32–4; limitations 36–7, 83–4, 84–5; local powers 33, 34–5; purposes 35, 56

Taylor & Francis
eBooks
FOR LIBRARIES

ORDER YOUR FREE 30 DAY INSTITUTIONAL TRIAL TODAY!

Over 23,000 eBook titles in the Humanities, Social Sciences, STM and Law from some of the world's leading imprints.

Choose from a range of subject packages or create your own!

Benefits for you
- Free MARC records
- COUNTER-compliant usage statistics
- Flexible purchase and pricing options

Benefits for your user
- Off-site, anytime access via Athens or referring URL
- Print or copy pages or chapters
- Full content search
- Bookmark, highlight and annotate text
- Access to thousands of pages of quality research at the click of a button

For more information, pricing enquiries or to order a free trial, contact your local online sales team.

UK and Rest of World: **online.sales@tandf.co.uk**

US, Canada and Latin America:
e-reference@taylorandfrancis.com

www.ebooksubscriptions.com

ALPSP Award for BEST eBOOK PUBLISHER 2009 Finalist

Taylor & Francis eBooks
Taylor & Francis Group

A flexible and dynamic resource for teaching, learning and research.